Marx's Labor Theory of Value

Marx's Labor Theory of Value

A Defense

Hayashi Hiroyoshi

*Translated
by Roy West*

iUniverse, Inc.
New York Lincoln Shanghai

Marx's Labor Theory of Value
A Defense

Copyright © 2005 by Roy West

iUniverse books may be ordered through booksellers or by contacting:

iUniverse
2021 Pine Lake Road, Suite 100
Lincoln, NE 68512
www.iuniverse.com
1-800-Authors (1-800-288-4677)

ISBN: 0-595-34600-6

Printed in the United States of America

Contents

Translator's Introduction

This book was published in Japan in 1998 as the first in a six-volume collection of Hayashi Hiroyoshi's writings from a period of over three decades.[1] The six chapters originally appeared as separate articles and essays in the publications of the Socialist Workers Party (Sharōtō) and its predecessor the Marxist Workers League (Marurōdō), which are organizations that Hayashi helped to create, and in which he played a leading role. His book is thus the "product" of the revolutionary socialist movement he has been an active participant in, and was written with a socialist audience in mind.

For Hayashi, Marx's labor theory of value is the core of a scientific understanding of capitalism, which in turn provides socialists with a needed sense of direction by elucidating the nature and limitations of bourgeois society, and bringing into view an essential image of socialism. But for the bulk of the past century most "Marxists" turned their backs on Marx's labor theory of value, which seemed to have been refuted by the existence of the law of value and widespread commodity production in the existing "socialist" countries. Despite this dominant view within leftist circles, Hayashi continued to adhere to Marx's theory of capitalism, and it is upon its basis that he developed his own theory of state capitalism to grasp the socio-economic system in the Soviet Union. This theory, which I will discuss a bit later, is one important example of the practical significance of studying Marx's *Capital*.

Marx's Labor Theory of Value: A Defense, examines some of the most fundamental aspects of Marx's theory of capitalism, beginning with a detailed discussion of his labor theory of value presented in part one of *Capital* (volume

---

1.   Please note that Japanese names throughout the book are listed with the
     family name first.

one). But instead of introducing the content of this book here, I want to focus on the socialist political movement that Hayashi has been involved in and continues to contribute to today as a leader of the Marxist Comrades Group. One reason to address this subject is simply because the Japanese postwar left may be unfamiliar to many readers. But more importantly, I think this merits attention because Hayashi's effort to develop a socialist movement that steers clear of both Stalinism and radicalism remains relevant today throughout the world. And I hope to illustrate how this movement has been based—in the most fundamental sense—on the scientific understanding of capitalism acquired from Marx.

"Marxism" and Postwar Japan

Hayashi Hiroyoshi, born in 1938, came of age at a time when Marxist thought exerted a powerful influence on workers, students, and intellectuals in Japan. During the roughly three decades after the end of the war, a familiarity with, if not sympathy for, Marxism was the norm among university professors, and Marxists occupied a nearly hegemonic position within academia. Itoh Makoto, an economist who himself claims to be a Marxist, wrote in 1980 that, "a knowledge of Marxist economics and a basic understanding of Marxism number among the almost essential prerequisites for membership in the Japanese intelligentsia."[2] Unlike many English-speaking countries, where even Keynes could dismiss Marx as a member of a sort of "intellectual underworld,"[3] bourgeois scholars in Japan have not had the luxury of being able to studiously ignore him.

At the same time, however, precisely because of the enormous prestige of Marx, the bulk of criticism aimed at his fundamental ideas has come from the pens of self-proclaimed Marxists! To begin with, most Marxists in the decade following the war were affiliated in some way or another with the Japanese Communist Party, and thus rejected elements of Marxism that contradicted their own Stalinist dogmas. But the anti-Stalinist "new left" that emerged in the late fifties, in some respects, moved even further away from Marx. For example, Kuroda Kan'ichi and (Itoh's teacher) Uno Kōzō, whose ideas were embraced by new left activists, attacked materialist philosophy and the labor

---

2.   Makoto Itoh, *Value and Crisis* (London: Pluto Press, 1980), 11.
3.   Paul Sweezy refers to this as Keynes' view in a 1986 interview with Sungar Savran and E. Ahmet Tonak.

theory of value, respectively, in the name of opposing Stalinism and developing Marxism.

Despite an abundance of such pseudo-Marxism, students of Marx in Japan have at least enjoyed access to a remarkable volume of resources. A visit to any decent used-bookstore in Tokyo provides some idea of the tremendous number of books related to Marx that were published in the past half-century. This can be seen, for example, in the existence of roughly a dozen different translations of *Capital*, two different translations of the first German edition of *Capital*, and an entire dictionary dedicated to Marx's famous work. There is also the impressive multi-volume *Marx-Lexicon zur Politischen Ökonomie*, edited by the economist Kuruma Samezō, that groups together passages from the entire body of Marx's work organized around a number of central themes. And in addition to the extensive work of Japanese Marxist scholars, an enormous number of works by foreign Marxists are available in Japanese translations.

Marxist thought, in some form or another, was thus very much in the air in postwar Japan. And when Hayashi entered Tokyo University in 1957, the interest in Marx was perhaps at its height. The late fifties also marked the moment when the student movement was breaking free of Stalinism, and the need for a new, revolutionary workers' party was keenly felt. The decision to reject Stalinism was the final outcome of a decade of friction between students and the JCP leadership. Students, taking the idea of communism more seriously than their leaders did, developed a radical *political* movement that often went beyond the narrow bounds of JCP reformism. The main vehicle for this movement was Zengakuren, a national organization formed in 1948 that grouped together all of the "student self-governing associations" into a national coalition.[4]

Workers, meanwhile, had already largely turned their backs on the JCP by the late forties, when the party proved itself more rearguard than vanguard during the turbulent, revolutionary period following Japan's surrender. With the Japanese bourgeoisie literally hanging on by a (red-white-and-blue) thread, the JCP continued, as in the prewar period, to call for a bourgeois-democratic revolution instead of a socialist one, proposing the formation of a "people's government" composed of a "broad united front of democratic

---

4. An overview of the history of Zengakuren up to the late sixties, including information on the various new left "sects," can be found in *Zengakuren: Japan's Revolutionary Students*, ed. Stuart Dowsey (Berkeley: The Ishi Press, 1970).

forces." Worker frustration with the JCP reached a peak when the party bowed to pressure from U.S. occupation authorities and called off a general strike scheduled for February 1, 1947.[5]

Developments in the early fifties contributed to a further erosion of confidence in the JCP, particularly among students. Young communists witnessed how, under criticism from the Soviet-led Cominform in 1950, the JCP in a matter of months completely altered its political tactics. After seeking to be a "lovable Communist Party," by advocating peaceful revolution and referring to the U.S. forces as an "army of liberation," the JCP suddenly began preparing for an "armed struggle" to achieve national liberation and free Japan from its status as a "semi-colony" of the U.S.[6] This head-spinning change, which marked the beginning of the party's so-called "Molotov cocktail period," gave students a first-hand glimpse of the unprincipled nature of the JCP. And those students who actually left their campuses to wage a "guerrilla struggle" in the countryside were left with the bitter memory of "squandering their youth" to engage in a caricature of Maoism that was doomed to fail, given the conditions in Japan at the time and the fictional goal that was being sought.

Student communists got another glimpse of the JCP's rotten core around the same time in the course of a power struggle within the party. In this factional dispute, many students sided with the "Internationalist faction," led by future JCP *supremo* Miyamoto Kenji, mistakenly believing that he was waging a principled struggle against the party's bureaucratic leadership. When the Cominform eventually sided with the existing leadership, many students were unceremoniously kicked out of the party for siding with the losing faction and forced to make a humiliating public "self-criticism" to regain entry. It came as a shock for many gung-ho student communists to be thrown out of a party they had worshipped as the result of a factional struggle they barely understood.

---

5. The expressions cited above are from Joe Moore's *Japan Workers and the Struggle for Power, 1945-1947* (Madison: University of Wisconsin Press, 1983), which provides a detailed examination of workers' struggles and the JCP's conservative response to worker militancy during the period immediately following Japan's defeat.

6. Despite its radical change in tactics, however, the JCP consistently stuck to a "two-staged revolution" strategy, merely adding "national liberation" as an additional task to be achieved within the bourgeois revolution.

The "ultra-left adventurist" line of the early fifties, as it came to be called, was rejected at the Sixth National Party Conference held in 1955, and the factional differences were patched over. But the damage had been done as far as student communist were concerned. The JCP's "criticism" of its own past mistakes merely opened the floodgates to more criticism from the lower ranks. Dissatisfaction reached a higher pitch the following year, when the Soviet invasion of Hungary starkly revealed the reactionary nature of Stalinism. The JCP responded by denouncing the Hungarian uprising as an "imperialist plot" and praising the "proletarian internationalism" of the Soviet response. Miyamoto and the party leadership even used the invasion as an opportunity to crack down on internal dissent, arguing that a lack of discipline within the Hungarian CP had been a cause of the "imperialist counter-revolution." This heavy-handed approach, needless to say, only deepened the students' sense of alienation.

A *New* Left Emerges

By the time Hayashi joined the JCP in 1958, the year after entering Tokyo University, the party "cell" on campus he became a member of was already largely functioning independently of, and often in opposition to, the central party leadership. Articles began to appear in *Marxism-Leninism*, the cell's theoretical journal, exposing the "betrayals" of the Stalinist-led communist movement. The increasingly critical view of Stalinism coincided with a significant upturn in the student movement, which had been moribund following the confusion and demoralization of the early fifties. And this period also marked a shift in the focus of student activists from the "peace movement" to the "class struggle."

During this "transitional" period, the ideas of Leon Trotsky exercised a powerful influence on radical students. The Japan Trotskyist Association (JTA) was formed in January 1957 by a handful of leftwing intellectuals (including Kan'ichi Kuroda). This organization, which changed its name to the Japan Revolutionary Communist League later the same year, was the first independent anti-Stalinist organization in Japan.[7] Despite a hysterical JCP

---

7.   Today there are three organizations bearing the name JRCL: the (Kuroda-led) Kakumaru-ha (Revolutionary Marxist faction), their hated rival, Chukaku-ha (Core faction), and a Trotskyist organization affiliated with the International Committee of the Fourth International.

campaign against Trotsky—who was labeled a "counter-revolutionary" if not worse—young communists seeking to understand Stalinism flocked to his works. Hayashi later recalled how he himself had "hungrily snatched up any of the often sloppily translated and poorly printed editions of Trotsky's writings made available," and that students at the time "read Trotsky prior to reading Marx or Lenin."[8] At the same time, however, students were reluctant to fully embrace Trotskyism, rejecting his emphasis on political maneuvering ("entry tactics," etc.) and sensing that he had tended to neglect Marx's economic theory.[9]

Thus, despite the significant influence of Trotsky's ideas, radical students sought to forge a path independent of both Stalinism and Trotskyism. Student JCP members—particularly those in the Tokyo University cell to which Hayashi belonged—formed the nucleus of this effort. These cell members and other student radicals critical of the JCP were able to seize control of the leadership of Zengakuren at its eleventh congress in May 1958, expelling a "right-wing opposition" faction obedient to the JCP. Following the congress the JCP summoned the new Zengakuren leaders to its headquarters to "straighten them out," but this only enraged the students, and an argument and physical scuffle ensued. After this so-called "June 1 Incident," the student rebels accelerated their activities in opposition to the JCP, issuing a newsletter entitled *Puroretaria tsūshin* (Proletarian Bulletin) in September to expand their faction. This culminated in December with the formation of an independent organization called the Communist League—in homage to Marx's Communist league—which commonly became known as "the Bund." Hayashi soon became a member of this new group.

The following month the Bund issued the inaugural issue of its theoretical journal *Communism*, including an article entitled "A Whole World to Win: Burning Tasks of the Proletariat," which can seen as the organization's founding manifesto. Clearly rejecting the JCP's two-staged revolutionary strategy

---

8. Hayashi Hiroyoshi,"1960 anpo tōsō to kyōsanshugidōmei" (1960 Anpo Struggle and the Communist League) *Rōdō to kaihō* June 1990: 15.
9. Hayashi has described his own critical view of Trotsky as being similar to Lenin's view of Rosa Luxemburg expressed in "Notes of a Publicist," where he refers to the Russian fable about how "eagles may at times fly lower than hens, but hens can never rise to the height of eagles." In other words, Trotsky—like Luxemburg—may be prone to error, but he also attains heights that low-flying Stalinists are unable to reach.

and nationalistic anti-Americanism, the Bund stated its aim as "rallying a revolutionary vanguard with the ability to successfully lead a socialist revolution." This road to socialism was seen as only being possible by "overcoming the crisis in proletarian leadership" and "liberating the proletariat from every illusion it holds in the leadership of the established communist movement, to create an independent revolutionary leftwing on the basis of the revival of truly revolutionary Marxism, and rally the revolutionary workers around this point." At the same time, the Bund made clear from the start that it was more interested in "praxis" than theory:

> We are opposed to those chattering bourgeois groups that seek to create something on the sole basis of debating ideas, theory and programs, and who call for a program to be in place prior to action, and instead say that the program for the emancipation of the proletariat can only emerge in the midst the trial by fire of praxis involving a response to the tasks of the class struggle that emerge every day.[10]

For an action-oriented radical group like the Bund, the year 1959 was ideal, as it marked a sharp upswing in political activism. In addition to various activities carried out to oppose the Teacher Efficiency Rating Law and the revision of the Police Duties Performance Law, there was a growing movement against the revision of the Japan-U.S. Security Treaty (Anpo) scheduled for the following year. The Bund (and Bund-led Zengakuren) would soon become synonymous with this movement—with the organization later being referred to as the "Anpo Bund."

The security treaty was opposed by the JCP as well as the Bund, but their positions were quite different. Stalinist opposition was based on the dogma that Japan was a "semi-colony" of the U.S., with the JCP arguing that the new treaty would only solidify this subordinate status. The Bund rejected this view, recognizing that Japan had already attained its political independence in 1952 and that the revised treaty was an imperialist alliance between two sovereign states, which actually reflected an increase in the strength of Japan relative to its ally. For the Bund, the treaty was the first step toward a revived Japanese imperialist state, and in this sense the first step toward future wars. By blocking the revision of the treaty, they reasoned, a political crisis for the bourgeoi-

---

10. Shima Shigeo ed., *Bunto no shisō* (Tokyo: Hihyōsha, 1992) 1: 15-16.

sie could be generated that might open up the path to revolution. Thus, for the Bund, this one movement was positioned as *the* decisive issue.

The radical Bund preferred to employ confrontational tactics to move this "decisive" movement forward, which contrasted sharply with the humdrum JCP approach. The group first gained national attention on November 27, 1959, when Bund-led Zengakuren members overwhelmed police barricades to break into the grounds of the Diet Building during a large-scale demonstration against the treaty. Hayashi participated in the action as one of the Bund leaders, and later described how JCP politicians were on hand with megaphones desperately pleading with the young rebels to behave themselves and go home. The JCP hysterically denounced the actions of these "ultra-left Trotskyists" in the pages of its newspaper *Akahata* and was not upset in the least when the government rounded up a number of Bund leaders, including Hayashi, a few days after the demonstration. Despite such arrests, the Bund carried out a number of spectacular actions the following year, such as the occupation of Haneda Airport, in an attempt to block Prime Minister Kishi's departure to the U.S. to sign the treaty, and several clashes with riot police outside the Diet Building.[11]

Buoyed by the strength of this mass-movement, and their astounding initial successes, Bund members were confident in the future revolutionary movement (and their own future within it). But once the movement opposing the security treaty petered out, following its ratification on June 16, 1960, it became clear that the Bund had little idea of "what was to be done." The following month, at the organization's fifth conference, the Bund leaders were subject to harsh criticism for the "failure" to block the treaty, and this quickly escalated to the point where the organization broke apart, with several competing factional groups emerging from out of the wreckage.[12]

---

11. At a protest outside the Diet Building on June 15, Hayashi's close friend, and fellow Bund member, Kamba Michiko was crushed to death in a clash with riot police. Since that day, her name has thus been closely linked to the "anti-Anpo" movement.

12. An English article on the history of the Bund by Hasegawa Kenji entitled "In Search of a New Radical Left: The Rise and Fall of the Anpo Bund, 1955-1960" appeared in the Spring 2003 issue of the *Stanford Journal of East Asian Affairs* (also available on-line at: http://www.stanford.edu/group/sjeaa/journal3/japan2.pdf).

"Against Right and 'Left' Opportunism!"

Hayashi, who was released from prison in July after being arrested a second time in May, was naturally shocked by the sudden demise of an organization that he and his comrades had placed so much hope in. Together with a handful of other former Bund members, Hayashi formed Kyosanshugi hataha (Communist Banner Group) in the spring of 1961. Their first important task was to make sense of what had just happened, which meant understanding why the Bund had collapsed, elucidating the historical nature of the movement against the security treaty, and most importantly grasping the limitations of petty-bourgeois radicalism. For Hayashi, the limitations of radicalism were apparent in terms of how the Bund positioned the security treaty, a single reformist issue, as being a "make-or-break" issue—as if the entire fate of the working class were riding on it—rather than viewing it within the larger context of the movement for socialism. The despair that the student radicals felt at the "defeat" of the movement against the treaty was in fact only the reverse-side of their earlier ultra-optimism.

Hayashi believed the way forward beyond such radicalism (and beyond Stalinism as well) would depend upon carrying out the theoretical "heavy lifting" necessary to build a strong foundation for a new workers' party. This meant a rejection of the one-dimensional new left approach of neglecting theory while focusing exclusively on "action." He took very seriously Lenin's statement that "without revolutionary theory, there can be no revolutionary movement." For new left activists, however, Hayashi's position seemed overly abstract and detached from political reality.

Despite such criticism, however, Hayashi's small group took the next step, in December 1963, of forming a "revolutionary circle" called Zenkokushaken (Nationwide Social Science Study Group). The group identified its immediate task as "preparing theoretically and practically to organize a mass communist party of the working class," and its critical view of both Stalinism and radicalism was reflected in its slogan: "Against Right and 'Left' Opportunism!"

In terms of the struggle against radicalism, Hayashi considered it particularly important to expose the superficiality of anti-Stalinist "Marxists," such as Uno Kōzō and Kuroda Kan'ichi, who were much in vogue at the time. The ideas of both of these theorists were attractive to students and workers who were disgusted with the JCP and seeking some alterative, but for Hayashi their theories were a theoretical dead-end, and the two were seen as having more in common with run-of-the-mill bourgeois scholars than Karl Marx.

Uno Kōzō's "unorthodox" reinterpretation of *Capital* first gained notice in the late forties, when he claimed that it is mistaken to abstract from use-value or the existence of the commodity owner when discussing value and the value-form. Echoing the views of Böhm-Bawerk, Uno's argument basically boiled down to the idea that the value of a commodity is "determined" subjectively by the owners and purchasers of it—and in the push and pull of supply and demand—rather than by the abstract human labor "objectified" within a commodity.[13] Uno, in other words, clearly rejected Marx's labor theory of value. There are other aspects of Uno's theory, including his three-staged "methodology" of economics, which takes an *a priori* model of "pure capitalism" as the object of study, as well as his dismissal of the materialist conception of history as a mere hypothesis with no scientific validity, which must instead be "demonstrated" by economic theory. But Hayashi discusses these and other points in some detail in this book, particularly the first chapter, so I will not touch on them further here.[14]

Unlike Uno, who kept his distance from politics, Kuroda Kan'ichi, until his recent retirement, has been the leader and theoretical guru of the Japan Revolutionary Communist League (Kakumaru-ha). In addition to developing a "theory of organization" related to these activities, his main area of concern has been philosophy. Kuroda has argued that "orthodox" (Stalinist) Marxists are guilty of "objectivism" in terms of neglecting the role of human subjectivity and viewing cognition as the "mirror reflection" of objective reality.[15] Indeed, Stalinism and "objectivism" were almost interchangeable terms (or insults) for those within the new left movement. For Hayashi, however, it was patently absurd to equate Stalinism with objectivism, considering that the JCP's funda-

---

13. Considering that Kuruma Samezō, in *Kachikeitai-ron to kōkankatei-ron* (1957), critically dissected Uno's subjective view of value, it is a bit astounding to hear the Unoist Sekine Tomohiko claim in his introduction to Uno's *Principles of Political Economy* (1980) that, "by the end of the 1950s Uno had won all arguments, amply demonstrating the impregnability of his theoretical position."

14. In addition to his *Principles of Political Economy*, readers interested in learning more about the views of Uno can consult a number of books in English written by his students Itoh Makoto and Sekine Tomohiko, as well as books by Robert Albritton, who learned what he knows about Uno from Sekine. Books by all of these authors are listed in the bibliography at the end of this book.

mental strategy has been based on the subjective, *a priori* idea that a bourgeois revolution is necessary in a highly developed capitalist country. Indeed, if this is the reflection of reality, it is through a "mirror darkly"! Not only did Hayashi reject this incorrect understanding of Stalinism, he defended the central materialist tenet that objective reality exists independent of human cognition, and that the aim of thought is to reflect this reality as fully and accurately as possible.

Hayashi's own approach to understanding Stalinism could hardly have been more different than the method of the "anti-Stalinist" Kuroda. As a materialist, Hayashi recognized immediately that one could not attain an understanding of Stalinism by treating it as a free-floating ideology that was not determined by anything more than Joseph Stalin's limited thought process. Instead of seeking out the reason Stalinism emerged, by ultimately identifying its connection to the material base (Soviet Union) from which it arose, new left theorists tended to speak in terms of Stalin committing an "epistemological error" that could be traced back, first to Lenin's understanding of materialism, and ultimately to Engels' misinterpretation of Marx. The members of Zenkokushaken, by contrast, sought a deeper understanding of Stalinism by first historically examining the Stalinist-led "communist" movement, and then clarifying the true nature of the socio-economic system in the Soviet Union, of which Stalinism was the ideological expression.

In order to gauge the impact of Stalinism on working class movements throughout the world, Hayashi and his comrades examined revolutionary movements in the twentieth century, as part of a larger study stretching back to the 1848 revolutions in Europe. This historical examination revealed exactly how disastrous the Stalinist leadership had been in one country after another. From this negative example—as well as the positive example of the Bolsheviks within the revolutionary movement in Russia—Hayashi and his group were able to learn a great deal that was applicable to the revolutionary movement in Japan. The Bolsheviks, for instance, had faced a similar struggle against "left" and right opportunism, avoiding the pitfalls of both rightwing

---

15. Kuroda defines "objectivism in Marxist materialism" as a "generic term signifying the tendency to reduce and dissolve the contents of cognition or reflection into their material bases, although these contents are those that have been cognized and reflected by the human Subject, as a social entity, who praxises, evokes emotion, and thinks." *Essential Terms of Revolutionary Marxism* (Tokyo: Kobushi Shobō, 1998), 84.

Menshevism and the superficial radicalism of the Social-Revolutionary Party. The Stalinists, meanwhile, as we have seen, adopted at different times *both* Mehshevik-style class-collaborationism and hysterical ultra-radicalism. Hayashi's group focused mainly on examining the class-collaborationist "popular front" of the Stalinist, because in the sixties the JCP was adopting this same tactic in tandem with the Socialist Party.

This did not mean, however, that Zenkokushaken veered toward the tactics adopted by the Stalinists prior to the popular front, namely, the theory of "social fascism" that was advocated in the late twenties and early thirties. This earlier theory had incredibly lumped together social-democratic parties with fascism, describing such reformists as the "moderate wing of fascism."[16] In this way, the Stalinists had ignored the crucial task of distinguishing between various bourgeois political tendencies, failing to recognize the specific role played by fascist parties, compared to bourgeois parties in general, and this contributed in no small measure to the victory of fascism in Germany.

The "popular front" is the polar opposite of this earlier theory—and the polar opposite error!—which involves reaching out to not only social-democratic parties, but even liberal bourgeois ones, in order to "fight fascism" or "defend democracy." To make the popular front as broad as possible, Communist parties happily kept to themselves whatever socialist ideas (or critical views of social democracy) they might have had, focusing solely on the immediate goal at hand. For bourgeois governments in the thirties, struggling for survival in the midst of an unprecedented economic crisis, the Stalinists' class-collaborationism was a veritable godsend, which helped to keep the lid on working class struggles and funnel the anger of workers into a nationalist direction.

Hayashi and his comrades noted that the popular front ran directly counter to the approach adopted by Lenin, both in the period leading up to the Russian Revolution and during the years he led the Communist International. Lenin insisted on the need for communists to expose the class nature of reformist parties, and in the 1920 "Terms of Admission to the Communist International" he drafted, noted that member-parties of the Third International must "expose systematically and relentlessly, not only the bourgeoisie

---

16. Hayashi examines this theory of social-fascism in "Fascism and the Communist International," which is on the MCG website (www.mcg-j.org).

but also its accomplices-the reformists of every shade" and make "a complete and absolute break with reformism and 'Centrist' policy."[17] This did not mean shunning all participation in reformist or trade-unionist struggles, but rather positioning them within the larger movement for socialism, as "by-products" of this revolutionary movement. Zenkokushaken, similarly, recognized that it was reactionary to form a semi-permanent alliance with petty-bourgeois political parties at the price of abandoning the struggle for socialism, particularly because only the proletariat, owing to its class interests, is able to fight against the rule of monopoly capital to the end.

Hayashi's critical view of the popular front did not mean, however, that he embraced Trotsky's "united front" between the Communist and Socialist parties, which was presented a sort of cure-all that could "unite" all of the different segments of the working class, defeat fascism, and even take the first steps toward socialism. Hayashi realized that the Socialist Party—today as in Trotsky's own day—represents the class interests of the (urban) petty-bourgeoisie, despite the party's name, so that a CP-JP "united front" is no different in essence from the class-collaborationism of the popular front.[18] (And here I am setting aside the question of whether Communist parties today or in the thirties can truly be considered parties that represent the interests of the working class.) Hayashi and his comrades noted that the emphasis of Trotskyists and Stalinists on a formalistic, numerical "unity" of the working class, ignores the content of this unity (i.e. its reformist leadership), and that there is little point in premising a movement upon the very opportunistic leadership that should be overcome in order to secure the political independence of the working class.

---

17. Lenin, *Collected Works*, vol. 31 (Moscow: Progress Publishers, 1966), 207.
18. Of course, Trotsky dressed up his theory, using typical leftist phrase-mongering, referring to it as a bottom-up alliance that would focus on the rank-and-file SP members, and claiming that the SP could be moved in a leftist direction because it organized a large number of workers. But Hayashi notes that according to such a view, openly bourgeois parties—such as the Christian Democrats in Europe or the U.S. Democratic Party—could be seen as have revolutionary potential on the basis of their "ties" to workers through the control of labor unions.

Hayashi's Theory of State Capitalism

Without doubt, the biggest step forward Hayashi and his group made in the late sixties—lifting them well beyond the theoretical level of Stalinism, radicalism, and Trotskyism—was their development of a theory of state capitalism to account for the socio-economic reality in the Soviet Union, China, and other supposedly "socialist" countries. Here I want to touch on some important aspects of this theory, which underscore the great practical significance of Hayashi's adherence to Marx's materialist conception of history and labor theory of value.[19]

Hayashi, of course, can hardly lay claim to inventing the term "state capitalism" to describe the Soviet Union, which many political groups and individuals have used, ranging from "left communists" in the twenties and the once "orthodox Trotskyist" Tony Cliff, to Maoists ("diehard Stalinists") in the sixties. In Japan, as well, there is the example of the theory of state capitalism presented by Tsushima Tadayuki in the mid-fifties.[20] Most of these theories, however, only noted the non-socialist nature of the Soviet Union, without providing a convincing explanation of *why* such a system arose—often blaming what was seen as a "reversion to capitalism" on the stupidity or malice of the Soviet leadership. Hayashi, by contrast, sought to elucidate the reasons underlying the emergence of state capitalism in Russia and elsewhere, describe how the system actually functioned, identify the historical tasks it accomplished, and also uncover the internal contradictions that determined its development (and in some cases—already—its collapse).

---

19. I have translated a number of essays on Hayashi's theory of state capitalism that are included in the book *Socialism: Stalinist or Scientific?—the Marxist Theory of State Capitalism* (Tokyo: Zenkokushaken-sha, 2000) and these essays also available on the MCG website.

20. Tsushima, who helped to popularize Trotsky's ideas in Japan after the war, introduced a theory of state capitalism in the fifties that most of the student radicals rejected at the time. For example, the official view of the Bund was that the Soviet Union was a country "fixed at a transitional period (to socialism)." Hayashi, for his part, was influenced by Tsushima's theory when still a member of Bund, and his own theory was developed in part through a critical examination of Tsushima's view. See "Tsushima's Theory of State Capitalism: The Limits of Wishful Theories of 'Socialism'" for Hayashi's view of the limitations of Tsushima's concept of state capitalism.

Looking back on the socio-economic conditions in pre-revolutionary Russia, with its overwhelmingly peasant population, it is clear—just as it was to Russian Marxists at the time—that the task facing the country was to sweep aside the old feudal structures in order to develop capitalism on a broader basis. Unlike the Narodniks, who hoped Russia could leapfrog over capitalism, straight to socialism, on the basis of an agrarian revolution, Marxists were convinced that capitalist development was both inevitable and historically progressive compared to feudalism. Moreover, they recognized that socialism is only possible on the basis of the material conditions put in place by capitalist development—through the enormous growth in the productivity and "socialization" of labor—and that socialism is ultimately the necessary "solution" to the fundamental contradictions of capitalism. On the basis of this understanding, it was obvious to Marxists at the time, as it should be today, that Russia was facing a "bourgeois" revolution, not a "socialist" (or proletarian) one.

Despite their broad agreement over the economic content of the coming revolution, however, Russian Marxists (Social-Democratic Party) disagreed sharply over the political strategy to pursue in order to carry out this revolution. Mensheviks insisted that the liberal bourgeoisie would (or should) take the leading role, with the working class in a supporting role. By contrast, Lenin's Bolsheviks argued that the Russian bourgeoisie, owing to its links with the existing system and fear of the working class movement, would behave similarly to the European bourgeoisie in 1848 and seek some compromise with the Tsarist state (such as a constitutional monarchy), so that the rotten feudal system could only be completely eliminated by the workers and peasants who shared a common opposition to the existing system, despite their different class interests.[21] Trotsky held a different view from both groups—his theory of "permanent revolution" accepted that the material conditions for socialism were not in place in Russia, but he argued that because the

---

21. Lenin presented this view in *Two Tactics* (1905), where he wrote: "We cannot jump out of the bourgeois-democratic boundaries of the Russian Revolution, but we can enormously extend these boundaries, and within these boundaries we can and must fight for the interests of the proletariat." *Two Tactics* (New York: International Publishers, 1989), 41.
Trotskyist claim that he later abandoned this view for that of Trotsky, citing his 1917 "April Theses" as evidence. But even in this short work, Lenin clearly states: "It is not our *immediate* task to 'introduce' socialism, but only to bring social production and the distribution of products at once under the control of the Soviets of Workers' Deputies."

proletariat would be compelled to seize political power (with the peasantry, who are seen as "incapable of taking an independent political role," in tow) this would mean the revolution would have to move forward toward socialism, with its ultimate success depending on successful revolutions in Western Europe.[22]

The situation facing Russia before the revolution was not unlike the one confronting Germany and Japan a few decades earlier, with the same task being how to accumulate (national) capital and industrialize in an extremely short period of time. In England and Holland, capitalism had emerged over an extended period of time, but a leisurely approach was not an option for capitalist upstarts if they hoped to avoid domination by foreign capital. In both Germany and Japan, a massive amount of centralized capital was created by concentrating small capital through a system of joint-stock companies and large-scale banks, with the state acting as the essential lever to foster this development and impede the entry of foreign capital.[23] But in the twentieth century, with the age of monopoly capital and advanced imperialism, the situation was even more problematic for "backward" countries, meaning that it was no longer an option to take the German or Japanese road.

As the Bolsheviks had anticipated, the liberal bourgeoisie, represented by the Cadet Party, proved incapable of leading the bourgeois revolution forward after forming a provisional government in February 1917 that was supported by the Mensheviks. The workers and peasants, who were organized under the Bolshevik Party, swept this bourgeois-led government aside in October. Given the Bolsheviks' political leadership, the Russian Revolution was widely seen as a proletarian or socialist revolution.[24] And this impression was later

---

22. This view of Trotsky, which blurs the essential distinction between proletarian and bourgeois revolution, is examined by Hayashi in the article "Trotsky's Theory of Permanent Revolution: A Marxist Expression of Romanticism."

23. The historian E. Herbert Norman notes that, "early Japanese capitalism may be described as a hothouse variety, growing under the shelter of state protection and subsidy." *Japan's Emergence as a Modern State* (Vancouver: HBC Press, 2000), 111.

24. During the period of "wartime communism," even Lenin was hopeful that the revolutionary state might be able to push on directly toward socialism. But by the early twenties, faced with the all-too-real lack of material conditions for socialism, Lenin abandoned this hope and introduced the New Economic Policy to avoid economic collapse and peasant revolts.

reinforced when the nationalization of large-scale industry and "collectiviza-tion" of agriculture carried out.

But for Hayashi the appearance of socialism was deceiving, since the nationalization of industry and radical agrarian reforms, as well as the "planned economy," were merely means of achieving the historical task, sketched out above, of rapidly accumulating national capital—or what Trotsky's "left-opposition" ally Preobrazhensky called "primitive socialist accumulation." Moreover, the Soviet Union was far from a classless society, or even a society on the path toward eliminating classes. The peasants on collec-tive farms were harshly exploited, with the state amassing enormous revenue for use in industrialization via the "turnover tax." Workers, meanwhile, sold their labor-power as a commodity for a wage, and were exploited to an extreme degree through the widespread use of the "piece-wage" system, which Marx called "a lever for the lengthening of the working day and the lowering of wages" during the "stormy youth of large-scale industry."[25] Hayashi's theory presents how the system of state capitalist production functions, examining both the industrial and agricultural sectors, and the relation between them, while also discussing the various forms of ownership in the Soviet Union. But here there is not enough space to adequately present a description of how the state capitalist system functioned.[26]

The historical necessity (and essentially bourgeois nature) of the socio-eco-nomic system in the Soviet Union is highlighted by the fact that it became an "economic model" for developing countries throughout the world. Even coun-tries where worker-peasant revolutions were not carried out to completely sweep aside feudal remnants, such as India or Egypt, employed state capitalist methods to develop their national economies and resist domination by imperi-alist powers. Hayashi notes, however, that the absence of a thorough "national-democratic" revolution in such countries meant that agriculture could not be incorporated within the system of state capitalism through agri-culture collectivization, leaving the feudalistic agricultural relations largely intact. As a result, instead of being able to rely on the agricultural sector to fuel their industrialization, such countries have been dependent upon foreign capi-tal, which has restricted their development. This fact alone illustrates the great

---

25. Karl Marx, *Capital*, vol. 1, trans. Ben Fowkes (London: Penguin Books, 1976), 698.
26. See Hayashi's "The Stalinist System: The Internal 'Evolution' Towards 'Liberalization'" in *Socialism: Stalinist or Scientific?*.

historical significance and progressive nature of the Russian and Chinese revolutions.

But the system of state capitalism that Hayashi describes is certainly not contradiction-free. With the rapid accumulation of state capital, the contradictions inherent to this system became increasingly apparent. Initially the only concern is to accumulate capital, but once this has been achieved to some extent, the intrinsic nature of capital begins to assert itself, and the freer flow of capital becomes a pressing issue. At this point, a system of state-directed production begins to act as a fetter to further development, and this has compelled every state capitalist country to carry out economic "liberalization." The Soviet Union struggled with this contradiction from around the time of Stalin's death, and made many attempts to resolve it—the final effort being of course Gorbachev's *perestroika*—but ultimately the Communist-controlled political system shattered under the pressure. China, of course, has continued to confront this challenge since the eighties, and the Chinese leadership is no doubt painfully aware that the transition from "socialism" to a "Western-style" capitalism, with its freer flow of capital, is fraught with dangers and difficulties.[27] In Russia, Yeltsin's privatization of state-owned industry, far from working miracles, resulted in the massive pillaging of the nation's wealth. Today, along with resurrecting the tune of the Soviet national anthem, Vladimir Putin has had to revive many of the state capitalist economic and political structures in a bid to stay afloat. The fact that the chief deputy of the arch "anti-Communist" Boris Yeltsin has reintroduced some of the "gains of October," once thought irretrievably lost, should give pause to Trotskyists and Stalinists everywhere, as it further demonstrates that nationalized industry and economic planning, in and of themselves, do not signify socialism.[28]

---

27. Maoists in the sixties, by contrast, paid little attention to Marx's warning that "the country that is more developed industrially only shows, to the less developed, the image of its own future," and lashed out at the "revisionism" of Soviet bureaucrats implementing economic liberalization. Little did these rebels realize that a decade or so later they would be forced to travel down the same "capitalist road." The Maoist concept of "state capitalism," incidentally is based on a simple equation of state capitalism prior to economic liberalization (i.e. the systems under Stalin or Mao) as being socialism.

Hayashi's theory, not surprisingly, was harshly criticized by Stalinists and Trotskyists. Both believed that calling the Soviet Union state capitalism was a "counter-revolutionary" rejection of the historical significance of the Russian Revolution. From the discussion thus far, however, it should be clear that this criticism is terribly misguided. Indeed, the very starting point of Hayashi's criticism is an understanding of the *historical necessity* of state capitalism in Russia. Hayashi, at the same time, has been criticized for defending Stalin and Stalinism by recognizing that state capitalism was not an aberration and indeed had historical necessity. From Hayashi's perspective, however, recognizing the essential nature of the state capitalist system, including its historical necessity and *limitations*, is the basis or starting point of the struggle against the Stalinist bureaucracy (ruling class) in these countries. This is similar to how Marx overcame "utopian socialism" to base the workers' movement on an objective understanding of capitalism—rather than upon mere subjective wishes—while recognizing the necessity and progressive nature of capitalism compared to feudalism. If accepting the historical necessity of capitalism is equivalent to glorifying it as a social system, then Marx is clearly the greatest bourgeois apologist the world has ever known!

In reality, the real apologists for the state capitalist regimes—setting aside the Stalinist bureaucrats—have been the Trotskyists themselves, who have glorified these regimes as post-capitalist "workers' states" or "transitional societies,"[29] on the basis of the nationalized means of production and "planned economy." They have only barely managed to maintain a critical stance toward Stalinism by describing workers' states as being "deformed" or "degenerated." Trotskyists have told the workers in state capitalist countries that the economic foundation of their societies is sound, albeit battered, and that a "polit-

---

28. Recent developments in Russia also reveal the real economic basis for the Cold War. That is, now that Putin is exercising greater control over the Russian economy and limiting the inroads made by foreign capital, the bourgeoisie in Western Europe and the United States are denouncing him as a Stalin-like dictator, which only exposes that their opposition to the Soviet Union was based less on ideology than a desire to penetrate the enormous Russian market.

29. If one expands the definition of a "transitional society" the Trotskyists are "correct" in a sense. That is, state capitalism, like capitalism in general, is one historical form of production (that will come to an end) that puts in place the material conditions making socialism possible.

ical revolution" to overthrow the bureaucratic Stalinist "caste"—not a ruling *class*, mind you—is all that is needed. But when workers in Eastern Europe did rebel against the Stalinist bureaucracies in the 1980s, they remained susceptible to illusions regarding Western capitalism, and were prey to reactionary ideologies such as religion and nationalism, precisely because they had not freed themselves from illusions regarding the non-capitalist nature of their own societies. Today, workers in China and other state capitalist countries can only benefit from a clearer understanding of the historical and class nature of their societies, which will help them wage a more resolute struggle against their rulers—a struggle aiming for socialism rather than *only* a "negative" movement against the status-quo.

My presentation of Hayashi's theory hopefully makes it clear how a historical approach—bearing in mind the panorama of human history and its stages provided by Marx's materialist conception of history—is essential to understanding why the Soviet Union was not a socialist society. But on a more essential level, it is Marx's labor theory of value that is the true basis of Hayashi's theory. This theory teaches us the most fundamental characteristics of the capitalist mode of production, which set it apart from previous socioeconomic systems as well as from the future socialist society. The first chapter of this book presents Marx's theory, and occasionally touches on the essential definition of socialism, so I will leave it to Hayashi himself to explain in greater detail this essential distinction between capitalism and socialism.

Let me just note, however, that it was none other than Joseph Stalin himself who provided us with the greatest hint—really a confession—that the Soviet Union was not socialist. In *Economic Problems of Socialism in the USSR*, published in 1952, Stalin openly states that commodity production not only exists in the Soviet Union, but is actually expanding. For Marx, however, the essential dividing line between capitalism and socialism is the existence or non-existence of commodity production, since "objects of utility" only necessarily take the form of commodities under certain historical conditions, i.e. when they are the products of the labor of private individuals or groups of individuals who work independently of each other. When the starting point is not this private labor, but directly social labor—as under socialism or "primitive communism"—where the means of production are the common possession of society (rather than being independently owned by state enterprises or joint-stock companies), there is no need for the products of labor to take the commodity-form or for societal needs to be satisfied via the roundabout way of commodity production and exchange.

Stalin's announcement should have been interpreted by Marxists at the time as evidence that the Soviet Union was not a socialist society in any sense, but their allegiance to Stalin was far greater than to Marx, and they concluded instead that Marx had been wrong about the law of value and commodity production having no basis to exist under socialism. Trotskyists, sadly, were no exception, offering views that differed in no essential way from those of Stalin and Stalinists. For example, the Trotskyist economist Ernest Mandel—in his introduction to *Capital*, no less!—informs us that the "phenomenon of commodity production obviously survive, at least partially in those societies in which the rule of capital has already been overthrown, but which are not yet fully-fledged classless, that is, socialist societies: the USSR and the People's Republics of Eastern Europe, China, North Vietnam, North Korea, and Cuba."[30]

In short, for more than half a century nearly the entire Marxist "camp" has been ignoring the most fundamental and *revolutionary* aspects of Marx's theory!

Creation of Marxist Workers League

After nearly ten years of existence, the members of Zenkokushaken decided that significant progress had been made on the theoretical front and that the time had come to create an organization that would play a more active *political* role. This resulted in the formation of the Marxist Workers League in July 1972 and the creation of a program for the new organization. Here I want to look at the MWL program because I think it clearly reflects the materialist approach of Hayashi and his comrades, and shows how their movement has been fundamentally centered on Marx's scientific understanding of capitalism. An examination of the MWL program thus underscores the connection—through several important mediating factors—between Marx's labor theory of value presented in *Capital* and the political struggle to achieve socialism.

The program is divided into seven sections, beginning with a description of the fundamental nature of capitalism and its contradictions and limitations. The first line states the aim of the working class as freeing itself from the chains of capital, noting that this objective is "determined by the nature of capitalism and its developmental process." This is a key point, I think, because

---

30. *Capital*, vol. 1, 16.

it indicates that socialism is not a mere product of human consciousness, and that the historical development of capitalism puts in place the objective and subjective conditions that make socialism possible and necessary.

The description of the characteristics of capitalism in this first section begins with the commodity, as the economic cell-form of capitalism, noting how the commodity-form is the outcome of private labor being expended in production on an independent basis, with capitalists owning the means of production, and workers selling their labor-power as a commodity and being exploited by capital. The profit (surplus-value) accumulated as capital confronts the workers as an alien force, and while this accumulation means a rapid development of technology and a rise in the productive power of labor, this only intensifies the exploitation of the working class. This development of capitalism thus puts in place the *objective*, material conditions necessary for socialism, with a rapid expansion of the productive power and socialization of labor, while at the same time the exploitation of workers drives forward class conflict and the class struggles of workers, bringing about a high level of socialist consciousness, and thereby creating the *subjective* conditions for socialism. This means the victory of socialism is not a moralistic demand or question of a choice, but a historical *necessity*. Socialist revolution, in turn, involves placing the privately owned means of production under "social ownership" and implementing a planned organization of the social production process so as to ensure the overall development and welfare of all members of society, while eliminating societal divisions and freeing humanity from exploitation.

This first section presents an understanding of capitalism and socialism at the most abstract and essential level, but it is no exaggeration to say that the rest of the program, and the political activity of the MWL as a whole, flows from this understanding, which provides the socialist movement with a sense of direction. We can compare this understanding of socialism as a historical necessity that is "determined" by capitalism and its contradictions, with the JCP's description in its current program of how a socialist society emerges:

> Such a [socialist] transformation begins with forming a consensus among a majority of the people in support of an advance toward socialism/communism; power aiming for socialism will be established with a backing of a stable parliamentary majority. Building a national consensus is prerequisite for taking action throughout these stages.[31]

Here we have the view of socialism as a "choice" mentioned above. That is, there is no objective reality making the move to socialism necessary, which can instead be arrived at any time, conveniently making use of the organs of bourgeois political rule to expropriate the bourgeoisie![32]

The first section of the MWL program, of course, remains at a high level of abstraction, and subsequent sections move toward a more concrete, historical understanding of capitalism (and its stages), by examining capitalist development throughout the world, and in Japan specifically, with the second section looking at the age of imperialism and the Russian Revolution, the third describing the "current world system" and the "prospects for world socialism," and the fourth section examining the development of Japanese capitalism and the nature of the coming revolution in Japan. In this fourth section, it is clearly stated:

---

31. Taken from the JCP website (www.jcp.or.jp).
32. Trotsky hardly provides a much better understanding of how socialism and class-consciousness are determined by capitalist development. His *Death Agony of Capitalism and the Tasks of the Fourth International*, which has served directly as a program or programmatic prototype for Trotskyist parties throughout the world, begins with a section entitled, promisingly enough, "The Objective Prerequisites for Socialism." But instead of providing us with a deeper understanding of how capitalist development determines socialism, he simply states that throughout the world the "economic prerequisite for the proletarian revolution has already in general achieved the highest point of fruition that can be reached under capitalism" and that these perquisites "have not only 'ripened'; they have begun to get somewhat rotten." This statement, of course, was only true at the time for countries in Europe and North America. But more importantly, for Trotsky the objective situation is merely a backdrop for the activity on the political stage, and he does not provide any understanding of the relation that exists between the two. His focus is on the "crisis of the revolutionary leadership" which underlies the "historical crisis of mankind," but for Hayashi and the MWL the "crisis of revolutionary leadership" is closely related to the inability of Stalinist (and Trotskyist!) parties to base the socialist struggle upon an objective understanding of capitalism, which accounts in no small part for the proclivity to engage narrow political maneuvering.

> Since the rule of monopoly capital is decisively established in Japan, and political democracy has been realized, the coming revolution in Japan can only be a *proletarian socialist revolution* to overthrow monopoly capital.

The working class is also described as naturally assuming leadership of the revolutionary struggle to overthrow monopoly capital and establish a proletarian government that would introduce a socialist system of production. Here, as in the first section, the understanding of the nature of the coming revolution emerges directly from the historical and theoretical understanding of capitalism in general and its concrete development in Japan.

The fifth section examines the content of the class struggles of workers and the tasks of the MWL. It begins by stressing that the trade union (economic) struggles of workers *alone* do not constitute a true class struggle, and that these struggles must develop into a comprehensive political struggle confronting the bourgeoisie as a whole and its state power. This is because, like all previous ruling classes, the class rule of the bourgeoisie is concentrated in its state apparatus, so that without assuming political power there is clearly no way for the working class to achieve socialism. This section then provides an overview of the political leadership of the working class throughout the world and in Japan since the nineteenth century. Finally the basic tasks of the MWL are listed, which include emphasizing international solidarity, propagating revolutionary ideas, developing the class-consciousness of workers, rejecting of class-collaborationism, and linking trade union struggles to the broader socialist movement.

This discussion is followed by a list of the policies to be immediately taken upon the formation of a revolutionary workers government in the sixth section, which provides a much clearer and concrete understanding of the significance of a socialist revolution and how socialism will differ from capitalism. The MWL offers no "minimum (reformist) demands," reflecting the fact that the clear aim of the MWL is socialism. This does not mean, however, that the MWL adopts an aloof attitude toward the various forms of "economic" or "democratic" struggles. The point emphasized in the MWL program, rather, is that such reforms should not be treated as goals in and of themselves, and instead positioned within, and connected to, the larger movement for socialism.[33]

---

33. This relation between reforms and the socialist movement is discussed in greater detail in the section on the Socialist Workers Party.

The program outlined above clearly places the emphasis on reaching theoretical clarity regarding a variety of aspects directly related to the socialist movement. This reflects the confidence of the MWL in the power of revolutionary ideas and the view that an objective analysis of capitalist society has revolutionary implications. This approach contrasted sharply with the new left's fetish of action and violence at the expense of theory, and with the JCP's parliamentarian approach of chasing after votes by appealing to (and representing) petty-bourgeoisie class interests. The basic "strategy" of the MWL was simply to spread revolutionary ideas among workers and organize them, with the means of accomplishing this including the publication of a central newspaper, handing out of flyers at demonstrations and trade union gatherings, and holding public meetings to address political and theoretical issues.

In addition to these sorts of activities, which were also employed by Zenkokushaken, the MWL set itself the goal of participating in the political struggle more actively by taking part in elections. The aim, again, was not simply to win votes in any way possible—or spread illusions that socialism was possible through the ballot box—but to spread revolutionary ideas among the working class. At the same time, the MWL did not adopt the "ultra-radical" (and self-contradictory) position of some new left candidates who entered election races only to denounce the absurdity of the parliamentarian system. The MWL, while having no illusions in bourgeois democracy and recognizing its clear limitations, sought to make use of this system as a means of advancing the socialist movement. A 1976 book explaining the MWL's election stance described this aim:

> It is this linking of the call for the overthrow of monopoly capital (=LDP) to the firm opposition to all opportunism...that is the strategic basis of the political struggles of the MWL. And it is no exaggeration to say that we measure the success of our election struggle on the basis of whether we have been able to connect these two struggles to the development and deepening of the class struggles and class-consciousness of workers.[34]

In its twelve years of existence, the MWL candidates participated in Diet elections six times, and published a number of books during election cam-

---

34. Hayashi Hiroyoshi, et. al. *Rōdō-ha, shakaishugi-ha no daihyō wo kokkai he!* (Tokyo: Zenkokushaken-sha, 1976) 51.

paigns to presents its political stance and criticize the positions of other parties.

Two Paths to Nowhere

By the time the MWL was formed, Hayashi could look back with some satisfaction on the fact that a fruitful path had been taken, or at least that it had been wise to avoid the sterile paths taken by the radicals and Stalinists. That is to say, by the early seventies it was quite clear, even to the casual observer, that the new left had lost its luster and was without direction, and that the JCP had crystallized as a purely petty-bourgeois, reformist party.

The only thing *new* about the radical movement since the collapse of the Bund was the large number of "sects" appearing on the scene, some created through splits and others being new tendencies (such as Maoism). The fragmentation of the radical movement could also be seen within the student movement itself, with a number of organizations connected to one sect or group of sects claiming to be the true "Zengakuren." Each of the major sects had strongholds in particular universities, and student activists tended to join whatever group happened to control the student self-governing association at their school or department.

But there seems little point in delving into this organizational labyrinth, because regardless of the nuances in their position, none of the sects were able to supercede the radicalism that characterized the activities of the Bund. And whereas the Bund was at least progressive for its time, in terms of exposing Stalinism *in practice*, the so-called "second radical movement" of the sixties, by not progressing one step further, became increasingly reactionary. Like the approach of the Bund, left radicals in the late sixties continued to seize upon any reformist movement that happened to spring up, blowing its significance completely out of proportion, and seeking to use such movements as a springboard to "revolution."

Following the collapse of the Bund, it was not until around 1965 that the radical movement began to pick up steam again. Some of the issues that sparked the revival were opposition to the bombing of North Vietnam and to the Japan-South Korea Normalization Treaty, but it was the campus struggles of the second half of the sixties that marked the true "high point" of the movement. The issues students were protesting differed depending on the particular university, but their demands generally centered on calling for greater student involvement in university administration. Many of the campus movements were led by "non-sect radicals," so-called because they did not belong to any particular new left group, but their political ideas and tactics clearly fell into the same general category of "radicalism." Often a campus struggle would begin over some relatively trivial issue, before escalating to the point where the student leaders themselves could scarcely articulate their own demands, and sweeping slogans such as "Dissolve the Universities!" were voiced. In this way, even though the "university struggles" mainly centered on campus-related issues, student activists dressed up their actions in ultra-revolutionary garb, even speaking of universities as "liberated zones" that could be used to wage revolution.

Hayashi was critical of the students' inability or unwillingness to connect their movement in any real way to the socialist movement, and he noted that workers were naturally ambivalent toward such a narrow movement. At the same time, however, he also noted that there was a "basis" for the students' rebellion. That is to say, the university system was expanding rapidly in the fifties and sixties to foster the wide managerial class that a rapidly-growing capitalist system required, and students were rebelling against their future class role within this system. Moreover, Hayashi was critical of the JCP position, which ignored the class nature of the universities, speaking of them as "places of pure learning," and only sought cosmetic reforms to give professors and students a greater role in administration. But even given this attitude, Hayashi (and Zenkokushaken) could not endorse a student movement that had no relation or connection to the working-class movement for socialism.

In addition to the campus rebellions, another issue that loomed large in the late sixties, at least in the minds of Japanese radicals, was the revision of the Japan-U.S. Security Treaty scheduled for 1970. Several years prior to this date, they were nearly salivating at the revolutionary opportunities that this much-advertised sequel to the 1960 struggle seemed to offer. In March 1970, a group calling itself the Japanese Red Army, attempted to give the "Anpo struggle" a morale boost by hijacking a plane and diverting it to Pyongyang. The (crazy) idea was to carry out a "simultaneous world revolution" using North Korea as a springboard, which was chosen after plans to set up a "revolutionary base" in Cuba fell through. Needless to say, this example of politics based solely upon *subjectivism* exposed the limitations of radicalism in Japan (and elsewhere). In the end, not surprisingly, the movement to block the treaty failed as it had a decade earlier, and the defeat of this "decisive struggle" once again plunged radicals into despair—but this time, the movement never fully recovered from this setback.

In the seventies, the only radical movement of any real importance or scale was the alliance between radicals and farmers to block the construction of a new international airport outside of Tokyo in Chiba Prefecture. The farmers, who were forced to sell their land, were obviously happy to find any allies they could, but they were solely concerned with holding on to their land and had no interest in socialism. The fact that new left groups unconditionally supported this movement of small landowners, and even argued in characteristic fashion that it had revolutionary potential, only revealed how comfortable they were within the confines of petty-bourgeois radicalism.

For the most part, the seventies were a period where new left sects channeled all of their frustration and anger at each other. Of course, even in the sixties it was not uncommon to see pitched battles between rival groups of students, armed with wooden sticks and sporting their distinctive helmets (featuring each group's trademark colors and "logos"), but this resulted mainly in concussions and the occasional broken bone. In the seventies, however, the conflict between sects—referred to as *uchi-geba* (internal violence)—greatly intensified. New left groups began assassinating activists from rival groups, usually by bludgeoning them to death with iron pipes, and in 1975 alone twenty new left activists were killed. This insanity was "justified" by the groups involved on the basis of claims that the other organizations were "tools of state power," "spy organizations," or "counter-revolutionaries." The sheer lunacy of the new left movement in the seventies no doubt contributed—along with the emergence of the "bubble economy"—to a significant drop in student activism during the eighties.

Even today, the feud between Kakumru-ha and Chukakku-ha continues—who were at the center of *uchi-geba* in the seventies—with over-heated name-calling in the pages of their newspapers, but in recent years such conflicts remain largely on this rhetorical level, and new left groups seem to have mellowed considerably. One example is the "Second Bund," which participated in the sixties university struggles and the movement to stop the airport. Today this group mildly states its aim as:

> We are going to change Japan to a complete republic without an Emperor.
> We will pursue the antiwar movement.
> We also act to build an environmentally sustainable society.[35]

---

35. From the (second) Bund's website (www.bund.org).

If there is any difference between such purely reformist demands and those advanced by the JCP I would be curious to know what it is.

Of course, even the new left is hard-pressed to outpace the JCP's move, further and further, to the right. Every few years, much to the delight of the bourgeoisie, the JCP announces that it is "softening" its political line by throwing out from its program some conspicuous remnant of its former left-wing rhetoric. The bourgeoisie would be wise, however, to be careful what it wishes for. That is to say, as far as class-conscious workers are concerned, the sooner the JCP completely drops its pretence of representing the working class, the better, since this would only facilitate the building of a new, revolutionary workers' party. Unfortunately, the JCP seems intent on holding on to the "communist" label a bit longer, whether out of nostalgia or a desire to drain the word of all meaning.

The position of the JCP since its last fling with radicalism in the fifties has been nothing if not consistent. The party continues to focus most of its energy on winning votes and parliamentarian seats, and it has also has not let go of its fixed idea that Japan is a "semi-colony" of the U.S. The coming revolution in Japan, according to the JCP, will be a "democratic" one that sweeps away this U.S. dominance. The JCP's newest program, adopted on January 17, 2004, describes the content of this revolution as follows:

> A change Japanese society needs at present is a democratic revolution instead of a socialist revolution. It is a revolution that puts an end to Japan's extraordinary subordination to the United States and the tyrannical rule of large corporations and business circles, a revolution that secures Japan's genuine independence and carries out democratic reforms in politics, the economy, and society...Success in achieving this democratic change will help solve problems that cause the people to suffer and pave the way for building an independent, democratic, and peaceful Japan that safeguards the fundamental interests of the majority of the people.[36]

In other words, the JCP continues to insist that Japan, which is one of the most highly developed capitalist countries on the planet, has yet to achieve a bourgeois revolution! The JCP does make mention of the future "socialist/communist society" in its program, but pours cold water on any enthusiasm we might have by informing us that the "socialist transformation will not be car-

---

36. From the JCP website.

ried out in a short period of time; it will be a long process that needs a stage-by-stage progress based on national consensus." Not only will this "transformation" take a long time, the JCP blandly insists, in the end life under socialism won't be all that different from capitalism. The JCP emphasizes, for example, that "socialist reforms" must be carried out that combine "elements of the planned economy and the market economy," and that "socialization of the means of production can take on a variety of forms of ownership." These are basically the same views the JCP held back in the fifties, but today at least their petty-bourgeois fantasies are expressed in a more open and "honest" form.

Socialist Workers Party (Sharōtō)

In 1984, the Marxist Workers League changed its name to the Socialist Workers Party (Sharōtō), reflecting the desire to function to an even greater extent as a revolutionary *political* organization. The political standpoint of the SWP was based largely upon that of the MWL, including a critical stance toward popular front tactics and "democratic coalition" governments, the view of the Soviet Union as state capitalism, and a rejection of reformism.

The program of the SWP[37] was structured similarly to the MWL program, beginning with an essential definition of capitalism, and then a more concrete analysis of capitalist development throughout the world, before moving on to a general description of socialism, the tasks to achieve it, and the "concrete demands" to be implemented with the victory of socialism. The first paragraph, for instance, sketches the essence of capitalism and its limitations:

> Under capitalism, labor products are produced not merely for their use-value—i.e. their quality of satisfying some human need—but as commodities for exchange. This is because capitalism is based on private property and the division of labor, where individuals pursue private interests from the starting point of general competition. Human beings have yet to bring social production under their own conscious control, and instead remain subordinated to the blind movement of the "economy." This reveals that we still remain in the stage of the "pre-history" of humanity.

---

37. An English translation of the SWP program is available on the MCG website.

Similarly, the program describes socialism in general terms, including the following overview that contrasts with the preceding description of capitalism:

> With the realization of socialist production, people will work collectively upon nature and refashion it to create wealth (objects of need) for the sake of consumption and the satisfaction of needs. These relations—between people and nature and between themselves—become perfectly transparent and plain. This will bring to an end the sort of "partial people" with narrow perspectives who are chained to one occupation or job throughout their lives for the sake of capital's profit. Under socialism, it will become possible for social interests and possibilities to branch out in all directions. As the subordination of people to capital and machines is done away with, it will becomes clear that people can use automation, robots and computers, rather than being used by them.

Like the MWL, the SWP emphasizes that the class struggle of workers is the means of achieving socialism, with the primary "moments" of this struggle being the propagation of ideas and organization of workers, and that the class struggle of workers only truly merits the name when it is raised to the level of being an overall political struggle aimed at ending class rule of the bourgeoisie. This means that the aim of the SWP is to strive to link everyday class struggles to the larger class struggle for the realization of socialism, with the former contributing to the development of the latter. Connecting these two levels of struggles does not mean, however, that the SWP looked down on, or shunned participation in, the everyday economic struggles of workers and the fight for democratic rights. The point the SWP program emphasizes, rather, is that such struggles should not be detached from the socialist movement and turned into autonomous goals.

To better understand why the SWP insisted on this position, and what it means in practice, it may help to consider the concrete example of the trade union movement. For the SWP, the economic struggles of the working class to improve wages and working conditions, typically led by trade unions, are seen as the starting point for the development of proletarian class struggle. The general position of the SWP toward these trade union struggles is the following:

> The SWP must rally a wide stratum of workers, be at the forefront of these struggles, foster the class power of the workers, and unite the party with the working masses. At the same time, the SWP needs to make clear that the

real solution to the workers' problems lies in the realization of socialism, and attempt to link everyday class struggles to the class struggle for socialism.

Underlying the assertion above that socialism is the "real solution" to the workers' problems is an understanding of the nature of exploitation under capitalism (discussed in detail in chapter one of this book). Somewhat simply put, even if capitalists pay workers the full value of their labor-power "commodity"—which is determined indirectly by the value of the commodities a worker consumes to "reproduce" this labor capacity—they are still able to obtain surplus-value (exploit labor) because the value of labor-power is not identical to the value that workers add to commodities in the production process. In other words, the "equal" exchange between worker and capitalist masks a relation of inequality that cannot be eliminated under capitalism, because capitalist production is carried out with the aim of producing surplus-value (profit). Although wages may at times even rise above the "value" of labor-power, they cannot rise to the point that the creation of surplus-value is eliminated, or even fundamentally threatened.

In other words, even if trade unions are able to force capitalists to pay a "fair wage" this does not mean that exploitation has been eliminated. Of course, recognizing this essential "limitation" of trade-unionist, economic struggles against capital does not mean that their importance is downplayed or that socialists should tell workers there is little point in fighting capital to maintain or increase wage levels. Indeed, Marx recognized the absolute necessity for workers' to fight what he called a "guerrilla war," using trade unions as "centers of resistance against the encroachments of capital"—but at the same time he never severs this defensive battle from the larger, revolutionary struggle:

> At the same time…the working class ought not to exaggerate to themselves the ultimate working of these everyday struggles. They ought not to forget that they are fighting with effects, but not with the causes of those effects…They ought, therefore, not to be exclusively absorbed in these unavoidable guerilla fights incessantly springing up from the never ceasing encroachments of capital or changes of the market. They ought to understand that, with all the miseries it imposes upon them, the present system simultaneously engenders the material conditions and the social forms necessary for an economical reconstruction of society. Instead of the conservative motto, "A fair day's wage for a fair day's work!" they ought to inscribe

on their banner the revolutionary watchword, "Abolition of the wages system!"[38]

Marx shows us that workers can "chew gum and walk at the same time"—or, more appropriately, they can fight the symptoms of a (social) disease while also seeking its cure—i.e. they can fight capitalists to get paid "fairly" while at the same time use their organizational strength to contribute to the movement to eliminate the entire unfair set-up altogether.[39]

The question of the attitude to take toward "reformist" everyday struggles is of course not limited to the trade union movement. The SWP, for instance, also emphasized the need to link movements opposing sexual or racist discrimination to the socialist movement, based on the recognition that full equality cannot be achieved under capitalism. This is because discrimination is not merely the outcome of outdated ways of thinking or inadequate laws, but has a "material" basis under capitalism. In the case of racial discrimination, it is obvious that dividing the working class along racial lines is strongly in the interests of the ruling class. But even sexual discrimination has a basis, with the natural functions of childbirth and pregnancy placing women in a position of disadvantage vis-à-vis capital, which is only concerned with obtaining profit. Discrimination must of course be resisted in the present, but at the same time it is only by uprooting its real basis—by overcoming class divisions and carrying out production for the needs of society and its members—that it can be fully and forever eliminated.

This understanding of the need to connect "everyday struggles" to the socialist movement is the reason that the SWP posed "concrete demands" to be realized along with the realization of socialism, rather than offering independent reformist demands that were severed from this movement and treated as independent goals. The SWP program notes that these demands "are pro-

---

38. Karl Marx, *Marx-Engels Collected Works* (New York: International Publishers, 1986), 149.
39. Here I won't discuss the manner in which this connection between the two levels is made, but this is touched on in the article "What Kind of Party is the SWP" (MCG website). One point to note, however, is that the SWP does not advocate *dissolving* the trade union movement directly into the socialist movement, so that trade unions would come under the direct control of a political party, nor is the position taken that labor unions should form their own political party.

posed within the struggle aiming for socialism, and are objectives or demands
to be realized along with the development of this struggle and the realization
of socialism." The first demand, for instance, is the realization of a four-hour
workday and the outlawing of nighttime labor. This demand is based on the
understanding that under socialism an increase in the productivity of labor is
the basis for dramatically shortening the working day, whereas this cannot be
achieved under capitalism given the aim of production being to generate
profit, which is obtained by squeezing more free labor from workers. Workers
obviously need to strive for shorter working hours today, but this struggle
should not be based on any illusions in the nature of the capitalist system.

Reflecting its attitude toward reformism, the SWP did not view participation in elections as a goal in itself, nor did they have any illusion that socialism
could be reached through achieving a parliamentary majority. For the SWP,
the struggle for greater "democracy" is an important task, but this cannot overlook the limitations of democracy under capitalism (i.e. "bourgeois democracy"), which is not in contradiction with the widespread exploitation of
workers. Thus, instead of making the fight for democracy a goal in itself, the
position of the SWP was to "make use of" bourgeois democracy in order to
advance the movement for socialism. This means, in particular, making use of
elections, which are the officially recognized platform for political struggle
under capitalism. This is different from the approach of the JCP, which only
aims to win votes, and either shuns talk of socialism or offers the fantasy that
it can be achieved through the ballot box. The aim of the SWP, by contrast,
was to use the election platform to spread socialist ideas among the working
class, while at the same time recognizing that the bourgeoisie can never be dis-
lodged through the election process alone.

With this basic approach in mind, the SWP focused considerable energy
on participation in elections. The organization fielded a number of candidates
in 1986 for the proportional representative elections and received about
140,000 votes. The SWP then set its sights on the 1989 elections, hoping for
a qualitative leap forward. But the result was nearly the same as three years
earlier, which led to considerable discouragement. This struggle to make significant progress on the election front was aggravated by subsequent revisions
to the election laws that made it increasingly difficult and expensive for small
political parties to participate.

At the same time, owing to its insufficient strength, the SWP was unable
to make progress in practically linking the trade union movement and various
"democratic" movements to the larger movement for socialism, apart from

efforts at the level of "propaganda" to clarify the necessity of this connection or the activities of individual party members within their own trade unions. By the mid-nineties, then, the SWP—despite its name—was functioning more as a revolutionary circle than a political party, with it being difficult to expand the scope of its influence. Of course, to a large extent both the MWL and the SWP faced the difficulty of advocating socialism during a period in Japan where, despite occasional problems such as inflation, capitalism was still largely "delivering the goods." Another factor, of course, was the negative influence of the JCP and infantile radicals, who contributed greatly to the tarnishing of both Marx's name and the very idea of socialism.

But there certainly had been an expectation among SWP members that the downturn in the Japanese economy in the nineties would lead to an upswing in the workers movement, making it easier to spread socialist ideas among workers. This, unfortunately, has not been the case, even as the economic crisis has now continued for over a decade, and the working class movement has remained largely stagnant. Of course, one cannot account for this situation without recognizing that the Japanese state has intervened on a massive scale to keep the economy afloat and blunt the effects of the crisis, accumulating an astounding debt in the process. In this sense, the bourgeois state is clearly living on borrowed time, and everyone recognizes that the situation in Japan—as elsewhere—is extremely volatile, with sudden change not only possible but likely. At the same time, the SWP at the turn of the century felt the need to make a decision regarding its current situation; namely, whether or not the organization should hold on to its current name and structure despite not functioning fully as a political party.

Creation of Marxist Comrades Group

The decision was made in November 2002 to dissolve the SWP and form a revolutionary circle called the Marxist Comrades Group. This was based on the conclusion that although the SWP had used the means at its disposal to clarify its political standpoint—exposing the government and opportunistic political groups—such activities remained within the limits of political statements, which, although one aspect of political activities, is a subordinate one that does not in itself signify a political struggle in the true meaning of the word. True political (or class) struggle, it was argued, involves leading a mass movement, including large-scale demonstrations and public meetings, as well as participating in nationwide elections. Instead of waiting longer, then, in the hope that the SWP would develop into a political party, the choice was made to "continue struggles in a different form" by creating a new organization.

The members of the SWP felt they had a responsibility to speak the truth to workers, which also meant telling them the truth about their own organization. If the SWP had carried on bearing the fictitious label of being a political party, it was seen as running the risk of decaying as an organization. As the founding statement of the organization noted:

> If we are to be an organization that bears a position of responsibility toward the working class, we must appear before the working class with the truth, and this is the path for us to win the confidence of workers and connect with them. We have no need to be concerned with vanity and appearances.[40]

Although the decision was clearly seen as a step backward, however necessary, Hayashi at the same time emphasized the opportunity that it presented in terms of members coming to a better understanding of the fundamentals of Marxism, specifically Marx's labor theory of value. The emphasis on Marxism is, of course, clear in the name of the organization itself, which was also emphasized in the founding statement:

> The name of the organization indicates that we fully base our theory and thought on Marxism [which] is certainly not outdated or bankrupt. Indeed, it is becoming increasingly clear that Marxism is the only system of thought and theory that can lead the liberation movement of the working class—the only scientific system that can provide a true understanding of present-day capitalist society and thus lead the class movement of the workers. For these reasons, we openly affirm the truth of Marxism. Vulgar petty-bourgeois political tendencies—such as the JCP, Social-Democratic Party, or new left sects—are increasingly bankrupt and feel free to attack or negate Marxism…But we will stick to the class standpoint of the workers and Marxism, and on this foundation we are seeking to reconstruct the movement and develop it further.

Hayashi, somewhat tongue-in-cheek, uses the expression "fundamentalist movement" to describe the new organization's emphasis on acquiring the fundamentals of Marxist thought, based on the recognition that it is not enough

---

40. Taken from the MCG website.

to pay lip-service to Marxism without being familiar with Marx's theory. The aim, however, is not to read Marx as a sort of intellectual pastime. Rather, Marx's theory is positioned as being important because it provides a clearer, scientific understanding of capitalism, starting with a grasp of capitalism at its most essential level.

The various branches of the organization have been involved in organizing study groups to read *Capital* or examine more specific topics related to capitalist society, and once a year a "Workers' Seminar" has been held to discuss theoretical topics in greater detail.[41] At the same time, many of the activities of the SWP have been continued, including the publication of a weekly newspaper that examines and exposes government policy and the positions of various political tendencies, and of a theoretical journal to examine issues in more depth. In this sense, the emphasis of the new organization remains spreading socialist ideas among workers and raising their class-consciousness.

The Breadth of Hayashi's Work

My discussion thus far, which has focused on issues related to the revolutionary socialist movement, does not provide a very good sense of the variety of topics that Hayashi has addressed over the more than four decades he has been active as a socialist. To begin with, as the editor of weekly political newspapers during this time, he has written countless articles dealing with pressing political and theoretical issues. Similarly, as an organizational leader, Hayashi has been involved in the writing of political flyers, has frequently made speeches at political rallies, and he has played a central role in drafting the political programs examined above.

In addition to all of this work related directly to political activities, Hayashi has dealt with more theoretical questions, which of course includes the content of this book. The interest in more fundamental theoretical questions often arose because of a given political task or some development within the organization. For example, the criticism of the philosophical subjectivism of the new left, particularly the theories of Kuroda Kan'ichi, raised a number of more general, fundamental questions related to materialism and idealism that were explored. Similarly, a debate within the SWP over Stalin's theory of the

---

41. In 2004, the MCG examined errors in Engels' editing of the third volume of *Capital* that came to light with the recent publication of Marx's original manuscript, particularly as they relate to Marx's theory of credit.

nation led Hayashi to examine this question in great detail and develop a theory of his own regarding the concept of the nation.[42] The development of capitalism itself has also necessitated a theoretical response, and since the seventies Hayashi has focused considerably energy on addressing issues related to the monetary system, including his examination of the phenomenon of inflation, criticism of the views of Keynes, study of the "managed currency system" and the gold standard, and research on Marx's theory of the money.

We can get an idea of the range of the theoretical topics Hayashi has addressed by looking at the content of the six-volume set of his selected writings published in the late nineties. In addition to this book (volume one) and another volume presenting his theory of state capitalism, there is a volume focusing on capitalism at a more concrete level, including his examination of the bubble economy, massive state debt, and the postwar IMF system, as well as criticism of Hilferding's theory of finance capital. Other volumes included articles and essays on philosophical idealism and religious superstition, women's liberation (and criticism of bourgeois "feminists"), education, the theory of the nation and nationalism, the Japanese emperor system, and the movement against the national flag and anthem.

The breadth of Hayashi's work is a reflection of the complexity of the socialist movement itself, and of how an organization representing the working class has a responsibility to gain the deepest possible understanding of capitalist society in all of its aspects. Without always striving for this understanding of objective reality—so that our thoughts "reflect" the reality of capitalist society as fully as possible—any organization can easily fall into dogmatism. At the same time, Hayashi's approach as a socialist is different from the approach of academics or "intellectuals," as he always bears in mind the ultimate aim of the movement—*socialism*. This means that rather than knowledge being pursued for its own sake, a given subject is examined because it has some "practical" significance in terms of moving the socialist movement forward.

---

42. A number of essays on the issue of the nation are available on the MCG website, including the key article "What is a Nation? Marxism and the Concept of Nation."

"Beginnings are Difficult"

In my overview of Hayashi's participation in the socialist movement, I have mentioned that an understanding of capitalism is the fundamental theoretical basis that guides the activities of a socialist organization, and offered some examples to demonstrate this. But even bearing this, revolutionary, significance in mind, I think many readers will find both *Capital* and this book difficult. Marx himself was well aware of the difficulty that *Capital*, particularly its first chapter, posed, and made every effort to popularize his presentation. But at the same time he recognized that it was impossible to eliminate this difficulty entirely, noting that "beginnings are difficult in all sciences." In the preface to the French edition of his book, moreover, Marx offers to "readers who zealously seek the truth" the following words of warning and encouragement:

> There is no royal road to science, and only those who do not dread the fatiguing climb of its steep paths have a chance of gaining its luminous summits.[43]

Some may wonder, however, what Marx means by science, and whether this term is appropriate to refer to the study of society (capitalism). One hint of Marx's understanding of the significance of science in general is reflected in his statement that, "all science would be superfluous if the form of appearance of things directly coincided with their essence."[44] In other words, a scientific understanding involves going beyond the appearance of things to arrive at a more essential level. But how can we do this? In the case of physical sciences, those wishing to grasp a given organism on a more profound level can, of course, physically dissect the organism or examine it on the cellular level using a microscope. But for the "social scientist," as Marx notes, "neither microscopes nor chemical reagents are of assistance," and both are replaced by "the power of abstraction."[45]

Normally, we tend to think of "abstract" and "concrete" as mere opposites, but for Marx it is only possible to arrive at the fullest understanding of concrete reality by first *abstracting* from it. He illustrates this point in a brilliant

---

43. *Capital*, vol. 1, 104.
44. Karl Marx, *Capital*, vol. 3, trans. David Fernbach (London: Penguin Books, 1981), 956.
45. *Capital*, vol. 1, 90.

explanation of his "method of political economy" in the introduction to *Grundrisse*. Marx explains that it seems natural to begin the study of political economy "with the real and the concrete," such as the "population" of a country, but that such concrete things or concepts contains various "determinations" and component parts. Without understanding this content, a "concrete" concept will, ironically, remain a mere abstraction. We can use the power of abstraction to "unpack" such concrete concepts, uncovering their essential determinations or "moments." In the case of "population," for example, further examination reveals that the population of a given capitalist country is composed of classes, which can only be grasped on the basis of understanding wage labor, capital, etc., and these concepts in turn contain their own determinations. One thus moves "analytically towards ever more simple concepts [*Begriff*], from the imagined concrete towards ever thinner abstractions" until arriving "at the simplest determinations."[46]

But the aim is not simply to arrive at this most abstract level. As Hayashi notes, abstract concepts, as such, although necessary to understand reality more deeply and essentially, still diverge from *direct* reality. Thus, just as a scientist cannot remain on the cellular level of an organism if the aim is to explain its functioning as a whole, so must the social scientist move from the abstract to the concrete. But when we arrive at the concrete again, it is no longer an "abstraction" as a "chaotic conception of a whole," but rather a "rich totality of many determinations and relations." Indeed, for Marx "the concrete is concrete because it is the concentration of many determinations, hence unity of the diverse."[47]

The difficulty at the beginning of *Capital*, therefore, is that we are dealing not with the concrete whole, but rather with the most abstract or "cellular" level of capitalism, i.e. with the commodity as the elementary form or "economic cell-form" of capitalism. This beginning is, at the same time, the endpoint of Marx's previous process of inquiry (abstraction), whereby he arrives at the simplest determinations of capitalist society. This is precisely why the beginning of the "science of capitalism" is *necessarily* difficult. That is to say, even if Marx had started with a more "concrete" concept, such as money or capital, he would still have been obliged to work his way back to the same

---

46. Karl Marx, *Grundrisse*, trans. Ben Fowkes (London: Penguin Books, 1973), 100.

47. Ibid., 101.

starting point, because these more complex concepts are themselves determined by simpler ones. Money, for example, can itself be reduced to the commodity, and the circuit of capital (M-C-M) is itself based upon commodity circulation (C-M-C).

But when we read *Capital* for the first time, we are largely unaware of the process of analysis and abstraction leading "down" to our starting point. The level of abstraction we are dealing and the relation of abstract concepts to more concrete reality are not necessarily clear. Moreover, Marx uses words we are familiar with—such as "commodity" or "value"—in unfamiliar and seemingly limited ways, so that we get the strong impression that he is randomly introducing *a priori* concepts. Marx himself recognizes the impression his book will likely have, noting that if the presentation is "done successfully" so that "the life of the subject-matter is now reflected back in the ideas, then it may appear as if we have before us an *a priori* construction."[48]

To some extent, then, first-time readers need to suspend their disbelief when reading chapter one of *Capital*, and resist the temptation to conclude that Marx is mistaken because the concepts he is introducing do not correspond *directly* to concrete reality as we know it. It is only after persevering somewhat, so as to arrive at more complex phenomena, that we are in a position to evaluate whether Marx is leading us in a fruitful direction or not. One such moment, I think, is when we arrive at Marx's explanation of how surplus-value is created in his discussion of the exploitation of labor. Here some important pieces fall into place, and we can appreciate why the effort to come to grips with concepts such as (exchange-) value and value-determination was worthwhile. This seems to be one of the "luminous summits" that Marx promises readers as a reward for their efforts.

To better understand the significance of Marx's "method" it may help to consider an *unscientific* approach to "political economy." Throughout his book, Hayashi refers to the example of Uno Kōzō and others who remain fixated at the phenomenal level, never arriving at the underlying concepts and laws. This is the reason Hayashi frequently refers to the thought of such scholars as being *mugainen* (non-conceptual or concept-free). Uno, for instance, speaks of the "value" of a commodity, but his understanding really corresponds to its *price* (exchange-value), which is the easily visible, phenomenal form of value. Never venturing beyond this level of appearance, Uno cannot grasp what "deter-

---

48. *Capital*, vol. 1, 102.

mines" the exchange-value (price) of a commodity or understand how exchange-value is the necessary "mode of expression" or "form of appearance" of the more essential concept of value.

It is from this phenomenal level that Uno offers a smug criticism of Marx, which boils down to rejecting Marx's concepts if they do not correspond *directly* to concrete reality. This view, however, ignores the need to first take a few steps away from concrete reality, through abstraction, in order to come to a richer understanding of its determinations, as mentioned above. One criticism that Uno is fond of repeating, for example, is that Marx was mistaken to assume that commodities exchange at their value because in reality this is not necessarily the case. Marx, however, was fully conscious of this fact, but in seeking to uncover the law that governs commodity exchange, he recognized the obvious need to set superfluous elements to one side and assume that a commodity is not being sold above or below its value. As Hayashi observes:

> In reality, commodities are not exchanged according to value. The law of value, as the essence of the price phenomenon (and exchange-value), only determines this from behind the scenes. When considering the essence of exchange-value—its determining law—there is little point in setting aside the law itself and pointing out that this does not appear as such in reality. At issue *is* the law, and it is for this reason that the object must be considered in its "pure form"!

Uno overlooks the theoretical issue Marx is examining here—and elsewhere—repeating *ad nauseam* that Marx has assumed something that "does not exist in reality." The fact is, however, that Marx does eventually account for how the prices of commodities can diverge from their intrinsic value, but this explanation is premised on the concept of value developed earlier in its "pure form," and upon more complex concepts such as production price. In short, this again reflects the "upward journey" from the abstract to the concrete. If we adopt the "method" of Uno instead, and impatiently try to explain everything at once, we end up understanding nothing at all, or simply describing reality as it appears phenomenally.

In addition to misunderstanding his method of abstraction, another way critics of Marx are "concept-free" is that they tend to ignore the significance of viewing capitalism as one *historical form* of society. This means that they only focus on the bourgeois or "formal" determinations of a concept, without considering the more fundamental or "original" determinations. The best example

of this is the commodity. Uno only looks at its "bourgeois" or "formal" determination as something with exchange-value (price), so that for him a commodity is nothing more than anything with a price that is exchanged, ignoring
the aspect of the commodity as the product of *labor*. Of course, it is true that
under capitalism many things that do not have value—such as land—come to
be "commodities," but Hayashi reminds us that Marx explains these "formal
commodities" as derivative phenomena that must be explained on the basis of
the more fundamental concept of the commodity presented in chapter one of
Capital. Marx's view reflects, on the most fundamental level, his (historical
materialist) understanding that the foundation of any historical form of society, including capitalism, is the material wealth that is fashioned by labor, and
that the commodity is merely the *historical form* that products of labor assume
under capitalism (and this fact also determines the "starting point" of *Capital*).
By losing sight of the relation between a "formal" determination and the more
general determination, Uno effectively severs capitalism from previous (and
subsequent) "modes of production."

Hayashi discusses, in detail, the relation between the formal, bourgeois
determinations (definitions) of a concept and its more fundamental aspects in
his examination of the concept of productive labor chapters five and six.
Hayashi shows how Marx examines productive labor under capitalism, and in
this sense is concerned with the bourgeois, formal definition of this concept—in terms of productive labor being that labor exchanging against capital
that creates surplus-value—but this does not mean that he severs productive
labor under capitalism from its more general or "original" determination as
human labor that works upon nature to create material wealth (use-values).
For Hayashi, it is important to not only grasp the formal and original definitions of productive labor separately, and not dissolve one into the other, but
also explain their essential unity. If we lose sight of this connection, we fall
into the trap of merely describing reality as it exists (under capitalism), and
thus, in a sense, glorifying this existing reality. In the case of productive labor,
for instance, we lose sight of the real material basis of human society if we
define productive labor as any sort of labor that generates profit for capital,
which would include, for example, the labor of prostitutes and mercenaries.
Hayashi makes a similar point in discussing the theory of rent. That is, if we
focus exclusively on the forms of rent under capitalism, overlooking that all
forms of rent are one (unearned) part of the total surplus-value of society, we
end up ignoring the essentially parasitic class nature of landowners.

This short discussion of "methodological" issues has probably raised more questions than it has answered, and I will leave it to Hayashi himself to better illustrate these fundamental points. But I do think that bearing in mind some of these issues regarding abstraction and historical forms will help readers, particularly newcomers to Marx, better navigate this book—as well as *Capital*.

Notes on the Translation

As mentioned above, all of the chapters in this book first appeared in various publications of the SWP and MWL. Chapters one and three were each published as a series of articles in the SWP newspaper *Henkaku* (Revolutionary Change), with the former appearing from October 1984 to April 1987 and the latter from April to September 1987.[49] The rest of the chapters were first published in the theoretical journals of the SWP or MWL, with chapter two appearing in the September 1997 issue of *Prometheus*, chapter four in the February 1983 issue of *Scientific Communism*, and the final two chapters appearing in the December 1996 and March 1997 issues of *Prometheus*.

The main liberty I have taken in my translation involves altering some of the paragraphs, which were extremely short in the two chapters that originally appeared in *Henkaku*, and italicizing some words to hopefully better convey meaning. I have also had to modify the English translations of *Capital* at times because of mistranslations, particularly when the translations veered off sharply from the Japanese versions that Hayashi was commenting on. In retranslating these passages, I have benefited from reading Hans G. Ehrbar's annotated translation of *Capital*, and on several occasions have relied on his translation.[50]

One advantage I have enjoyed in my "struggle" to complete this translation was the opportunity to meet frequently with the author to pester him with questions and seek his help in tracking down elusive passages from Marx. (This is not meant to suggest, of course, that he bears any responsibility for whatever mistakes may remain in the translation or for the content of this introduction.) I owe a debt of gratitude to the author as well for all of his help

---

49. This accounts, incidentally, for the extreme regularity of each of the chapter's sub-sections, which were each published as separate newspaper articles.
50. Hans Ehrbar's translation is available at http://www.econ.utah.edu/ehrbar/akmk.pdf.

over the roughly seven years that I have known him, and even more so for the great amount that I have learned from reading his articles and essays. Despite there being no "royal road" to science—as Marx reminds us—it has been tremendously beneficial to have a reliable guide to indicate, first of all, where this road begins, and then to help lead the way.

February 15, 2005

Preface to the Japanese Edition

This is a book intended to defend Marxism and its most fundamental aspects. To be honest, I had nearly forgotten that I had written some of the essays included in this book. In fact, when I was searching for various papers that deal with fundamental theoretical issues to include in this book, the series of articles I wrote on the commodity [chapter one] did not spring to mind at all. Kamezaki Kanji, who was helping me with that effort, mentioned the series might be worth including in the book.

Rereading the various articles and essays, I had the feeling that our organization has done a good job of defending the theoretical foundations of Marxism, and thus carrying out our struggles upon a solid basis, and it seemed that there was a need to publish the works together as a book. That is to say, with the collapse of the "socialist" Soviet Union, and the appearance of China as an openly capitalist state, as well as the noisy talk today about the breakdown and collapse of Marxism, it is more necessary than ever to firmly defend the theoretical basis of Marxism.

From the book's title—*Marx's Labor Theory of Value: A Defense*—it is clear that I set out to defend the foundation of Marxism, but in order to do this it has been necessary to not only criticize blatantly bourgeois theorists, but also to oppose the vulgar Unoist and Communist scholars. Although such scholars place Marxism on a pedestal and praise it, they are in reality "professional" critics of Marx, who attack, revise, and distort his theories, and in this sense are nothing but two-faced hypocrites.

On occasion we are asked to clarify the tasks of our struggle or the prospects for socialism, as well as define the sort of socialism we are aiming for. With the collapse of the Soviet Union, and the failure of Stalinistic "socialism," these are indeed crucial questions. Part of the response to such questions can be found within the defense of the labor theory of value. Of course, I am only referring to the most fundamental and essential concepts.

For a long time, the Soviet Union and China were seen as socialist states and treated as absolutes, while Stalin (who "constructed socialism" in the Soviet Union) and Stalinism were glorified. Indeed, for a period of time after the Second World War, Stalin was praised as a sort of god. Today Stalinists have modified their position to a certain extent—and been obliged to do so, as it is no longer possible to conceal the terrible, fundamentally bourgeois nature of Stalin and Stalinism—and along they way they have submitted to capital. Stalinists still pay lip-service to Marxism, refer to Marx and communism, and "strike a pose" by holding on to the "Communist" label, but already there is not a trace of a proletarian basis or any Marxist elements within the actual politics and ideology of this party. The members of the Japanese Communist Party have progressed from being Stalinists to end up as run-of-the-mill, vulgar bourgeois specimens.

Of course, the JCP is not alone in terms of publicly or covertly fleeing from Marxism, and "radical" factions (new left) are no different in this sense. Radicals have rapidly undergone a conversion to liberalism, sliding into every variety of the "civic movement" [*shimin undō*] and trade-unionism. This reflects that they were never consistent champions of class struggle in the first place, but rather covert liberals (and petty bourgeois), and today they no longer feel the need to conceal this fact.

Class-conscious workers today need to defend Marxism in opposition to such irresponsible and unreliable elements, and take up the task of preparing the way for a new workers' party and resolute class struggles, reconstructing the foundation for these developments. This is the task that we are undertaking now, and I view this book as one reinforcing link in this effort.

We raise high the banner of defending Marxism and struggle to achieve this. Unlike others, we have not been surprised by the collapse of the Soviet Union or the increasing bourgeois nature of China, nor have we felt a sense of despair or defeat. This is because in the past we had already consistently indicated and exposed the capitalist foundation of the socio-economic systems in these countries. (And in response to this, the JCP labeled us "counter-revolutionaries" who were attacking the socialist states and seeking their downfall.) The collapse of these systems—far from revealing the bankruptcy of Marxism or socialism—demonstrated the correctness of our position, which is firmly based upon a Marxist standpoint.

This book, I believe, is a useful introductory, reference text for workers and young people seeking to learn more about Marxism. If examined in study groups and the like, I think readers can benefit from it in terms of learning more about the theoretical foundations of Marxism and assimilating this knowledge for themselves. My sincere hope is that readers will put this book to good use.

June 8, 1998

Preface to the English Edition

I have some doubts about whether a book on Marxism will be welcomed in the United States, or anywhere else, at this point in time—even among a small number of people. I say this because Marxism seems to have lost much of its popularity because of the historical experience of Stalinism, and this trend further accelerated in the 1990s following the collapse of the Soviet Union. Even workers have, for the most part, turned away from Marxism, which is commonly seen as a failed or "dead" ideology.

In recent years the strength of Marxism has been on the wane not only in countries where it had wielded relatively little influence to begin with, such as the United States, but also in Japan, where Marxist thought had a significant impact on society. The Japanese Communist Party already is not a Marxist party in any sense of the word. Not only has the JCP approved of the market economy in recent years, which is incorporated within their concept of "socialism," but it has also changed its position so as to recognize the Japan-U.S. Security Treaty, the emperor system, the "Self Defense Forces," as well as the *hinomaru* flag and *kimigayo* anthem. Clearly, the JCP no longer feels even the slightest need for Marxism. At the same time, this is a party whose strength and influence is on the decline. (It would be an interesting, theoretically, to consider whether this recent decline is the result of the JCP's opportunism and bourgeois corruption, or rather has occurred despite their class-collaborationism.)

Regardless of these objective and subjective conditions, however, what has consistently sustained me while attempting to make practical and theoretical steps forward is the idea of the "historical necessity" for humanity to break free of the chains of capital. In this sense, Marxism has not "died" or lost its significance, and will not as long as capitalism continues.

With this perspective as the starting point, I have sought, together with my comrades, to reveal the "secrets" of the Stalinist systems, and we have exposed the fact that the socio-economic systems in the Soviet Union and China were in fact not socialism, but state capitalism. Already in the 1960s, we defined both countries as state capitalist, thus treating Stalinism is as the ideological expression of these systems. Our standpoint regarding this issue is presented in a number of essays that Roy has translated and presented in the book *Socialism: Stalinist or Scientific?*

The fact that Russia (Soviet Union) and China emerged as capitalist superpowers indicates to us that the world is increasingly ripe for socialism, which also confirms the Marxist "formula" that socialism and communism are arrived at only after society has passed through capitalism.

In addition to the essays on state capitalism, Roy has translated a number of other things that I have written, including articles dealing with the most fundamental questions—namely, the defense of the "labor theory of value," which is the foundation of Marxist thought. Marx's labor theory of value exposes the fact that wealth in capitalist society is the outcome of the labor of workers, elucidating that the value of commodities is in fact labor.

I have set out to defend Marxism, not only against bourgeois scholars, but also against the stale theories advanced by self-proclaimed "Marxist" scholars, such as Uno Kōzō and his followers, who have dedicated themselves to attacking Marx and sunk deep roots in Japanese academia. This is similar to the efforts of Marxists in the past to expose pseudo-Marxists. That is to say, Marxists are obliged to discuss Marxism in relation to the time period and environment within which they happen to find themselves, and apply this to the living, political and theoretical reality within their own country.

In this sense, I do not have the slightest intention of concocting some sort of new, unique theory. My only desire is to resolutely defend Marxism and apply it for the sake of the critical analysis and understanding of reality, given the historical and practical circumstances we are facing, in the hope that this will form one "moment" in opening up and developing a new socialist movement of a different dimension from the one led by social-democratic and Communist parties in the past. Since the age of nineteen, having come of age during the struggle against the 1960 Japan-U.S. Security Treaty, I have been faithful to this task, and it is with this goal in mind that I have lived my life over the past decades.

This struggle of ours is a difficult one, with advances made a single step at a time. But not only am I certain that this struggle is a worthwhile one, I believe that far from being an isolated effort, it has a universal and international character and will ultimately contribute to the emancipation movement of workers throughout the world. I say this because the working class, just like capital—and even more so qualitatively—is universal and internationalist in the truest sense of the word. And the liberation from the rule of capital, on a global scale, is historically inevitable, regardless of how many years it may take to achieve this.

September 12, 2004

1

The Meaning of the Commodity
(Why does labor take the form of value?)

The following is a series of articles, first published in the newspaper *Henkaku* (Revolutionary Change) over a period of two-and-a-half years, whose aim is to provide a "simple" explanation of Marxist economics. The main object of study here is the theory of the commodity developed by Marx in part one of the first volume of *Capital*. I have adopted the "method" of not simply providing an explanation of Marx's own work, but also introducing various examples of criticism aimed at his economic theory (and responses to such criticism) in an attempt to clarify the correctness, effectiveness, and significance of Marxist concepts. The bulk of the criticism of Marx introduced here comes from the Uno school—a truly contemptible group of university professors who make their living peddling criticism of Marx—but I also examine significant examples of criticism from bourgeois scholars. My sincere hope is that those striving to understand *Capital* and Marxist economic thought, particularly young people, will find this examination of Marx's ideas to be beneficial.

1. A Word on "Methodology"

Materialist Conception of History and "Economics"

Before beginning our examination of the commodity, I would like to first consider some "methodological" questions—and here I am referring to methodology as it relates directly to Marxist economics. Throughout this series of articles we will be examining Marx's "method" in its various forms, depending on the particular issue at hand, but here I are speaking of the question of methodology *in general*, such as the relation between *Capital* (economics) and the materialist conception of history (or historical materialism), and the methodological significance of *Capital* (whether it is a "principle theory" of "pure" capitalism as Uno Kōzō claims). The views expressed by the Unoists on general questions of methodology are essentially the same regardless of the particular scholar we may happen to be dealing with, and we can begin by looking at a passage from Ōuchi Hideaki's *Keizai genron* which I happen to have near at hand.

> In the case of economics in the narrow sense of the term, economic laws are explained by taking modern capitalism as the object of study, and then economics in the wider sense, which encompasses the entire history and development of humanity, including capitalist society, can be positioned "on top of this." This is the correct methodology for economics as a historical science. Accordingly, Marx's "ultimate aim" in *Capital* is to is "lay bare the economic law of motion of modern society," taking as his object, not ancient or medieval society, but rather the modern capitalist economy.[1]

Frankly, I find it rather astonishing that university professors are able to make a living by dishing up such ideas! The fact that *Capital* takes "capital" as its object of analysis—rather than ancient or medieval society—is obvious, even a tautology, since otherwise Marx surely would not have chosen the title *Capital* in the first place. Ōuchi has written such foolishness because he—along with the Uno school in general—denies or obscures the independent significance of the materialist conception of history, claiming that it is nothing more than an "ideological hypothesis" whose correctness must be "demonstrated" by Marx's *Capital*.

Needless to say, it is completely nonsensical to argue, in the manner of Ōuchi, that the economic laws of capitalism must first be clarified, and then the materialist conception of history or "economics in the wider sense" positioned "on top of this." Clearly a scientific understanding of capitalist production can contribute to the establishment of historical materialism, but historical materialism itself is derived from a general overview of the historical,

---

1.   Ōuchi Hideaki and Kamakura Takao, eds., *Keizai genron* (Tokyo: Yuhikaku, 1976), 191.

social development of humanity. One would have thought this point self-evident, but Uno reasons as follows:

> The materialist conception of history clarifies that the economic process of society is a materialistic process that itself develops; whereas it is the task of economics to demonstrate this scientifically...Economics is not able to provide this theoretical basis by means of the materialist conception of history. Unless a demonstration can be provided that people will accept regardless of whether or not they adhere to the materialist conception of history, it cannot be deemed scientific...If economics were to attempt to provide this demonstration by means of the materialist conception of history, both economics and the materialist conception of history would be unable to claim objectivity.[2]

Uno Rejects the Materialist Conception of History

Uno states that the task of economics is provide a scientific demonstration of the materialist conception of history. He places economics and the materialist conception of history in a relation of opposition, claiming that it is economics that "demonstrates" the materialist conception of history, rather than the materialist conception of history providing economics with a theoretical basis. In short, what exists for Unoists is "economics"—the meaning of which will become progressively clear—not the materialist conception of history, since they claim that an overview of human history can only be derived from the analysis of capitalism.

We must point out, however, that the materialist conception of history clarifies the fact that human history develops via the reciprocal relation between productive power and production relations, with certain production relations (and therefore social relations) being formed to correspond with the productive power of human labor, and a "superstructure" (state apparatus, "culture," and ideological relations) in turn developing that corresponds to these relations; and that as productive power develops further it comes into contradiction with the existing relations of production, ushering in a turbulent period of revolutionary change that does not come to an end until the relations of production and productive power are once again brought into correspondence with each other. According to Marx's materialist conception of history,

---

2.   Uno Kōzō, *Kachi-ron no kenkyū* (Tokyo: University of Tokyo Press, 1952), 144-5.

human history to date has, fundamentally, developed by passing through slave-based, feudal, and capitalist social systems, and in the future humanity will be compelled to shift to a system of socialism.

The twentieth century has been an age of turmoil and revolution, a period of deep crisis, which stems from our arrival at a stage where no forward progress is possible without solving the enormous and historically unprecedented task of achieving a transition from capitalism to socialism on a worldwide scale. By studying the materialist conception of history, we can come to know the major, necessary historical currents that run through human history, as well as the laws of human development, and become aware of the reason why we must oppose capitalism and fight for socialism. This is precisely why petty-bourgeois Unoist intellectuals have a deep loathing for the materialist conception of history, and try to keep it at arm's length by referring to it as an "ideological hypothesis" or by claiming that priority must be given to the objective, scientific analysis of economics. In this way, they hope to escape from the psychological "pressure" exerted by the materialist conception of history. It is clear why Uno makes the materialist conception of history dependent upon the "demonstration" of capitalism. He prefers "pure" scientific logic, as a sort of intellectual game, while viewing the solution to the real contradictions of capitalism—by realizing socialism and liberating the working class—as matters of complete indifference.

Uno offers the plausible argument that making economics dependent upon materialism would result in both economics *and* the materialist conception of history forfeiting the claim to objectivity, but in reality he is advocating vulgar, "objective" economics while denying the objectivity of the materialist conception of history by dissolving it into the realm of economics. Uno argues that economics cannot be provided a theoretical basis by means of the materialist conception of history, but who on earth is he debating here? His opponent is a windmill not an actual Marxist. A Marxist would say that the general historical laws of the materialist conception of history also penetrate capitalist society, but that the scientific elucidation of capitalism cannot be directly deduced, derived, or "demonstrated" from the materialist conception of history, requiring instead an independent analysis and the study of the development of capitalist economic relations.

To Unoists, however, who base themselves upon the dogma that economics (the analysis of capital) provides a theoretical basis for the materialist conception of history, such a view appears equivalent to saying that economics is "theoretically demonstrated" by means of the materialist conception of history.

They are unaware of the simple truth that capitalism is also one historical form of human society and is therefore subject to the general developmental laws of human history. Saying that *Capital* must provide a demonstration "that people will accept regardless of whether they adhere to the materialist conception of history," is nothing more than rotten bourgeois "scientism" [*kagakushugi*] and fashionable "positivist" nonsense.

Uno's View of the "Economic Process"

In explaining the materialist conception of history, Uno says that the "economic process of society is a materialistic process that itself develops." This may sound very much like a materialist explanation, but we need to consider the content of this, as there are various brands of materialism. Uno's view of materialism as it is applied to human society (historical materialism) is as follows:

> We set out to elucidate the economic laws that penetrate capitalist society in general. This is an attempt to systematize the structure so that the process of social metabolism occurs in a purely capitalistic manner...What we intend to clarify by this are the economic laws of capitalist society as manifested as an independent materialistic process.[3]

> The commodity economy, which is the object of economics, particularly the capitalist-commodity economy, is a society in which, unlike past historical societies, the economic process is treated as a pure economic form.[4]

Setting aside the inane expression that the economic process "is treated as a pure economic form," what does Uno mean by "economic process" here?

> Man is in fact a thing...Everyone knows that human beings live by consuming things. And everyone understands that the consumption of things cannot continue without the production of things. It is also clear that the production of things must be carried out through the labor of human beings. There is a so-called process of social metabolism in which things become human, while at the same time human beings become things. No society can be formed without this economic process...Economics clarifies

---

3.   Uno Kōzō, *Shakai kagaku no konpon mondai* (Tokyo: Aoki Shoten, 1966), 45.
4.   Ibid., 109.

how this process is carried out as a capitalist-commodity economy. This is a social metabolic process that possesses its own independent movement. And *Capital* is the basis upon which materialism can be coherently established.[5]

Just as a commodity is not simply a thing (use-value), capital is also not merely a thing (means of production; e.g. machinery, etc.), but rather essentially involves certain relations of production. Machinery, for instance, is only capital under certain production relations. Uno, however, views commodities and capital directly as things and believes that the aim of economics is to analyze the movement (or "economic process") of these things. *Capital* is thus said to be the analysis of the commodity *qua* thing.

There is a significant difference, however, between saying that relations between people *appear* as relations between things under capitalist relations of production, and saying that the production relations themselves *are* relations between things. People today, as in the past, have never experienced production relations that are not in fact relations between human beings. The development of capital is also the development of the relationship between capital and wage-labor, not merely an absurd "development of things." Uno speaks of a "pure" economic process, but forgets that economic relations are relations between human beings within the production process, and that even economic categories such as the commodity, money, and capital are nothing more than human relations concealed behind relations between "things."

The "economic process" for Uno is one in which people consume and thereby live, and this process is "carried out as a commodity-economy." Uno says that because *Capital* elucidates this process it is able to ultimately establish a theory of materialism. But he does not even attempt to explain *why* the social metabolic process can only occur via a commodity-economy, merely pointing out instead that this occurs. Uno simply states that this is the metabolism of society, which demonstrates a relationship between things, and that this therefore establishes materialism.

For Uno, human beings are simply things, not the *subject* that creates society and history by means of labor and social praxis. He sees the economic process as primarily involving consumption as well as the activity needed for this consumption, rather than being a social relation that connects people through labor and production. We have nothing in common with such a crude view of

---

5.   Ibid., 127-8.

the materialist conception of history. This is a confused, vulgar brand of materialism that is really nothing more than a parody of the materialist conception of history. With no understanding of the theory of materialism applied to the particularity of human history (the materialist conception of history), Uno attempts to dissolve this directly into a general theory of materialism, namely a relation between human beings as "things" and "things" as objects of consumption!

Subject Matter of *Capital*

One would have thought it self-evident that Marx sets out in *Capital* to analyze and scientific elucidate capitalism as one historical form of production relations, and that the subject matter of this work is simply capitalist production. But even on this point there are differences of opinion. According to Uno, the subject matter of *Capital* is only one stage of capitalism, the stage of industrial capitalism, as distinguished from both the earlier stages of capitalism and the latter stage of finance capitalism. Uno makes this claim because he believes that only at this one particular stage did capitalism unfold while eliminating elements that are not pure to capitalism, strengthen the "trend toward approximating a so-called purely capitalist society," and show a "tendency toward purification," whereas in the earlier and later stages this capitalistic purification does not occur (and that in the monopoly stage a "reversal" takes place so that capitalism becomes even less pure). Uno makes use of the following passage from Marx's preface to *Capital* as the grounds of his argument.

> The physicist either observes natural processes where they occur in their most significant form, and are least affected by disturbing influences, or, whenever possible, he makes experiments under conditions which ensure that the process will occur in its pure state. What I have to examine in this work is the capitalist mode of production, and the relations of production and forms of intercourse [*Verkehrsverhältnisse*] that correspond to it. Until now, their *locus classicus* has been England. This is the reason why England is used as the main illustration of the theoretical developments I make.[6]

As we can see, the question of purity or impurity does not even enter the equation for Marx here. Rather, he is saying that in studying capitalism other rela-

---

6.   Karl Marx, *Capital*, vol. 1, trans. Ben Fowkes (London: Penguin Books, 1976), 90.

tions must, for the moment, be placed out of consideration. And, realistically speaking, England is always presupposed by Marx since it was the typical capitalist country of the time. Everyone knows that a "pure" capitalist country is not something that actually exists. What exists in reality is capitalist production that is connected to, or intertwined with, various elements that are more or less "impure" (feudalistic or petty-bourgeois elements). This fact, however, presents no real challenge in terms of abstracting the laws of capitalism once capitalist relations of production have become the dominant relations and this predominance increases.

Uno says that the subject matter for Marx is a stage of capitalism which, despite not being purely capitalistic and containing some impure elements, has a *tendency* toward purification. Marx's model is said to be England, and thus *Capital* is seen as having decisive limitations in terms of the historical era it treats. But even though actual capitalism contains various impure elements, there is no need to presuppose any sort of pure model in order to grasp the concept of capital; all that is needed is the premise that capitalism is the dominant mode of production. One would have thought this a simple truth but the idealist Uno Kōzō is quite incapable of grasping this.

Marx speaks of "classical" capitalism but he never raises the issue of "pure" capitalism. Moreover, even though Marx notes in the preface to the first German edition of *Capital* that England has been the *locus classicus* of capitalist relations of production "until now," this certainly does not mean that countries other than England were seen as somehow being "impure" capitalist countries. Rather, Marx expected that in the near future Germany (and indeed all nations throughout the world) would follow behind England and similarly enter the path of capitalist development. This is the reason why Marx, in the same preface, notes that "the country that is more developed industrially only shows, to the less developed, the image of its own future."[7] And apart from particular differences in detail or form, the history of humanity *has* essentially advanced as Marx noted, with every country entering, or being compelled to enter, the path of capitalist development. The deepening development of capitalism has occurred within every country and continues to move forward in the age of monopoly capital. This is certainly not something that occurred solely in England or only during the stage of industrial capital.

---

7. Ibid., 91.

A "Pure" Model of Capitalism

Uno's discussion of "pure" capitalism is completely idealistic.

> Marx, for his theoretical development in *Capital*, naturally clarifies the dominant laws of the capitalist mode of production, as they should purely unfold, whereas in reality they only exist as an approximation of this. Marx, however, believed that with the development of capitalism this would become increasingly pure, as impurities resulting from the previous production mode were eliminated.[8]

> In the concrete process of the development of capitalism, however, this pure capitalist society that was the theoretically premise did not come about, and in the late nineteenth century the new stage of finance capital was reached so that the purification process of capitalism was obstructed—in England this was because of external relations with its colonies, etc., and in less advanced countries because of the internal problem of the old agricultural system impeding capitalist development. In any event, the process of developmental change from the period of industrial capital to that of finance capital did not consist of the internal development of a pure commodity-economy process.[9]

The position expressed by Uno here represents a slip into idealism. He says that there is a "pure" principle theory and "impure" reality, and that reality is nothing but an "approximation" of the pure theory. Uno lacks the elemental materialist awareness that a theory can only be scientific if it correctly reflects reality, and that the actual relations precede the theory!

What exactly does Uno mean by "pure" capitalism? Is the concept of capital discussed in the first chapter of *Capital* an example of a theory of pure capitalism? Is pure capitalism somehow distinct from actual capitalism? According to Uno's view, pure capitalism, which is the theoretical object, is not actual capitalism because capitalism in reality can only exist while containing various "impure" elements. A Marxist, however, would say that *Capital* is the theory and correct understanding of capitalism. Even accepting the fact that actual capitalism contains elements that are more or less impure, this does not prevent *Capital* in any way from being the correct, scientific understanding of the real content and laws of motion of modern bourgeois society. This is theory as

---

8.   *Shakai kagaku no konpon mondai*, 20.
9.   Ibid., 120.

the reflection of reality, and there is no need to presuppose some sort of model (e.g. "pure capitalism").

Of course, since Marx does "purely" consider capitalism as such, whereas what exists in reality is "impure" capitalism, some may imagine that Uno is making a valid point in claiming that Marx's object of study is some sort of intermediary, theoretical model posited as an *ideal type* instead of actual capitalism. This view, however, is a superficial one. The power of abstraction employed to analyze real social relations is certainly not equivalent to establishing a theoretical model which then becomes the object of examination. Uno needs to reflect on Marx's comment that in the analysis of social relations "neither microscopes nor chemical reagents are of use."[10]

In the first place, presupposing a model of pure capitalism and then taking the model as the object of analysis cannot be considered a materialistic approach. To establish this model a certain understanding (concept) of capitalism is necessary to begin with, but according to the premise above, the analysis of "capital" begins with this model, so at this stage we are not yet supposed to be in possession of a true concept. What sort of model of "pure" capitalism, then, could we possibly establish? Uno's "method" is completely idealistic and bourgeois in nature, and this is the same sort of roundabout method typical of modern bourgeois philosophy.

Marx wrote *Capital* to expose the *reality* of capitalist production. This is precisely why those suffering from the contradictions of capitalism, and those who have decided to fight against the rule and exploitation of capital, need to study *Capital*.

Adopting Max Weber's Idealistic Method

Certainly, in the third volume of *Capital*, Marx notes that "in theory, we assume that the laws of the capitalist mode of production develop in their pure form" whereas "in reality, this is only an approximation."[11] But is this view really identical to Uno's methodology? Marx emphasizes that "in theory" the laws of capitalism operate purely, but this is related to the nature of theory in general and does not imply anything strange or mysterious (although Uno apparently hopes to mystify this).

---

10. *Capital*, vol. 1, 90.
11. Karl Marx, *Capital*, vol. 3, trans. David Fernbach (London: Penguin Books, 1981), 275.

Capitalism in reality always contains some other, pre-capitalist elements. Within the realm of theory, however, such impure elements are abstracted from, and this is because the theoretical task is to grasp the concept of capital and the essence of capitalist production. To assume that "in theory" the laws of capital operate purely certainly does not mean that one presupposes, in the fashion of Max Weber, an "ideal type" of capital that is then taken as the object of analysis. For Marx, the object of analysis is real capitalist production, not some sort of ideal type. It is illogical and self-contradictory to assume the existence of pure capitalism or construct this notion upon a subjective basis, and then make this product of human subjectivity the object of analysis. What exists in reality is capitalism as the dominant and historically inevitable mode of production. In analyzing this we make use of abstraction (the functioning of our brains) as a tool. The power of abstraction is utilized to "purely" define capital and establish it as a category, and herein lies the real meaning of the passage of Marx cited above.

In a profound sense, Uno's position is close to Weber's notion of an ideal type. According to Weber, an ideal type is not a general idea or category, but rather something extracted from the various elements comprising the actual social and cultural formations, as most typically embodying the characteristics of these formations. Such an ideal type, however, would not be the *concept* of capital.

Neo-Kantians have generally argued that social science should not seek universally applicable laws and that it is only possible to grasp the "laws" pertaining to individual, concrete phenomena and the types that commonly appear with them. Weber uses the term "ideal type" to describe a model that is constructed for a particular phenomenon in this manner, and Uno's so-called "pure capitalism" (or "principle theory") closely resembles such an ideal type.[12]

Uno's "pure capitalism" is a type of model that is derived through the "idealization"—taken to its ultimate point—of a supposed tendency toward "purification" within the stage of actually existing nineteenth century industrial capitalism, and he claims that *Capital* should be the theoretical consideration of this model, which means that *Capital* needs to be rewritten in a "pure" form. This model, thus, does not (and is unable to) provide a theory of capitalism in general. This is not the intention, from the very outset, and ultimately

---

12. Uno denies this, claiming that it is his "stage-theory"—not the "principle theory"—that is the same as Weber's ideal type.

it remains nothing more than a Unoist model ("principle theory"). Uno's "theory" is fundamentally determined by his illusion—his upside-down, irrational and idealistic view—that some sort of "scientific" theory can be constructed by means of assuming a subjectively-based construct ("pure capitalism") which is then analyzed. This alone reveals the emptiness of Uno's theory and the fact that he is incapable of offering anything more than mere speculation.

Nothing better indicates the reactionary nature of Uno's theory than the fact that his "method" is essentially borrowed from neo-Kantians and Max Weber.[13] Uno's "theory" represents an attempt to revise Marxism by making use of the philosophy and economics of modern monopoly capital, and in this sense it perfectly suits the disposition of intellectuals dependent upon bourgeois academia for their livelihood.

Uno's Irrational Three-stage Theory

Uno's so-called "stage-theory" is self-contradictory and irrational from the outset. He says that his stage-theory method amounts to a negation of general concepts. "Finance capital," for instance, rather than being considered a category of capital common to economically advanced countries from the nineteenth to twentieth centuries, is said to merely represent a "type." Uno claims that there can be a German finance capital or an English finance capital, but that there is no such thing as a concept of finance capital in general, and it is from this perspective that he criticizes Lenin in a manner closely reassembling the method of neo-Kantians.

> It seems to me like a case of rather forced logic to suggest that the use of the term finance capital means that it possesses some general, common quality, and that to the extent that it has this general common quality, finance capital is a general principle similar to the general principles of capitalism...To view scientific elucidation in this manner amounts to losing sight of the significance of economics as a historical science. And speaking of science, it is fundamentally problematic to proceed on the basis of the perspective of commonsensical, natural science.[14]

---

13. Later we shall see that Uno's theory of value is essentially borrowed from the marginal utility school.
14. Uno Kōzō, *Keizaigaku no hōhō* (Tokyo: Hosei University Press, 1963), 18.

We should note here that in explaining modern capitalism, Uno begins from the notion of "heavy industry" as a natural thing. But considering the noticeable existence of heavy industry in England, the United States, and other countries, one would have thought Uno would be compelled to recognize the existence of some "general, common quality." We can see the essence of Uno's "methodology" of tailing after the neo-Kantians in his stage-theory, where imperialist states only exist as "separate entities" in this manner.

The concentrated expression of the reactionary essence of Uno's theory is his view that modern capitalism, basically speaking, cannot be scientifically or rationally (theoretically) grasped on the basis of *Capital*; and instead can only be phenomenally or empirically described as a "type." However, present-day capitalism—as capitalism—necessarily includes the principles and essential nature of capitalism elucidated by Marx in *Capital*. Present-day capitalism has, of course, undergone various transformations since the age of "free competition," with many new characteristics appearing, and there is no doubt that one independent theoretical task is to provide an overview of such new characteristics as Lenin did in *Imperialism*, but this is completely different from what Uno is saying.

Some may generously interpret Uno's standpoint as being a reaction against those who find it sufficient to directly trim present-day capitalism to fit the mold of a general theory of capital (and this is how Uno and his followers view their role). But in fact Unoists are denying the possibility of attaining a fundamental, scientific understanding of modern capitalism, thus reflecting the frivolous standpoint of petty-bourgeois intellectuals who seek refuge in the "analysis of the current situation"[15] where phenomena are merely described as such. It is obvious that the various phenomena related to modern capitalism (such as monopoly price, etc.) cannot be directly grasped with only a general theory of capital, and phenomenally speaking can even appear to be in contradiction with this general concept. Despite this, new phenomena *can* be explained by reducing them to the general concepts of capital, passing through various levels of mediation, and this is how we must proceed. In the case of Uno's irrational and idealistic theory, however, present-day capitalism is detached from capitalism in general, and thus is already treated as something other than capitalism.

---

15. [This refers to the third ("empirical") level of Uno's three-staged theory.]

In our discussion of Marx's *Capital* in this chapter, there is no specific need to assume nineteenth century England as Uno recommends, since we find present-day Japan, as a highly developed monopoly capitalist state, to be sufficient. We view the study of *Capital* as being connected to our examination of the capitalist society in which we live, and this is precisely why we believe it necessary to thoroughly study *Capital* and view this endeavor as having decisively important practical significance. Thus, firmly bearing in mind the theoretical task at hand, I would like to move on to examine the commodity and the theory of value.

2. The Commodity at the Beginning of *Capital*

Bourgeois Claims that "*Capital* is Contradictory"

Marx's *Capital* begins with the following well-known paragraph:

> The wealth of societies in which the capitalist mode of production prevails appears as an "immense collection of commodities"; the individual commodity appears as its elementary form. Our investigation therefore begins with the analysis of the commodity.[16]

Perhaps it was inevitable, considering the great historical significance of *Capital*, but this short opening paragraph has been the object of great debate and

---

16. *Capital*, vol. 1, 125. [Since this section examines controversies related to Japanese translations of this opening passage, it is important to consider the accuracy of this English translation by Ben Fowkes. Hans Ehrbar in his "Annotations to Marx's *Capital*" notes for instance that the two "appears" in the passage have separate meanings in the original German, with the first meaning "takes the form of" and the second referring to a "form of appearance." Moreover, the pronoun "its" in "appears as its material form," is somewhat ambiguous, whereas in the original German the pronoun clearly refers to the elementary form of *wealth*. Ehrbar thus translates the opening passage as follows: "The wealth of those societies, in which the capitalist mode of production reigns, presents itself as an 'immense heap of commodities.' The analysis of the individual commodity, the *elementary form* of this wealth, will therefore be the starting point of our investigation." Hans Ehrbar, "Annotations to Marx's 'Capital'" (2004). http://www.econ.utah.edu/ehrbar/akmc-a4.pdf]

endless discussions. Innumerable interpretations of its meaning have been offered and fierce arguments waged over how to interpret it. This issue was first raised by bourgeois scholars. Already at the end of the nineteenth century, when *Capital* was beginning to make inroads among the working class and the workers movement was joining forces with scientific socialism, Eugen von Böhm-Bawerk, who had made a name for himself as a critic of Marx, launched an attack on the labor theory of value in his book *Karl Marx and The Close of His System*. In the book, Böhm-Bawerk argues that a contradiction exists between the first volume of *Capital*, where commodities are exchanged according to their value, and the third volume where they are exchanged according to production prices that deviate from value.[17] From this fact, he triumphantly declares that Marx's theory is confused and pronounces the labor theory of value bankrupt. Böhm-Bawerk, for instance, writes:

> In the first volume it was maintained, with the greatest emphasis, that all value is based on labor and labor alone, and that values of commodities were in proportion to the working time necessary for their production...And now in the third volume we are told briefly and dryly that...individual commodities do and must exchange with each other in a proportion different from that of the labor incorporated in them, and this is not accidentally and temporally, but of necessity and permanently."[18]

In response to Böhm-Bawerk's criticism, the Austrian Marxist Rudolph Hilferding argued that there was no contradiction within Marx's "system" because the first volume of *Capital* presupposes "simple commodity production," whereas the third volume deals with capitalist-commodity production.[19] This debate also reached the shores of Japan in the 1920s, with the bourgeois scholars Koizumi Shinzō, Takata Yasuma, and Hijikata Seibi rehashing Böhm-Bawerk's criticism of Marx, and in turn being staunchly opposed by the Marxists Kawakami Hajime and Kushida Tamizō.

---

17. According to Marx, a capitalist commodity is exchanged on the basis of its cost price plus average profit, not on the basis of its "value." He calls this price the "production price," and this is a category particular to Marxism.

18. Eugen von Böhm-Bawerk, *Karl Marx and the Close of His System*, ed. Paul Sweezy (Philadelphia: Orion Editions, 1949), 30.

19. Rudolph Hilferding, "Böhm-Bawerk's Criticism of Marx" in *Karl Marx and the Close of His System*, 184.

Closely connected to this debate on the nature of the commodity at the beginning of *Capital* is Böhm-Bawerk's comment on the following passage he cites from the third volume of *Capital*:

> It is, therefore, altogether in keeping with fact to regard the values as not only theoretically but *historically* prior to the prices of production. It holds good for circumstances where the means of production belong to the worker.[20]

Böhm-Bawerk criticizes Marx, calling this a "hypothetical style" that "contains no shadow of proof, or even an attempt at proof" and is "only hypothetically deduced from [Marx's] theory." According to Böhm-Bawerk, this is "inherently improbable" and "even experience is against it."[21] In other words, he is saying that, "experientially" speaking, exchange "according to value" does not exist anywhere.[22]

Böhm-Bawerk's criticism of the "contradictions" of Marx's system—the supposed contradiction between the first and third volumes—raises the question of the nature of the commodity analyzed at the beginning of *Capital*. In other words, is this commodity a capitalist commodity, and if so in what sense, and why does it differ from the commodity discussed in the third volume? Or, is it not directly a capitalist commodity, but rather a "simple commodity" such as could actually be found in pre-capitalist society?

Kushida's "Historical Simple Commodity"

Kushida Tamizō was the first to respond to the attacks aimed at Marx by bourgeois scholars such as Koizumi Shinzō. Kushida interpreted the commodity at the beginning of *Capital* as being fundamentally a "historical simple commodity." At the same time, however, he also understood this as being a "theoretical hypothesis," or rather we might say that he increasingly adhered to the view of the commodity as an actual (historical) pre-capitalist simple commodity *because* he was compelled to clearly recognize it as a "theoretical hypothesis":

---

20. *Karl Marx and the Close of His System*, 26. [This citation from chapter ten of the third volume of *Capital* is taken from the Kerr edition.]
21. Ibid., 42-43.
22. Today the Unoists repeat, almost word for word, the similarly inane views of the marginal utility school.

If it can be said that the individual commodity is arrived at here by abstracting from the characteristic of [forming an] "immense collection," doesn't this already mark a divergence from the capitalistic properties of the commodity? The "individual commodity," in the sense of diverging from its capitalistic properties, is not simply an abstraction, but, seen historically, seems to be something with real significance as a commodity under the period of so-called simple commodity production that existed prior to capitalism...It is possible to offer a logical explanation of this as an abstract concept, but it is also possible to think of this as historical reality in terms of a simple commodity that does not appear as a capitalist commodity.[23]

Kushida says that there are two ways of interpreting the opening passage of *Capital*. Let's begin by looking at Kushida's own view:

The first explanation involves interpreting "the individual commodity" as something not directly related to the "collection of commodities," but rather as an independent form that is its *opposite*. In this case, the term "the individual commodity" refers to the individual commodity in a relation of opposition to the "collection of commodities," and therefore [?] *seine Elementarform*, translated as "the primitive form (of social wealth)," must be interpreted, from the beginning, as a primitive form [*genshi keitai*], or in some other historical sense, and cannot be considered in the non-historical or logical sense of being an elemental form [*seiso/genso keitai*]. Given this, the "individual commodity" here becomes the commodity in the pre-capitalist period of simple commodity production, and the commodity that is analyzed subsequently is the so-called simple commodity; and therefore it can be supposed that the law of value derived from this also more or less has such significance. Read in this manner, commodities here are already classified into two types: the capitalist commodity and the simple commodity. However, the historical relation between the two is revealed by referring to the latter as the "primitive form" of the former.[24]

As we can see, Kushida places the "collection of commodities" and the "individual commodity" in a relation of opposition, and thus the term *seine Elementarform* at the beginning of *Capital* is translated as "primitive form" [*genshi keitai*]. Kushida interprets the commodity as being the basis and starting point of capital only in a historical sense. There are serious problems with this view,

---

23. Kushida Tamizō, *Kachi oyobi kahei* (Tokyo: Kaizōsha, 1934), 154.
24. Ibid. 69-70.

but Kushida does display a certain degree of "understanding" in presenting the other explanation he thinks possible.

This second explanation is the view that the "individual commodity" can also be understood as one part of the "collection of commodities." But Kushida insists that "even if this logical explanation is a correct reading of the text, there is no reason to say that the commodity analyzed subsequently by Marx is necessarily a capitalist commodity."[25] Here, at the very least, Kushida has some inkling that in terms of a strict reading of the text, it is not appropriate to place the "collection of commodities" and the "individual commodity" in opposition to each other and translate *Elementarform* as "primitive form," but he still insists that this is not a capitalist commodity but rather a historical simple commodity.

To support this view, Kushida argues that "when one abstracts from the capitalistic properties of the capitalist commodity, the property of being a large quantity of products of capital is also abstracted from at the same time, so that this must be referred to as a simple commodity." He adds that, "when the quantitative property of the capitalist commodity is abstracted from, we are left with a simple commodity as an individual commodity."[26] Kushida thus concludes "this must signify not only a logical fiction but at the same time a historical fact."[27] In other words:

Its so-called "value" is abstracted from the particular properties of the capitalist commodity, which is subject to capitalistic limitations and includes capitalist surplus-value. Thus, if this commodity is compared to an actual commodity in capitalist society, it is merely an individual, abstract commodity, nothing more than an ideological hypothesis or the philosophical construct of *als-ob* [as if].[28] However, thought of in terms of historical reality, this is a pre-capitalist simple commodity.[29]

A "Simple Commodity" in What Sense?

To say that the commodity at the beginning of *Capital* is simply a theoretical hypothesis, while at the same time defining it in reality as a historical simple

---

25.   Ibid.
26.   Ibid., 172.
27.   Ibid., 173.
28.   [In German and English in the original.]
29.   Ibid., 178, 183.

commodity, is extremely one-sided and trivializes the significance of the analysis of this commodity, misunderstanding the very meaning of *abstraction*, which is a particularly important tool for social science. Engels, in response to Conrad Schmidt's view of the law of value as a mere "scientific hypothesis," wrote the following:

> Schmidt declares that the law of value in the capitalist form of production is a fiction, though a theoretically necessary one. In my opinion, however, this conception is completely inapposite. The law of value has a far greater and more definite importance for capitalist production than that of a mere hypothesis, let alone a necessary fiction...what is involved is not just a logical process but a historical one, and its explanatory reflection in thought, the logical following-up of its internal connections.[30]

(It should be noted, however, that Engels displays a strong tendency toward explaining the commodity at the beginning of *Capital* as a historical simple commodity.) Marx, for his part, recognizes that "the exchange of commodities at their values, or at approximately these values" corresponds to historically simple commodity production, but in this case as well he also explains that "it is also quite apposite" to recognize the value of commodities as being not only "theoretically prior to the prices of commodities, but also as historically prior to them."[31] For Marx, first there is the "theoretical" and on top of this the "historical" is placed.

Kushida, to return to our discussion, recognizes the commodity at the beginning of *Capital* as not directly being a capitalist commodity (a commodity exchanged as a product of capital), but rather a simple commodity, a pure commodity, or the commodity *per se*. Therefore, the question that remains is whether this is a simple commodity in terms of abstracting from the properties of the capitalist commodity and the fact that the commodity is produced capitalistically, or rather a pure commodity in the historical sense. Kushida, for his part, basically adheres to the latter position.

But is this really the case? When Marx says "our investigation therefore begins with the analysis of the commodity," is the "commodity" being placed in opposition to the "immense collection of commodities" so that it would be

---

30. Frederick Engels, "Supplement to Volume 3 of *Capital*," in *Capital*, vol. 3, 1032-3.
31. *Capital*, vol. 3, 277.

correct to translate *Elementarform* as "primitive form"? Furthermore, can we be satisfied with the explanation that if the aspect of a large quantity of commodities is abstracted from, to arrive at the individual commodity, this then represents a historical simple commodity? Is this really a question that hinges solely on such a quantitative issue?

When Marx says that the wealth in which the capitalist mode of production prevails appears as a "collection of commodities" with the individual commodity as its "elementary form," he is saying two important things. First of all, this indicates that the wealth of bourgeois society as a whole appears as a *collection of commodities*. Secondly, however, this means that in bourgeois society, the collection of commodities is not directly the wealth of society. Rather, this wealth exists as a collection of *individual commodities*, and this point is the most essential characteristic of the wealth of bourgeois society.

By understanding these two points, we can naturally understand the word "therefore" in the opening passage of *Capital*. Wealth in bourgeois society does not exist directly, but rather as an immense collection of commodities with the individual commodity being its formative element; thus in order to know the nature of wealth in this historical form of society, one must begin with the analysis of the commodity. What must be examined is the commodity as an *elementary form*, the commodity simply as such, since what is at issue here is not the question of whether wealth is produced capitalistically or not, but whether wealth is produced in the form of commodities. In this case, capitalist production is only the object of consideration in terms of being commodity production.

Capitalist production is also commodity production as one form of the production of wealth, and it is this aspect of capitalist production that is being examined. Thus, the commodity at the beginning of *Capital* is the commodity abstracted from being a capitalist commodity produced under capitalism, and in this sense is a simple commodity. To this extent it is an abstract commodity, but it is not correct to refer to this as a "theoretical hypothesis" since this is also very much a reality of capitalist production, one of its essential moments or inseparable aspects.

Kushida's "Epistemological" Error

An "epistemological" error can be said to underlie the one-dimensionality of Kushida's theory. He says that the method of abstraction for Marx is "ultimately a question of the identity of things, and is nothing more than abstraction in the sense of abstract truth actually existing as the commodity *qua* object of cognition and its properties."[32] Kushida adds that, "abstraction in Marx's theory of value means nothing more than abstraction in the sense of abstract reality as it actually unfolds day after day within economic society."[33] But is this view held by Kushida correct, "philosophically" speaking?

To begin with, in terms of the relation between our cognition and reality, a perfect agreement between the two is, by nature, impossible. This is not meant to suggest, however, adherence to the agnostic view that cognition cannot approximate reality. Rather, this means that reality is limitlessly rich and our cognition certainly cannot fully assimilate it. By means of the functioning of our brains, we are able to move closer to reality, even if we cannot understand it completely. This is not a question of the identity of reality and cognition. The correct perspective, as Lenin emphasized, is to view our cognition as the *reflection of reality*—an increasingly correct and profound reflection.

Kushida cannot properly understand the meaning of abstraction because he is unable to adopt a correct, materialist viewpoint. He basically forgets that abstraction is our method of cognition, the operations of the human brain, and insists instead that abstraction is possible because "abstract truth" actually exists. Therefore, when Kushida finds that an "abstract truth" does not exist within reality—such as the fact that the "simple commodity" is not a direct reality within capitalism—he is easily prone to seek it out in the historical past.

But what is an "abstract truth"? Kushida provides the example of abstract human labor as the substance of value. Certainly, abstract human labor is a really existing thing and not merely a theoretical hypothesis, but it is not correct to consider this as a direct entity. Abstract human labor exists as such as the substance of value and is in fact the outcome of commodity exchange. What exists within reality is not necessarily an abstract truth but *concrete truth*—and it is only through the power of human abstraction that the underlying truth is uncovered. Here "abstract truth" is distinct from concrete truth, and the two are not in direct agreement

It cannot be said that because abstract truth exists within reality we are able to "abstract" it out. Rather, we extract (abstract) one particular relation or aspect from out of the various concrete relations of reality, which form the object of our cognition, depending on the theoretical task at hand. If we only

---

32. *Kachi oyobi kahei*, 23.
33. Ibid., 26.

regard this one extracted aspect alone, reality is abstract—i.e. understood in an abstract form—and therefore is not concrete reality. Kushida has overlooked the provision, or necessary limitation, that only one aspect of reality is seen. To abstract is to understand reality more deeply and essentially, but on the other hand this represents a divergence from *direct* reality. To reach a concrete understanding of the totality of capitalism, we cannot remain fixated on the concept of abstract value, but must make the "ascending journey,"[34] i.e. the theoretical pursuit of moving closer to concrete reality. Still, abstract concepts do form the starting point or basis for a correct understanding of reality.

An abstract concept cannot be considered a mere "theoretical hypotheses" concerning the cognition of reality, but at the same time abstract concepts, as such, in addition to being profound truths, are also one-sided and restricted, and we need to be aware of these limitations as well. Kushida is unable to correctly understand that an abstract concept is part of the reality of capitalism—although a one-dimensional abstraction from this reality. Since he recognizes that such truths cannot exist *as such* under capitalist relations of production, he seems to seek refuge in the notion of a historical simple commodity. In this sense, although Kushida speaks of abstraction, he ultimately fails to truly understand its significance.

Kawakami's Response to Kushida

Kushida's views were squarely opposed by Kawakami Hajime, who emphasized that "the commodity at the outset of *Capital*, as the most abstract category of capitalist society, is one aspect extracted out from this society, something abstracted from capitalist society, which is our object of study."[35] No one more clearly and firmly rejected the theory of a "historical simple commodity than Kawakami:

---

34. [The "ascending journey" here refers to the method outlined in Marx's introduction to *Grundrisse* where he says that once the "simplest determinations" of a given object (in this case "population") have been arrived at by means of abstraction, "the journey would have to be retraced until I had finally arrived at the population again, but this time not as the chaotic conception of a whole, but as a rich totality of many determinations and relations."]

35. Kawakami Hajime, *Shihon-ron nyūmon*, 3 vols. (Tokyo: Sekaihyōron-sha, 1946), 1: 94.

Generally the more abstract category will historically precede the more concrete category. Therefore, although the "history of the modern life of capital"—and therefore the capitalist commodity—begins in the sixteenth century, the commodity first made its appearance on the planet some seven or eight thousand years earlier. But the commodity that appears at the beginning of *Capital* is not the same as the most embryonic commodity that first appears within history. Rather, this is a contemporaneous entity that is totally inseparable from the capitalist society that is the object of study in *Capital*.[36]

The commodity at the beginning of *Capital* is the commodity as the most abstract category of capitalist society. Thus, at the same time, here the *capitalistic* determination of the capitalist commodity is abstracted from so that we have a *simple commodity*, but on the other hand, since this is the most abstract category of capitalist society...it is something that exists simultaneously in this society as one aspect of the exceedingly concrete capitalist society.[37]

Kawakami is perfectly justified in emphasizing that the commodity, as the most abstract category of capitalist society, is an external phenomenon that is given prior to thought."

In a society where the system of capitalist production prevails, the wealth of this society—socially-produced wealth—consists almost entirely of commodities. When we seek to acquire any part of the wealth that is socially produced, i.e. when we act in a practical [*jissenteki*] way upon this, we always discover these goods are commodities. Our first discovery is this actual manner in which the wealth of capitalist society exists.[38]

Kawakami, unlike Kushida, recognizes that an abstract category is not directly reality itself, but rather one aspect of a richer, whole entity—an inseparable and internally necessary aspect of this. He quotes a passage from D.I. Rozenberg's[39] book on *Capital* where Rozenberg says that "an abstract thing is pos-

---

36. Ibid., 105.
37. Ibid., 105-6.
38. Ibid., 88.
39. [David Iokhelevich Rozenberg (1879-1950)] is a Soviet economist well known among Japanese Marxists for his introduction to Marx's *Capital*, *Shihon-ron chūkai*, 5 vols. (Tokyo: Aoki Shoten, 1962). The passage here is translated from this Japanese edition.]

ited by experience, but for the aims of science this is considered as a particular cross-section, as reality that is subject, so to speak, to particular operations."[40] For this reason, Kawakami places a strong emphasis on Marx's idea that "in the theoretical method, too, the subject, society, must always be kept in mind as the presupposition,"[41] and he focuses attention on the following passage from Marx's introduction to *Grundrisse*:

> The method of rising from the abstract to the concrete is only the way in which thought appropriates the concrete, reproduces it as the concrete in the mind. But this is by no means the process by which the concrete itself comes into being. For example, the simplest economic category, say e.g. exchange value, presupposes population, moreover a population producing in specific relations; as well as a certain kind of family, or commune, or state, etc. It can never exist other than as an abstract, one-sided relation within an already given, concrete, living whole.[42]

In dealing with the issue of the historical validity of economic (simple) categories, Kawakami also quotes Marx's statement that "the simpler category can express the dominant relations of a less developed whole...to that extent the path of abstract thought, rising from the simple to the combined, would correspond to the real historical process,"[43] in order to emphasize that the various categories are first and foremost categories of bourgeois society.

As we can see, Kawakami's viewpoint is an extremely principled one that is not plagued by Kushida's vagueness and eclecticism. However, we must point out that at the end of the section where he presents his views on the commodity at the beginning of *Capital*, Kawakami needlessly introduces the idea that a line can be drawn between the first two sections of chapter one and the third section (on the value form), arguing that the first two sections when "applied to actual history" refer to the commodity prior to capitalism, whereas the commodity in section three corresponds to the exchange of products that first occurred thousands of years ago, and therefore the "orientation toward historical development begins from this section."[44]

---

40. Ibid., 92.
41. Karl Marx, *Grundrisse*, trans. Ben Fowkes (London: Penguin Books, 1973), 102.
42. Ibid., 101.
43. Ibid., 102.
44. *Shihonron nyūmon*, 118.

Rejecting the "Simple Commodity"

Uno Kōzō completely discards the prewar debate outlined above, arguing that the commodity at the beginning of *Capital* is merely a "circulation-form." He claims that the commodity, money, and even capital already appeared in pre-capitalist society, and that these "forms" can be "posited regardless of the type of production relations under which production takes place," and are thus simply circulation-forms which are not determined by the relations of production. For Uno the term circulation-form signifies a thing that has no actual basis in the relations of production, and therefore lacks a substance (or is something that is not provided a basis through having a substance). From this perspective, Uno criticizes Marx for carrying out a "demonstration" of the labor theory of value in his analysis of the commodity at the beginning of *Capital*. His argument is that since a commodity is simply a substance-less circulation-form, no demonstration or proof of it can be provided.

According to Uno, the entire debate since the time of Böhm-Bawerk over the nature of the commodity at the beginning of *Capital* can be "transcended" by referring to the commodity as a circulation-form, since commodities in the market, as well as commodities in the circulation process, are able to exist regardless of the particular type of production relations. Thus, no distinction can be drawn between commodities in a society of small producers and commodities within capitalist-production society. In the book where Uno first expressed this idea (dogma), there is the following passage:

> The commodity at the outset of *Capital*...naturally is something abstract that is extracted from capitalist relations, but what sort of characteristics does this abstract commodity have?...This, of course, is something that does not have concrete qualities like the so-called simple commodity."[45]

Although Uno speaks of the abstract quality of the commodity at the beginning of *Capital*, he claims that this "is not something that has concrete qualities like the so-called simple commodity." This rather pathetic excuse for a scholar even lacks the elementary understanding that an abstract category exists as such for the very reason that it does not have "concrete qualities" as a direct entity. He can only imagine the simple commodity, or the commodity

---

45. Uno Kōzō, *Kachi-ron* (Tokyo: Iwanami Shoten, 1973), 312.

per se, as a historical simple commodity,[46] which exposes his complete inability to understand the meaning of abstraction and the fact that he is a "vulgar" scholar. In order to refute the existence of the "simple commodity" category, Uno begins by arguing that a simple-commodity society did not exist historically. But what is at issue is the "simple commodity" as an element of capital, not simple-commodity production, historically speaking. In eagerly refuting the actual existence of a simple-commodity society, and claiming to have somehow surpassed Marxism as a result, Uno appears strikingly similar to Don Quixote waging an absurd and comical battle against a windmill.

It may seem that Uno is saying that the commodity at the outset of *Capital* is an abstract commodity arrived at by abstracting from the fact that the capitalist commodity is produced under capitalism, but his actual view is quite different. Uno is in fact arguing that when one abstracts from capitalist production, what remains is not the simple commodity or the commodity in general, but the commodity as a "means of circulation." But this commodity as "simple circulation-form" is nothing more than the commodity in its direct existence as a thing with a price, having no content apart from this. This is completely different from our consideration of the simple commodity, and is not the commodity in terms of being what Marx calls the elementary form of wealth in bourgeois society.

Uno does not recognize the formation of the category of a simple commodity or the fact that the commodity in general, although existing in various historical societies, is the outcome of certain production relations. In other words, he does not understand that commodity production itself is the outcome of private labor, or a system of private ownership—the expression of this system—and that capitalist society is also a society of commodity production, and therefore a society of private ownership (developed to its highest level!). Uno claims that in *Capital* "it is not made clear under which production relations the commodity at the beginning of *Capital* is produced,"[47] but in actual fact Marx very clearly says that "objects of utility become commodities only because they are the products of the labor of private individuals who work independently of each other."[48]

---

46. Or more precisely, he raises the issue of what he calls "simple-commodity society."
47. Uno Kōzō, *Kachi-ron no mondai ten* (Tokyo: Hosei University Press, 1963), 8.
48. *Capital*, vol. 1, 165.

Uno's "Simple Commodity Society"

Uno says that there is no so-called "simple-commodity production society," and he criticizes the advocates of a theory of a historical simple commodity. He adds that commodity production under slave-based and feudal systems only took place in the interstices of these societies, and only to a partial extent, whereas the overall development of commodity production only occurs in capitalist society. Uno thus emphasizes that even if the commodity in pre-capitalist societies can be called a "simple commodity," this is certainly not an entity that exists on a society-wide basis. Under capitalism, by contrast, the commodity becomes the form of wealth of the entire society, but it appears as a capitalist commodity, not a simple commodity. In short, according to the view of Professor Uno, one cannot suppose the existence of a simple-commodity society.

What Uno fails to realize (or feigns ignorance of), however, is that defending the category of the simple commodity is totally different from defending the existence of a society of simple-commodity production. He takes aim at the notion of a historical simple-commodity economy, but in reality the question of whether a simple-commodity society actually existed—i.e. a society in which commodities are basically exchanged according to "value"—is beside the point, and even our renowned professor cannot refute the fact that in pre-capitalist societies commodity production was carried out widely over a period of thousands of years. Who could deny that along with commodity exchange one also has the existence and functioning of the "law of value"—although it has yet to undergo various modifications and appears in an undeveloped and rudimentary form.

> Initially the commodity-form...emerged in the interstices between two communities, and gradually penetrated into the community itself, so value from the outset is not something that developed on the basis of having a substance. For the commodity, the uniformity of value is, so to speak, naturally required by the form itself. This is because exchange cannot occur if uniformity is not anticipated.[49]

---

49. Uno Kōzō et al., *Shihonron kenkyū* (Tokyo: Chikuma Shobō, 1967), 1: 123-4.

Here Uno introduces the "historical" fact of extremely underdeveloped commodity exchange. In the case of commodity exchange which has just emerged from barter, the value-relation is still extremely diluted. This is the superficial phenomenon that allows Uno to say that the commodity-form itself "requires uniformity [?] of value." In other words, within the development of exchange *itself* the value-relation develops and the law of value becomes more deeply-rooted and penetrates overall. This issue, however, is completely separate from the question of our understanding (cognition) of the nature of the law of value. It is only on the basis of the concept of the law of value that we are first able to come to an understanding of the nature and significance—and limitations—of commodity exchange in its initial historical form. This concept of the law of value can only be obtained by means of a rational method. In short, it is a waste of effort to chase after every sort of historical phenomenon (or phenomenon related directly to capitalist reality). Rather, what is needed is a scientific method and a certain, necessary process of cognition (our logical pursuit). Uno speaks of a pure theoretical process, but in reality he adopts the extremely vulgar standpoint of being taken in by phenomena or only being able to focus on direct historical reality.

From the passage above, it is clear that Uno believes the commodity exchange occurring between communities or within a slave-based or feudal society is somehow unrelated to private ownership. However, the analysis of commodities makes clear that even if products are exchanged between communities, to the extent that this is commodity exchange, each community confronts the other as a "private" producer. The only reason that they do not appear as purely private producers is that commodity exchange has just begun and this relation is still extremely undeveloped. With the development of the exchange of products, the circulation of commodities also rebounds back into the community itself, as historical research makes clear, leading to the disintegration of the community and the emergence of a society that is increasingly composed of private owners. To say that the commodity "has no relation at all to production relations" is simply an expression of Uno's own ignorance.

Significance of Studying the Commodity

Already we have devoted a number of pages to discussing the commodity at the beginning of *Capital*. The reason for focusing so much attention on this topic is that differences in the understanding or awareness of the commodity at the outset of *Capital* can soon lead to completely different interpretations of the commodity subsequently discussed by Marx.

We have made it clear that the commodity at the beginning of *Capital* is not a capitalist commodity in terms of its direct concrete nature, nor is it a "historical simple commodity," but rather it is a simple commodity or the commodity *per se*. Still, when it is a question of the nature of this commodity (or its position and significance within the totality of *Capital*), we must emphasize that it should be understood as the commodity as the origin, element, or basis of capital. The commodity as the element of capital, however, is the simple commodity, the commodity in general. Therefore, the commodity at the beginning of *Capital* is at the same time the concept of the commodity in general.

We have also emphasized that the commodity is the outcome of certain historical production relations. A product only becomes a commodity in cases where it is the outcome of private labor. As the result of private property and a division of labor, private labor at the same time must be realized as (one part of) social labor, and in this case the only means open to the private producers is the exchange of their own products (the transformation of these products into commodities). Capitalism, as Marx emphasizes, is the most highly developed commodity-production society, and only under capitalism is wealth generally produced as commodities.

This leads us to one significant aspect of the analysis of the commodity at the beginning of *Capital*, namely, the question of what it means that wealth is generally produced in the form of commodities. Is this the production of wealth carried out according to some sort of suprahistorical, universal method; or is this a limited, historical form that can only exist at a certain stage of human history?

If the production of wealth as commodities is only necessary and realistic at a certain historical stage, ceasing to exist in a more developed society (socialism), then the analysis of the commodity product—such as its value, the magnitude of this value, and the commodity-form—precisely reveals the historical limitations of capitalist society, its temporary nature, and clarifies the contradictions of the society of capital and the origins of these contradictions The limitations and contradictions of the commodity are the basis or starting point of the limitations and contradictions of capital, representing one of its historical aspects. For this reason, at the beginning of *Capital* Marx writes:

The value-form of the product of labor is the most abstract, but also the most universal form of the bourgeois mode of production; by that fact it stamps the bourgeois mode of production as a particular kind of social production of a historical and transitory character. If then we make the mistake of treating it as the eternal natural form of social production, we necessarily overlook the specificity of the value-form, and consequently of the commodity-form together with its further developments, the money form, the capital form, etc.[50]

Marx says that the "value-form [commodity-form] of the product of labor" already "stamps the bourgeois mode of production as a particular kind of social production of a historical character." What could be a more clear and definitive statement than this? Indeed, it is in this sense that we need to come to an understanding of the nature of the commodity from Marx's analysis of the commodity at the beginning of *Capital*. As Marx notes:

The economic concept of value does not occur in antiquity...The concept of value is entirely peculiar to the most modern economy, since it is the most abstract expression of capital itself and of the production resting on it. In the concept of value, its secret betrayed.[51]

A truly critical awareness of value is thus at the same time a critical awareness of capital, marking the starting point of this awareness.

3. "Demonstration" of the Labor-Theory of Value

Marx's "Demonstration"

It seems that Marx himself never referred to his theory of value as a "labor theory of value"; the term apparently being coined instead by bourgeois critics of Marx and gaining wider currency shortly after the turn of the century when Rudolf Hilferding came to the defense of this theory. From the perspective of the marginal utility school,[52] Marx's theory of value is merely a *labor* theory of value because he considers labor as the *sole* factor determining the rate of commodity exchange, ignoring various other elements. Böhm-Bawerk in criticiz-

---

50. *Capital*, vol. 1, 174.
51. *Grundrisse*, 776.

ing Marx's theory of value speaks of "the naïve juggle by means of which the property of being a product of labor has been successfully distilled out as the common property of a group from which all exchangeable things which naturally belong to it, and which are not the products of labor, have been first of all eliminated."[53]

> [If use-value is disregarded] is there only one other property [i.e. the attribute of being a product of labor]? Is not the property of being scarce in proportion to demand also common to all exchangeable goods? Or that they are the subjects of demand and supply? Or that they are appropriated? Or that they are natural products?…Or is not the property that they cause expense to their producers—a property to which Marx draws attention in the third volume—common to exchangeable goods?[54]

Böhm-Bawerk criticizes Marx for what he says is the deceptive or circular logic of limiting the object of analysis to those commodities that are products of labor, i.e. excluding non-labor products, and then discovering as the outcome of his analysis the commodity as a product of labor. But is this really the case?

Marx's "demonstration" or "proof" itself is quite simple. Already in the famous opening paragraph of *Capital* he declares his intention of analyzing the commodity as the elementary form of capitalist wealth. From this starting point, Marx launches his investigation. He first of all discovers that a commodity is a useful object, a use-value ("a thing which through its qualities satisfies human needs of whatever kind"), and immediately following this ascertains that the commodity is at the same time an exchange-value ("the proportion in which use-values of one kind exchange for use-values of another kind").

Marx raises the example of the given exchange-value of a certain commodity, and indicates that this has two aspects:

---

52. As the reader may know, the marginal utility school is a bourgeois tendency that has generated a mountain of meaningless theories from the starting point or basis of mixing up value and use-value in an incredibly simple-minded and careless fashion.
53. *Karl Marx and the Close of His System*, 73.
54. Ibid., 75.

It follows from this that, firstly, the valid exchange-values of a particular commodity express something equal, and secondly, exchange-value cannot be anything other than the mode of expression, the "form of appearance," of a content distinguishable from it.[55]

Marx sets out to clarify what this "equal thing" or "content" is. In order to purely carry out his analysis, he introduces an equation involving two commodities: 1 quarter of corn = x cwt of iron.

As long as the corn and iron are equivalent to each other, there must be something they share in common, but this cannot be use-value (since if their use-values were identical there would be no point in exchanging them for each other in the first place), and therefore this cannot be some physical property of the commodities. Marx notes that "clearly, the exchange relation of commodities is characterized precisely by its abstraction from their use-values,"[56] and thus concludes:

> If we then disregard the use-values of commodities, only one property remains, that of being products of labor...There is nothing left of them in each case but the same phantom-like objectivity; they are merely congealed quantities of homogeneous human labor; i.e. of human labor-power expended without regard to the form of its expenditure. All these things now tell us is that human labor-power has been expended to produce them, human labor is accumulated in them. As crystals of this social substance, which is common to them all, they are values—commodity values [*Warenwerte*].[57]

Fundamentally speaking, this is Marx's famous "demonstration of the labor theory of value," which, by itself seems quite simple.

Uno's Circular Argument

We have already introduced Böhm-Bawerk's criticism of Marx's theory of value, but in Japan there is also the example of Uno Kōzō's incoherent criticism of Marx. For instance, Uno writes:

---

55. *Capital*, vol. 1, 127.
56. Ibid.
57. Ibid., 128.

Certainly in the exchange relation of commodities, we have equal commodities with different use-values, and it can thus be said that this is characterized by an "abstraction from the use-value of a commodity." However,
a commodity can definitively not be exchanged in abstraction from its use-
value. Moreover, a commodity cannot be directly exchanged with every
other commodity. As Marx himself considers in detail in the second chapter of *Capital*, the exchange of commodities is carried out as commodity
circulation mediated by money. The direct exchange indicated in the equation between corn and iron is nothing more than so-called barter, and does
not signify the exchange of commodities. For exchange as a commodity, a
commodity owner that desires another commodity must be able to freely
carry out exchange regardless of whether the other commodity owner
wishes to exchange his own commodity for this commodity or not, but this
is impossible since the same relation is sought by all commodities, and thus
one commodity among all others becomes money, whereas commodities as
such are passively purchased with money, so that the exchange for the
desired commodity can be accomplished not as direct exchange but rather
through circulation mediated by money. To immediately seek within the
equation between corn and iron some "commonality" amounts to overlooking the particular quality of commodity exchange. What actually appears as
the "commonality" between the two is not direct value but rather their
money price. These two commodities are often exchanged more or less in
divergence from their values and it is only a matter of chance if they happen
to coincide directly, but this is carried out as exchange realized from either
side [?]. Moreover, this divergence of price from value is adjusted by means
of the relationship of supply and demand, and through production itself,
but this adjustment through production, furthermore, is only ensured in a
commodity-economy manner through grasping production via capital that
is based upon the formal development of the commodity and money.[58]

Could any Marxist read this passage without feeling a bit stunned? This is
being peddled as "Marxism that goes beyond Marx," but not even an ounce of
Marxism is on display here! What Uno is saying—and here we have all of the
essential characteristics of Unoist theory, its "secrets" laid bare—is the following: (1) Since the commodity "can definitely not be exchanged in abstraction
from its use-value," one cannot speak of exchange-value while excluding use-
value; (2) commodity exchange is in fact the exchange relation between two
commodities, therefore (?) it is not barter but "commodity circulation mediated by money," and that to extract the substance of value, as Marx does, from

58. Uno Kōzō, *Keizaigaku hōhō-ron* (Tokyo: University of Tokyo Press,
    1962), 173-4.

the exchange of two commodities (barter?) is incorrect; (3) moreover, commodity exchange is not merely an exchange of commodities (?) but rather is carried out as a purchase made with money, whose point of origin is the money-owner's desires, so that one cannot ignore this fact and seek a "commonality" in the equation between two commodities; (4) thus, even if there can be said to be a commonality, this is not value (objectified human labor) but simply price; (5) Marx's approach ignores the characteristic of commodity exchange in which value and price diverge, and he fails to see that this is "adjusted" via the relationship of supply and demand; and finally (6) the "demonstration" of the labor theory of value must be mediated by the commodification of labor-power.

This theory is quite ridiculous from top to bottom, however. First of all, although he sets out to analyze the commodity, Uno presupposes the category of money—as well as price (which is the expression of a commodity's value through money). However, in order to rationally understand—as a concept—money or money price, it is first necessary to clarify the meaning of value. Uno, by taking as his premise categories that must be elucidated within the unfolding of the theory of value, falls into hopeless confusion and is trapped within a circular argument.

We have already briefly looked at Böhm-Bawerk and Uno's criticism of Marx, but now we will need to move on to a more detailed examination of various issues related to the "demonstration" of the law of value.

Products Taking the *Historical Form* of the Commodity

Bourgeois scholars claim that Marx merely took as his object of analysis the commodity as a product of labor, and then proceeded to analyze this commodity, finding the substance of its value or content to be labor. These scholars claim that this is a circular argument or theoretical sleight of hand. They wonder why Marx did not consider commodities in general, that is to say, all commodities, including those that are not products of labor, such as land, "nature," securities, works of art, rare goods with particularly high prices, labor-power, or even "sex." Had Marx done this, these scholars argue, the weakness of his "demonstration" would have been exposed, since it is perfectly clear that no labor is objectified in such commodities, or that they are not exchanged in proportion to the labor objectified in them.

As a sort of "complement" to these views, we have Unoists who argue that Marx was criticized by bourgeois scholars because of the defect in his demonstration, and because he explained the substance of value as labor from the relation of equivalence between two commodities at the beginning of *Capital*. They add that Marx would not have been criticized had he said that the two commodities merely share the trait of having general exchangeability.

This criticism stems from a lack of understanding—or inability to understand—that the commodities Marx is analyzing are certainly not lacking a premise. Marx clearly says that what is being analyzed is the commodity as the elementary form of wealth in capitalist society. Here "wealth" refers to the material wealth that sustains human life. Social "wealth" by nature is the outcome or product of human labor, whereas natural things, such as air, despite being indispensable to human beings, clearly do not make up one part of this wealth.

This does not mean, however, that things such as land cannot *become* "commodities" (assume the commodity-form). Marx later clarifies how things which are not products of labor, such as land, are commodified under capitalism. However, the seemingly irrational price of land can only be explained in a truly scientific (rational) manner through the mediation of first positing the concept of the commodity in general and then establishing the concepts of capital and rent. The analysis of the commodity in *Capital* does not lack a premise, and underlying this is the magnificent analysis carried out in Marx's mind, his process of abstraction (the so-called "downward journey").[59]

Wealth in capitalist society is composed of capital, money, and commodities, but Marx discovers that capital and money can also be reduced to the commodity. Thus, the issue for Marx is the significance or content of wealth in capitalist society—i.e. products of labor—assuming the commodity-form. This is the theoretical task of the entire first chapter of *Capital*, with the first section ("The Two Factors of the Commodity") dealing with one aspect of this and representing the point of departure.

Is it really so peculiar or strange that the commodity considered by Marx is the commodity as the historical form taken by products of labor, which is thus distinguished from non-labor products that assume the commodity-form in a derivative manner? It seems that those who find this strange or a "theoretical sleight of hand" are in fact under the sway of bourgeois prejudices. They fail to recognize that products of labor are transformed into commodities, and that only from this fundamental social relation can land and other things be "com-

---

59. [See Marx's introduction to *Grundrisse*.]

modified" in a derivative sense. They have given no thought to what the foundation of human society is, what supports this society, and this is because they are members of the bourgeoisie (or petty bourgeoisie), rather than workers, and occupy a parasitical position within society. Marx pointed out the basic perspective that such people lack in a famous letter written to Ludwig Kugelmann in 1868:

> Every child knows that any nation that stopped working, not for a year, but let us say, just for a few weeks, would perish. And every child knows, too, that the amounts of products corresponding to the differing amounts of needs demand differing and quantitatively determined amounts of society's aggregate labor. It is self-evident that this necessity of the distribution of social labor in specific proportions is certainly not abolished by the specific form of social production; it can only *change* its form of manifestation. Natural laws cannot be abolished at all. The only thing that can change, under historically differing conditions, is the form in which those laws assert themselves. And the form in which this proportional distribution of labor asserts itself in a state of society in which the interconnection of social labor expresses itself as the private exchange of the individual products of labor, is precisely the exchange-value of these products.[60]

Uno Emphasizes Commodity Exchange is Not "Barter"

Uno concerns himself with exchange mediated by money, or more precisely "purchases with money." However, why does he begin by looking at purchases? In *Theories of Surplus Value*, Marx criticizes Berry in the following way:

> His entire wisdom is, in fact, contained in this passage. "If value is nothing but power of purchasing" (a very fine definition since "purchasing" [pre]supposes not only value, but the representation of value as "money"), "it denotes," etc. However, let us first clear away from Bailey's proposition the absurdities which have been smuggled in. "Purchasing" means transforming money into commodities. Money already presupposes value and the development of value. Consequently, out with the expression "purchasing" first of all. Otherwise we are explaining value by value. Instead of purchasing we must say "exchanging against other objects."[61]

---

60. Karl Marx, *Marx-Engels Collected Works* (hereinafter *MECW*), vol. 43 (New York: International Publishers 1988), 68.
61. *MECW*, vol. 32 (1990), 237.

If one correctly refers to "exchange" rather than the vulgar term "purchasing," it becomes immediately apparent that at issue is the exchange-value of commodities, and therefore the relation between one commodity and another (a relation of equivalents). Uno, however, uses the expression "purchasing commodities with money," and for this reason becomes caught up in the direct phenomenon of the mediation of money, failing to understand that the problem centers on the exchange-value of commodities and a relation of equivalence.

It does not require much "wisdom" to understand that the exchange between commodity and money is also an exchange of commodities, being nothing more than its developed form. (Marx says that it is more difficult, rather, to understand that a commodity *is* money.[62]) By sticking to the vulgar perspective of "purchasing with money," Uno is unable to understand that money is also a commodity, and that in section one of the first chapter of *Capital* no distinction is made between commodities and money in terms of their being commodities, and therefore it is correct to view commodity A = commodity B as the basic form, rather than the special, developed form of commodity exchange (exchange-value), namely: commodity = money.[63]

Needless to say, nothing changes when we are dealing with the exchange-value between commodity and money (i.e. *a* cwt. of iron = *b* ounces of gold), but in this case gold is a "normal" commodity rather than money. In order to not generate confusion and misunderstanding, Marx avoided introducing gold into the simple form of value. But Uno says that it is necessary for the com-

---

62. [Hayashi is referring to chapter two of *Capital* where Marx writes: "The difficulty lies not in comprehending that money is a commodity, but in discovering how, why and through what a commodity is money."—Here I am following Hans Ehrbar's translation, which is similar to most of the Japanese translations and accurately reflects the original German. Ben Fowkes' translation, perhaps drawing on the French translation of *Capital*, replaces "is" with "becomes" so that the passage reads: "The difficulty lies not in comprehending that money is a commodity, but in discovering how, why and by what means a commodity becomes money." Ehrbar also notes in his annotated translation that the word "means" should be removed because "a commodity does not need an external means to become money, but it has inner money traits."]

63. In sections three and four of chapter one, by contrast, the theoretical issue revolves around the particular significance of money.

modity to be directly "equivalent" to money, and even adds that this is not merely "equivalence" but a "purchase with money."

Uno also claims that Marx analyzed "simple barter" rather than commodity exchange, and failed to understand the particular form of commodity exchange. For Marx, however, *a* cwt. iron = 1 coat is not simply barter, but commodity exchange and the basic form of exchange-value. Marx recognizes that all exchange-value can ultimately be reduced to this most basic form, whereas Uno's attention is fixated on the direct form of commodity = money.

In the first section of chapter one, Marx introduces the most basic form of exchange-value. He notes that the commodity is the elementary form of capitalist wealth, and must therefore be examined. Following this, he says that since value is manifested or exists in reality as exchange-value, the examination of exchange-value will elucidate the mystery of value, and he proceeds to examine exchange-value. To begin with, exchange-value is the array of exchange ratios between various use-values, but the basic element of this is the exchange-value between two commodities. Viewing the exchange relation of the commodity at the beginning of *Capital* as merely *barter*, represents a complete misunderstanding of Marx's method, reflecting the workings of a vulgar mind incapable of understanding that exchange-value in its elementary form is the exchange-value between two commodities.

"Abstracting" Use-Value

Bourgeois scholars continue to be perplexed by the abstraction from use-value in the so-called "demonstration of the law of value," and this point has also tripped up the Unoists. It is natural that the bourgeois marginal utility school of the late nineteenth century criticized Marx's theory of value for having "abstracted from use-value." This vulgar school of thought argued that the value of a commodity is determined by the relation between the subjective evaluation of the purchaser and the commodity's "utility," confused value with price, failed to distinguish between value and use-value, and focused attention on the most superficial and direct phenomena of exchange-value, thus fashioning an ideology suitable for an increasingly parasitic monopoly-capitalist society in decline, as is clear from the fact that the consumer, rather than the producer, is taken as the subject.

A reflection of this vulgar theory can also be found within "Marxist economics" (the Uno school). Very little of the Unoist criticism of Marx is more than a simple aping of the work of bourgeois scholars, and the most conspicuous example of this is their condemnation of Marx for abstracting from use-value. Uno argues that the demonstration of the theory of value cannot abstract from the use-value of the commodity and that the seller's commodity is the natural premise, just as the desires or "demand" of the buyer (money) are also presupposed. He says that buyers, through the repeated purchases of a commodity, provide an "objective" evaluation, and that this is what determines value (really price!). As we can see, this approach is essentially the same as that of Böhm-Bawerk and the marginal utility school.

We feel obliged to ask why, however, it is necessary to raise the question of use-value in order to understand "value"? Marx was also perfectly aware that a commodity exists as the unity of use-value and value, but who can deny that value itself is something totally distinct from use-value, and does "not contain an atom of use-value."

Marx recognizes that the commodity is a material thing that satisfies some human need, has many attributes that are useful to human beings, and has "utility" as a desired object. Of course, it is the "work of history" to determine in what way or to what degree these attributes of the commodity-body *qua* thing are useful. Use-value is one element of the commodity, and without this a commodity cannot exist as such, but use-value itself is totally distinct from value and is nothing more than the "material bearer" of exchange-value. Whereas use-value is an attribute of the commodity as thing, value is a social substance that is separate from the commodity as thing; namely, the human labor that is "objectified" or crystallized in the commodity-body. What is at issue in the analysis of the commodity is *value*, not use-value, because the existence of the commodity as use-value is self-evident and it is sufficient to merely assume it as such.

Therefore, in the analysis of commodity-value, use-value is disregarded since the relation of commodity-exchange itself is the abstraction from the use-value of the commodity. Within the equation x commodity A = y commodity B, a certain proportion of two different use-values are equivalent, but their relation of equivalence bears no relation to use-value *per se*. For example, iron and corn are not equal in terms of use-value, nor are they exchanged because they have the same weight. The two are equivalent because they share something in common, and it is perfectly clear that this is not their use-value (or any property they may have as material things). Commodities can be exchanged as mutually equal things because they have equal value, and the content of this value is *objectified human labor*. Here the only role of use-value is to serve as the bearer of value. If one understands that value and use-value are totally distinct, and that in this way the contradictory nature of the commodity is generated, then the abstraction from use-value poses no particular difficulty. As Marx notes, "so far no chemist has ever discovered exchange-value either in a pearl or a diamond."[64]

"Formal Determination" of the Commodity

Unoists repeatedly criticize Marx for failing to understand the particularity of commodity exchange, arguing that in his demonstration of the theory of value (and throughout *Capital*) he adopts the incorrect "method" of developing his theory on the basis of value and price coinciding, despite recognizing that the "quantitative incongruity between price and magnitude of value" is "not a defect" of this mode of production, thus overlooking the particularity of commodity production and its "formal determination" [*keitai-kitei, Formbestimmtheit*] and taking as his object something other than commodity production (i.e. barter exchange).

In reality, however, no theorist penetrated the historical character of commodity production more profoundly than Marx. The extent to which he perfectly understood and emphasized human labor being "objectified" as the value of a commodity—and therefore grasped the significance of labor assuming the formal determination of value—should be clear to anyone who has read the third and fourth sections of the first chapter of *Capital*. In the first German edition of *Capital* Marx writes:

> If one considers only the quantitative relationship in the simple, relative value-expression: x commodity A = y commodity B, then one finds also only the laws developed above concerning the motion of relative value, which all rest upon the fact that the amount of value of commodities is determined by the labor-time required for their production. But if one considers the value relation of both commodities in their *qualitative* aspect, then one discovers in that simple expression of value the mystery of the value-form, and hence, *in nuce* of money.[65]

In *Capital* Marx notes:

---

64. *Capital*, vol. 1, 177.
65. Karl Marx, *Value: Studies by Marx*, trans. Albert Dragstedt (London: New Park Publications, 1976), 22.

> Political economy has indeed analyzed value and its magnitude, however, incompletely, and has uncovered the content concealed within these forms. But it has never once asked the question why this content has assumed that particular form, that is to say, why labor is expressed in value, and why the measurement of labor by its duration is expressed in the magnitude of the value of the product. Note: It is one of the chief failings of classical political economy that it has never succeeded, by means of its analysis of commodities, and in particular of their value, in discovering the form of value which in fact turns value into exchange-value.[66]

As we can see, the formal determination of the commodity emphasized by Marx has a content totally different from the explanation of Uno, who can only offer the completely vulgar view that the "value-determination" refers to the fact that there are price fluctuations and price is thus "determined" by supply and demand and competition. For Marx, by contrast, the fundamental question is essentially why and how human labor comes to take the objective form of *value*.

Uno spills forth endlessly about the "formal determination" but fails to understand the actual content and significance of the term. Moreover, as we can see from the fact that he concerns himself exclusively with the "determination of value," Uno concentrates on what Marx considers a quantitative issue. For Marx, however, the formal determination is a qualitative question, which is not the theoretical task of the first section of chapter one where he is primarily concerned with the quantitative aspect of what determines exchange-value, which had already been dealt with, albeit insufficiently, by the classical school of economics. This is the theoretical framework of the first section.

Uno does not recognize that each part of *Capital* has its own particular theoretical task, and that this is also true of the first chapter. The first section focuses mainly on the substance of value and its magnitude. Of course, in terms of saying that the substance of value is labor, this also enters into a qualitative question, but this is merely stated as a fact, whereas the main task concerns the fundamentally quantitative aspect of what determines exchange-value (or the exchange relation of commodities). The third section, by contrast, explains the character of the labor that takes the material form of value, and the fourth section clarifies why human labor must take the objective, material form of value. In section one, Marx is merely indicating, as a fact,

---

66. *Capital*, vol. 1, 173-4.

what forms the substance of value, and naturally here the question of the formal determination is not raised. To call for an examination of this issue here reflects a failure to understand Marx's method and theory (and an underlying bourgeois, vulgar consciousness).

Value and the Relation of Supply and Demand

Another criticism of Marx, common to both bourgeois scholars and the Uno school, is the notion that a theory of value cannot be developed while overlooking the relation of supply and demand. Everyone knows that the price of a given commodity will rise if the demand for it expands while its supply remains limited (and fall in the opposite case). Those who focus exclusively on this phenomenon believe it is impossible to speak of the value of a commodity while disregarding the relation of supply and demand. Bourgeois scholars, for their part, have elevated this slanted view to the level of "theory" and claim that "value is a function of supply and demand."

But what is taken for "value" here is in fact price. The historical appearance of the concept of value is the outcome of scientific insight stemming from the experience of human beings over a long period of time. People recognized that although prices do fluctuate due to supply and demand, seen over the long-term a certain price exists, and that different types of commodities have different magnitudes of price. The awareness thus emerged, correct as such, that "price" itself is exchange-value, one of its forms (namely the exchange ratio between money and commodity).[67] The question then became: What is nature of this exchange-value? Commodities clearly exchange at a certain rate, but what determines this rate? The view arose that this rate is determined by the cost expended on the production of a commodity, but since this cost itself is composed of commodities, ultimately this was a circular argument. It was Ricardo who offered the final word from the perspective of the classical school by concluding that exchange-value is determined by the labor included in commodities, i.e. the labor expended on their production.

Most people would say that if there is no demand for a commodity and it cannot be sold, it cannot be said to have value no matter how much labor may be objectified in it, and that a "labor theory of value" could certainly not demonstrate this. Setting aside the confusion expressed here between value and

---

67. But present-day bourgeois economists and the Uno school even lack this elementary understanding!

price, there are two comments we can make. First of all, things that are not objects of need and for which there is no demand will not be produced to begin with and therefore will not become commodities. For this reason, we find no need to devote much attention to commodities in this sense. Second, there is the case of overproduction where the lack of demand is due to some social cause (what Keynes calls "insufficient effective demand"). But this is related to the temporary phenomenon of crisis, and when seen from a long-term perspective, the disequilibrium is forcefully "adjusted" and the shift made back to equilibrium—albeit equilibrium as a temporary, transitional state. The equilibrium of supply and demand is always penetrated by fluctuations and cases of disequilibrium, since under capitalism "laws can only assert themselves as blindly operating averages between constant irregularities"[68]—and this is precisely the characteristic of bourgeois production.

> What initially concerns producers in practice when they make an exchange is how much of some other product they get for their own; in what proportions can the products be exchanged?…The production of commodities must be fully developed before the scientific conviction emerges, from experience itself, that all the different kinds of private labor (which are carried out independently of each other, and yet, as spontaneously developed branches of labor, are in a situation of all-round dependence on each other) are continually being reduced to the quantitative proportions in which society requires them. The reason for this reduction is that in the midst of the accidental and ever-fluctuating exchange relations between the products, the labor-time socially necessary to produce them asserts itself as a regulative law of nature…The determination of the magnitude of value by labor-time is therefore a secret hidden under the apparent movements in the relative values of commodities. Its discovery destroys the semblance of the merely accidental determination of the magnitude of the value of the products of labor, but by no means abolishes that determination's material form.[69]

Experience fosters the understanding that price fluctuations are not merely an "accidental" determination, and that underlying this is an essential relation. But Böhm-Bawerk and Uno turned their back on the development of such an understanding (which is the deepening of scientific cognition). This type of

---

68. Ibid., 196.
69. Ibid., 167-8.

attitude is shared by today's corrupt bourgeois intellectuals and can be considered one of their characteristic traits.

Supply and Demand Cannot Explain Value

One fundamental view held by bourgeois economists today is that value is *determined* within the relation of supply and demand, and this view is also shared by the professional critics of Marxism grouped within the Uno school. Marx, however, clearly states that the law of value can certainly not be explained on the basis of the mechanism of supply and demand.

> If demand and supply coincide, they cease to have any effect, and it is for this very reason that commodities are sold at their market value. If two forces act in opposing directions and cancel one another out, they have no external impact whatsoever, and phenomena that appear under these conditions must be explained otherwise than by the operation of these two forces. If demand and supply cancel one another out, they cease to explain anything, have no effect on market value and leave us completely in the dark as to why this market value is expressed in precisely such a sum of money and no other. The real inner laws of capitalist production clearly cannot be explained in terms of the interaction of demand and supply...since these laws are realized in their pure form only when demand and supply cease to operate, i.e., when the coincide.[70]

Prices of commodities are always fluctuating in relation to the demand and supply for them, so that a given commodity may sell for 10,000 yen on one occasion and for 30,000 yen on another. However, although the price of the commodity might be 20,000 yen on average, it certainly could not fall to 10 or 100 yen, or even 1,000 yen. This is something that we can notice at any given time. Supply and demand, then, cannot explain why this commodity sells for 20,000 yen rather than 100 or 1,000 yen. The relation of supply and demand is able to account for the price fluctuating above or below the 20,000-yen range, but it is quite incapable of explaining why the point around which the price fluctuates is 20,000 yen rather than 100 or 1,000 yen. And this is precisely the question that concerns us; namely, the question of why the exchange-value of a particular commodity is 20,000 yen rather than 100 yen (despite the fact that many commodities that *are* sold for 100 yen). Our response to this question is that commodities can differ greatly in price

---

70. *Capital*, vol. 3, 290-1.

because of differences in their value. Unoists and others, however, argue that these differences are the outcome of supply and demand. We must note, however, that some commodities differ greatly in terms of exchange-value despite having the *same* level of supply and demand. In various sections of *Theories of Surplus Value*, Marx touches on the question of supply and demand:

> The twaddle about the law of demand and supply of course does not help us out of this *cercle vicieux*. For the "natural price" or the price corresponding to the value of the commodity is supposed to exist just when demand meets supply, i.e., when the price of the commodity does not stand above or below its value as a result of fluctuations in demand and supply; when, in other words, the cost-price of the commodity (or the value of the commodity supplied by the seller) is also the price which the demand pays.[71]

> Here we have the gist of the matter. [This is said by] Mill who, as a zealous Ricardian, proves that although demand and supply can, to be sure, determine the vacillations of the market price either above or below the value of the commodity, they cannot determine that value itself, that these are meaningless words when applied to the determination of value, for the determination of demand and supply presupposes the determination of value![72]

One would have thought it self-evident that fluctuations resulting from the relation of supply and demand can explain nothing more than the divergence or inconsistency between price and value, but bourgeois scholars seem totally incapable of recognizing this plain truth. This is related to the fact that they lack any sort of concept of value. What they refer to as "value" is in fact price, and (at best) nothing more than the concept of average price. We say that price is equal to value when supply and demand coincide. If bourgeois scholars are going to bother to discuss value, they are obliged to explain the significance of price (exchange-value) when supply and demand are in agreement, and account for why a commodity is exchanged at a certain rate rather than another. But this is precisely what they refuse to do or are incapable of doing!

---

71. *MECW*, vol. 30 (1988), 401.
72. *MECW*, vol. 32, 284-5.

At Issue is the "Pure Form"

Another major issue concerning the "demonstration of value" is the Unoists criticism of Marx for having demonstrated the substance of value from the very beginning *of Capital*. At the same time, they also take Marx to task for having explained commodity exchange from the beginning as a relation of equivalence. Unoists claim, holding fast to direct phenomena, that since value and price diverge due to price fluctuations, and actual exchange is not carried out according to value (or only randomly so), "theory" should not disregard this reality by explaining exchange as being generally carried out according to value.

Uno and his followers, however, have failed to understand the crux of the issue. Marx is not saying that exchange is carried out according to value in reality. Rather, he recognizes that the price-expression of value can itself include a divergence between value and price. Still, Marx emphasizes that to the extent that there is an exchange of commodities, some commonality must exist and that this does not concern their use-values.

Having said this, what is this common element? Marx, basing himself on the findings of Ricardo and other classical economists, responds by saying that it is *human labor* (or more precisely, human social labor "objectified" in the commodity). The point he is insisting on here has nothing to do with claiming that commodity exchange is actually carried out "according to value" or that this must occur, which everyone knows is not the case in reality. Here the issue being addressed is a completely different one. Marx, for instance, notes the following in his discussion of simple commodity circulation:

> If we consider this in the abstract, i.e. disregarding circumstances which do not flow from the immanent laws of simple commodity circulation, all that happens in exchange (if we leave aside the replacing of one use-value for another) is a metamorphosis, a mere change in the form of the commodity. The same value, i.e. the same quantity of objectified social labor, remains throughout in the hands of the same commodity-owner, first in the shape of his own commodity, then in the shape of the money into which the commodity has been transformed, and finally in the shape of the commodity into which this money has been re-converted. This change in form does not imply any change in the magnitude of the value…In so far, therefore, as the circulation of commodities involves a change only in the form of their values, it necessarily involves the exchange of equivalents, provided the phenomenon occurs in its purity…It is true that commodities may be sold at prices which diverge from their values, but this divergence appears

as an infringement of the laws governing the exchange of commodities. In
its pure form, the exchange of commodities is an exchange of equivalents,
and thus it is not a method of increasing value.[73]

In reality, commodities are not exchanged according to value. The law of
value, as the essence of the price phenomenon (and exchange-value), only
determines this from behind the scenes. When considering the essence of
exchange-value—its determining law—there is little point in setting aside the
law itself and pointing out that this does not appear as such in reality. At issue
is the law, and it is for this reason that the object must be considered in its
"pure form"!

The question for us is why two commodities, when exchanged for each
other, are exchanged as equivalent, equal things. Given this theoretical task,
the issue of whether the ratio of exchange in reality is strictly carried out
according to value is a secondary one. Prior to this, there is the *qualitative*
question of what the two commodities share in common, and it is important
to note that the two commodities can be considered as equivalents and
exchanged with each other precisely because of their commonality. Critics of
Marx are unable to realize that if exchange is not conceived of as being in
accordance with value, then the essence of exchange-value becomes something
without a concept. Unoists do not recognize the human labor objectified in a
commodity determines its exchange-value, and for this precise reason they do
not accept that commodity exchange—in its "pure form," understood
abstractly in a form suitable to science—is an exchange of equivalents.

"Demonstrating" Value via the Labor-Power Commodity?!

To bring our discussion of the demonstration of the labor theory of value to an
end, I would like to take a look at the "demonstration" offered by the Uno
school in criticizing Marx. Unoists say that it is not possible to demonstrate
the labor theory of value in the case of the simple commodity or individual
commodity, arguing that this must instead be mediated by capitalist-commodity production, i.e. the "law of surplus-value" and the commodification of
labor-power. They claim that "the worker buying back through labor-power
the things he has made" must be made the basis of a demonstration of the law
of value. Uno argues that this demonstration must be based upon "the funda-

---

73. *Capital*, vol. 1, 260-1.

mental relation of workers, in the production process of capital, producing commodities and then buying back the means of livelihood from out of the commodities produced." Based on this view, Ōuchi Hideaki offers the following:

> The value of the labor-power commodity is determined by necessary labor...Moreover, it is precisely in terms of the worker buying back what he has made via labor-power, since it is bought back through the production process, that the value relation can in fact have come to have a necessary connection to the substance of labor, and here the substance of value can be very clearly explained.[74]

Who can be expected to make sense of such incoherent sophistry? This superficial and formalistic theory is pure nonsense. Unoists think that the law of value amounts to "the value relation having a necessary connection with the substance of labor." But the value-relation of commodities is an exchange of equivalents, and the law of value explains the basis of this equivalence. This is not merely a matter of "having a connection."

Even though Ōuchi is obliged to explain value, he presupposes the value of the labor-power commodity, since he claims that "the value of the labor-power commodity is determined by necessary labor." However, the value of the labor-power commodity is the necessary labor-time to reproduce the labor-power, and the labor-power is not produced from direct labor. The reproduction of labor-power is only reproduced through the consumption of consumption means (commodities), such as food, clothing, and lodging. Therefore, the value of the labor-power commodity is the value of the commodities (consumption means) needed to reproduce this labor-power, so that the value-determination of the labor-power commodity, unlike commodities in general, is *mediated* and thus commodity-value is determined through commodity-value, which in a sense may seem to represent a circular argument. The value-determination of the labor-power commodity already presupposes the value-determination of general commodities, i.e., the concept of value.

Having rejected the concept of value, however, how can Unoists then say that the value of the labor-power commodity is necessary labor? Saying that the value of the labor-power commodity is "necessary labor" is based on the value of the commodities necessary for the reproduction of labor-power being

---

74. *Shihonron kenkyū*, 1: 240.

the necessary labor, which can only be said based on the assumption of the concept of value.

According to the theory held by Uno and his followers, labor is the substance of value simply because the "worker buys back what he has made," but for workers it will remain an eternal mystery how it could be said that labor is the substance of value if "bought back." The expression "buying back" does not help to clarify at all what determines the magnitude of the value of the consumption-means commodities that are "bought back." Ultimately, the Unoist view forms a superficial connection between the clear fact that workers produce commodities and the fact that they also purchases commodities, and this is said to demonstrate the labor theory of value. But this theory completely lacks rational content or "logic." The fact remains that it is only through first establishing the concept of value that the value of the labor-power commodity can be explained, and the concept of value cannot be arrived at through the mediation of the commodification of labor-power.

Even if workers do not "buy back" the commodities that they (and their class) have produced—as in the case of small farmers purchasing rice—they still very much remain workers, and there is no reason why this would change the value-determination of the labor-power commodity. This is because the value-determination of the labor-power commodity and the worker "buying back" commodities—or more correctly, the exchange between the labor-power commodity and the consumption-means commodities—are two separate issues. By mixing up and confusing the two, Unoists only manage to muddle the thinking of workers.

4. Complex labor and simple labor

Complex Labor Reduced to Simple Labor

The question of complex and simple labor, i.e. the question of the reduction of complex labor to simple labor, has been at the center of a historically significant debate.

> [Human labor] is the expenditure of simple labor-power, i.e. of the labor-power possessed in his bodily organism by every ordinary man, on the average, without being developed in any special way...More complex labor counts only as *intensified*, or rather *multiplied* simple labor, so that a smaller quantity of complex labor is considered equal to a larger quantity of simple

labor. Experience shows that this reduction is constantly being made. A commodity may be the outcome of the most complicated labor, but through its *value* it is posited as equal to the product of the simple labor. The various proportions in which different kinds of labor are reduced to simple labor as their unit of measurement are established by a social process that goes on behind the backs of the producers; these proportions therefore appear to the producers to have been handed down by tradition. In the interests of simplification, we shall henceforth view every form of labor-power directly as simple labor-power; by this we shall simply be saving ourselves the trouble of making the reduction.[75]

Commodities as values are nothing but crystallized labor. The unit of measurement of labor itself is the simple average-labor, the character of which varies admittedly in different lands and cultural epochs, but is given for a particular society. More complex labor counts merely as simple labor to an exponent or rather to a multiple, so that a smaller quantum of complex labor is equal to a larger quantum of simple labor, for example...A commodity may be the product of the most complex labor. Its value equates it to the product of simple labor and therefore represents on its own merely a definite quantum of simple labor.[76]

The fact that Marx's explanation presupposes the concept of value is indicated by his statements that "experience shows" that this reduction is made, that complex labor is "considered" as intensified simple labor, and that the proportion of this reduction being established by "a social process that goes on behind the backs of the producers." These, in other words, are theoretical tasks that cannot yet be explained in this section. Bourgeois scholars, however, are unable to understand this, and thus direct criticism at Marx. Here, as elsewhere, the attack was spearheaded by Böhm-Bawerk:

The fact with which we have to deal is that the product of a day's or an hour's skilled labor is more valuable than the product of a day's or an hour's unskilled labor [simple labor]; that, for instance, the day's product of a sculptor is equal to the five days' product of a stone-breaker.[77]

He claims that the view above violates the basis of Marx's theory, where it had been argued that the product of one day's labor-time exchanges with the prod-

75. *Capital*, vol. 1, 135.
76. *Value: Studies by Marx*, 9.
77. *Karl Marx and the Close of His System*, 81.

uct of the same single day of labor. According to Böhm-Bawerk, Marx's theory addresses the issue of a special type of labor rather than "labor in general" and thus does not have general validity. His argument boils down to the following:

> If we look at this dispassionately, however, it fits still worse, for in sculpture there is no "unskilled labor" at all embodied, much less therefore unskilled labor equal to the amount in the five day's labor of the stone-breaker. The plain truth is that the two products embody *different kinds* of labor in *different amounts*, and every unprejudiced person will admit that this means a state of things exactly contrary to the conditions which Marx demands and must affirm, namely, that they embody labor of the *same kind* and of the *same amount*![78]

A Reduction Shown "By Experience"

Marx says "experience shows" that complex labor is reduced to simple labor, while Böhm-Bawerk counters by saying that experience does not show this, as no unskilled labor (simple labor) at all is embodied in a sculpture, for example. But what exactly is Böhm-Bawerk trying to say here? He seems to be doing no more than pretentiously stating the fact that skilled or high-grade labor exists as such rather than being simple labor.

But this fact is perfectly clear, and we hardly need Böhm-Bawerk to point this out for us. His criticism of Marx only exposes the fact that he has missed the point. Böhm-Bawerk thinks in terms of skilled labor (power) being directly reduced to simple labor (power). But at issue here is the value of the commodity, as well as the law that determines commodity exchange, and it is in relation to this that Marx speaks of the reduction of complex labor to simple labor.

Our own everyday experience shows us that products of complex labor and products of simple labor are equivalent *as value* and exchanged at certain proportions, so that, for example, one day of complex labor may be equal to three days of simple labor. And as long as such equivalent exchange is carried out, one day of complex labor corresponds to three days of simple labor. This theory presents little difficulty if one understands the law of value and the fact that the substance of value is abstract human labor,.

---

78. Ibid., 82.

Actual commodities are not limited to products of simple labor, and include various products of complex labor as well. But to the extent that commodities are exchanged as value, the labor that produces commodities only exists and is equated as abstract, human labor. This is what Marx's expression "experience shows" refers to. This does not mean that complex labor is *directly* simple labor, or that it is directly dissolved into simple labor. Here Marx is merely making a passing reference to the issue of complex labor on the basis of the concept of value already established.

It is clear that Marx goes to the trouble of addressing this issue here because he already foresees the possibility of a vulgar criticism—actually voiced by Böhm-Bawerk—that would consider his theory of value as being unable to account for one day of some particular labor (complex labor) exchanging for five days of another type of labor (simple labor). Since Marx already clarifies that the substance of value is abstract human labor, he is able to clearly state that even though one day of complex labor may exchange for three days of simple labor, this is already a question of quantity rather than quality; that is to say, this is simply the fact that one day of complex labor is reduced to three days of simple labor. Despite this, however, Böhm-Bawerk has no qualms about offering the following:

> Marx certainly says that skilled labor "counts" as multiplied unskilled labor, but to "count as" is not "to be," and the theory deals with the beings of things. Men may naturally consider one day of a sculptor's work as equal in some respects to five days of a stone-breaker's work, just as they might also consider a deer as equal to five hares.[79]

This criticism of Marx reveals to us that Böhm-Bawerk has absolutely no concept of value. Already in the first German edition of *Capital*, Marx wrote "counts as," which merely refers to the fact, on the basis of the theory of value, that complex labor is quantitatively reduced to simple labor. This, however, bears no relation to the arbitrary reduction of considering "a deer as equal to five hares." Marx is merely indicating that products of complex labor at a certain proportion are equal, as exchange-value, to the products of simple labor, i.e. the fact that complex labor can also be reduced to simple labor. But he is not saying anything beyond this—such as how the ratio of reduction is determined, etc.

79. Ibid., 82.

What is "a Social Process"?

Marx says that the "various proportions in which different kinds of labor are reduced to simple labor as their unit of measurement are established by a social process that goes on behind the backs of the producers"; while Engels, for his part, notes in *Anti-Dühring* that the "different proportions in which different sorts of labor are reduced to unskilled labor as their standard, are established by a social process that goes on behind the backs of the producers, and, consequently, appear to be fixed by custom."[80] But what exactly is this "social process"? Marx has already provided us with a hint of what this means in the footnote immediately following his first reference to the reduction of complex labor in *Capital*:

> The reader should note that we are not speaking here of the wages or value the worker receives for (e.g.) a day's labor, but of the value of the commodity in which the day of labor is objectified. At this stage of our presentation, the category of wages does not exist at all.[81]

Marx thus suggests that the law determining this reduction is connected to the law that determines the value of labor-power. He says that complex labor, by its nature, will create more value in the same one-hour period than simple labor does. This is because complex labor is the manifestation of complex labor-power, which requires a greater degree of cost than simple labor-power, and thus has greater value.

> In order to modify the general nature of the human organism in such a way that it acquires skill and dexterity in a given branch of industry, and becomes labor-power of a developed and specific kind, a special education or training is needed, and this in turn costs an equivalent in commodities of a greater or lesser amount. The costs of education vary according to the degree of complexity of the labor-power required. These expenses (exceedingly small in the case of ordinary labor-power) form a part of the total value spent in producing it.[82]

> We stated on a previous page that in the valorization process it does not in the least matter whether the labor appropriated by the capitalist is simple

---

80. *MECW*, vol. 25 (1987), 183.
81. *Capital*, vol. 1, 135.
82. Ibid., 275-6.

labor of average social quality, or more complex labor, labor with a higher specific gravity as it were. All labor of a higher, or more complicated, character than average labor is expenditure of labor-power of a more costly kind, labor-power whose production has cost more time and labor than unskilled or simple labor-power, and which therefore has a higher value. This power being of higher value, it expresses itself in labor of a higher sort, and therefore becomes objectified, during an equal amount of time, in proportionally higher values.[83]

This is how Marx explains the "social process that takes place behind the backs of the producers." It now becomes clear that Marx did not offer this explanation in the discussion of the commodity at the beginning of *Capital* because such an explanation cannot be carried out without the value-determination of the special commodity called *labor-power*. Marx took the approach of first simply indicating this reduction as a fact, leaving to more appropriate, subsequent sections the explanation concerning the proportion of this reduction and why complex labor can exist. Böhm-Bawerk, however, fails to grasp this, and he attacks Marx in the following way:

> We will only inquire a little more closely in what manner and by what means we are to determine the standard of this reduction, which, according to Marx, experience shows is constantly made. Here we stumble against the very natural but for the Marxian theory the very compromising circumstance that the standard of reduction is determined solely *by the actual exchange relations themselves*.[84]

> Under these circumstances what is the meaning of the appeal to "value" and the "social process" as the determining factors of the standard of reduction? Apart from everything else it simply means that Marx is arguing in a complete circle...They exchange in this way, Marx tells us, though in slightly different words, because, according to experience, they do exchange this way.[85]

Is Marx's Argument Circular?

Marx points out that the reduction of complex labor to simple labor is revealed as a fact within commodity exchange, and this was done in order to explain

83. Ibid., 304-5.
84. *Karl Marx and the Close of His System*, 83.
85. Ibid., 83-4.

that the existence of complex labor does not violate or contradict the law of value. Marx also notes that the proportion of this reduction—i.e. why and how one day of complex labor corresponds to two, three, or perhaps five days of simple labor—is naturally not determined by the commodity-exchange process, but rather is determined at a completely different level and therefore he provides no "demonstration" of this when explaining the law of value.

Böhm-Bawerk, however, fails to grasp Marx's theory and just offers up random comments about "the very natural...circumstance [?] that the standard of reduction is determined solely by the actual exchange relations themselves."[86] Of course, Marx never says, and has no reason to say, that the standard of reduction is determined by the exchange relation *itself*. Had he said such a thing, this would certainly amount to a circular argument. In fact, however, Marx is saying that the reduction of complex labor to simple labor does not take place within the exchange relation, but rather via a separate, *social process*, and that the fact that this occurs is made clear empirically within commodity exchange. Böhm-Bawerk twists this view around to claim that Marx, without any theoretical basis, is saying that this reduction occurs *through* the "experience" of the exchange relation.

Böhm-Bawerk convinces himself that "a certain social process" does not, as Marx later explains, concern the formation of high-grade (complex) labor-power, being instead simply a question of the proportion at which commodities are exchanged. This is natural in his case, since it is well known that Böhm-Bawerk is the great representative of the marginal utility school, which ultimately believes that no concept of value can exist apart from exchange-value. For those adhering to this view, the concept of value directly concerns the determination of the magnitude of value (price). But since they lack the concept of value—that is, the determination of what is the substance of value or what value is essentially speaking—in raising the issue of the determination of the magnitude of value, they are only able to say that this magnitude is determined by some circumstance within the exchange process, such as the subjective views or needs of purchasers or the relation of supply and demand.

Böhm-Bawerk says that Marx's argument is circular on the basis of the idea that Marx, in his discussion of the reduction of complex labor, argues that this reduction is determined in line with the exchange relation, whereas he had

---

86. Ibid., 83.

claimed in his theory of value that the exchange ratio of commodities is determined by labor. Of course, this is a misinterpretation of Marx's views.

In speaking of the reduction of complex labor, Marx already bases himself on the labor theory of value. Indeed, without this premise, why would the issue of the reduction of labor be raised in the first place? Even from the perspective of formal logic it is clear that in order to compare two things quantitatively they must first be reduced to some qualitatively identical aspect (in this case abstract human labor). Böhm-Bawerk does not raise the issue of the reduction of complex labor to simple labor in the original sense, and is unable to do so. Böhm-Bawerk, in calling into question why and how it can be said that one day of labor performed by a sculptor or lawyer can be reduced to five days of labor performed by a "stone-breaker" or "factory hand"—i.e. how the labor of the former can be calculated to be five times more intensified than the latter—reveals that he has understood nothing at all of the theoretical task at hand.

The magnitude of value is *revealed* in the exchange of commodities, but what *determines* this magnitude is not the exchange process itself but rather the production process—since value is nothing more than the social labor objectified in the commodity. If one has this essential understanding, it will be perfectly clear that even though the reduction of complex labor to simple labor is *made clear* by experience in the exchange of commodities, this certainly does not mean that the rate of reduction is actually *determined* by the exchange process of commodities. Since Böhm-Bawerk lacks a correct concept of commodity-value, he seeks a standard of reduction within the relation of commodity exchange, thus mistaking an effect for the cause.

Simple Labor Actually Exists

We have seen that complex labor is reduced to simple labor, but the standard of measurement—*simple labor*—is not merely something abstract that is found within the analysis of exchange-value. Rather, this is a real category within bourgeois society, as the so-called existence-form [*jitsuzon-keitai*] of abstract human labor. In *A Contribution to a Critique of Political Economy*, Marx writes:

> This abstraction, human labor in general, *exists* in the form of average labor which, in a given society, the average person can perform, productive expenditure of a certain amount of human muscles, nerves, brain, etc. It is *simple* labor [note: English economists call it "unskilled labor"] which any average individual can be trained to do and which in one way or another he

has to perform. The characteristics of this average labor are different in different countries and different historical epochs, but in any particular society it appears as something given. The greater part of the labor performed in bourgeois society is simple labor as statistical data show.[87]

In *Capital*, Marx provides one statistical example in a footnote:

> Moreover, we must not imagine that so-called "skilled" labor forms a large part of the whole of the nation's labor. Laing estimates that in England (and Wales) the livelihood of 11,300,000 people depends on unskilled labor. If from the total population of 18,000,000 living at the time when he wrote, we deduct 1,000,000 for the "genteel population," 1,500,000 for paupers, vagrants, criminals and prostitutes, and 4,650,000 who compose the middle class, there remain the above-mentioned 11,000,000. But in his middle class he includes people who live on the interest of small investments, officials, men of letters, artists, schoolmasters and the like, and in order to swell the number he also includes in these 4,650,000 the better paid portion of the "factory workers"! The bricklayers, too, figure, amongst these "high-class workers."[88]

In the same footnote, Marx quotes a passage from the *Supplement to the Encyclopaedia Britannica*, where James Mills says that the "great class who have nothing to give for food but ordinary labour, are the great bulk of the people."[89] Marx also emphasizes that simple labor is the natural outcome of modern industry and the "automatic workshop":

> Does not this reduction of days of compound labor to days of simple labor suppose that simple labor is itself taken as a measure of value? If the mere quantity of labor functions as a measure of value regardless of quality, it presupposes that simple labor has become the pivot of industry. It presupposes that labor has been equalized by the subordination of man to the machine or by the extreme division of labor; that men are effaced by their labor; that the pendulum of the clock has become as accurate a measure of the relative activity of two workers as it is of the speed of two locomotives. Therefore, we should not say that one man's hour is worth another man's hour, but rather that one man during an hour is worth just as much as

---

87. *A Contribution to a Critique of Political Economy*, in *MECW*, vol. 29 (1987), 272-3.
88. *Capital*, vol. 1, 305.
89. Ibid.

another man during an hour. Time is everything, man is nothing; he is, at the most, time's carcass. Quality no longer matters. Quantity alone decides everything; hour for hour, day for day; but this equalizing of labor is not by any means the work of M. Proudhon's eternal justice; it is purely and simply a fact of modern industry.

In the automatic workshop, one worker's labor is scarcely distinguishable in any way from another worker's labor: workers can only be distinguished one from another by the length of time they take for their work. Nevertheless, this quantitative difference becomes, from a certain point of view, qualitative, in that the time they take for their work depends partly on purely material causes, such as physical constitution, age and sex; partly on purely negative moral causes, such as patience, imperturbability, diligence. In short, if there is a difference of quality in the labor of different workers, it is at most a quality of the last kind, which is far from being a distinctive specialty. This is what the state of affairs in modern industry amounts to in the last analysis. It is upon this equality, already realized in automatic labor, that M. Proudhon wields his smoothing-plane of "equalization," which he means to establish universally in "time to come"![90]

Simple labor is an undeniable reality of bourgeois society, and this highlights the indifference of workers toward the content of their own labor, and thus all of the work-related prejudice of workers also comes to be dissolved. This predominance of simple labor also has enormous significance for the realization of socialism.

Theory of "High-Grade Labor-Power"

In the 1960s, a "theory" arose in Japan which claimed that Marx believed "complex labor" should naturally receive higher payment because "all labor of a higher, or more complicated, character than average labor is expenditure of labor-power of a more costly kind, labor-power whose production has cost more time and labor than unskilled or simple labor-power, and which therefore has a higher value."[91] At the time, coinciding with changes in labor resulting from technological innovations, a system involving greater pay differentials for workers at a given workplace began to be introduced—particularly at large enterprises—and intellectuals adhering to "structural

90. Karl Marx, *The Poverty of Philosophy* (New York: International Publishers, 1992), 41-2.
91. *Capital*, vol. 1, 304-5.

reformism"[92] attempted to apply Marx's theory of "high-grade labor" to provide this new wage system with a "Marxist" basis.

These intellectuals argued that since the wage is the price-form of the value of labor-power as a "commodity"—being the payment for this commodity—it is natural that the greater the value of the labor-power, the greater the wage should be. In other words, it is natural or justified for there to be wage differences between professions. This was said to correspond to Marx's theory of value, and therefore to the scientific theory of wages, so that high-grade labor-power receives higher payment while simple labor-power receives lower payment.

Of course this structural reformist view is a bourgeois theory that represents the interests of the technicians, specialists, and researchers—not to mention the vast array of non-productive management "workers"—who receive a greater degree of education so that their labor-power is sold at a higher value. Structural reformists defended and justified the payment of higher wages to such workers.

They gave no thought, however, to the issue of how high-grade workers came to possess their high-grade labor-power. The cost of fostering high-grade labor-power ultimately depends on the financial means of the individuals and is connected to the financial resources of their families. High-grade labor-power exists as such, as Marx points out, because its "production has cost more time and labor,"[93] and it is the result of a certain quantity of "accumulated" social labor (of other people).

Structural reformists failed to understand that the labor-power commodity differs from commodities in general and that it is a mistake to view the labor-power commodity as being directly identical to commodity-value as a thing in which social labor is objectified. They also did not grasp that there is naturally a difference between what remains when the "value-determination" of this

---

92. [The structural reformists represented a faction within the JCP that emerged around 1956. The group was strongly influenced by the program of the Communist-led Italian Federation of Labor and the views of Italian CP leader Palmiro Togliatti. They argued that socialism could be achieved through a combination of parliamentarianism and gradual reformism that would lead to a qualitative change in the power structure. The faction later split with the JCP.]

93. Ibid., 305.

labor-power commodity is stripped away and what remains when the value-determination of a general commodity is stripped away.

Since commodities are exchanged in correspondence to their value, it is also thought natural that the labor-power commodity be compensated at its value. But in the case of the labor-power commodity, we are dealing with a completely bourgeois "law"—whereas the law of value is a bourgeois law in a slightly different sense, and moreover is a bourgeois "law" in a more direct way. In connection with this, Engels says the following:

> How then are we to solve the whole important question of the higher wages paid for compound labor? In a society of private producers, private individuals or their families pay the costs of training the qualified worker; hence the higher price paid for qualified labor-power accrues first of all to private individuals: the skilful slave is sold for a higher price, and the skilful wage-earner is paid higher wages. In a socialistically organized society, these costs are borne by society, and to it therefore belong the fruits, the greater values produced by compound labor. The worker himself has no claim to extra pay. And from this, incidentally, follows the moral that at times there is a drawback to the popular demand of the workers for "the full proceeds of labor."[94]

Marx argues that complex labor is the outcome of the expenditure of complex (high-grade) labor-power, but that this does not justify high payment, and from the perspective of scientific socialism this is natural.

Does Marx Clarify the "Basis for Reduction"?

I would like to bring this section on complex and simple labor to a close by introducing the views on this topic held by Uno and his followers, which should help reveal the silly and hollow nature of the Unoist theories being bandied about by those within the new left movement. Uno, after quoting the passage from Marx that we examined at the very beginning of this section, offers the following "explanation":

> The "reduction" [Marx is speaking of] here is nothing more than the fact of being "equated to the product of simple labor" at the time of commodity exchange, but the basis for this "reduction" is not made clear at all...At issue is complex labor itself being "reduced" to simple labor under the capi-

---

94. Frederick Engels, *Anti-Dühring*, in *MECW*, vol. 25, 187.

talist production method [?!] This is not merely the "reduction" of being "equated" within commodity exchange [?!], but the fact that products of complex labor come to be produced by simple labor [?!]. Labor-power purchased as a commodity—on the basis of the relation of being made to carry out certain production within a given production process—comes for the first time to be distributed throughout society as a whole, but even if this is realized through the production method under a capitalist-commodity economy, this is certainly not a method of "reduction" particular to a commodity economy. Rather, this is one abstract aspect of labor that is able to generally determine human labor.[95]

This is a bad piece of writing that is extremely hard to understand since every sort of distorted view and vulgar notion is jumbled together. If we attempt to bring a bit of order to this, Uno's argument could be expressed as follows. In Marx's explanation the basis of the "reduction" is not made clear, but the actual basis for this is capitalist production, not the fact that complex labor is reduced by being equated in the exchange of commodities[96]; and historically speaking, products that had been produced by complex labor come to be produced by simple labor, which is the basis of the "reduction" of complex to simple labor.

Uno, like bourgeois scholars in general, clearly understands very little of Marx's theory. He attacks Marx, saying that "to explain the reduction of complex labor to simple labor, in the manner of Marx, as something that takes place via commodity exchange amounts to saying that the duality of labor itself is also particular to a commodity economy,"[97] but we have seen that Marx clearly states that within exchange-value the fact that one day of complex labor can be "reduced" to three days of simple labor is manifested, but that what *determines* the rate of reduction (its magnitude) is a "certain social process" completely independent of the exchange process, and we have already touched on the nature of this process. Uno adopts Böhm-Bawerk's manner of argument, because—apart from their superficial differences—in the most profound sense the two men are strongly taken in by the hopelessly vulgar view

---

95. Uno Kōzō, *Keizai genron* (Tokyo: Iwanami Shoten, 1977), 84-5.
96. Of course, as we have seen, Marx says that the fact that the "reduction" takes place is *indicated* in the commodity-exchange relation, *not* that the exchange process itself determines the proportion of this "reduction."
97. Ibid.

that the value of a commodity (its magnitude) is determined within commodity exchange.

Uno's view that the reduction of complex labor to simple labor is historically connected to complex labor being driven out and replaced by simple labor makes us wonder if he has any awareness of what a theory actually is. It is strange that he can consider this to be the "reduction" of complex labor to simple labor. If complex labor over the course of history is replaced by simple labor, the question of "reduction" would not be relevant at all. This is yet another example of how incredibly dim-witted he can be!

Uno notices the fact that under capitalism, generally speaking, the concept of abstract human labor emerges, and therefore the category of simple labor can also be established (of which Marx was also aware). He then directly and mechanically connects this fact to the question of the "reduction" of complex labor to simple labor, just as he connects the question of the labor theory of value to the question of the commodification of labor power. Needless to say, the reduction of complex labor to simple labor bears no relation whatsoever to the distribution of labor "throughout society as a whole." He is not aware that in order to obtain a particular theory, one must assume various relations that make the theory necessary. By contrast, merely juxtaposing every sort of relation that lies outside of the realm of the theory amounts to drowning science in a sea of confusion.

5. What is the "Value-form"?

Theoretical Task of Section Three

In *Capital*, the theory of the value-form is presented in section three of the first chapter, and we need to consider the theoretical task of this section. The first chapter on the commodity, as is well known, is composed of four sections. The first section starts out from exchange-value and analyzes value itself, and we thus come to know the substance of value and discover that its actual content is the human labor objectified in the commodity. Here we uncover the essence of value, as well as exchange-value as its phenomenal form. What regulates or governs the exchange of commodities is the "law of value," i.e. the labor objectified in the commodity. In the second section, Marx examines the character of the abstract human labor that forms the substance of value, providing a more profound determination of this. This section also contains an essential explanation of the relation between simple labor and complex labor.

Like these first two sections, the third and fourth sections also address their own, independent theoretical tasks related to uncovering the essential nature of the commodity, and here we need to consider the independent theoretical task of the third section.

Marx says in *Capital* that he "started from the exchange-value, or the exchange relation of commodities, in order to track down the value that lay hidden within it."[98] Here he is referring to the theoretical task of the first section, where we come to know about the value of a commodity. This is something essential in terms of our understanding of the commodity. Yet this alone is far from being sufficient for a solid understanding of the character of the commodity and the nature of value. Even if it is understood that the value of a commodity (its substance) is human labor, this does not elucidate at all the social character of the human labor that takes the form of commodity-value, or explain why human labor necessarily takes the form of value. These are in fact the tasks set for sections three and four. In the first section it was already shown that human labor takes the form of value, but this was only indicated as a fact. And the content of this first section had already been elucidated, albeit insufficiently, by Ricardo and the classical school. The content presented in sections three and four, however, leaves these bourgeois scholars—as well as the Uno school!—far behind. This section presents aspects that only Marx analyzed and elucidated.

> Everyone knows, if nothing else, that commodities have a common value-form which contrasts in the most striking manner with the motley natural forms of their use-values. I refer to the money-form. Now, however, we have to perform a task never even attempted by bourgeois economics. That is, we have to show the origin of this money-form, we have to trace the development of the expression of value contained in the value-relation of the commodities from its simplest, almost imperceptible outline to the dazzling money-form. When this has been done, the mystery of money will immediately disappear.[99]

Marx says that the task of the third section is to "show the origin of [the] money-form." But we need to consider why, and for what purpose, this is necessary.

---

98. *Capital*, vol. 1, 139.
99. Ibid.

The world of commodities is at the same time a *money* economy, with all commodities existing as such to the extent that they are exchanged for money. As a precondition for exchange, all commodities must have a money-form, i.e. that their own value is expressed through money, having a price-form (such as 1 television = x grams of gold, or x thousand yen). We need to consider why this is necessary, and what is its significance.

What Marx calls the value-form, expressed in simpler terms, could be called the money-form. But we must note that the money-form is the most highly developed form of the value-form, its ultimate form. The issues to be addressed are why human labor proceeds to the point of taking the money-form and what is the mechanism that makes this necessary. If these points are understood, we can also understand what money is. Since the phenomenon of money is a common, everyday matter, most people view it as a natural fact and do not give it a second thought. There are relatively few people in bourgeois society who, if asked, could correctly define money.

Simple Commodity-Form

It is immediately apparent that the question of the value-form also concerns the *expression* of value. All commodities express their own value relatively through money, in the form of being equal to a certain amount of money. The theory of the value-form is thus, from the outset, a question of how the expression of value is carried out. In analyzing the value-form, Marx does not directly take up the money-form. Rather than examining the money-form, which is the developed form of value, he analyzes in detail the simple form of value, namely: x quantity of commodity A = y quantity of commodity B (e.g. 25 yards of linen = 1 coat).

Marx had Engels read and criticize the first edition of *Capital*, and in particular Marx rewrote the section on the form of value. In June 1867, he wrote to Engels regarding the revisions that had been made:

> With regard to the development of the form of value, I have both followed and not followed your advice, thus striking a dialectical attitude in this matter, too…It is not only the philistines that I have in mind here, but young people, etc., who are thirsting for knowledge. Anyway, the issue is crucial for the whole book. The [classical] economists have hitherto overlooked the very simple fact that the equation *20 yards of linen= 1 coat* is but the primitive form of *20 yards of linen = £2*, and thus that the simplest form of a commodity, in which its value is not yet expressed in its relation to all

other commodities but only as something differentiated from its own natural form, embodies the whole secret of the money form and thereby, *in nuce*, of all bourgeois forms of the product of labor. In my first presentation [*Contribution to the Critique of Political Economy*], I avoided the difficulty of the development by not actually analyzing the way value is expressed until it appears as its developed form, as expressed in money.[100]

This represents an extremely valuable statement by Marx himself on the development (description) of the value-form. He discusses why, and in what way, the description changed over the period of time from the publication of *A Contribution to the Critique of Political Economy* to the appearance of the first German edition of *Capital* and the subsequent editions of *Capital*. The most important point to note is that in *A Contribution*, the money-form is posited from the outset and then "the way value is expressed" is presented. In this way, Marx "avoided the difficulty," whereas in *Capital* the money-form only appears at the end of the analysis of the value-form. What is directly examined in *Capital* is not the money-form but the simplest form of a commodity—the value relation between two commodities—and from this the value-form and the expression of value are uncovered.

Those reading *Capital* for the first time are often perplexed by the analysis and description of the value-form. It appears that what Marx is saying is purely speculative or abstract. By contrast, it seems easier to understand the approach adopted in his earlier work, where he posited or presupposed the money-form from the onset, and then on the basis of this "actually analyze[d] the way value is expressed." At least in this case it is easy to grasp what is at issue and what is being discussed.

In *Capital*, however, Marx discards the approach employed in his earlier work, feeling that it is incorrect or a sort of circular logic to presuppose the emergence of the money-form. In place of his earlier presentation, Marx shows that the simple value-form develops, and that as the outcome of this the money-form becomes necessary. This is not merely the case historically speaking but also theoretically. Ultimately "the whole mystery of the form of value lies hidden in this simple form,"[101] and although the developed form (money-form) directly indicates the operations of the value-form, it also conceals its true significance. From the analysis of the money-form alone it is not possible

---

100. *MECW*, vol. 42 (1987), 384-5.
101. *Capital*, vol. 1, 139.

to elucidate why the relation of value seen in the money-form is necessary. This money-form is necessary precisely because a product is not merely the product of labor, but a commodity and thus a value. The generation of the money-form, or its necessity, must therefore be sought from the perspective of the exchange relation of commodities and the value-relation.

Different Roles of the Two Commodities

Marx discovers that the money-form is the developed value-form, with the simple form of value as its basis. For this reason, in section three he analyses the same equation as section one, where x commodity A = y commodity B (20 yards of linen = 1 coat). In section three, Marx carries out of the analysis of the form of value—and therefore the examination of the expression of value—in its simplest (and purest) form. The same equation as section one is introduced, but this time the perspective of analysis has changed. Whereas in the first section the emphasis was placed on both commodities being equivalent, section three focuses attention on the fact that each of the two commodities in the equation plays a different role.

> Here two different kinds of commodities (in our example the linen and the coat) evidently play two different parts. The line expresses its value in the coat; the coat serves as the material in which the value is expressed. The first commodity plays an active role, the second a passive one. The value of the first commodity is represented as relative value, in other words the commodity is in the relative form of value. The second commodity fulfils the function of equivalent, in other words it is in the equivalent form.[102]

Marx says that in the relation between the two commodities as value, each commodity plays a different role. However, many readers may have difficulty understanding what this means, exactly. And it is natural to find this difficult to understand, since even Rosa Luxemburg failed to recognize the significance of this third section, considering it to be nothing more than a scholastic manner of speaking. For Marx, however, it is merely recognition of fact to say that each of the two commodities, in their value-relation, plays a different role. It is of course possible for the commodities to play the opposite roles, but once the equation has been established, the role of each commodity within this framework cannot be changed.

---

102. Ibid.

Where, then, did Marx discover that within the exchange relation each commodity plays a different role? Clearly, this stems from the exchange relation between a commodity and money, such as 20 yards of linen = 2 pounds of gold.

> The only difficulty in the concept of the money-form is that of grasping the universal equivalent form, and hence the general form of value as such, form C. Form C can be reduced by working backwards to form B, the expanded form of value, and its constitutive element is Form A: 20 yards of linen = 1 coat or x commodity A = y commodity B. The simple commodity-form is therefore the germ of the money-form.[103]

Several concepts that we have not referred to at all, such as the general form of value or forms B and C appear here, so it is somewhat difficult to understand, but we mainly need to note that Marx is saying that the "difficulty in the concept of the money form" can ultimately be reduced to the simple commodity-form.

Marx views the money-form as the form of expression of commodity-value, where the value of a commodity is expressed through money, and this expression occurs in the form of the value of one commodity being equal to a certain quantity of money (gold). In other words, the two commodities (the normal commodities and money) are clearly playing different roles. The commodity (linen) expresses its value in money, so that money plays the role of being the material in which this value is expressed. The linen plays an "active role," while the money plays a "passive role."[104]

When Marx says that the linen and the coat play two different roles, he is considering the manner in which commodity-value is expressed. The coat is merely the undeveloped form of money. When Marx says that the two commodities play different roles, he is simply recognizing, as a fact, this relation that is included within commodity-exchange. The question concerns the significance of this fact.

---

103. Ibid., 163.
104. Uno however says that money plays an active role and the commodity a passive role, but we will examine this view later.

The "Roundabout Way"

How, then, is the value of the linen expressed through the coat? This is the question we need to examine. We have seen that the value of the linen *is* expressed through the coat—20 yards of linen being equal to 1 coat—but we need to consider what mechanism makes this possible. This involves the mediation of the coat becoming or being posited as—within the value-relation of the two commodities—the existence-form of value, i.e. a value-thing [*Wertding*]. The coat is only identical to the linen as the value-thing. The following passage by Marx discusses the basis for this mechanism of value-expression:

> If we say that, as values, commodities are simply congealed quantities of human labor, our analysis reduces them, it is true, to the level of abstract value, but does not give them a form of value distinct from their natural forms. It is otherwise in the value relation of one commodity to another. The first commodity's value character emerges here through its own relation to the second commodity.
>
> By the coat, for example, being equated to the linen as the value-thing, the labor embedded in the coat is equated with the labor embedded in the linen.[105] Now it is true that the tailoring which makes the coat is concrete labor of a different sort from the weaving which makes the linen. But the act of equating tailoring with weaving reduces the former in fact to what is really equal in the two kinds of labor, to the characteristic they have in common of being human labor. This is a roundabout way of saying that weaving too, in so far as it weaves value, has nothing to distinguish it from tailoring, and, consequently, is abstract human labor. It is only the expression of equivalence between different sorts of commodities which brings to view the specific character of value-creating labor, by actually reducing the different kinds of labor embedded in the different kinds of commodity to their common quality of being human labor in general.[106]

---

105. [I have modified the English translation somewhat here because English translations of *Capital* insert a subject that is equating the value with the linen—an ambiguous "we" in the case of Ben Fowkes or "the commodity owners" in Hans Ehrbar's translation. But in the original German (and Japanese editions of *Capital*) no such subject is inserted. Hans Ehrbar admits that he has translated this sentence "more freely," and certainly this is more readable in a sense, but I have preferred to stick more closely to the German and the Japanese.]

106. Ibid., 141-2.

Marx's passage describing the "specific character" of the labor that produces commodities, and therefore the labor that develops into money, has rarely been understood correctly and generally misunderstood completely (by Unoists and others).

In the passage above, Marx ascertains that the exchange relation between two commodities is at the same time the form of value-expression, and he explains *how* value is expressed. In other words, the value of the linen is expressed in the natural form of the coat, but what makes this possible is first of all that the linen equates the coat to itself, positing the coat as the pure embodiment of value or the value-thing (value-form). This also means that the tailoring labor of the coat and the weaving labor of the linen are reduced to the "characteristic they have in common of being human labor." In this way, the tailoring labor of the coat is posited as the representative of abstract human labor in which the character of commodity-producing labor is manifested.

> We see, then, that everything our analysis of commodities previously told us [sections 1 and 2] is repeated by the linen itself, as soon as it enters into association with another commodity, the coat. Only it reveals its thoughts in a language with which it alone is familiar, the language of commodities. In order to tell us that labor creates its own value in its abstract quality of being human labor, it says that the coat, in so far as it counts as its equal, i.e. is value, consists of the same labor as it does itself.[107]

For the value of the linen to be expressed in the coat, first of all the labor that creates both commodities must be reduced to something qualitatively equal, and this is done by the linen positing the coat as being equivalent to itself in terms of value. Following this "roundabout way," the linen for the first time is able to express its own value, relatively, in the natural body (use-value) of the coat, since the coat already only exists as the value-thing, with the tailoring labor of the coat representing abstract human labor.

From Private Labor to Social Labor

This issue of the "roundabout way" can be explained in simpler terms as follows. At issue is the nature of the labor that takes the form of the value of a commodity. In other words, what exactly does the relation between the linen

---

107. Ibid., 143.

(relative value-form) and the coat (equivalent-form) signify? The linen, by equating the coat to itself, transforms the coat into the value-thing and through this mediation is able to express its own value using the coat (20 yards of linen = 1 coat, or developed further, 20 yards of linen = 2 grams of money-gold). Marx also says that in this relation between the two commodities, "the labor embedded in the coat is equated with the labor embedded in the linen" and that this is reduced to "their common quality of being human labor in general."

It is well known that commodity-producing labor is private labor, and not socially abstract, general labor, directly speaking. As a product of private labor, even though the commodity has a certain use-value, it is not necessarily guaranteed, or even possible, for it to be transformed into any other use-value. A commodity, as such, must be able to be transformed into any other use-value, which means that private, individual labor must be transformed into its opposite (abstract labor in general). In discussing the relation between the linen and the coat, Marx says that linen, as the product of private labor, only has a social character within its relationship with the coat, where it is able to express its own labor as general, abstract human labor, and therefore as social labor.

The linen, in equating the coat to itself, posits the value-thing, thus providing the form of value, and this means that the coat is posited as the "determinate being" [*teizai*; *Dasein*] of general labor. This is made possible because the linen is also a value, a thing in which human labor with the historical quality particular to commodity production is objectified. The linen is thus able to express its own value relatively through the coat. This is because the coat is already the value-thing, and its natural form—as is—becomes the value-form of the linen and is (the origin of) the general equivalent. Marx says that "this necessity to express individual labor as general labor is equivalent to the necessity of expressing a commodity as money."[108]

If the linen is able to express its own value in the coat, and in the developed relation all commodities are able to express their value in money, so that all commodities acquire a money-expression (price) for their own value, then every commodity is expressed as socially-abstract general labor and can thus be exchanged for every other commodity. A commodity is indicated as a certain quantity of social labor, but of course few people are aware of this or reflect on

108. *MECW*, vol. 32, 323.

this fact, since it is difficult to come to such a realization without studying Marx.

For example, a 1,000-yen commodity and a 10,000-yen commodity share a money-expression in common, making it possible to exchange them directly. Ten 1,000-yen commodities can be exchanged for one 10,000-yen commodity, since they share a common value-expression. Through this price, commodities manifest themselves as the "materialization"[*busshitsuka*] of the same social labor or as the expression in different quantities of the same substance.

Money, as well as the money-expression of the commodity, is something essential and necessary for a society of commodity production and exchange. This is because private, individual labor in this society must be transformed into social labor, and human labor does not exist directly as social labor, but rather starts off as private, individual labor which at the same time must also be social labor. Value elucidates the historical character and limitations of labor in this bourgeois, commodity-production society, and is not merely a quantitative relation, as Ricardo believed or the Uno school loudly proclaims.

Development and "Reversal" of the Value-Form

Even though linen expresses its own value in the coat, this does not mean that the particular, historical character of commodity-producing labor fully emerges. This is only a "social character" to the extent that the two commodities are placed in relation to each other. Within this relationship the labor of both commodities can be said to be human labor in common, but the social character of the two commodities is still extremely narrow.

What is important in the relation between the two commodities, however, is that it represents the most essential mechanism of value-expression, and therefore this is where the analysis of this mechanism is carried out. This narrow, "insufficient" relation must move on to a more complete form, overcoming its limitations. This is the movement from the "total or expanded form of value" to the "general form of value." With the development of the value-form, and the progression to the general form of value, the character of value-producing labor for the first time becomes clear overall. The shift to the general equivalent form of value is the famous "reversal" of the equation. That is, the linen, which had been in the position of the relative form of value, is placed in the position of equivalent form (general value form). Marx, after pointing out that the "expanded" form of value "has no single, unified form of appearance," writes:

The expanded relative form of value is, however, nothing but the sum of the simple relative expressions or equations of the first form, such as:
20 yards of linen = 1 coat
20 yards of linen = 10 lb. of tea, etc.

However, each of these equations implies the identical equation in reverse...

In fact, when a person exchanges his linen for many other commodities, and thus expresses its value in a series of other commodities, it necessarily follows that the other owners of commodities exchange them for the linen, and therefore express the values of their various commodities in one and the same third commodity, the linen. If, then, we reverse the series 20 yards of linen = 1 coat, or = 10 lb. of tea, etc. i.e. if we give expression to the converse relation already implied in the series, we get:

(c) The General Form of Value

$$\left.\begin{array}{l} \text{1 coat} \\ \text{10 lb. of coffee} \\ \text{1 quarter of corn} \\ \text{2 ounces of gold} \\ \text{1/2 ton of iron} \\ x \text{ commodity A etc.}[109] \end{array}\right\} = \text{20 yards of linen}$$

In this way, the linen becomes the general form of value, and by replacing linen with gold we arrive at money.

There has been a debate among scholars on this "reversal" of the equation, with some, starting with the Uno school, criticizing Marx's "method" (saying, for example, that it has little significance if the equation can be reversed at any time). But it makes no difference whether the linen is placed in the position of relative value-form or equivalent value-form. Once this position is decided, one must proceed from this as the assumption, but this position itself can always be reversed.

From the perspective of the development of the value-form, the second form (expanded form of value) is a quantitative development of the first (simple form of value). In this second form, the value of the linen is expressed in an infinite number of other commodity bodies, so that the linen acquires a social relation with the entire world of commodities, not just with any single commodity.

---

109. *Capital*, vol. 1, 162.

In the second form, the linen expresses its own value in any of the other commodities, but in the third form (general form of value) the other commodities express their value in the linen, and the linen generally becomes the value-form (equivalent form). The second and third forms are the same in terms of private labor appearing as social, general labor, but the third form is different in terms of being a "unified" expression.

Thus, at issue in the case of the third form, is that one commodity is "excluded" as the general equivalent form, and provides a "unified expression" for the world of commodities. Formally speaking, this "excluded" commodity could be anything. As Marx points out above, the precondition for the linen to be excluded is that a person has to exchange linen for a large number of other products so that other people also exchange their commodities for linen, and in this way linen expresses the value of the other commodities.

Money vs. Physical Measurements

One aspect of Uno's criticism of Marx is his view that money as a measure of value is different than a physical measure. In *Kachi-ron no mondai-ten*, for instance, there is the following conversation between Uno and one of his students:

> *Uno*: In the case of weight or length, there is at any rate a certain standard that can be set so that there is no real problem when it comes to measurement, but in the case of value, no such standard can be directly established. Even in the case of gold-money, this is a measure whose value fluctuates, which is a problem of a different order than weight or length.
>
> *Student A*: In the case of weight, both objects have the shared attribute of weight, don't they?
>
> *Uno*: That's right. And in this case, through a unilateral commitment it is possible to have a general standard. By means of this one can measure the other object. However, this does not mean that this relation can be applied, as is, to the case of the value-form. If the labor theory of value is understood as explaining in advance that there is an equal amount of labor objectified in both commodities, one forfeits an understanding of the particularity of the commodity-form, which is different from the case of measuring weight or length. Interpreters [of Marx] seem unable to grasp this point. And Marx himself was not immune to this pitfall.[110]

Since the conversation above involves an essential aspect of the commodity-form, and also exposes the truly vulgar nature of the Uno school, I cannot let this pass without comment. In the passage below, Marx explains what is at issue. In his explanation of the equivalent form, he says that commodities cannot express their own value using their own commodity body, and "therefore must make the physical shape of another commodity into its own value-form." He then offers the following comparison:

> Let us make this clear with the example of a measure which is applied to commodities as material objects, i.e. as use-values. A sugar-loaf, because it is a body, is heavy and therefore possesses weight; but we can neither take a look at this weight nor touch it. We then take various pieces of iron, whose weight has been determined beforehand. The bodily form of the iron, considered for itself, is no more the form of appearance of weight than is the sugar-loaf. Nevertheless, in order to express the sugar-loaf as a weight, we put it into a relation of weight with the iron. In this relation, the iron counts as a body representing nothing but weight. Quantities of iron therefore serve to measure the weight of the sugar, and represent, in relation to the sugar-loaf, weight in its pure form, the form of manifestation of weight. This part is played by the iron only within this relation, i.e. within the relation into which the sugar, or any other body whose weight is to be found, enters with the iron. If both objects lacked weight, they could not enter into this relation, hence the one could not serve to express the weight of the other. When we throw both of them into the scales, we see in reality that considered as weight they are the same, and therefore that, taken in the appropriate proportions, they have the same weight. Just as the body of the iron, as a measure of weight, represents weight alone, in relation to the sugar-loaf, so, in our expression of value, the body of the coat represents value alone.[111]

Marx's comparison is quite easy to understand and also clarifies the particularity of the expression of value. The iron is compared to the commodity in the equivalent form (the coat), and it only represents *weight* just as the coat only represents *value*. Because of this, the weight of the sugar is able to be expressed by means of the iron, just as the value of the linen can be expressed through the coat, thereby positing the form of value. In the same way as the sugar's weight can be expressed by means of the iron (phenomenal form of

---

110. *Kachi-ron no mondai-ten*, 63-4.
111. *Capital*, vol. 1, 148-9.

weight) since both are qualitatively equal in terms of weight, the linen's value can be expressed through the coat (equivalent form) since both are identical as value. The comparison is perfectly appropriate. It is incredibly crude of Unoists to criticize Marx by claiming that money as the measure of value differs from a physical measurement, and to argue that the value of a commodity is "measured" when it is "purchased with money."

Echoing the Marginal Utility School's Views

As we have seen, the theoretical issue regarding the value-form and exchange-value (section three of chapter one) concerns how value is expressed. Simply put, all commodities express their value in the form of price, i.e. in the form of a certain quantity of money (gold). Section three examines how this takes place.

At the same time, this section clarifies how money is necessary. In other words, commodities are able to express their own value for the first time by pushing forward a single commodity as the general equivalent form (money). Furthermore, the general equivalent form—or money-form—of the commodity also clarifies the thoroughly social and common, abstract character of the labor that forms the substance of commodity-value. Therefore, at issue in the case of the value-form is certainly not a qualitative relation, which is instead a secondary aspect. The fundamental issue revolves around *how* the expression of value is carried out and *what* is the character of the particular historical labor that produces commodities; in other words, this is a question of quality not quantity.

A commodity cannot use itself to express its own value. For this reason, a commodity must express its value within its value-relation with another commodity through the mediation, or roundabout way, of equating itself with the other commodity so that this commodity only exists as the "equivalent" or value-thing. When all of the commodities carry this out in relation to one particular commodity, that commodity becomes money. By pushing forth this one particular commodity so that it becomes the general equivalent (money), all of the other commodities are able to *generally* express their value through money. This means that all of the commodities come to have a form (or expression) of value that is socially recognized, i.e. the price-form of being worth so many hundred or thousands of yen, dollars, etc. Within the value-relation between two commodities, the expression of value cannot yet take this sort of general form, since the relation remains individual and narrow. However, the mechanism of value-expression is the same, with the fundamental content being purely expressed in this simple form of value.

Value is of course a social category, and in this sense differs from length or weight. Human labor, as the substance of value, is a social substance. But if it is presumed that commodity-value is objectified human labor—and this already is the assumption when the value-form is discussed—then there is no difference between the expression of a commodity's value being posited within its exchange relation with another commodity and the weight of a given thing being posited within its weight-relation with some other thing.

Uno criticizes Marx for discussing the expression of the social substance of value as if it were the same as weight or length. For Uno, since gold-money is "a measure whose value fluctuates," it is said to be different from the measurement of weight or length. However, when a commodity becomes the equivalent form vis-à-vis another commodity, and value is expressed through this mediation, this is not directly related at all to the quantity (magnitude) of value. Whether the value is great or small, or whether it fluctuates or does not, the mechanism of value-expression clearly remains the same.

Uno is thinking of something quite different from what Marx is addressing. This vulgar scholar views the expression or measure of value in terms of the magnitude of price being determined by the competition, bargaining, and transactions between buyers and sellers, and therefore he raises the issue of the purchaser's money or desires and focuses on the process whereby the magnitude of the value (i.e. price) of a commodity is established by being purchased with money, offering the ridiculous theory that the discussion of the value-form or expression of value centers on this issue.

Uno noisily discusses the establishment of the magnitude of value, but not only does he lack a concept of value, he does not even possess a concept of price. He also fails to reflect fundamentally on the fact that Marx provides us with the concept of price in his discussion of the value-form (section three) and the closely connected discussion of money as the measure of value (chapter three, section one), and that this is the precise issue Marx is attempting to elucidate. Uno has no concept of price and only considers how the magnitude of price is determined. In other words, he essentially remains within the realm of the modern bourgeoisie's vulgar economics (theory of marginal utility, etc.).

The Genius of Aristotle

The money form—i.e. human labor taking the form of money—clarifies the historical character of commodity-producing labor, where concrete labor becomes abstract human labor, and private labor becomes social labor. In connection with this, Marx speaks of the "genius" of Aristotle who noted that 5 beds = 1 house is indistinguishable from 5 beds = a certain amount of money, and pointed out that "there can be no exchange without equality, and no equality without commensurability." In this way, Aristotle is even able to recognize that the equation 5 beds = 1 house includes the expression of value (no different from 5 beds = a certain quantity of money), and that for the house to express the value of the beds, the thing expressed must be common to both. Ultimately, however, Aristotle concludes that this is not possible and that therefore the equivalent is "only a makeshift for practical purposes." This was because, as Marx points out, he was not familiar with abstract human labor:

> Aristotle himself was unable to extract this fact, that, in the form of commodity-values, all labor is expressed as equal human labor and therefore as labor of equal quality, by inspection from the form of value, because Greek society was founded on the labor of slaves, hence had as its natural basis the inequality of men and of their labor-powers. The secret of the expression of value, namely the equality and equivalence of all kinds of labor because and in so far as they are human labor in general, could not be deciphered until the concept of human equality had already acquired the permanence of a fixed popular opinion. This however becomes possible only in a society where the commodity-form is the universal form of the product of labor, hence the dominant social relation is the relation between men as possessors of commodities. Aristotle's genius is displayed precisely by his discovery of a relation of equality in the value-expression of commodities. Only the historical limitation inherent in the society in which he lived prevented him from finding out what "in reality" this relation of equality consisted of.[112]

I have quoted this at length since it is one of my favorite passages from *Capital*. Marx is saying that human labor assuming the money-form shows us that it is equal as abstract human labor, and to this extent "men and their labor-powers" are perfectly equal. And, more importantly, Marx elucidates that here labor is not something individual, but rather something that has become thoroughly social.

---

112. Ibid., 151-2.

What lies in front of our eyes is a general commodity-economy, a money-economy, but we tend to give little thought to the crucial significance this has in terms of revealing that human labor has become something thoroughly social, and that to this extent the real conditions for socialism have been formed (in the most abstract, and therefore the most essential sense). In Aristotle's time socialism was not yet feasible, as labor at the time was not abstract (qualitatively equal), nor had it become a social thing.

This provides us with an idea of what equality means under socialism, its significance, as well as its limitations. This means that each person is equal as a member of society engaged in carrying out one part of the total social labor. This is the foundation of socialism. Such equality is not some sort of abstract ideal, and this is already a reality in the case of the value-form of the commodity within general commodity-production society. The existence of money (the general equivalent form) clarifies this point. Today, unfortunately, there are "Marxists economists" (Unoists) with a level of understanding far below that of Aristotle, who argue that it cannot be said "from the beginning" that there is something equal within the value-relation of 5 beds = 1 house.

What is the *Qualitative Aspect*?

We have seen that the relation between commodities is not only one of equivalence, but also includes the expression of value, which must advance toward the emergence of the general equivalent form (money), and that this clarifies the special historical character of commodity-producing labor. Simply put, money reveals to us the character of the labor that produces commodities as labor that is concrete and at the same time thoroughly abstract, labor that is private and at the same time thoroughly social. Money is necessary as the outcome of these contradictions inherent to commodity-producing labor. Marx, in criticizing Ricardo, explains the necessity of the money-form within commodity society, and its significance, in the following passage from *Theories of Surplus Value*, which I will quote at length because of its importance:

> But to say that "value" is not an absolute, is not conceived as an entity, is quite different from saying that commodities must impart to their exchange-value a separate expression which is different from and independent of their use-value and of their existence as real products, in other words, that commodity circulation is bound to evolve money. Commodities express their exchange-value in money, first of all in the price, in which they all present themselves as materialized forms of the same labor, as only

quantitatively different expressions of the same substance. The fact that the exchange-value of the commodity assumes an independent existence in money is itself the result of the process of exchange, the development of the contradiction of use-value and exchange-value embodied in the commodity, and of another no less important contradiction embodied in it, namely, that the definite, particular labor of the private individual must manifest itself as its opposite, as equal, necessary, general labor and, in this form, social labor. The representation of the commodity as money implies not only that the different magnitudes of commodity values are measured by expressing the values in the use-value of one exclusive commodity [gold-money], but at the same time that they are all expressed in a form in which they exist as the embodiment of social labor and are therefore exchangeable for every other commodity, that they are translatable at will into any use-value desired…But the labor embodied in them must be represented as social labor, as alienated individual labor. In the price this representation is nominal; it becomes reality only in the sale. This transformation of the labor of private individuals contained in the commodities into uniform social labor, consequently into labor which can be expressed in all use-values and can be exchanged for them, this qualitative aspect of the matter which is contained in the representation of exchange-value as money, is not elaborated by Ricardo. This circumstance—the necessity of presenting the labor contained in commodities as uniform social labor, i.e., as money—is overlooked by Ricardo.[113]

I think that it has finally become clear why Marx carried out such a detailed examination of the value-form in section three. In this section, he considers the exact character of labor as the substance of value, which was noted in section one, and the form this character takes. Thus, it should be perfectly clear that section three is premised on the "magnitude of value" from section one.

Marx clearly states that what is at issue in section three is not a quantitative problem but a qualitative one. The "quantitative" problem, needless to say, refers to the question of the substance of value and its magnitude discussed in section one. In the discussion of the value-form in section three, by contrast, the theoretical task is no longer to grasp that it is the (magnitude of) human labor objectified or absorbed in the commodity that determines its exchange-value. Section three does not concern the basis upon which commodities are exchanged, but rather the transformation of private labor into social labor, and concrete labor into abstract labor, and the manner in which this occurs. Unoists, however, only see a problem that concerns quantity, remaining quite

---

113. *MECW*, vol. 32, 317-8.

unaware of what Marx is discussing in this section and how he is carrying out his theoretical discussion.

6. Fetish Character of the Commodity

Theoretical Task of Section Four

Here we will begin by considering the fourth section of chapter one, entitled "The Fetishism of the Commodity and its Secret," which in a sense is the most important part of *Capital* since it reveals the contradictions and nature of the commodity, clarifying its historical limitations. Section four thus provides us with an overview of the first chapter of *Capital*.

As we have seen, the first section of chapter one reveals that the substance of commodity-value is abstract human labor. Here, human labor taking the form of value is first of all confirmed as a fact, which had already been pointed out, albeit inadequately, by classical economists such as David Ricardo. In section two, Marx goes on to provide a more in-depth definition of the labor that forms the substance of value. This, in turn, is followed by an exploration of the form of value in section three, where it is shown that commodity-producing labor is private labor that at the same time becomes social labor, concrete labor that is also abstract labor, so that the world of commodities must necessarily progress toward the formation of a general equivalent, i.e. money must emerge.

What, then, is the particular theoretical task of section four that sets it apart from these first three sections? In a word, this can be said to revolve around *why* human labor takes the form of value. Already in the first section, labor taking the form of value is indicated as a fact, with Marx analyzing the value-relation (a relation of equivalence) between two commodities and explaining that the content of this is the relation between the labor objectified (absorbed) in the commodities. In other words, we already recognize, as a fact, that value is human labor, its "objectified" or "material" form.

The form of value is also analyzed in the third section, and we have seen that this form develops into the money-form, which is the independent material form of value. But in this third section as well Marx is simply recognizing this as a fact. In the fourth section, by contrast, he fundamentally explores why human labor takes the form of commodity-value and appears as value, why the properties of human labor take on the appearance of the properties of material things; and the underlying reason why human labor presents itself as an out-side, genuine "thing" (money).

Despite being surrounded by a world of commodities in daily life, most people give little thought to the meaning of the commodity. Even with the great advances in science and civilization, people are blind to this everyday, familiar world, and commodities are treated uncritically as a sort of natural thing. No consideration is given to what a commodity is, the basis upon which commodities are exchanged, or the significance of the value-form (price). While we can see everyday that commodities have prices and are exchanged on the basis of such prices, no one is aware that this represents an important the-oretical question!

The reason for this lack of awareness is that an understanding of the con-tradictions and essence of the world of commodities depends on a certain class standpoint (whereas the bourgeoisie and petty bourgeois are blinded by their class interests), and that this understanding also requires a scientific consider-ation of the problem. Even in the case of workers, if this conscious scientific pursuit is abandoned, so that they become submerged in the "common sense" of bourgeois society, it becomes impossible to understand the essence of the commodity and its significance.

To begin by stating our conclusion; products of human labor take the form of commodity-value because production is carried out on a private basis. In a society based on private labor (private ownership) and a division of labor, commodities are necessary as a manifestation of the contradictions of this his-torical society, and therefore if production is transformed into production in common, so that the labor of each person is directly social labor, labor is not turned into commodity-value. Here we have the very root of the question.

In section four, therefore, Marx carries out a profound analysis of the essence of the commodity in this sense, which serves as an overview of the entire theory of the commodity presented in chapter one. This is more than simply a theory of fetishism, but rather the basis and starting point for the criticism of commodity-capitalist production as a historical form of society. By studying the fourth section, we can gain an understanding of the commodity, the historical stage of a society that produces commodities, and come to know the basis of this society's contradictions.

The Term "Fetishism"

What exactly is the fetish character of the commodity or commodity fetishism? Why does Marx entitle the fourth section, which provides an overview of chapter one, "The Fetishism of the Commodity and its Secret"? Marx's intention, clearly, is to elucidate the upside-down nature particular to a commodity-production society (and therefore to bourgeois society). Marx says that the world of commodities has a mysterious, enigmatic nature. But the average person, based on "common sense," is not even aware of the extremely mysterious nature of the world of commodities. Here we need to consider the source of the enigmatic nature of this world.

We have seen that commodities have value (exchange-value), but the issue here concerns what this value is and how ordinary people view this value. Based on the examination of *Capital* up to this point, we would probably say that the value of a commodity (its substance) is human labor, and that what is manifested as exchange-value is the (proportion of) labor that is "objectified" in the commodity. For those lacking this understanding, however, the value of a commodity seems to be some sort of quality inherent to the commodity-body *as a thing*.

The third section of chapter one of *Capital* taught us that the social character and relations pertaining to the commodity do not stem from its character as a thing, but rather that value exists as such as the substance of social labor. What directly enters people's field of vision, however, is only the character or relations of the commodity as thing. A social relation between people—a relation between different labor engaged in production—is disguised as a relation between things.

Labor, of course, is the substance of value and has no relation to the commodity-body as thing. But in reality this appears to be a property of things—and this is precisely what Marx refers to as the "fetishism" or "mysterious character" of the commodity. Clearly this is an upside-down relation. What actually exists is a production relation between people, a relation between people connected to each other via social labor, but this appears "as social relations between things, between the products of labor."[114]

Originally the term "fetishism" refers to the primitive religious belief that material things such as stones or trees are inhabited by spirits and have the power to bring happiness or misery to human beings. Marx uses the term to

---

114. *Capital*, vol. 1, 170.

describe the bourgeois view of the commodity within developed, modern society, since the same upside-down quality of primitive religious beliefs is manifested.

The idea that stones or trees possess spirits was merely a product of human consciousness (illusions), but this belief then came to govern the behavior of human beings. Similarly, it is an illusion of "modern man" that the commodity has value *qua* thing, and Marx caustically notes that this upside-down consciousness is no different from the fetishism of primitive people. He looks down on "modern" bourgeois consciousness as being no different from that of primitive man.

The fetish character of the commodity is not merely a question of ideas, however. The relation between commodities is a real one. Even though a relation between human beings connected via labor is disguised as a relation between "things," there is a realistic basis for this. This fetishism arises from people being uncritically taken in by the visible relations, and in this sense can be considered the inevitable consciousness or "superstructure" within commodity-production society. Marx as well says that "fetishism" becomes the general illusion of people living in bourgeois society, and that these fetishized forms are assimilated in their given state by bourgeois scholars, who treat the commodity-economy as an absolute, so that the "categories of bourgeois economics consist precisely of forms of this kind."[115]

In this society, human labor is manifested in a material form as value, and therefore as money. Normally we do not consider this fact to be particularly mysterious. Most of us are not even conscious of this mystical nature, but if asked to explain the value of a commodity our difficulty in responding would immediately reveal the extent to which we are under the sway of commodity fetishism. Consider for example how we might explain *why* an apple would have a price (exchange-value) of 100 yen?

The Basis of Commodity Fetishism

Why does a relation involving human social labor take on the form of a relation between things? The reason is simple, says Marx:

---

115. Ibid., 169.

As the foregoing analysis [section 3] has already demonstrated, this fetishism of the world of commodities arises from the peculiar social character of
the labor which produces them.

 Objects of utility become commodities only because they are the products of the labor of private individuals who work independently of each
other. The sum total of the labor of all these private individuals forms the
aggregate labor of society. Since the producers do not come into social contact until they exchange the products of their labor, the specific social characteristics of their private labors appear only within this exchange.[116]

What is being said here is quite straightforward. In capitalist (private-owner-
ship) society the starting point is individual labor as private labor. Those
engaged in production are not aware of their own individual labor as being one
part of the total labor of society. And all of these people enter into a social
relation not directly through the "exchange" of their labor, but rather through
the exchange of products that are the outcome of their labor. In this sense, it is
perfectly natural that a social relation between producers would present itself
as a social relation between products in their given state.

 It is only through or within the exchange of private products that it is made
clear that private labor becomes social labor and that it is one part of the total
labor of society. The relation involving private labor is only manifested as a
relation of things, as the exchange-value of commodities, and hence the commodity becomes a mysterious thing, a "sensuous thing" that "transcends sensuousness."[117]

 Value is basically nothing more than a social "substance." An apple as a
commodity is certainly produced by human labor, but no matter how thin one
may slice it, its value as human labor will not be revealed. The apple as value is
a completely suprasensual thing. It is an illusion to think of value as somehow
being objectified or accumulated as a "mass" or energy within the apple. Even
if one says that human labor is objectified and the substance of value is human
labor—and this is indeed the correct definition—this human labor is not
"objectified" as a thing. Still, this is manifested as a relationship of things, and
it is precisely for this reason that the commodity displays a mysterious character. One can only truly grasp the significance of the "objectification" of human
labor within the commodity by understanding that value is the expression or

116. Ibid., 165.
117. Ibid., 163.

reflection of historical production relations of human beings. By doing this, the commodity's mysterious nature is dispelled.

Of course, it would be incorrect to think that this justifies viewing value as a mere logical fiction or some sort of convenient hypothesis (model). The substance of value, its magnitude, has a real existence. It is important to realize that a material [*jibutsuteki*] form itself is real, and not simply a sort of ideal-form created by human beings. This is because such forms are the expression of historical production relations. Indeed, the fact that human labor takes the objective [*taishōteki*] form of value and a material form reveals the limitations and contradictions of commodity-producing labor.

The young Marx referred to commodity-producing labor as "alienated [estranged] labor," and it could be said that this more or less intuitive (and essential) criticism of capitalism and commodity production also penetrates his later work *Capital* in a richer and more profound form. Labor only takes the objective and material form of value within capitalist-commodity production. In a society where the division of labor and private ownership have been overcome, so that individual labor is one part of the social labor from the outset, i.e. socialism, labor will not take the form of value, and indeed would have no need to so since this would not be private production and therefore there would be no necessity to exchange products. This is precisely the essential point we need to grasp.

Money Fetishism

We also need to consider the fetishism of money. As long as we possess money—and particularly gold-money—we are able to buy anything. Money has the property of direct exchangeability with every commodity. Here the issue revolves around this character of money. Where does this character come from? The typical response would likely be that it stems from the original, inherent character of money (gold), the character of gold as a thing. Such a response, however, is a classic example of the fetishism of money!

Marx says "the riddle of the money fetish is therefore the riddle of the commodity fetish, now become visible and dazzling to our eyes."[118] We have already learned about commodity fetishism and seen that the commodity takes the material form of value in which human labor is objectified in a thing and social relations between human beings appear in the form of social relations

---

118. Ibid., 187.

between things, leading to the upside-down view of value as a natural property of things.

If we reflect further on the analysis of the value-form, we can easily understand that fetishism is more clearly manifested in the case of the commodity in the equivalent form, which is the archetype of the money-form, than for the commodity in the relative form of value. In other words, the commodity in the position of the relative form of value (linen) expresses its own value using the commodity in the equivalent form (the coat), and it does this through the mediation of equating the coat to itself as value, thus "positing" the coat as value-thing (a natural form that expresses value). The coat becomes the equivalent form *within* this value-relation, and this is not due to some intrinsic property of the coat itself. Within the value-relation, the value of the linen is expressed using the use-value of the coat—in other words, in the form: 20 yards of linen = 1 coat.

> The equivalent form consists precisely in this, that the material commodity itself, the coat for instance, expresses value just as it is in its everyday life, and is therefore endowed with the form of value by nature itself. Admittedly, this holds good only within the value-relation, in which the commodity linen is related to the commodity coat as its equivalent. The coat, therefore, seems to be endowed with its equivalent form, its property of direct exchangeability, by nature, just as much as its property of being heavy or its ability to keep us warm. Hence the mysteriousness of the equivalent form, which only impinges on the crude bourgeois vision of the political economist when it confronts him in its fully developed shape, that of money.[119]

> [The equivalent form] consists precisely in the fact that the corporeal- or natural-form of a commodity counts immediately as social form, as value-form for another commodity. Within our traffic with one another it thus appears as [a] social natural property of a thing, as a property inhering in it from nature, the property of possessing equivalent-form, consequently of being—just as it exists in sensible manner—immediately exchangeable with other things. Because, however, within the value-expression of [a] commodity the equivalent-form inheres in Commodity B from nature, it appears to belong to the latter from nature, even outside this relationship. Hence, for example, the riddling character of gold, which appears to possess along with its other nature-properties (its color, its specific gravity, its non-oxydizability-in-air, etc.) also the equivalent-form from nature; that is,

---

119. *Capital*, vol. 1, 149.

the social quality of being immediately exchangeable with all other commodities.[120]

This is not a particularly easy explanation to understand, but Marx is saying that money's capability of purchasing anything only exists within the world of commodities where one commodity (gold) is made the general equivalent by the other commodities. This is only the case within this relation, and bears no connection to the material properties of gold. (Fetishism refers precisely to the worship of gold on the basis of the belief that its power stems from some material property.)

Capital Fetishism

Commodity fetishism appears in a developed form as money and further as capital. If confronted with the question of what is capital, bourgeois scholars would likely say that it is one of the elements necessary for production, a means to this end, and in this function it is a "thing" that has a claim to profit. Already in 1847, however, Marx criticized this vulgar view in *Wage Labor and Capital*:

> Capital consists of raw materials, instruments of labor, and means of subsistence of all kinds, which are employed in producing new raw materials, new instruments, and new means of subsistence. All these components of capital are created by labor, products of labor, accumulated labor. Accumulated labor that serves as a means to new production is capital.
> So says the economists.
> What is a Negro slave? A man of the black race. The one explanation is worthy of the other.
> A Negro is a Negro. Only under certain conditions does he become a slave. A cotton-spinning machine is a machine for spinning cotton. Only under certain conditions does it become capital. Torn away from these conditions, it is as little capital as gold is itself money, or sugar is the price of sugar.[121]

Just as seeing sugar as the price of sugar, or gold itself as money, are examples of the fetishism of the commodity and money, respectively, the view that production means, in and of themselves, are capital is the fetishism of capital.

---

120. *Value: Studies by Marx*, 60.
121. *MECW*, vol. 9 (1978), 211.

Here certain social relations between people appear as the properties of the "things" themselves (in this case the means of production).

Marx criticized bourgeois economists for holding such views regarding capital and emphasized that the means of production *per se* are not capital, and are only transformed into capital (self-valorizing value) under certain historical relations of production; stressing the need to distinguish between the material elements of capital and capital itself. He points out in *Theories of Surplus Value*, for instance, that a distinction must be made between the "material element of capital" and "its social form—with its antagonistic character as the product of labor dominating labor."[122]

> Capital, land, labor! But capital is not a thing, it is a definite social relation of production pertaining to a particular historical social formation, which simply takes the form of a thing and gives this thing a specific social character. Capital is not the sum of the material and produced means of production. Capital is the means of production as transformed into capital, these being no more capital in themselves than gold or silver are money. It is the means of production monopolized by a particular section of society, the products and conditions of activity of labor-power, which are rendered autonomous vis-à-vis this living labor-power and are personified in capital through this antithesis…Here we therefore have one factor of a historically produced social production process in a definite social form, and at first sight a very mysterious form.[123]

When capital becomes "interest-bearing capital," the fetish character of capital appears in its completed form as M-M' (money and a greater sum of money), which Marx calls the capital relation in "its most superficial and fetishized form."[124] In the case of interest-bearing capital, the fetish character of capital appears directly as M-M', i.e. as self-valorizing value, so that self-valorization is seen as an attribute of money. Money as a thing appears to be capital, with self-valorization being its attribute as such. Even though interest is a part of profit, and nothing more than one part of the surplus-value extracted from workers, it appears instead to be something inherent to capital.

---

122. *MECW*, vol. 31 (1989), 248.
123. *Capital*, vol. 3, 953-4.
124. Ibid., 516.

In M-M' we have the irrational form of capital, the misrepresentation and objectification of the relations of production, in its highest power: the interest-bearing form, the simple form of capital, in which it is taken as logically anterior to its own reproduction process; the ability of money or a commodity to valorize its own value independent of reproduction—the capital mystification in the most flagrant form."[125]

This mystification of capital is of course in the interests of the bourgeoisie since it blurs the true source of the self-valorization of capital—namely, the exploitation of labor—so that capital itself is directly seen as the creator of value.

Essential (But Abstract) Concept of Socialism

When examined closely, one can understand how extremely peculiar it is that products of labor take the form of value. A commodity, on the one hand, is a use-value, "an ordinary, sensuous thing," but on the other hand it is also "a thing which transcends sensuousness" and as the bearer of an abstract, social relation (i.e. as value) it evolves "grotesque ideas."[126] Even though it is a product made by human beings, as a thing it has an independent social character and it seems to forge the social relations itself. This inevitably emerges from private ownership (private labor) and the division of labor in society where products of labor are produced as commodities.

One can indeed point to several examples in *Capital* where Marx notes that "the whole mystery of commodities" and "all the magic and necromancy"[127] that surrounds products as commodities will vanish if we shift our attention to other forms of production.

Marx first of all looks at the world of Robinson Crusoe, who is shipwrecked on a remote island and forced to survive on his own. With the aim of providing for his own needs, he divides up his labor and distribution. "All the relations between Robinson and these objects that form his self-created wealth are [extremely] simple and transparent...and yet those relations contain all the essential determinants of value."[128]

---

125. Ibid.
126. *Capital*, vol. 1, 163.
127. Ibid., 169.
128. Ibid., 170.

Even in feudal society, human relations are not concealed by the commodity-form. Labor directly takes a social form and the relation between landlords and peasants is transparent, but in this case labor does not have a general quality as in commodity-production society. In considering "labor in common, i.e. directly associated labor," Marx says that there is no need to go all the way back to the primitive system of production in common, and he raises instead the example of "a peasant family which produces corn, cattle, yarn, linen and clothing for its own use."[129]

> The fact that the expenditure of the individual labor-powers is measured by duration appears here, by its very nature, as a social characteristic of labor itself, because the individual labor-powers, by their very nature, act only as instruments of the joint labor-power of the family.[130]

Finally Marx speaks of "an association of free men," in other words a society that has yet to be attained by humanity, and provides us with the essential content of socialist society, which exists beyond the development of capitalist-commodity production, emerging from the sublation of capitalism.

> Let us finally imagine, for a change, an association of free men, working with the means of production held in common, and expending their many different forms of labor-power in full self-awareness as one single social labor force…The total product of our imagined association is a social product. One part of this product serves as fresh means of production and remains social. But another part is consumed by the members of the association as means of subsistence. This part must therefore be divided amongst them. The way this division is made will vary with the particular kind of social organization of production and the corresponding level of social development attained by the producers. We shall assume, but only for the sake of a parallel with the production of commodities that the share of each individual producer in the means of subsistence is determined by his labor-time. Labor-time would in that case play a double part. Its apportionment in accordance with a definite social plan maintains the correct proportion between the different functions of labor and the various needs of the associations. On the other hand, labor-time also serves as a measure of the part taken by each individual in the common labor, and of his share in the part of the total product destined for consumption. The social relations of the

129. Ibid., 171.
130. Ibid.

individual producers, both towards their labor and the products of their
labor, are here transparent in their simplicity, in production as well as in
distribution.[131]

It may seem strange that Marx would speak of the most essential content of
socialism in relation to the commodity rather than capital, but there is a strong
necessity underlying this. In every type of society, wealth (use-values) must be
produced to sustain life, and the question is how this is carried out. We need
to bear in mind, however, that the concept of socialism provided by Marx in
section four is limited in terms of still being an abstract concept.

Commodity Production and Socialism

Marx emphasizes that products of labor assuming the commodity-form is particular to capitalist society—or more precisely to a society of private ownership
with a division of labor—and that in socialist society, or for collective production in general, this form does not exist and has no reason to exist. However,
within "leftist" circles in Japan and elsewhere (both the Communist Party and
radical groups), this view has been tossed aside, and this has been the "tradition" since the time of Stalin.

Since Stalin's 1952 declaration in *Economic Problems of Socialism in the
USSR* that commodity production remains under socialism, Socialist and
Communist parties have insisted that commodity production and socialism
are not incompatible; a view which is also based on the general existence of
commodity production in the actual "socialist" states (Soviet Union and
China). The new left, for its part, has done nothing more than fill in the gaps
of Stalinist theory, claiming that commodity production also exists during a
"transitional period."

Recently the Chinese Communist Party declared that Marx's theory is not
correct and that there is a socialism" particular to China, even bragging that
they have gone beyond Marx. In 1983, Sun Shangqing, one of the heads of
the Chinese Academy of Social Sciences, responded in the following way
when asked by a reporter for the Mainichi Shimbun whether socialist China is
incompatible with a commodity economy:

---

131. Ibid., 171-2.

From the perspective of traditional Marxist theory, this can certainly be said. But seen from the practice of China, socialism and a commodity economy are not in contradiction. Commodity production is not a particular type of social system, but rather is common to both capitalism and socialism. Even under socialism, commodity production can be fully developed on the basis of a system of state ownership. Thus, there can be competition between companies, the cost of products can be brought down, and the needs of the market met [!!]. Previous centrally planned economies did not vitalize companies, and they produced and consumed labor without regard for market needs. In order to develop a commodity economy, we want to study the economic management techniques of advanced capitalist states. This, however, is a common method for both systems and does not represent a shift to capitalism. China will not employ the approach of traditional socialist states [the Soviet Union?]. Since Marx died over one hundred years ago, we, as his pupils, must advance beyond our teacher...We must make a further effort so that the so-called "Chinese model" can succeed.[132]

The students may conceitedly feel they have surpassed their teacher, but in reality this only means that conditions in China have made commodity production necessary and that the requirements for overcoming commodity production (and therefore capitalism)—such as the development of productive power and the transformation of direct producers into wage-workers, etc.—have yet to come into general existence there.[133]

Labor products assuming the commodity-form, as we have already seen, signifies that products are reduced to equivalents as value, i.e. as abstract human labor, because the various types of labor performed by human beings are not yet directly social labor, and as long as society is based upon private ownership and the division of labor this is unavoidable. In the Soviet Union and China, however, although the means of production are formally "nationalized," appropriation is still private and has been unable to become social. For example, in economically backward China or the Soviet Union, land, which represents the bulk of the means of production, has been subject to either collective ownership (ownership by cooperative unions), individual ownership, or

---

132. [Exact date of *Mainchi Shimbun* article is not listed.]
133. [Hayashi wrote this in the mid-eighties, and it should of course be noted that following the explosive capitalist development in China in recent years, these objective conditions have clearly changed significantly.]

exclusive use.[134] Even factories were positioned as independent enterprises—as "companies"—and were expected to operate on a profitable basis.

In the Soviet Union and China, products of labor take the form of commodities because labor is not directly social, but rather individual labor, and thus only through the exchange of products as "value" does this appear as abstract human labor. This reveals that production and labor are carried out spontaneously (unconsciously), and signifies that the Soviet Union and China are not socialist but rather bourgeois societies. Consequently, the Communist parties in these countries have been obliged to revise or reject Marx.

Commodity Production and Religion

In connection with the "fetishism of the commodity and its secret," Marx refers to the question of religion. The term fetishism originally refers to the worship of a "fetish" in primitive religions. According to such religious beliefs, material things such as rocks or pieces of wood possess spirits with the power to determine human happiness or misery. Marx notes the similarity between "definite social relations between men themselves [assuming] for them the fantastic form of a relation between things" and the "misty realm of religion." He points out that in religion "the products of the human brain [gods, Buddha, etc.] appear as autonomous figures endowed with a life of their own which enter into relations both with each other and with the human race," and "so it is in the world of commodities with the products of men's hands."[135] In other words, both religion and the world of commodities represent upside-down illusions.

Marx also notes that a necessary relation exists between the development of commodity production and Protestantism, which emerged in the middle of the sixteenth century.

> For a society of commodity producers, whose general social relation of production consists in the fact that they treat their products as commodities, hence as values, and in this material [*sachlich*] form bring their individual, private, labors into relation with each other as homogeneous human labor, Christianity with its religious cult of man in the abstract, more particularly

---

134. This was overwhelmingly the case in China after the collapse of the "people's communes."
135. Ibid., 165.

in its bourgeois development, i.e. in Protestantism, Deism, etc., is the most fitting form of religion.[136]

Prior to capitalism and general commodity production, the relation between man and nature, as well as the relation between human beings, were narrow and limited, and "these real limitations are reflected in the ancient worship of nature, and in other elements of tribal religions."[137] However with the development of capitalism, so that commodity production becomes general, Protestantism emerges. Abstract human labor is objectified within the commodity, and for this reason in capitalist society Protestantism becomes the "most fitting form of religion" and historically necessary. In this section of *Capital*, Marx also indicates the conditions necessary for the disappearance of religion.

> The religious reflections of the real world can, in any case, vanish only when the practical relations of everyday life between man and man, and man and nature, generally present themselves to him in a transparent and rational form. The veil is not removed from the countenance of the social life-process, i.e. the process of material production, until it becomes production by freely associated men, and stands under their conscious and planned control. This, however, requires that society possess a material foundation, or a series of material conditions of existence, which in their turn are the natural and spontaneous product of a long and tormented historical development.[138]

Religion, particularly modern religion, is a reflection of the "real world," a reflection of a society in which the relation between man and nature, as well as the social relation between human beings, take on the mystical form of value, not appearing as the rational relation that remains hidden in the shadows. Therefore, religion can only ultimately be eliminated through a revolutionary change of the "real world" so that the actual relations are reorganized in a rational form.

In the passage cited above, Marx also presents the important idea that in order for the social production process to "come under the conscious control" of human beings, and for us to be freed from all social illusions and upside-down consciousness, certain "material conditions" are necessary; namely, the

---

136. Ibid., 172.
137. Ibid., 173.
138. Ibid.

great development of productive power, which is the "natural and spontaneous product of a long and tormented historical development." From this perspective (the materialist conception of history), one can easily understand why Christianity has not disappeared in the Soviet Union, and in fact has grown increasingly strong there. This is the reflection or outcome of the fact that the Soviet Union is a type of capitalist society (state capitalism).

Classic Example of Fetishized Consciousness

We also need to consider, concretely, the type of form in which "fetishized consciousness" is manifested, and we can take the Uno school as one typical example. Uno Kōzō says that it is incorrect for Marx to deal with the issue of fetishism in the chapter on the commodity, claiming that the mystery surrounding the commodity is "perfectly elucidated" once it is understood that the substance of value is human labor in general, but that this substance of value should not yet appear in the discussion of the commodity. Uno insists that the fetish character actually appears in the case of money, namely in the form of "gold becoming the value-thing because of its particular use value."[139] This is what Unoists claim is the fetish character of the commodity.

In *Shihon-ron kenkyū*, Uno argues that "the fetish character as such first appears in reality in the case of money" and that "the theory of the commodity should be carried out in terms of the fetish character of money." For Uno, money fetishism refers to "the value of a commodity being expressed in the use-value of another commodity," and he claims that Marx's theory of the fetishism "is somewhat unclear because he focuses mainly on revealing its basis by means of the [commodity's] substance."

If one sets aside the typical Unoist nonsense expressed here—such as the idea that the substance of value should not be clarified in the theory of the commodity, and that it is sufficient to merely analyze the commodity as a form—what remains is the view that the fetish character refers to one commodity expressing its value in the use-value of another *particular* commodity (money). This, however, is a classic case of fetishized consciousness, although Uno and his followers seem oblivious to this fact!

In an unmediated fashion, Unoists say that the value of one commodity is expressed in another commodity's use-value (in its character as a thing). Uno is even considerate enough to fully reveal his own fetishized consciousness by

---

139. This expression is taken from the Unoist Furihata Setsuo.

saying that "gold, because of its particular use-value, becomes the value-thing, and on this point the fetish character of the commodity appears in a concrete form." But on what basis can Uno make this claim? No matter what "particular" quality it may have, use-value *as such* cannot become the value-thing, just as length cannot suddenly become weight!

As we already noted in our discussion of the theory of the value-form, the fact that a particular commodity (the commodity in the position of equivalent form) becomes the value-thing (or value-body) stems from the relation between the two commodities, and does not—and could not!—bear any relation to the particular use-value of the commodity. With the development of the value-form, however, so that we arrive at the general equivalent, gold comes to play this role. In this case, the character of gold as a "thing" comes to have important meaning, but this is the *outcome* of gold being pushed forward in the role of general equivalent through the "joint action"[140] of all of the other commodities, certainly not the other way around. This is perfectly clear if we note that historically money has not always existed in the form of gold. Precious metals *come to be* money precisely because they are "commodities which are by nature fitted to perform the social function of a universal equivalent."[141]

Uno fails to understand that whether a commodity expresses its value in one *shō* [1.81 liters] of rice or a gram of gold makes no essential difference, and therefore bringing up the question of the "particular use-value of gold" reflects a terribly fetishized consciousness. Uno claims that gold is money because of its particular use-value, and for this reason it is able to measure the value of other commodities and purchase anything! This view is no different from how most people are dazzled by the fetish character of gold, which is worshiped and turned into a mystical thing.

Despite the fact that the fetishism of money centers precisely on money *qua* thing (use-value) seemingly having the ability to measure the value of all other commodities and being exchangeable with them (thus appearing all-powerful), Uno can do nothing more than offer up a plausible version of this idea! In reality, the fact that all commodities can express their own value in money—that is, in a quantity of the use-value of money—is because all of the

---

140. [I have taken the term "joint action" (of the whole world of commodities) from the Samuel Moore and Edward Aveling translation (International Publishers). Ben Fowkes' translation (Penguin edition) uses the term "joint contribution" and Hans Ehrbar prefers "joint work."]
141. Ibid., 183.

commodities have already pushed forward gold as the general equivalent, posited it as the value-thing, which thus allows them to express their own value in the use-value of gold (as so many yen or thousands of yen). If this mediation is lacking, however, the completely illogical mystification of equating or comparing value with use-value, and saying that value is expressed as a use-value (as a thing!), will go unchallenged. (And this is the way reality presents itself under capitalism, so that this society is overrun with a fetishized view of money).

No Need for Value Under Socialism

This is the final section dealing with the first chapter of *Capital*. Our study of the commodity has allowed us to become more familiar with capitalism, its basis and starting point, since wealth under capitalism is generally produced in the commodity-form. Thus, we have also come to a better understanding of socialism as the solution to the contradictions of capitalism, as the superceding of capitalist limitations.

We have seen, for example, that products take the historical, social form of the commodity when production is carried out in a private rather than a social form, with private ownership and the division of labor as the starting point; that the commodity is the inevitable outcome of a stage of society in which people engaged in private production form a social connection through the exchange of their products; and that therefore if people no longer proceed from the starting point of private labor and the need to exchange products comes to an end, the commodity-form would also be eliminated. With the overcoming of private ownership, the individual labor of human beings already no longer appears as private labor, but rather as directly social labor (as one of its parts or appendages), and therefore there is no need for the exchange of products to mediate the social relations of human beings. As Marx notes: "Objects of utility only become commodities because they are the products of the labor of private individuals who work independently of each other."[142]

The magnitude of value is expressed relatively through money (as price), but value is nothing more than social human labor. When labor becomes directly social, rather than being private labor, there is no need for people to measure the magnitude of products "in a roundabout way, through the medium of exchange, relatively" and this can instead be carried out "directly, absolutely...in labor-hours or days."[143] With the shift to production in com-

---

142. Ibid., 165.

mon, "society can easily measure" how much social labor on average is necessary to produce a certain use value, and for this there is no need for value, as Engels points out:

> The useful effects of the various articles of consumption, compared with one another and with the quantities of labor required for their production, will in the end determine the plan. People will be able to manage everything very simply, without the intervention of much-vaunted "value." [Engels' footnote:] As long ago as 1844 [in the *Deutsch-Französische Jahrbücher*] I stated that the above-mentioned balancing of useful effects and expenditure of labor on making decisions concerning production was all that would be left, in a communist society, of the politico-economic concept of value.[144]

Those taken in by the reality of so-called "actually-existing socialism" in the Soviet Union have advanced the theory that production and distribution cannot be smoothly carried out without economic accounting, and that socialism cannot be constructed without at least effectively "utilizing" such accounting. Engels, however, argues that without resorting to economic accounting, things would be managed "very simply." Which of these views, then, is the correct one?

Consider the following example. Let us say that four hours of labor a day are needed to sustain the present level of life and consumption of a group of people, but these people wish to possess a car. According to calculations, it is known that an additional ten minutes of labor per day for a period of ten days would be necessary to acquire this car. Thus, these people could work four hours and ten minutes over a period of ten days. The "calculation" here, of course, is not "economic accounting" and there would be no appearance of the "economy." This is not economic but rather *technical* accounting. In this example it is already a question of the relation between the means of production, raw materials, labor time, and products. Human beings, not capital, are the subject. At issue is how much production, and thus expenditure of labor, is necessary for the people's lives and consumption. The notion that production and consumption are impossible without recourse to the "economy" is a view

---

143. *Anti-Dühring*, 292.
144. Ibid., 295.

tainted by the traditions of bourgeois society, and merely exposes a narrow-mindedness incapable of thinking beyond the relations of capitalist society.

7. The Exchange Process—The Site of Money Formation

Theoretical Task of Chapter Two

Right in the middle of the three chapters that compose part one of *Capital* comes the chapter "The Exchange Process," as the dividing point between the first chapter "The Commodity" and the third chapter "Money, or the Circulation of Commodities." The position of this short second chapter tells us something about the theoretical task it addresses. In his earlier work, *A Contribution to the Critique of Political Economy*, just prior to the section that corresponds to the second chapter of *Capital*, Marx wrote the following:

> So far two aspects of the commodity—use-value and exchange-value—have been examined, but each one separately. The commodity, however, is the direct unity of use-value and exchange-value, and at the same time it is a commodity only in relation to other commodities. The exchange process of commodities is the real relation that exists between them.[145]

Marx's examination of the commodity in the first chapter is *analytical*. That is, at times he examines the commodity as use-value, while at other times (and for the most part) the focus is on the aspect of exchange-value. In reality, however, the commodity exists as such as the unity of use-value and exchange-value, and in the second chapter Marx directly examines the commodity in this sense. The commodity appears as such in the process of exchange, and Marx considers the contradictions of the commodity within this process, the contradiction of the commodity as a totality composed of use-value and exchange-value.

Some may be wondering, however, whether the first chapter of *Capital* is indeed analytical. Granted, Marx did quickly abstract from (or ignore) the issue of use-value in the first section of chapter one, after briefly discussing the use-value of the commodity, in order to uncover the substance of value, which

---

145. *A Contribution to the Critique of Political Economy*, 282.

certainly is an example of an analytical method. And section two is likewise analytical, with Marx separately analyzing labor in terms of creating use-value and in terms of creating value. But what about section three? Since the value of commodity A is expressed in the use-value of commodity B, and thus value and use-value are treated as being inseparable, can we really refer to this as analytical? (This seems like the sort of question that the Unoists would be likely to raise.)

In fact, however, such questions are based upon a complete misunderstanding of the theoretical task of section three. Certainly it can be said that the value of commodity A is expressed in the use-value of commodity B, but in this case the use-value of commodity B itself becomes the form of value. For this precise reason, commodity A is able to express its own value relatively through the use-value of commodity B, and thus comes to assume the form of value. Thus, section three ultimately focuses on value and analyzes the form of value (and how this form is possible). The use-value of the commodity in the *original sense* is not a matter of concern here.

As long as a commodity exists as such it will have a form of value—such as 1,000 yen—and section three aims to clarify *how* this is possible. This is a question of the value-form; that is to say, the value of a commodity acquires a form separate from its existence as a use-value, and therefore it is clear that this is analytical and one-dimensional. Section four on commodity fetishism is also, fundamentally speaking, an examination of the nature of value, with the question centering on *why* human labor necessarily takes the form of value and the significance of this.

Seen from this perspective, chapter one on the commodity is analytical as a whole, and to this extent is one-dimensional. This is natural in a sense considering that the commodity is "value," but in terms of considering the commodity as it actually exists, this examination alone is insufficient. Actual commodities exists as such not merely as use-value or value, but rather as the unity of the two. In considering the commodity as it actually exists, the issue of use-value, which has barely been considered up to this point,[146] becomes an issue of equal importance to that of value.

---

146. Here I am referring to consideration of use-value in the original sense of being a desired object.

Contradictions in the Exchange Process

In the process of exchange, the commodity appears as the unity of use-value and exchange-value, and must be considered as such. However, as a unity of use-value and exchange-value the commodity is a contradictory thing. This contradiction actually unfolds within the process of exchange. Here we need to consider what, exactly, is the real contradiction between use-value and exchange-value.

It is self-evident that the use-value of a commodity is not a use-value for its owner, and only actually is treated as a use-value after being handed over to another person. In the hands of its owner, the commodity is not directly a use-value but simply an exchange-value. Thus, as a use-value, the commodity must be transferred into the hands of another party. At the same time, the commodity as exchange-value is qualitatively identical to other commodities, only differing in terms of quantity, and must therefore be replaced, at a given proportion, for another commodity. The process of exchange is the process of the realization of the commodity as use-value and at the same time the process of its realization as exchange-value, but these two processes harbor a fundamental contradiction, which Marx refers to as a "vicious circle."

As a commodity owner, for example, I might have one kilogram of tangerines I would like to exchange for a copy of Marx's *Capital*. If I then happen to come across a person who has a copy of *Capital*, it would be ideal, of course, if the person were interested in acquiring tangerines, but such a lucky encounter would be extremely unlikely. The owner of the copy of *Capital* might wish to exchange it for a bottle of bourbon, not a kilogram of tangerines, and in this case exchange would be impossible. This is the manner in which the realization of use-value and the realization of exchange-value are in contradiction.

> One and the same relation must therefore be simultaneously a relation of essentially equal commodities which differ only in magnitude, i.e., a relation which expresses their equality as materializations of universal labor-time, and at the same time it must be their relation as qualitatively different things, as distinct use-values for distinct needs, in short a relation which differentiates them as actual use-values But equality and inequality thus posited are mutually exclusive. The result is not simply a vicious circle of problems, where the solution of one problem presupposes the solution of the other, but a whole complex of contradictory premises, since the fulfillment of one condition depends directly upon the fulfillment of its opposite.[147]

A commodity owner hopes to realize a commodity as value, i.e. realize this in relation to any other commodity of the same value regardless of its use-value. However, commodities as use-values come in an infinite variety, and since it is not possible to directly exchange the commodity with all other commodities, commodity owners are not able to exchange commodities with each other. Other commodity owners also hope to realize their own commodities as value with any other commodity, but at the same time they only want commodities whose use-value suits their own needs. This is the same for all commodity owners, so that the exchange process is deadlocked and commodity production becomes impossible.

This means that commodities "do not confront each other as commodities, but as products or use-values only."[148] This is because, from the perspective of the realization of a commodity's use-value, the process of exchange is an individual process, but from the perspective of its realization as value it is a social process. "But the same process cannot be simultaneously for all owners of commodities both exclusively individual and exclusively social and general."[149] Some mediation is needed to resolve this contradiction, since without it commodity production becomes generally impossible. We will now consider the form that this solution takes.

Dual Nature of the Commodity

We have seen that the realization of a commodity's use-value and the realization of its exchange-value are actually in contradiction and mutually exclusively, and that without resolving this contradiction commodity-production society is not possible. This contradiction is resolved, needless to say, through the appearance of money. With money's appearance, commodity owners are able to realize their own commodities as both use-value and exchange-value.

Some readers may be thinking: "Is that it? Everyone knows this, and we encounter this fact every day, so there is no need for Marx's splendid yet difficult-to-grasp theory."

But hold on a second! The matter is not quite so simple!

We have said, for example, that as long as a person has money the contradiction inherent to the process of exchange is resolved, but what does it mean

---

147. Ibid., 285.
148. *Capital*, vol. 1, 180.
149. Ibid.

to have money—and what is money in the first place? Generally speaking, people do not consider such questions. The use of money to mediate commodity exchange is considered normal, a natural process that goes unquestioned. Bourgeois scholars often state that commodity exchange has always occurred and will continue far into the future, and that money is simply a convenient means or tool that was "discovered" for the sake of such exchange. Those who superficially read Marx's chapter on the exchange process (Unoists!) are able to come up with nothing more than such arguments of bourgeois scholars. Marx, however, writes:

> Money necessarily crystallizes out of the process of exchange, in which different products of labor are in fact equated with each other, and thus converted into commodities. The historical broadening and deepening of the phenomenon of exchange develops the opposition between use-value and value which is latent in the nature of the commodity. The need to give an external expression to this opposition for the purposes of commercial intercourse produces the drive towards an independent form of value, which finds neither rest nor peace until an independent form has been achieved by the differentiation of commodities into commodities and money. At the same rate, then, as the transformation of the products of labor into commodities is accomplished, one particular commodity is transformed into money.[150]

The contradiction between the use-value and exchange-value of commodities develops along with the expansion of commodity production, and the impetus to resolve this contradiction does not cease to exist until an "independent commodity-value"—an independent form of value as money—emerges. We must begin by recognizing that money is the differentiation of commodities into commodities and money so that a certain commodity takes on the independent form of value, as the general equivalent form, and is separated out from the other commodities. Thus, money is not a tool that is "discovered" and brought in from outside of commodity circulation. For this precise reason, immediately following the passage above, Marx ridicules "the craftiness of petty-bourgeois socialists" (Proudhon et al.) who hope to abolish money while perpetuating commodity production. To eliminate the money-economy—the world where money is all-powerful—it is necessary to overcome commodity production and shift to socialist production.

---

150. Ibid., 181.

We have seen that the money-form is merely the reflection thrown upon a single commodity by the relations between all other commodities. That commodity is therefore only a discovery for those who proceed from its finished shape in order to analyze it afterwards. The process of exchange gives to the commodity which it has converted into money not its value but its specific value-form. Confusion between these two attributes has misled some writers into maintaining that the value of gold and silver is imaginary.[151]

Here Marx is merely saying that money is also a commodity, and it is as such that it first comes to have value. What the process of exchange provides is not value but merely the value-form. This is an extremely important point considering the prevalence of Uno's upside-down view that to begin with the commodity has a value-form, and that this provides the commodity with a value within the process of exchange.[152]

Relation to Section Three

The next problem we need to consider is how we should understand the distinction and connection between the examination of the formation of money in section three (value-form) and the discussion in chapter two (exchange process). In both sections the issue of money is raised, and it seems that both discuss how money comes to appear, but the manner of carrying out this discussion is quite different. This issue is elucidated in the following passage from *Capital* where Marx, after referring to the contradictions of the exchange process, solves the problem of how commodity owners act before thinking:

> In their difficulties our commodity owners think like Faust: "in the beginning was the deed." They have already acted before thinking. The natural laws of the commodity have manifested themselves in the natural instinct of the owners of commodities. They can bring their commodities into relations as values, and therefore as commodities, by bringing them into an opposing relation with some one other commodity, which serves as the universal equivalent. We have already reached that result by our analysis of the commodity. But only the action of society can turn a particular commodity into the universal equivalent. The social action of all other commodities, therefore, sets apart the particular commodity in which they all

---

151. Ibid., 184-5.
152. There is also Uno's idea of the *a priori* existence of money, which basically amounts to the same thing.

represent their values. The natural form of this commodity thereby becomes the socially recognized equivalent form. Through the agency of the social process it becomes the specific social function of the commodity which has been set apart to be the universal equivalent. It thus becomes—money…Money necessarily crystallizes out of the process of exchange.[153]

This passage is quite difficult to understand by itself. Here after mentioning the contradiction of the exchange process—i.e. the contradiction between the realization of the commodity as use-value and as exchange-value—Marx is noting that this contradiction can be resolved to the extent that a general equivalent (money) is posited, and that this problem was already dealt with in section three of the first chapter.

In other words, in his theory of the value-form—based on the understanding that there is no essential difference between the equation x commodity A = y commodity B, and the equation x commodity A = z gold—Marx demystifies the strangeness of commodity A expressing its value in a quantity of gold *as a thing*, as well as the mystery of the money-form by tracing this back to the initial form of x commodity A = y commodity B. Marx finds that commodity B, in its relation to commodity A, is made the value-body or value-form, and through this mediation the value of commodity A is expressed using commodity B. And if this same thing occurs in the case of all commodities—in other words, the development of the value-form—a general equivalent is formed, and this general equivalent is in fact money. In his theory of the value-form, Marx shows how, formally speaking, a certain commodity (linen), through the development of the value-form, becomes the general equivalent (money), but he does not mention the "moment" that makes this necessary. His discussion in section three is limited to the form of value (and its development). Kuruma Samezō explains this point in the following way:

> It can be said that prior to the theory of the exchange process, the theory of the value-form clarifies how the general equivalent is formed, and how by means of this the relation of commodities as value, and therefore as commodities, is mediated, and thus in the theory of the exchange process the development of the contradiction of the commodity is traced back…The path to break through this deadlock is already clarified in the theory of the value-form. Even though this is already clarified in the theory of the value-

---

153. Ibid., 180-1.

form, however, it is the joint action of the world of commodities that actually sets apart a particular commodity which in reality becomes the general equivalent, and this joint action is made necessary by the deadlock of the unmediated exchange process and the various contradictions of this process, which necessitates some sort of mediation. Along with tracing back these contradictions, the theme particular to the theory of the exchange process involves the discussion of the necessity of the general equivalent to mediate the exchange process, i.e. the formation of money, and this falls outside of the sphere of the theory of the commodity-form.[154]

"How, Why, and Through What"

Toward the end of his discussion of the exchange process, Marx writes:

> The difficulty lies not in comprehending that money is a commodity, but in discovering how, why, and through what a commodity is money."[155]

Samezō Kuruma argues that these three points—"how, why, and through what"—correspond to section three (value-form), section four (commodity fetishism), and chapter two (exchange process), respectively. In other words, in the theory of the value-form Marx indicates *how* a commodity's value is expressed through the use-value of another commodity, in the form of a certain quantity of the money-commodity. In the theory of fetishism, the question revolves instead around *why* this occurs and why this cannot be directly expressed as labor-time. Finally, the chapter on the exchange process indicates the necessity of money in the exchange process as the solution to the real contradiction inherent to the commodity, as use-value on the one hand and exchange-value on the other; i.e. *what* makes money necessary. The second chapter then clarifies the real "moment" that determines this.[156]

Kuruma's view is very clear and convincing, but Unoists have attacked it. Ōuchi Hideaki, for instance, believes that "this is just a case of Marx's employ-

---

154. Kuruma Samezō *Kachikeitai-ron to kōkankatei-ron* (Tokyo: Iwanami Shoten, 1957), 23.
155. [This is taken from Hans Ehrbar's translation of *Capital* which is a more accurate translation of the original German.]
156. In the discussion of the *substance of value* in the first section of chapter one, Marx also considers *what* value is, i.e. what is expressed in the relationship of equivalence between the two products, and he discovers that this is socially abstract human labor.

ing a type of rhetoric," and that "the only way to have known if it has more profound meaning would have been to ask Marx himself." Ōuchi adds that, "it seems best to view Marx as having used the expression 'how, why, and through what' to emphasize the importance of the value-form and how the commodity necessarily comes to take the form of money." Furihata Setsuo, another follower of Uno, writes:

> In short, since it is insufficient to merely understand that money is a com-modity, it is necessary to clarify the logical connection by means of which the commodity becomes money, and in saying that he already made this clear in the theory of the value-form, Marx adds on this part about the "how" etc. Given the context, I think it is safe to say that each of these three words cannot be seen as posing a separate [theoretical] question.[157]

Both Ōuchi and Furihata are confused and lack an elementary understanding of the fact that the passage in question does not concern the value-form at all, and that, to begin with, the second chapter as a whole is a discussion of the exchange process, and thus there is no reason to examine the form of value here. Kuruma, for his part, has the following to say about Marx's famous sentence:

> Here I want to note incidentally that these three problems were not posed by Marx as a sort of logical schema or in a frivolous manner, and that with-out solving each one of them we cannot come to an adequate understand-ing of money. Indeed, there is the real problem of earlier political economy slipping into a variety of errors by failing to solve these problems. First of all, one must pose the realistic problems to be solved, and then the issue becomes how one should solve them, the question of where and how they should be discussed, not the other way around. Therefore, it would be like "casting pearls before swine" if we were to present the solution to someone who has not even grasped the problem itself. Some may believe [however] that Marx is merely engaging in a frivolous discussion here, while others focus their attention on this as the penetration of a Hegelian "logical pro-cess."[158]

This brings to a close our look at the exchange process, and now I would like to turn to the third chapter, "Money, or the Circulation of Commodities." As

---

157. *Shihon-ron kenkyū*, 1: 253.
158. *Kachikeitai-ron to kōkankatei-ron*, 41.

in the first two chapters, money appears in this chapter, but here it is playing the leading role, whereas the commodity was the main focus in the first two chapters with money playing a supporting role.

8. Functions of Money and the Phenomenon of "Price"

First Function is the "Measure of Value"

Here we will examine money, the economic category that symbolizes bourgeois society and expresses its social relations. Today, however, money no longer appears directly, but rather takes a "proxy" form, so that to some extent its functions are no longer easily understood.

Marx speaks of the three main functions of money: (1) money as a measure of value, (2) money as the means of circulation, and (3) money as money (as the independent crystallization of value). According to Marx, the first or primary function of money is as "a measure of value," but the meaning of this expression may be somewhat difficult to understand. Literally, this means to measure or gauge a commodity's value, but since this involves the value of a commodity this is not "measured" or expressed in the direct form of some quantity of social labor-time.[159] Marx has the following to say about the function of money as a measure of value:

> The first main function of money[160] is to supply commodities with the material for the expression of their values, or to represent their values as magnitudes of the same denomination, qualitatively equal and quantitatively comparable. It thus acts as a universal measure of value, and only through performing this function does gold, the specific equivalent commodity, become money.[161]

---

159. Incidentally, Unoists object to Marx's view and claim that the first function of money is as a "means of purchase" rather than a measure of value. This view that "value is expressed by purchasing something with money" represents, in a condensed form, the truly vulgar and reactionary (parasitic!) standpoint of the Unoists, and this is a point we will examine in more detail later.
160. Here gold is presupposed as the money-commodity.
161. *Capital*, vol. 1, 188.

We all know that commodities have prices (as so many yen, dollars, pounds, etc.), so that their value is represented "as magnitudes of the same denomination, qualitatively equal and quantitatively comparable." The question is what is this "price" and what sort of mechanism exists for the price-expression of value. The term "measure of value" refers to the expression of value, the role of money in expressing value in terms of price. The measure of value is the "gauging" of the value of a commodity in gold *qua* money, just as the length of something can be gauged using a ruler or the weight of a thing measured using a balance—and we have already touched on the significance and limitations of this comparison in our discussion of the value-form.

Would the reader be surprised by the idea that *price* concerns the value of a commodity being expressed in a quantity of gold? For example, the fact that this book is worth two thousand yen. This, in other words, signifies that the book expresses its own value in the form of being equal to x grams of gold. The concept of yen is connected to a certain amount of gold. In the prewar period (under the gold standard), this was clearly indicated legally as: 1 yen = to 2 *fun* (0.75g) of gold.[162] Today, however, under the managed currency system, where central banknotes circulate that to a large extent function as paper money—the quantity of gold equivalent to yen is not necessarily clear, since it is always fluctuating and changing, and this is a point that we will touch on later.

It would seem quite obvious that the role of gold as money involves the use of its own physical body to express the value of a commodity, thus becoming the material through which value is expressed, but in fact this has sparked significant debate. This is evidenced by the complete failure of Unoists to understand the significance and content of the function of money as a measure of value, which again exposes how incredibly dim-witted they can be. Gold can "measure" a commodity's value and express this because all commodities are equal as value and commensurate, and because gold is the general equivalent, the independent existence form of value. Without understanding this, even if one speaks of the measurement of a commodity's value through money, it becomes nothing more than a meaningless arrangement of words. And the arguments of the Uno school provide us with a perfect example of this.

---

162. [Under the traditional system of Japanese measurement, 1 *fun* is equal to 0.375 g.]

The Illusions of John Gray

In the previous section I mentioned that the first function of money is to provide a commodity with the material for the expression of its value and that this value is expressed in the form of the commodity being equal to a certain quantity of gold. This, in other words, is the transformation of value into price, or the price-expression of value. The value of a commodity is expressed in the relative form of being equal to x grams of gold (in its exchange relation with another, special commodity, i.e. money).

x commodity A = y money-commodity

In this equation, the value of a commodity is indicated in a socially recognizable and valid form. Some may wonder, however, why this sort of expression of value is necessary. In other words, since the value of a commodity is the labor (time) objectified in it, why can't this value be directly expressed as labor-time? Marx responds to this question in the following way:

> Money as a measure of value is the necessary form of appearance of the measure of value which is immanent in commodities, namely labor-time. [Footnote:] The question of why money does not itself directly represent labor-time, so that a piece of paper may represent, for instance, x hours' labor, comes down simply to the question why, on the basis of commodity production, the products of labor must take the form of commodities. This is obvious, because their taking the form of commodities implies their differentiation into commodities [on the one hand] and the money commodity [on the other]. It is the question why private labor cannot be treated as its opposite, directly social labor.[163]

Under capitalism, products take the form of commodities, and because of this a commodity can only express its own value relatively within its exchange relation with a special commodity (gold-money). The situation is different under socialism, but in capitalist society, where the fact that private labor is also social labor must be revealed *within* the exchange of products, it is not possible for value to be expressed directly as labor-time.

---

163. *Capital*, vol. 1, 188. [The final sentence in this passage is taken from Hans Ehrbar's translation of *Capital* which is closer to both the Japanese translation Hayashi cites and to the original German.]

We need to consider the following questions (which Marx answers): Why, in capitalist society, is value not measured directly as labor-time, making use instead of an external measure; why do all commodities have their value evaluated through one, excluded commodity; and why is this excluded commodity transformed into money?

Marx notes that the English economist John Gray, starting from the discovery that labor-time is the direct unit of the measure of money, arrives at the following idea:

> [John Gray] proposes that a national central bank should ascertain through its branches the labor time expended in the production of various commodities. In exchange for the commodity, the producer would receive an official certificate of its value, i.e. a receipt for as much labor time as his commodity contains, and this bank note of one labor week, one labor day, one labor hour, etc. would serve at the same time as an order to the bank to hand over an equivalent in any of the other commodities stored in its warehouses.[164]

Marx criticizes Gray's idea in the following manner:

> As Gray presupposes that the labor-time contained in commodities is immediately social labor-time, he presupposes that it is communal labor-time or labor-time of directly associated individuals. In that case, it would indeed be impossible for a specific commodity, such as gold or silver, to confront other commodities as the incarnation of universal labor and exchange-value would not be turned into price; but neither would use-value be turned into exchange-value and the product into a commodity, and thus the very basis of bourgeois production would be abolished. But this is by no means what Gray had in mind—goods are to be produced as commodities but not exchanged as commodities.[165]

Proudhon was also under the sway of this sort of illusion, and the bankruptcy of such views is immediately exposed in practice. Commodity-producing labor is private labor, not directly social labor in common. For this reason, the value of a commodity cannot be expressed directly as labor-time, but rather only *relatively* within the exchange relation. This is why the idea of "labor money" on the basis of commodity production is a shallow fantasy. Before getting swept

---

164. *A Contribution to the Critique of Political Economy*, 320-1.
165. Ibid., 321.

up by such fantasies, we need to understand the price-expression of commodities and why it is necessary.

Relation to the Value-Form

Anyone who has read *Capital* has probably noticed the strong relation between the theory of money as a measure of value (section one, chapter three) and the theory of the value-form (section three, chapter one). In analyzing the value-form, Marx also considers the manner in which value is expressed, and the theoretical task of section three is to clarify the fundamental mechanism of value-expression by tracing it back to the simple form of value.

Even though both of these sections deal with the expression of value, they pursue fundamentally different theoretical questions. In section three of chapter one, Marx discusses the process and mechanism whereby one commodity (gold) becomes the general equivalent (money) by means of the "joint action" of the world of commodities, and thus the focus is on the expression of value (and the development of the value-form). In considering money as a measure of value, however, it is already presupposed that gold has become money and exists as such, and Marx examines instead how a commodity expresses its own value as price through money and the role of money in this process. Although Marx speaks of the "expression of value" in section three, money is not playing any role. Rather, this section deals with the expression of value in terms of the formation of money. Regarding this, Marx has the following to say:

> The expression of the value of a commodity in gold—x commodity A $= y$ money commodity—is its money-form or price. A single equation, such as 1 ton of iron $=$ 2 ounces of gold, now suffices to express the value of the iron in a socially valid manner. There is no longer any need for this equation to figure as a link in the chain of equations that express the values of all other commodities, because the equivalent commodity, gold, already possesses the character of money. The general relative form of value of commodities has therefore resumed its original shape of simple or individual relative value.[166]

The equation 1 ton of iron $=$ 2 ounces of gold, seen formally, is the same as the equation in chapter one of 1 quarter of wheat $= x$ cwt. of iron (section one) or 20 yards of linen $=$ one coat (section three). The equation in section three, in

---

166. *Capital*, vol. 1, 189.

particular, when written as 20 yards of linen = x ounces of gold, is exactly the same, formally speaking, as the equation in the first section of chapter three.

From a theoretical perspective, however, there is an essential difference. Even when gold is introduced into the equation in chapter one, it is certainly not gold as money, but rather as a "normal" commodity that is exactly equivalent to the linen and other commodities. In chapter three, by contrast, gold as the general equivalent is already gold as money, and for this reason each commodity already expresses its own value directly by means of the gold. In other words, "there is no longer any need for this [value] equation to figure as a link in the chain of equations"[167] as it had in section three of the first chapter, and Marx thus consciously clarifies the relation and distinction between chapter three and this earlier section.

Despite this, however, Unoists claim that Marx's discussion of money as the measure of value is strange because it presupposes that exchange is carried out according to value.[168] They argue that the function of money as the measure of value refers to a buyer making a purchase with money and the seller setting a price-level that takes the buyer into consideration, and that since this is what determines the purchase price, it can be set at various levels depending on the will of the seller. As a result, commodity prices fluctuate and tend to depart from value rather than commodities being exchanged according to value. In other words, Unoists consider the function of money as a measure of value to merely be the seller assigning a price to his own commodity. If this were the case, however, how could one speak of the value of a commodity being expressed in money? Even without the premise of this function of money, Uno's theory would be fully possible.

Uno understands nothing about money and fails to grasp, in any sense, the significance of a commodity expressing its own value through money. Precisely because he fails to understand this essential question, he focuses exclusively on the determination of the magnitude of price and its quantitative aspect. Marx, by contrast, prior to considering the magnitude of price, raises the question of what is price. Thus, in this first part of chapter three, he temporarily sets aside the quantitative question, deeming it sufficient for matters to proceed in the normal form of exchange according to value.

---

167. Ibid.
168. Regardless of the particular issue, Unoists advance this stupid, one-track criticism that fixates on the fact that commodities, in reality, are not necessarily exchanged according to their value.

Measure of Value and the Measurement Standard

In Marx's discussion of the function of money as the measure of value, the function as the standard of price (standard of measurement) naturally emerges, but he says that these two functions are entirely distinct from each other. In the case of money as the measure of value, the commodity's price is expressed in a certain quantity of gold, or in silver or copper if they happen to be used as money. On the other hand, money as a standard of measure is money as a definite quantity of gold functioning as the measurement standard of price.

When commodity-value comes to be expressed as a certain quantity of gold, so that commodities are mutually comparable and measurable, there is a "need to compare them, for technical reasons, with some fixed quantity of gold as their unit of measure."[169] When this unit of measure is separated and fixed as the standard unit, it is called the "standard of measure." In prewar Japan, for example, the gold standard was set at "2 *fun* (0.75g) = 1 yen" In other words, one yen was the name for gold weighing 2 *fun*, and therefore 4 *fun* of gold was 2 yen, and so on. "It is owing to this," as Marx points out, that "in all metallic currencies, the names given to the standards of money or of price were originally taken from the pre-existing names of the standards of weight."[170] The monetary unit of *pound* in England, for instance, is also the name for a unit of measurement. Marx explains the difference between the function of money as measure of value and as standard of price in the following way:

> As a measure of value, and as standard of price, money performs two quite different functions. It is the measure of value as the social incarnation of human labor, it is the standard of price as a quantity of metal with a fixed weight. As the measure of value it serves to convert the values of all the manifold commodities into prices, into imaginary quantities of gold; as the standard of price it measures those quantities of gold. The measure of values measures commodities considered as values; the standard of price measures, on the contrary, quantities of gold by a unit quantity of gold, not the value of one quantity of gold by the weight of another. For the standard of price, a certain weight of gold must be fixed as the unit of measurement. In this case, as in all cases where quantities of the same denomination are to be measured [e.g. weight or length], the stability of the measurement is of decisive importance. Hence the less the unit of measurement (here a quan-

---

169. Ibid., 191.
170. Ibid.

tity of gold) is subject to variation, the better the standard of price fulfils its office.[171]

Fixing the standard of price involves making a certain quantity of gold, as the measure of value, the measurement standard of price (e.g the form of 2 *fun* = 1 yen). In this way, all other quantities of gold can be compared to this standard quantity of gold. If commodity B expresses its value in a quantity of gold ten times that of commodity A, then its price is 10 times that of commodity A, while commodity C would have a price twenty times that of commodity A if its value were expressed in twenty times the quantity of gold—i.e. "when we are dealing with prices we are only concerned with the relation between different quantities of gold."[172]

Even if the price of gold fluctuates, the various quantities of gold always maintain the same proportion to each other, so clearly this does not impede in any way its function as the standard of price. Ten grams of gold, no matter how much the value of gold may change, will still have a value that is ten times that of one gram of gold. Of course, fluctuations in gold-money can bring about changes in price, but this does not mean that the function of gold as a measure of value or price as a standard of measurement are impeded or rendered ineffective. Rather, it can be said that price fluctuations are the form through which these functions are carried out.

The function of money as standard of price is also essentially connected to inflation, and I will discuss this in more detail later. Inflation can be fundamentally defined as an "economic" devaluation of the measurement standard of price. For example, the quantity of gold that represents 1 yen might drop by one-half or two-thirds. By means of the function of money as a measure of value and price as the measurement standard, commodity-value is transformed into the price form that we encounter every day.

Divergence between Value and Price

Uno and his followers are ridiculously fond of saying that price (money-expression of value) and value do not coincide, never tiring of quoting the following passage from *Capital*:

---

171. Ibid., 192.
172. Ibid.

The magnitude of the value of a commodity therefore expresses a necessary relation to social labor-time which is inherent in the process by which its value is created. With the transformation of the magnitude of value into the price this necessary relation appears as the exchange-ratio between a single commodity and the money commodity which exists outside it. This relation, however, may express both the magnitude of value of the commodity and the greater or lesser quantity of money for which it can be sold under the given circumstances. The possibility, therefore, of a quantitative incongruity between price and magnitude of value, i.e. the possibility that the price may diverge from the magnitude of value, is inherent in the price-form itself. This is not a defect, but, on the contrary, it makes this form the adequate one for a mode of production whose laws can only assert themselves as blindly operating averages between constant irregularities.[173]

According to Unoists, Marx in this passage is explaining the constant fluctuation of prices and the mechanism of capitalist-commodity production—the strange and ethereal *invisible hand!*—where the magnitude of value is determined by such fluctuations. They conclude, therefore, that it is incorrect to attempt to analyze commodity exchange in terms of value and price coinciding from the outset (i.e. exchange according to value). The correct approach, rather, is to start out from the divergence between the two, and then "logically" demonstrate their agreement somehow.

This view, however, is nonsense. Even if the price-expression does not coincide exactly with value, this does not alter the fact that it is the expression of value. The question Marx raises here is the role of money in the expression of value and the price-expression of value—this does not pertain to whether value and price are in *quantitative* agreement.

Value and price may or may not coincide, but even if they do not, price still remains the money-expression of value. What Marx pursues in his examination of money as the measure of value is this *qualitative* question, not a quantitative one. What is important here is that the value of a commodity "expresses a necessary relation to [the] social labor-time" needed for its production, and that with price this [necessary relation] "appears as the exchange-ratio between a single commodity and the money commodity that exists outside it."[174]

---

173. Ibid., 196.
174. Ibid.

To follow the Unoists' train of thought would result in losing sight of what price is in the first place. They directly presuppose both value and price. In other words, they discuss price without having a *concept* of price (and the same is true of their treatment of value). Marx naturally recognizes that price is the expression of value, but this is "the exponent of its exchange-ratio with money"[175] and thus there is the possibility of a quantitative disagreement between the two, and this inevitably emerges from the concept of price. Despite lacking the concept of price, Unoists talk about a divergence between price and value. On top of this, they also lack a concept of value. They say that prices do not coincide with value because they fluctuate every day, but in that case they should also recognize that value is not something that is eternally fixed.

Marx is well aware of the fundamental contradiction of commodity production, where value must be expressed as price in terms of the rate of exchange with money. This is also the contradiction inherent to a society where products are produced as commodities. Under this mode of production, the value of a commodity is expressed relatively as price in the rate of exchange with money, rather than directly as labor-time. On the basis of an awareness of this profound contradiction inherent to this mode of production, Marx says that this price-expression of value—and the possibility of a divergence between value and price—is "not a defect, but on the contrary, it makes this form the adequate one for [the capitalist] mode of production,"[176] since this corresponds to the anarchic nature of this form of production. This has nothing in common with the views of Unoists, which amount to a prettifying of commodity production by treating it as something eternal.

Phenomena Should be Purely Considered

Here we need to consider why Marx, while fully recognizing the possibility of a divergence between value and price, proceeds on the basis of the premise that the two are in agreement. In the second section of chapter three, which discusses money as a means of circulation, Marx addresses this issue in the following way:

175. Ibid.
176. Ibid.

Of course, it is also possible, that in C-M-C the two extremes C and C, say corn and clothes, may represent quantitatively different magnitudes of value. The peasant may sell his corn above its value, or may buy the clothes at less than their value. He may, on the other hand, be cheated by the clothes merchant. Yet, for this particular form of circulation, such differences in value are purely accidental. The fact that the corn and the clothes are equivalents does not deprive the process of all sense and meaning, as it does in M-C-M. The equivalence of their values is rather a necessary condition of its normal course.[177]

And in chapter five he writes:

It is true, commodities may be sold at prices which diverge from their values, but this divergence appears as an infringement of the laws governing the exchange of commodities. In its pure form, the exchange of commodities is an exchange of equivalents, and thus it is not a method of increasing value.[178]

In other words, Marx is saying that the transformation of a commodity is mediated by money and at issue is this transformation, not whether it is carried out according to value or not, and thus equivalence between the two is "a necessary condition of its normal course." This is a sound view that is easy to understand, and it is perplexing that Unoists are incapable of understanding such a simple point.

It is also natural that the "exchange of commodities….is not a method of increasing value." To argue that commodity exchange is a means of increasing value, rather than essentially an exchange of equivalents, represents a return to the view held by the mercantilists, which is a theory that exists at a level below that of the classical school, not to mention Marx. It is certainly no accident that Unoists make scant mention of the real source of augmenting value, namely, the exploitation of labor.

The division of labor converts the product of labor into a commodity, and thereby makes necessary its further conversion into money. At the same time, it makes it a matter of chance whether this transubstantiation succeeds or not. Here, however, we have to look at the phenomenon in its pure shape, and must therefore assume it has proceeded normally. In any case, if

177. Ibid., 252.
178. Ibid., 261.

the process is to take place at all, i.e. if the commodity is not impossible to
sell, a change of form must always occur, although there may be an abnormal loss or accretion of substance—that is, of the magnitude of value.[179]

Uno and his followers raise a big fuss, as a sort of leftwing pose, by claiming
that it would amount to beautifying or eternalizing capitalist production to
presuppose that the circulation and metamorphosis of commodities occurs
"normally" or somehow progresses smoothly. In reality, however, they are
completely overlooking one of the fundamental contradictions of capitalist-
commodity production—namely, the contradiction involving the production
of labor-products as commodities and labor taking the form of value.

Obsessed with a superficial, formalistic "contradiction," Unoists criticize
Marx for trivializing or ignoring the fact that there is a quantitative disparity
between value and price, saying that he barely pays any attention to this even
though it represents a fundamental contradiction of capitalist production!
However, the fact that Unoists focus so exclusively on the question of the dis-
crepancy between value and price, only reveals that they adhere to the exceedingly bourgeois position of seeking (the magnitude of) the value-
determination of a commodity within the relations of price fluctuations, supply and demand, subjective desires, and consumption. In believing, mistakenly, that the *magnitude of value* is the central issue, Uno and his followers end
up exposing their fundamentally bourgeois nature!

A Qualitative Contradiction: Price Without Value

At the end of our discussion of money as a measure of value, I would like to
take a look at Marx's idea, expressed in the following passage, that the price-
expression of value "harbors a qualitative contradiction":

> The price-form, however, is not only compatible with the possibility of a
> quantitative incongruity between magnitude of value and price, i.e.
> between the magnitude of value and its own expression in money, but it
> may also harbor a qualitative contradiction, with the result that price ceases
> altogether to express value, despite the fact that money is nothing but the
> value-form of commodities. Things which in and for themselves are not
> commodities, things such as conscience, honor, etc., can be offered for sale
> by their holders, and thus acquire the form of commodities through their

---

179. Ibid., 203.

price. Hence a thing can, formally speaking, have a price without having a value. The expression of price is in this case imaginary, like certain quantities in mathematics. On the other hand, the imaginary price-form may also conceal a real value-relation or one derived from it, as for instance the price of uncultivated land, which is without value because no human labor is objectified in it.[180]

Without the concept of value, as well as the concept of price, the idea that the price-form "harbors a qualitative contradiction"—i.e. that some prices lack the "substance" of value—must seem to be complete gibberish, and this is the perspective of the Uno school and Böhm-Bawerk. Unoists attack Marx's concept of value and badmouth the idea that its substance is determined "from the beginning" as being social human-labor. Their concept of "value" is taken directly from price as it is posited in reality, as a common quantity of a certain magnitude (in yen, dollars, pounds, etc.). They even say that if Marx had defined "value" in this way, his views would never have been subject to the criticism of Böhm-Bawerk and other bourgeois scholars! Incidentally, Böhm-Bawerk's criticism of Marx is as follows:

> From the beginning [Marx] only puts into the sieve those exchangeable things which contain the common property which he desires finally to sift out as "the common factor" [social labor], and he leaves all the others outside....he limits from the outset the field of his search for the substance of the exchange value to "commodities"...and limits it to products of labor as against gifts of nature. Now it stands to reason that if exchange really means an equalization, which assumes the existence of a "common factor of the same amount," this common factor must be sought and found in every species of goods which is brought into exchange, not only in products of labor but also gifts of nature, such as the soil, wood in trees, water power, coal beds, stone quarries, petroleum reserves, mineral waters, gold mines, etc. To exclude the exchangeable goods which are not products of labor in the search for the common factor which lies at the root of exchange value is, under the circumstances, a great error in method.[181]

Not only bourgeois scholars but also Unoists have repeated this view held by Böhm-Bawerk. Uno and his followers insist that what should be examined is not merely the commodity-form of labor-products, but goods in general, any-

180. Ibid., 197.
181. *Karl Marx and the Close of His System*, 70.

thing in general that has a price. They note that natural objects that are not products of labor can also have a price, and therefore profit can be obtained through them. They claim that Marx has thus committed a "methodological" error in dealing only with the commodity as the product of labor, rather than goods in general, or in examining just one part of the wealth of bourgeois society rather than its entirety. This view of Uno and his followers, however, starkly reveals their own theoretical weaknesses, which stem from an inability to distinguish between value and its price-expression or to consider the "quantitative contradiction" that this "harbors." The fact that Unoists completely lack a concept of value accounts for their tendency to spout such nonsense.

Unoists' Theory of Money as the Measure of Value

The views of the Uno school on money as a measure of value are expressed in the following passage of Kamakura Takao:

> Owing to the fact that a commodity cannot indicate its reality as value by itself, the expression of commodity-value by means of money, i.e. price, is nothing more than the unilateral, subjective expression of the commodity's value in a certain quantity of the use-value of gold. Therefore, in terms of this determination, the value of a commodity, as a matter of course, first enjoys a social appraisal when its price is actually expressed and it is transformed into a certain quantity of money. Moreover, since every commodity is fixed in the relative form of value, commodities are unable to actively transform themselves into money. The value of a commodity can only first receive a social evaluation or have its value measured when it is actually purchased for money, which monopolizes the position of being the socially equivalent form and can thus possess the form of being directly exchangeable. Therefore, if the function of the measure of value is unfolded starting from the explanation of the value-form, it is necessary to determine the function of money as a measure of value in terms of being the active function of purchasing commodities with money. But Marx was unable to truly establish the function of money as a measure of value in terms of the unfolding of the determination of the value-form.[182]

Certainly in his theory of the value-form of the commodity, Marx discusses the expression of value, but the commodity is consistently the subject. He clarifies the fact that the commodity-exchange relation is at the same time the

---

182. *Shihon-ron kenkyū*, 1: 151-2.

expression of value, and that with the development of this relation money becomes necessary as the general equivalent form. This is different from pre-supposing money and then saying that by means of money the commodity expresses its own value "ideally" as price (i.e. the function of money as measure of value). Unoists do not understand the distinction between the two at all.

Of course, in terms of dealing with the expression of value, the two sections of *Capital* bear a close relation to each other. Despite this, however, the value-form, where the commodity is the subject, concerns the logic of how the development of the mechanism of value-expression makes money necessary, whereas in the case of the latter, money is the subject, and the question centers on how, as a function of money, the value of a commodity is expressed. The two are inseparable—two sides of the same coin—but at the same time each logically pursues a separate theoretical task.

For Uno, however, the theory of the value-form is said to directly be the expression of the value of a commodity through money. If we look at this alone, it seems that Uno is speaking of the same theoretical task that Marx sets for his theory of money as the measure of value. But in fact Uno is saying something quite different; namely, despite speaking of the price-expression of a commodity's value, Uno sees this as the unilateral, subjective expression of the commodity owner rather than a social appraisal.

But what on earth is Uno trying to say? Formally speaking, this is similar to Marx's theory of money as the measure of value, but in terms of actual content this is nothing more than a commodity owner attaching a price to a commod-ity as an arbitrary, subjective "evaluation" that bears no relation to value—not the "objective" content of the price-expression of value.

Uno, who lacks a concept of value, should not speak of price separate from value, but since his thought is quite alien to scientific logic, such "mundane details" are a matter of complete indifference. In this way, Uno forces a com-pletely distorted theory of the measure of value upon the theory of the value-form, declaring that money as the measure of value concerns measurement by means of purchases, involving the function of money as a means of purchase. By reducing the question of the measure of value to a purely subjective expres-sion on the part of the commodity owner, Uno introduces a nonsensical theory that bears no relation to Marx's own ideas.

9. Money as the Circulating Medium and Inflation

Formal Transformation of the Commodity

One would have thought that the function of money as the means of circulation would be relatively easy to understand, as it involves money's role in mediating the metamorphosis of the commodity, but apparently this is not the case. Many "scholars" are even unable to understand this simple matter (and I am referring of course to the Unoists).

At the beginning of the second section of chapter three, where money's function as a means of circulation is discussed, Marx says that the "exchange of commodities implies contradictory and mutually exclusive conditions" and that the "further development of the commodity does not abolish these contradictions, but rather provides the form within which they have room to move."[183] Here the "exchange of commodities," needless to say, refers to chapter two of *Capital* where Marx discusses how the commodity, as the unity of value and use-value, involves a relation that "implies contradictory and mutually exclusive conditions," and how the formation of money mediates this contradiction.

The passage quoted above, however, already is premised on the formation of money and the transformation of value into price, and discusses instead how this contradiction is resolved or provided the form within which it has the "room to move." Stated in this manner, the issue may sound terribly complicated, but Marx is basically saying that since exchanging commodity A for commodity B—i.e. exchanging one commodity, as is, for another—is problematical directly speaking, this is carried out in the form: C^A-M-C^B.

With the formation of money, exchange is divided into two processes: a sale (C^A-M) and a purchase ($M-C^B$). In this way, the commodity owner does not directly exchange his own commodity for the desired commodity, but rather first exchanges it for money, and through this mediation the money is then used to carry out an exchange for the desired commodity.

Explained in this way some readers may be wondering what all of the fuss is about, since this is a very ordinary act that people engage in every day. But the point here is to "reflect" on this phenomenon. Already we are familiar with the

183. *Capital*, vol. 1, 198.

significance of the transformation of the commodity into money as well as the nature of money. In handing over a commodity as a use-value, the labor that is expended on the production of the commodity is demonstrated to be socially-useful labor, and thus the commodity takes on the socially appropriate form of value, becoming money. This is precisely why the commodity owner, by transforming his own commodity into money, is now able to exchange the money for any desired commodity. It is true that this is something we do on a daily basis, but here, instead of simply discussing this as a phenomenon, Marx is considering, among other things, what money is and the significance of the transformation of value into price, thereby profoundly reflecting on the commodity and commodity-exchange. He notes, for example:

> This change of form has been very imperfectly grasped as yet, owing to the circumstance that, quite apart from the lack of clarity in the concept of value itself, every change of form in a commodity results from the exchange of two commodities, namely an ordinary commodity and the money commodity. If we keep in mind only this material aspect, that is, the exchange of the commodity for gold, we overlook the very thing we ought to observe, namely what has happened to the form of the commodity. We do not see that gold, as a mere commodity, is not money, and that the other commodities, through their prices, themselves relate to gold as the medium for expressing their own shape in money.[184]

This passage seems to have been almost expressly written to enlighten Uno and his followers. At issue is not, for example, that C^A–M is a "purchase with money," but that the price of C^A is realized, and gold is precisely the shape of the value of the commodity itself. In other words, it is important to understand that C^A–M is not merely one commodity being exchanged for gold as another commodity, but rather is the commodity's *change of form*, as the actual transformation of the shape of the commodity's own value, which had already existed ideally.

Is the "Subject" the Commodity or Money?

In discussing money as a means of circulation, Unoists adopt the peculiar approach of considering whether the "subject" is the commodity or money. They criticize Marx for having obscured the fact that money is naturally the

---

184. Ibid., 199.

subject, and for having focused mainly on the commodity instead. This is the idea, in other words, that the latter half of the formula C^A–M–C^B—namely, the purchase—is of greater significance.

> When the commodity is sold and turned into money, this cannot be said to be the metamorphosis of value because the initiative here is not on the side of the commodity. Since C–M is carried out as the reverse side of M–C, and it is the side of M–C that brings about the active movement, the commodity is unable to change into money on its own initiative, whereas it can be said that money is transformed into a commodity.[185]

Unoists say that M–C^B is the "active" side of the formula, compared to C^A–M, and thus the significance of money is made clear. They emphasize that in the case of C^A–M, there is no possible way for the commodity to seek out its own exchange with money, and claim that, "precisely by clarifying that the M–C link of money for commodity completes the circuit of C–M–C, money as the circulating medium is also elucidated."[186] But these Unoist scholars are quite incapable of understanding that the question here concerns a "social metabolism"(and its bourgeois form) and therefore Marx only considers "the whole process in its formal aspect, that is to say, the change in form or the metamorphosis of commodities through which the social metabolism is mediated."[187]

The commodity producer cannot personally consume the commodity produced, because although it is a value for the producer it is not a use-value for him. This commodity, therefore, has to undergo the metamorphosis of C^A–M–C^B, and as long as a commodity exists as such this is self-evident. When dealing with this issue of the form of metamorphosis, it is completely beside the point to bring up the issue of whether the amount of value changes in this process or not, or whether or not this transformation will actually takes place. These points, in other words, are abstracted from. It is for this reason that Marx describes the quantity of value as remaining unchanged in this transformation process, saying that the process must be considered in its pure form.

If we are going to bring up the question of what is the "subject"—commodity or money?—naturally this would be the commodity. Unoists expose an

---

185. *Shihon-ron kenkyū*, vol. 1: 284.
186. Ibid.
187. *Capital*, vol. 1, 198-9.

inability to grasp the theoretical task being addressed when they criticize Marx on the basis of their view that the active side of the formula is $M–C^B$ because the central moment concerns "purchasing with money" and it is money that is being discussed. They display an irrational attitude on an essential level, adopting a view premised on purchases without sales (or people who buy without selling anything), the *a priori* existence of the possession of money. Marx, however, notes:

> The conversion of a commodity into money is the conversion of money into a commodity. The single-process is two-sided: from one pole, that of the commodity-owner, it is a sale, from the other pole, that of the money-owner, it is a purchase. In other words, a sale is a purchase, C-M is also M-C.[188]

Unoists completely lack such awareness, and thus one-dimensionally emphasize the purchase even though this at the same time is a sale.

> Up to this point we have considered only one economic relation between men, a relation between owners of commodities in which they appropriate the produce of the labor of others by alienating [*entfremden*] the produce of their own labor. Hence, for one commodity-owner to meet with another, in the form of a money-owner, it is necessary either that the product of the latter should possess by its nature the form of money...or that his product should already have changed its skin and stripped off its original form of a useful object.[189]

There is no room within this for the introduction of people who possess money without working themselves, or those who earn a "wage" by depending upon the bourgeoisie (such as Unoist university professors!)—that is to say, people who buy without selling, and consume without producing. This, incidentally, happens to be an apt description of the parasitical class within modern monopoly capitalism, i.e. the petty bourgeoisie and their theoretical champions!

---

188. Ibid., 203.
189. Ibid., 203-4.

Quantity of the Means of Circulation

Is there a quantity of the means of circulation in Japan, or any given country, that could be said to be necessary, objectively speaking? The answer, of course, is *yes*. And this is natural as long as commodities are circulating. One would have imagined that this point is self-evident, but apparently this is not the case.

Raising the question of the socially necessary volume of the circulating medium also naturally brings up the issue of the total price of commodities. Because price is the ideal expression of commodity-value through money, here the volume of the means of circulation is already posited. In other words, the volume of the means of circulation is determined by the sum of the prices of commodities to be realized.

But some are perplexed by this view. The Uno school, for example, does not recognize this concept of the objective sum of the prices of commodities. They claim, first of all, that the price of a commodity is something subjective, which stems from competition between buyers and sellers, rather than being determined as a social, objective thing. Needless to say, if the objectivity of the sum of commodity prices is rejected in this way, the idea of a necessary quantity of circulation means becomes a completely empty concept.

In addition to the sum of commodity prices, the quantity of the circulating medium is also determined by the *velocity* at which money circulates. If the sum of the prices of commodities is one million yen, and this is realized in five consecutive transactions of 200,000 yen, the total amount of money necessary would be 200,000 yen rather than one million yen. Thus, the quantity of money functioning as the means of circulation for a given period of the circulation process is determined by the sum of the prices of the commodities in circulation divided by the average velocity of the circulation of money.

The volume of the necessary means of circulation will be greater to the extent that the sum of commodity prices in the numerator is greater, the prices of the individual commodities are greater, and/or the speed of money circulation is slower. Needless to say, the opposite would result under the opposite circumstances, and there are a variety of combinations that determine the quantity of money actually needed.

Marx emphasizes that first there is the sum of the prices of commodities, and that this then determines the quantity of money necessary—rather than the quantity of money determining the sum of commodity prices.

The law, that the quantity of the circulating medium is determined by the sum of the prices of the commodities in circulation, and the average velocity of the circulation of money, may also be stated as follows: given the sum of the values of commodities, and the average rapidity of their metamorphoses, the quantity of money or of the material of money in circulation depends on its own value. The illusion that it is, on the contrary, prices which are determined by the quantity of the circulating medium, and that the latter for its part depends on the amount of monetary material which happens to be present in a country, had its roots in the absurd hypothesis adopted by the original representatives of this view that commodities enter into the process of circulation without a price, and money enters without a value, and that, once they have entered circulation, an aliquot part of the medley of commodities is exchanged for an aliquot part of the heap of precious metals.[190]

The illusion that prices are "determined by the quantity of the circulating medium, and that the latter for its part depends on the amount of monetary material which happens to be present in a country," is generally referred to as the *quantity theory of money*. According to this view, the price of commodities is determined by the quantity of money. In other words, if the quantity of money were doubled, commodity prices would also double, whereas if the quantity of money were cut in half, commodity prices would also be reduced by half. This sort of illusion arises, of course, because the concept of commodity-value is either lacking or vague.

The notion that a commodity without a price and money without value enter into circulation, come into contact with each other and are exchanged, which at the same time "determines" price, is nonsensical—from both a realistic and a theoretical standpoint. But in criticizing Marx, the Uno school comes very close to the vulgar quantity theory of money in insisting that the commodity itself has no price without being purchased with money. (Incidentally, this issue of the quantity of the means of circulation is closely connected to the understanding of inflation, and thus has particularly important significance.)

Substitution of Tokens of Value

Up to now, we have discussed money as a metallic substance, whereas today the money actually in circulation does not appear as such. Metallic money has

---

190. Ibid., 219-20.

been replaced by Bank of Japan notes. Strictly speaking, paper money and Bank of Japan notes (banknotes) are quite different—both in their origin and nature—but Bank of Japan notes have become a *quasi* paper money, and for the time being we will discuss such banknotes as if they circulate as paper money.

Paper money, unlike money with intrinsic value, is of course valueless, but this does not prevent it from being a means of commodity exchange, referred to by Marx as "tokens of value." Since the replacement of money by such tokens is the absolute precondition for inflation, we need to look at this in some detail.

Marx says that the potential for money to be transformed into tokens of value already exists when money takes the form of coins. Coins appear, not as gold bullion, but as pieces of gold bearing a money-name of so many yen, dollars, etc. Here a quantity of gold is given a certain name. Thus "the business of coining, like the establishment of a standard of price, is an attribute proper to the state."[191] To take a concrete example, 1 yen is set at 2 *fun* (0.75g) of gold, so that 2 *fun* of gold is called 1 yen. This means that a commodity equivalent to 2 *fun* of gold will have a price of 1 yen.

In the course of circulation, however, coins are gradually worn down so as to "transform the coin into a symbol of its official metallic content." In other words, a 1-yen coin, which is supposed to weigh 0.75g of gold, will in fact only weigh 0.7g. In this way the "function of gold as coin becomes completely independent of the metallic value of that gold" and therefore "things that are relatively without value, such as paper notes, can serve as coins in its place."[192]

It is possible for gold to be replaced by tokens that are themselves lacking in value because "the function of gold as coin becomes completely independent of the metallic value of that gold." In the process of commodity exchange, money only functions momentarily. For this reason, it is possible for money to separate from its metallic substance and take on a "purely functional mode of existence."[193]

> The presentation of the exchange-value of a commodity as an independent entity is here only a transient aspect of the process. The commodity is immediately replaced again by another commodity. Hence in this process

191. Ibid., 222.
192. Ibid.
193. Ibid. 223.

which continually makes money pass from hand to hand, it only needs to lead a symbolic existence. Its functional existence so to speak absorbs its material existence.[194]

Thus it becomes possible for the circulation of paper money to replace the circulation of gold. Of course this is possible, but for this to *necessarily* occur certain historical conditions must emerge, including the shift to the monopoly-stage of capitalism and the abnormal intensifications of capitalist contradictions and disequilibria. Unlike metallic money, Marx says that tokens of value render the reality of capitalism even more complicated and difficult to understand.

> In the circulation of tokens of value all the laws governing the circulation of real money seem to be reversed and turned upside down. Gold circulates because it has value, whereas paper has value because it circulates. If the exchange-value of commodities is given, the quantity of gold in circulation depends on its value, whereas the value of paper tokens depends on the number of tokens in circulation. The amount of gold in circulation increases or decreases with the rise or fall of commodity-prices, whereas commodity-prices seem to rise or fall with the changing amount of paper in circulation. The circulation of commodities can absorb only a certain quantity of gold currency, the alternating contraction and expansion of the volume of money in circulation manifesting itself accordingly as an inevitable law, whereas any amount of paper money seems to be absorbed by circulation
>
> These laws indeed appear not only to be turned upside down in the circulation of tokens of value but even annulled; for the movements of paper money, when it is issued in the appropriate amount, are not characteristic of it as token of value, whereas its specific movements are due to infringements of its correct proportion to gold, and do not directly arise from the metamorphosis of commodities.[195]

These points raised by Marx are extremely important, and are essential to the discussion of inflation.

---

194. Ibid., 226.
195. *A Contribution to the Critique of Political Economy*, 356.

Definition of Inflation

A theoretical explanation of inflation is already provided, in a classic form, in both *Capital* and *A Contribution to the Critique of Political Economy.*

> If the quantity of paper money represents twice the amount of gold available, then in practice £1 will be the money-name not of 1/4 of an ounce of gold, but 1/8 of an ounce. The effect is the same as if an alteration had taken place in the function of gold as the standard of prices. The values previously expressed in the price of £1 would now be expressed by the price of £2.[196]

> Let us assume that £14 million is the amount of gold required for the circulation of commodities and that the State throws 210 million notes each called £1 into circulation: these 210 million would then stand for a total of gold worth £14 million. The effect would be the same as if the notes issued by the State were to represent a metal whose value was one-fifteenth that of gold or that each note was intended to represent one-fifteenth of the previous weight of gold. This would have changed nothing but the nomenclature of the standard of prices…As the name pound sterling would now indicate one-fifteenth of the previous quantity of gold, all commodity-prices would be fifteen times higher and 210 million pound notes would now be indeed just as necessary as 14 million had previously been. The decrease in the quantity of gold which each individual token of value represented would be proportional to the increased aggregate value of these tokens. The rise of prices would be merely a reaction of the process of circulation, which forcibly placed the tokens of value on a par with the quantity of gold which they are supposed to replace in the sphere of circulation."[197]

This passage may be difficult to understand since it refers to English currency and prices, and because Marx is referring to the quantity of money in England at the time, but what he is saying is quite simple.

Suppose, for example, that 100,000kg of gold are necessary for commodity circulation and there is one trillion yen of paper money in circulation (so that 1 yen = 1mg of gold), and that the government issues another one trillion yen of paper money, with which various things are purchased. There is now two trillion yen of paper money in circulation, and 1 yen is equal to 0.5mg of gold

---

196. *Capital*, vol. 1, 225.
197. *A Contribution to the Critique of Political Economy*, 354.

rather than 1mg, meaning that there has been a *depreciation* in the value of money. The amount of paper money circulating has increased from one to two trillion yen, but the necessary money for circulation remains 100,000kg of gold. Thus, 1mg of gold now represents 2 yen of paper money rather than 1 yen.

When such a depreciation of the value of currency occurs, commodity prices will naturally appreciate. The value of a commodity becomes a price by being expressed in a certain quantity of gold, but now since 1 yen is equal to 0.5mg of gold rather than 1mg, commodity prices undergo a two-fold increase. The exact same commodity now exchanges for twice the amount of money. This is not, however, the result of an increase in the value of the commodity or because the value of gold has fallen, as the premise here is that both of these have remained unchanged. Rather, this is the result of 1 yen now being the monetary name for 0.5mg of gold instead of 1 mg of gold, so that the same value once expressed in a price of 1 yen is now expressed as 2 yen.

Although it can thus be said that inflation is an appreciation in prices due to the depreciation of money, which stems from paper money being thrown into circulation in excess of the volume of money necessary for circulation, if we look at the content of inflation itself, this only means that there has been a change in the method of designating the measurement standard of price.

We have already spoken of the role of money as a standard of price. That is, with the value of a commodity coming to be manifested in a quantity of gold (i.e. "price"), a unit of calculation is necessary to compare such quantities of gold, which results in the need to set some standard of price, such as 1mg of gold being equal to 1 yen, etc. The example above, where this standard changes from 1mg of gold being equal to 1 yen, to 0.5mg being equal to 1 yen[198]—a *de facto* devaluation of the standard of price—concerns the fundamental definition of inflation.

Inflation is certainly not merely a price appreciation or a value depreciation of gold-money. Prices can increase as a result of an increase in the value of commodities, but inflation is characterized instead by price increases without any change in the value of commodities.

---

198. This takes place naturally or "economically" rather than by legal means.

Inflation Benefits Debtors

We have noted that, abstractly speaking, inflation is an actual decrease in the standard of price, that is to say, a simple rise in prices. This is the fact, for example, that a product that once sold for 10,000 yen, now comes to have a price of 20,000 yen despite its value remaining unchanged. One would imagine, then, that inflation would have no real impact. But this is certainly not the case. Indeed, inflation has an enormous and complex impact on both society as a whole, and on the various social classes within society. Inflation is a process, namely a continual rise in prices, but rather than affecting all commodities simultaneously, the increase will be more pronounced for certain commodities and slower for others, and this is a fundamental aspect of inflation. We now need to take a look at the direct impact inflation has on economic relations.

Consider, for example, the relation between debtors and creditors, which is directly affected by inflation. Generally speaking, inflation benefits those who have borrowed money (debtors), while it harms those who are lending it out (creditors). A person who has borrowed one million yen will thus benefit from a drop in the value of money. If the value of this sum of money is cut in half by inflation, the debt will also in fact be reduced by half, so it is as if that portion of the debt were eliminated altogether. This means that interest rates will increase under inflation, but in the event of rampant inflation such increases cannot keep pace with the depreciation of paper money, and ultimately there will no longer be anyone willing to loan money. If this occurs, not only normal economic accounting, but also credit relations would come unhinged and collapse. This means that promissory transactions, sale on credit, and monthly installment sales would become extremely risky. And if the credit system collapses, it is clear that bourgeois society would likewise be in a state of collapse.

Various types of people borrow money, but the largest and steadiest debtor is the bourgeois state itself. Today the state does not directly put paper money into circulation, but through the issuing of state bonds (borrowing) it is able to cover its enormous budget deficits. The Japanese state is already burdened with an enormous debt (in national bonds) totaling hundreds of trillions of yen. This is roughly equivalent in scale to three annual budgets.[199] With the

---

199. Today [1998] this figure is over 200 trillion yen. [By the end of 2003, outstanding government debt in Japan reached a total 670.12 trillion yen.]

advance of inflation, however, an enormous state debt can be turned into nothing. And in fact this policy of borrowing prepares the way for inflation and encourages it (to the extent that this is connected to the increased issuing of currency). The bourgeois state has the convenient method of borrowing a large sum of money and then wiping it out on its own.

This is clearly not just simply a question of abstract theory. In the past, the imperialist bourgeois state of Japan borrowed enormous sums of money to fund its war effort—through the issuing of war bonds, etc.—but following the war rampant inflation wiped the slate clean and freed the state from its burden of massive debt. In this sense, the state became "free" and unencumbered, and this was one of the key moments constituting postwar capitalist development and prosperity. But those who believed they were helping the war effort, giving up their yen to buy war bonds or deposit money in postal accounts, were treated as fools. The government paper that was supposed to have great value became completely worthless just a few years after the war.

Under inflation, creditors definitely come out on the losing end. In the case of large finance capital, however, it is both a creditor and a debtor, and even as a creditor receives trillions of yen in interest from the state every year, thus making out quite well. The ones who suffer the most are those who have their small savings in bank accounts, those small-scale capitalists and members of the petty bourgeoisie who purchase state bonds, i.e. the "middle-classes." Under the imperialist state, there is an increase in the number of people who live off of interest, but inflation deals them a heavy blow. This is why Keynes referred to inflation as the "euthanasia of the *rentier* class."

Inflation and Social Classes

It is clear that the greatest beneficiary of inflation is the bourgeois state. If one trillion yen is in circulation, and then an additional one trillion yen is added, the value of money would be halved (and prices doubled), but the state would be able to make one trillion yen in purchases (free of charge!). This method can be used for the sake of waging war or dealing with an economic crisis, etc. As Keynes noted, a state that should collapse is able to survive using this method. This is in fact nothing but taxation in a different form. The characteristic of such taxation is that no one is aware of its exact rate or when it is levied, and it takes place on an unprecedented scale. Compared to the sort of plunder carried out via inflation, even a large increase in the general consumption tax appears as nothing.

In an inflationary period, the industrial bourgeoisie and farmers tend to fare well. With prices constantly rising, they are able to obtain a special profit. Before they sell their products they must make purchases, but with inflation they are able to sell products at high prices that would have been unthinkable at the time raw materials and production means were purchased, and this contributes to their profits. Thus an increase in prices has always been a great stimulus to the business activities of the bourgeoisie. In this way, even if a company runs up a huge debt, enormous profits can be made. An inflationary period is thus a period of thriving business and booms (if we set aside the question of whether this is long-lasting or simply an economic bubble). New members of the bourgeoisie enter the scene in search of quick profits, while some of its established members, particularly small-scale money capitalists, are ruined.

How does the class of wage-workers, those who make a living by selling their own labor-power, fare under inflation? Workers sell the only commodity in their possession, their labor-power, but increases in the price of this commodity tend to lag behind the price increases of other commodities. A rise in wages does not keep up with the increase in product prices, always lagging behind instead. Moreover, unlike capitalists, workers are not in a position to stock up on raw materials. Most of their food necessities are purchased on a day-to-day basis, meaning that workers suffer mercilessly from inflation.

Of course, the impact from inflation does not hit every segment of the working class equally. In postwar Japan, for example, under the system of "priority production," workers in the steel, coal, and electric industries—those productive workers supporting the basis of social life—were guaranteed special incentive wages, whereas school teachers and other "civil servants," who receive more favorable treatment today, had very few pay raises. Moreover, compared to the wages of organized workers who were able to fight against capitalists for increases in pay, the wages of unorganized workers at small- and medium-sized companies were very slow to rise.

Already in 1923, Keynes wrote that "inflation is unjust and deflation is inexpedient" but that "of the two perhaps deflation is, if we rule out exaggerated inflations such as that of Germany, the worse; because it is worse, in an impoverished world, to provoke unemployment than to disappoint the *rentier*."[200] Both inflation and deflation are a problem, but Keynes felt that inflation was preferable—particularly in the case of "limited and flexible" currency inflation—because, despite harming the *rentier* class, it is a means of maintaining business prosperity and countering unemployment.

Today reformists and trade unionists (the "centrist" Socialist and Communist parties) cite this same reason in support of inflationary policies over deflationary ones, while keeping up appearances by claiming that this is a policy to expand domestic demand "for the sake of the people" rather than being in the interests of capital.

But in reality, inflation by fiscal and circulatory means is the plundering of the masses on an enormous scale, and is indeed a manifestation of the sort of exorbitant taxation that typifies or symbolizes modern-day capitalism. The basis for this is paper money taking the place of money tokens. Inflation generalizes to all classes the contradictions of capitalism, intensifies class divisions, propels forward the dissolution of society, and thus paves the way for a major social transformation.

10. The Exploitation of Labor

Contradictions of the Concept of "Capital"

The end of the examination of the commodity marks the beginning of the examination of capital—the question of the commodification of labor-power, the exploitation of labor, and the mechanism of this exploitation. Based of our examination of the commodity up to this point, we now need to move on to address these topics.

In its most abstract form, capital is M–C–M', or self-valorizing value. Given the prevalence of vulgar Unoist theories today, we need to begin by recognizing that the existence of capital is completely dependent upon commodity circulation. The direct form of commodity circulation, as we have already seen, is C–M–C, but commodity circulation also has another aspect, M–C–M (buying in order to sell). At first glance this latter form seems to lack content, since if we purchase a commodity for one million yen and sell it for the same sum of money, we obviously end up with the one million yen that we started off with. In the case of C–M–C, it is clear that the commodity a person comes away with is different from the initial commodity, whereas M–C–M by itself is completely vacuous, since no person is willing to carry out a sale and purchase to end up with the same amount of money. Thus, M–C–M

---

200. John Maynard Keynes, *A Tract on Monetary Reform* (Amherst: Prometheus Books, 2000), 40.

must necessarily move on to M–C–M' (so that, for example, the initial 1 million yen becomes 1.15 million yen). In this sense, M–C–M itself can already be considered capital in terms of its nature; that is, capital can only emerge and develop based on the condition of C–M–C (commodity circulation).

> The circulation of commodities is the starting-point of capital. The production of commodities and their circulation in its developed form, namely trade, form the historic presuppositions under which capital arises. World trade and the world market date from the sixteenth century, and from then on the modern history of capital starts to unfold.[201]

Against the Uno school, we must emphasize that the commodity forms the starting point of capital, both historically and as the practical—and therefore theoretical—premise. Unoists, however, insist on explaining "capital" without first establishing the concept or definition of the commodity.[202] And we can only respond to such an approach by saying that their understanding of "scientific theory" has no connection to actual social relations, and amounts to nothing more than a meaningless and idealistic theory. Any Marxist would know that the commodification of labor-power is a direct moment determining the existence of capital as such, but it would be ridiculous to think that this is possible apart from commodity circulation or without the real historical conditions of commodity circulation.

The first phenomenal form of capital is money, but this is actually the final outcome of commodity circulation. The development of commodity circulation is the development of the value-form, and therefore money becomes necessary, and historically this is connected to the development of merchant capital and interest-bearing capital. Marx points out, however, that in order to recognize money as the first phenomenal form of capital it is not necessary to review the history of the formation of capital, because:

---

201. *Capital*, vol. 1, 247.
202. For instance, Unoists play around with the plausible yet empty notion that the commodification of labor-power (which "was not originally a commodity") is the moment that determines capital as such, or argue that the concept of the commodity is only posited through establishing the concept of capital (which is also said to make the determination of value possible), etc.

Every day the same story is played out before our eyes. Even up to the present day, all new capital, in the first instance, steps onto the stage—i.e. the market, whether in the commodity-market, the labor-market, or the money-market—in the shape of money, money which has to be transformed into capital by definite processes.[203]

In a sense, commodity circulation and the movement of capital are exact opposites. Commodity circulation is a "metabolism" involving objects that are useful to human beings, and when commodities are thrown out of circulation to enter the consumption process they are also divested of their commodity determination, whereas money *qua* capital appears as a body in perpetual motion that continues its self-valorization. Here the social metabolism or metamorphosis of the commodity is not the aim, but rather a means of self-valorizing capital.

However, as we have seen, the exchange process of commodities is an exchange of equivalents, and this process itself does not increase value. Surplus-value cannot be derived from the process of circulation. Even if one brings up the fact of nominal price hikes it is of little use, since this only benefits one party at the expense of another. Such a method—i.e. the theory of "profit upon alienation"—cannot scientifically account for surplus-value, which does not emerge from the circulation of commodities. The circulation of commodities as the exchange of equivalents cannot create surplus-value, and this is a major contradiction that we now need to consider.

Commodification of Labor-Power

Even though capital must emerge within commodity circulation, which it then mediates, as long as the circulation of commodities is an exchange of equivalents, capital (or self-valorizing value) is not possible. This means that the capitalist must be fortunate enough to find within the market "a commodity whose use-value possesses the peculiar property of being a source of value, whose actual consumption is therefore itself an objectification [*Vergegenständlichung*] of labor, hence a creation of value."[204]

Does such a commodity actually exist? We have already seen that commodities exist as such as the unity of use-value and (exchange-) value. But use-value and value are qualitatively distinct from each other, and cannot be

---

203. Ibid., 247.
204. Ibid., 270.

reduced to a common factor. Is it truly possible for a commodity to exist whose "use-value is the source of value"?

Marx shows us that such a commodity does indeed exist! This commodity is "labor capacity" or what he simply refers to as "labor-power." Since the use-value of labor-power is "labor" itself, this is certainly the source of value. The money-owner purchases the labor-power commodity on the market, and through the (productive) "consumption" of this commodity he is able to generate surplus-value, and in this way the money-owner emerges as a capitalist.

For labor-power to emerge on the market as a commodity various conditions must be met. Marx notes that workers must appear who are free in a double sense. This means that the worker "as a free individual can dispose of his labor-power as his own commodity, and that, on the other hand, he has no other commodity for sale, i.e. he is rid of them, he is free of all the objects needed for the realization [*Verwirklichung*] of his labor-power."[205] In one respect workers are "free" personalities compared to serfs in feudal society. They are human beings who have been freed from the fetters of feudal rank and possess the right to "freely" sell their own labor-power. This indicates the superior position of the wage-worker compared to the feudal serf, which represents a great historical advance.

At the same time, however, workers are severed from the means of production (land, machinery, and raw materials), and in this sense are also "free." Without these means of production at their disposal, workers are unable to work or make a living, and for this reason in Japanese they were [once] referred to as *musansha*.[206] In order to survive, the only recourse for workers is to somehow be united with the means of production and subsistence, but workers exists as entities that have been "freed" from the actual resources needed to directly realize their own labor-power. This second sense of being "free" determines the position of the worker in capitalist society as a wage-laborer or "civilized slave."

Although the expression "free in two senses" is used, this can be understood as two sides of the same coin in terms of the position of wage-workers. On the one hand, historically speaking, wage-workers are "free" and liberated com-

---

205. Ibid., 273.
206. [*Musansha* is the Japanese word for "proletariat" that was commonly
      used in the early twentieth century, which literally means "a person with
      no property." Today the foreign loan word *puroretaria* is more commonly
      used.]

pared to the direct producers under feudalism, and this represents a step forward. But seen from another angle, workers lead a wretched existence since they are "free" of the means of production and subsistence, and can only survive by selling their labor-power as a commodity.

When the owners of money, who are thus the owners of the means of production and subsistence, find this kind of "free worker" on the market, capital is established. Thus, although capital presupposes commodity circulation and the circulation of money, it cannot emerge on this basis alone. This is clear from the fact that ancient civilizations, such as Greece and Rome, fell into decline prior to the development of capitalism despite the existence of commodities and the circulation of money (this is a point Unoists in particular should note). In other words, as Marx points out, the capitalist epoch is "characterized by the fact that labor-power, in the eyes of the worker himself, takes on the form of a commodity which is his property; his labor consequently takes on the form of wage-labor."[207]

Particularity of Capitalist Exploitation

In reading Marx's explanation of the exploitation of labor, some may find it strange that he brings up the issue of labor-power being a commodity, and thus also having an exchange-value and use-value, or that he feels it necessary to use the roundabout expression of labor being the use-value of the labor-power commodity, "whose use-value possesses the peculiar property of being a source of value."[208] It may seem adequate, in a more straightforward manner, to say that capital exploits workers and extracts surplus-value by forcing them to perform labor in the production process that exceeds necessary labor.

The question here, however, is not exploitation in general, but capitalist exploitation, and we need to consider the *form* in which the exploitation of labor is carried out. If one only says, in general terms, that surplus-labor is extracted in the production process, it would not be clear how this differs, for instance, from the exploitation of serfs by feudal landowners. And without clarifying this specific difference, the working class certainly cannot become aware of its own real historical position so as to correctly and resolutely wage its struggles.

---

207. Ibid., 274.
208. Ibid., 270.

The particularity of exploitation under capitalism centers on the fact that it is concealed by the surface "economic relations" (market relations). Here "economic relations"—as we must clearly point out for the sake of Unoists—refers to the principles of commodity exchange, where the relation between capitalists and workers appears to be a relation based on equal exchange between owners of equivalent commodities, an exchange-relation of equivalents. Exploitation is concealed by this commodity-exchange form, which is a decisive characteristic of capitalist exploitation.

Workers sell labor-power as their own commodity to capitalists, and the wage that is paid to them by the capitalist is equivalent to this commodity. In this sense, the capitalist here cannot be said to be tricking the workers or exploiting them. The worker, in turn, uses the money received from the capitalist as the equivalent of labor-power in order to purchase means of consumption from other capitalists, and in principle this exchange is carried out according to value with no exploitation taking place. This exchange relation functions completely in accordance with the law of value, and to this extent is no different from the exchange of normal commodities between two commodity owners. The worker, personally speaking, is "free" and only connected to the capitalist through the exchange relation. In other words, this is not a relation of personal dependence but rather a "contractual relation" whereby the worker sells the labor-power he possesses rather than selling himself as a commodity.

The fact that the relation between capitalists and workers is hidden by an "economic relation" is manifested not only in the relation between both parties in the market but also in the outcome of exploitation. That is, one decisive characteristic of capitalist exploitation is that surplus-labor takes the form of being one part of value, i.e. the form of surplus-value (profit).

Few are aware of the fact that surplus-labor takes the form of surplus-value (profit), or even that profit is, to begin with, a particular historical form of surplus-labor. Thus, even if people are able to see that labor-power appears as a commodity, they cannot understand the profound significance of this, only viewing it as an example of human alienation. Members of the Uno school even say that "the fundamental contradiction of capitalism is the commodification of labor-power, which was originally not a commodity," which is essentially an example of their liberal "humanism."

The fact that labor-power appears as a commodity in the first place is ultimately the outcome of value being transformed into a subject *qua* self-valorizing value (capital), so that all other commodities (machinery, raw materials, etc.) are forced into the role of merely being a means of self-valorizing value. Both capital and the commodification of labor-power are made necessary by the broad development of commodity production and circulation, while on the other hand the commodification of labor-power makes it possible for commodity production to become generalized. Precisely because capitalist production is the production of commodities (value), it is also the production of capital (surplus-value). Everything is reduced to the relation of value, which is one of the reasons why labor-power must also present itself as a "commodity" (as a value-thing!).

Value-Determination of Labor-Power

In the previous section we saw that in capitalism the human labor capacity—"the aggregate of those mental and physical capabilities existing in the physical form, the living personality, of a human being, capabilities which he sets in motion whenever he produces a use-value of any kind"[209]—becomes a "commodity," which is to say it becomes a value-thing [*Wertding*]. However, since human labor-power itself is neither a "thing" nor a product (useful object), it is not directly the outcome of social labor. Here we need to consider what form, exactly, the value-determination of labor-power takes, since without a value-determination it cannot be a value-thing.

To the extent that labor-power is also a commodity, its value-determination is like that of commodities in general, with the value of the labor-power commodity being the social labor necessary for its reproduction. What is necessary for the "reproduction" of labor-power, however, is not social labor directly speaking, but the materials of subsistence consumed by the worker. In capitalist society these means of consumption also assume the commodity-form. This means that the value of labor-power can be reduced to the value of a certain sum of the means of subsistence, and thus labor-power also has a value-determination (in this "roundabout way").

We can see that the value-determination of labor-power presupposes the value-determination of general commodities—or what could be called the "law of value"—and that this determination is carried out indirectly through this mediation, rather than directly as in the case of commodities in general. This is natural, if one stops to consider it, since labor-power is not the outcome of human productive activity, but rather its *subject* or premise (although

---

209. Ibid., 270.

in a sense labor-power can also be considered the outcome or fruit of human productive activity).

Unoists fail to grasp this particular character of the labor-power commodity. Instead, they randomly offer up the silly notion—which they consider to be "true science"—that the value-determination of the labor-power commodity is the premise for the value-determination of commodities in general. This, in other words, is the idea that one must first determine the value of the labor-power commodity, and this then "spreads out" to include the value-determination of commodities in general. Here we cannot examine this view in detail, but it is worth noting that this is similar to the view held by Adam Smith and Thomas Malthus.[210]

The fact that the value-determination of the labor-value commodity is mediated by the value-determination of the means of subsistence that workers consume naturally adds a certain quantitative particularity to this value-determination, in addition to its qualitative particularity.

> His natural needs, such as food, clothing, fuel and housing vary according the climatic and other physical peculiarities of his country. On the other hand, the number and extent of his so-called necessary requirements, as also the manner in which they are satisfied, are themselves products of history, and depend therefore to a great extent on the level of civilization attained by a country; in particular they depend on the conditions in which, and consequently on the habits and expectations with which, the class of free workers has been formed. In contrast, therefore, with the case of other commodities, the determination of the value of labor-power contains a historical and moral element. Nevertheless, in a given country at a given period, the average amount of the means of subsistence necessary for the worker is a known *datum*.[211]

This passage is extremely important. The value of labor-power is reducible to the value of its reproduction, i.e. the value of the minimum means of subsistence necessary for its reproduction, but this magnitude is flexible and changeable to some extent, unlike the value of general commodities, which scientifically speaking concerns the social labor "objectified" in them. Of course, this value cannot rise to the point that the exploitation of labor—the

---

210. On this point Uno does not hesitate to say that his views are the same as those of Adam Smith.
211. Ibid., 275.

extraction of unpaid labor—becomes impossible, or is even fundamentally threatened, but it can change to some extent depending on the "cultural and moral" factors in a given country, as well as the power-relation between capital and wage-labor.

This is precisely the reason why Marxists, who explain the value of labor-power as an objective thing, reject the "iron-law of wages" espoused by Proudhon or Ferdinand Lasalle (which only serves the interests of capital), and recognize the significance of labor unions and workers' economic struggles. Marx's theory, at the same time, clarifies the limitations of the trade-union movement and underlines the necessity for workers to advance toward revolutionary political struggles.

"Labor-Power Not Originally a Commodity" (Uno)

Uno and his followers go on at great length about the labor-power commodity, claiming that the fundamental contradiction of capitalism is the commodification of labor-power, which was not "originally" a commodity. The Unoist view that the labor-power commodity is not an "original commodity" in fact presupposes the concept of commodities in the original or genuine sense, i.e. the commodity in general as essentially determined by the labor theory of value. It would seem encouraging that they have managed to draw some distinction between the commodity in general and the labor-power commodity.

At the same time, however, Unoists consistently emphasize that anything with a price is a commodity. Along with Böhm-Bawerk, they attack Marx's labor theory of value, saying that Marx, by providing the value-determination of the commodity "from the beginning" of *Capital*, is unable to determine other types of commodities. According to this line of reasoning, had Marx simply defined the commodity as anything with a price—i.e. defined it as a "circulation-form"—he would not have been criticized by Böhm-Bawerk.

This logic implies that it is *not* possible to draw a distinction between general commodities and the labor-power commodity, with the former being original commodities and the latter not being original commodities. Clearly, a distinction between general commodities and the labor-power commodity—or commodities *sui generis* such as land—can only be drawn on the basis of the labor value theory. But Unoists claim that anything with a price is a commodity, while at the same time saying that one must distinguish between general commodities and the labor-power commodity. We must thus ask our esteemed professors to explain how this is not a blatant contradiction! If one says that the commodity is defined essentially as a thing with a price, then the labor-power commodity certainly qualifies and would not be distinguished in any way from general commodities. Why on earth do Unoists argue, in somewhat plausible fashion, that the labor-power commodity "was not originally a commodity." In a society where products of labor are generally produced as commodities, if labor-power is also commodified, it is sufficient to correctly define the particularity of this commodity, and there would be little sense in saying that it was "not originally a commodity."

Has Uno introduces this manner of expression in order to distinguish between commodities in general and the labor-power commodity? If we reflect on this more essentially—setting aside the fact, as we have just seen, that Uno also views such a distinction as a deception and a self-contradiction—it also becomes clear that commodities in general are *not* "originally" commodities. (Or is Uno so deluded as to think that products are *intrinsically* commodities!?)

In a society with private ownership and a division of labor, the products of human labor become "commodities" and appear as such. In such a society, people are not directly social entities, but rather private producers and isolated entities. The social connection between these people is only made possible through the exchange of their own private products as commodities. Since people cannot directly exchange social labor, which this is carried out instead through the mediation of the exchange of products. This is the well-known "exchange-value"—the "market economy"!—and its secret.

If capitalism were overcome, it would soon become apparent that products of labor are not commodities by nature. What is there left to say about the vulgar bourgeois character of Uno, when he implies—perhaps through carelessness—that products of labor are commodities by nature, thus treating commodity production as something eternal? Even if Unoists set out to distinguish between general commodities and the labor-power commodity, by using the expression that "labor-power is not a commodity by nature," such an expression is completely inappropriate and not correct in any sense, because not only the labor-power commodity but commodities in general are "not commodities by nature." And this point should be perfectly clear to a Marxist. For Unoists to attach the label "Marxism that goes beyond Marx" to this pile of nonsense is similar to an unscrupulous salesman trying to pass off a pebble as a piece of gold! How different are these rotten intellectuals, really, from financial swindlers who rob the elderly of their savings?

Marx's Explanation of Exploitation

Marx says we must take leave of the "sphere of circulation or commodity exchange" where the sale and purchase of labor-power is carried out, which is a "a very Eden of the innate rights of man"—a place overrun by petty-bour-geois "communists"—and travel to the abode of production where "the secret of profit-making must at last be laid bare." According to Marx, the sphere of circulation is "this noisy sphere, where everything takes place on the surface and in full view of everyone," whereas the abode of production is a place "on whose threshold there hangs the notice 'No admittance except on business'" and where "we shall see, not only how capital produces, but how capital itself is produced."[212]

In his explanation of exploitation, Marx uses the example of the production process to turn cotton into yarn. Since this explanation is somewhat difficult to understand on its own, I have created a table to help explain it.

Marx's Explanation of Exploitation

		Means of labor	Raw materials	Labor-power (1 day)	Product	Surplus-value
A: 6 Hours of Labor	Materials	Amount of wear of the spindles	10 pounds of cotton	(6 hours of labor)	10 pounds of yarn	
	Value (Shillings)	2	10	3	15	0
B: 12 Hours of Labor	Materials	Amount of wear of the spindles	20 pounds of cotton	(12 hours of labor)	20 pounds of yarn	
	Value (Shillings)	4	20	3	30	3

Note: It is presupposed that the daily value of labor-power is 3 shillings, and that 3 shillings is equivalent to the product of six hours of labor.

Marx contrasts the case of six hours of labor where absolutely no surplus-value is created, and the case of twelve hours of labor which creates three shillings of surplus-value. Thus, the capitalist receives no surplus-value if the worker only works six hours a day, so that surplus-value can only be obtained if the worker is compelled to work beyond this six-hour period. This is because the single-day value of labor-power is three shillings, and three shillings is the quantity of

---

212. Ibid. 298-80.

gold for the product of six hours of labor. In working for six hours, the worker performs labor for the capitalist that corresponds precisely to the amount of value (labor-time) paid to him by the capitalist.

The case of twelve hours of labor, however, is completely different. This is twice the amount of labor as the first case, so that there is twice the wear-and-tear on the means of labor and twice the amount of raw material, and therefore this represents twice the amount of value. The value of labor-power, however, since it is a daily value, remains the same whether the working day is six hours or twelve hours, namely three shillings. In the second case, the worker labors for twelve hours in production, resulting in the creation of six shillings of value, but in return only receives payment worth six-hours of labor (three shillings). The magic trick has thus been performed, with the capitalist managing to extract three shillings of surplus-value.

Upon reading this, the immediate impression many may have is that the figures and calculations Marx introduces are totally arbitrary. Certainly, at first glance, Marx's argument does generate the feeling that it is arbitrary and formalistic. For six hours of labor, the cost is 15 shillings and the value is also 15 shillings, whereas in the case of a twelve-hour working day the cost is 27 shillings and the value 30 shillings, so that there remains three shillings of surplus-value. Some may wonder, however, whether in the meantime the value of the means of labor or the raw materials would have changed, whether the product would actually sell at its value, or why ten pounds of cotton is set at ten shillings (the product of 20 hours of labor time) in the first place. All of this seems quite arbitrary, and some may think that the whole issue simply revolves around such arithmetic, and the like.

Marx's argument, however, is arbitrary in appearance only. The task he sets himself is to scientifically explain the reality of profit for capital (surplus-value). Moreover, everything, including the commodification of labor-power, is determined strictly by the labor theory of value. Only based on the premise of the labor theory of value does the logical nature and profound significance of this argument become clear. Without this premise, Marx's explanation would appear to be completely formalistic and empty. It is thus natural that those who fail to understand the labor theory of value, such as bourgeois scholars and Unoists, would also be incapable of understanding Marx's explanation of capitalist exploitation.

Formal Equality of Exchange

The fact that capitalists are able to augment value by purchasing labor-power ultimately stems from the fact that the value of labor-power and the daily expenditure of this labor-power "are two totally different things."[213] The former is the daily maintenance cost of labor-power (the value of the daily necessary means of subsistence for the sake of production), whereas the latter is a day of labor (the augmentation of value in the production process).

If we use the figures that appeared in the previous section, the value of labor-power is three shillings (six hours of labor), whereas six shillings of value (12 hours of labor) are created in the production process. Three shillings of surplus-value have thus been formed as the difference between these two figures; that is to say: "The fact that half a day's labor [6 hours] is necessary to keep the worker alive during 24 hours does not in any way prevent him from working a whole day [12 hours]."[214]

Marx emphasizes here that the capitalist does not commit any "injustice towards the seller [worker]" and only "acts in accordance with the eternal laws of commodity exchange." The worker selling his labor-power, like all sellers of commodities, "realizes its exchange-value, and alienates its use-value."[215] On the other hand, since the money-owner (capitalist) pays the worker for the value of labor-power, he acquires the right to use this labor-power, which is freely put at his disposal. Thus, in forcing the worker to labor in excess of the value of his labor-power (six hours of labor), the capitalist is not departing from the law of commodity exchange in any way. Moreover, the fact that a commodity a capitalist only expends 27 shillings on sells for 30 shillings also corresponds to its value, rather than from the commodity being sold at a price that exceeds its value. Without going beyond the realm of circulation to elucidate the mystery of surplus-value, the best a person can come up with is the superficial explanation of "profit upon alienation" (buying low and selling high).

Seen from its result, however, the exchange relation between the capitalist and worker is "unequal exchange," so that the law of commodity exchange (equal exchange) is transformed into its opposite, namely unequal exchange. The capitalist, despite only paying the worker a value of three shillings, can

---

213. Ibid., 300.
214. Ibid.
215. Ibid., 301

compel the worker to labor until six shillings of value (12 hours) are created—and this is what occurs in reality. Thus the worker provides the capitalist six shillings while only receiving three in return.

The fact that the relation between capitalists and workers *formally* appears
to be a relation of commodity exchange is an important particularity of capitalist production relations, and this is the real basis for the prevalence of the
ideology of "freedom" and "democracy" under capitalism. On the surface, in
the realm of circulation alone, the relation between capitalists and workers is
one that involves the owners of equal commodities exchanging "equivalents"
in the role of "free" independent personalities. Of course, in the case of equal
exchange between producers of general commodities this is certainly not a
mere formal equality. But in the case of the relation between capitalists and
workers, "equality" *is* merely formal and superficial, and the actual relation
between the two—involving the exploitation of labor, "unequal exchange,"
and the subordination of workers to capital—is concealed.

Marx discusses the relation between law of private property based on (simple) commodity production and the law particular to capitalism, and he says
that the laws pertaining to the former "become changed into their direct
opposite through their own internal and inexorable logic." Marx then notes:

> The relation of exchange between capitalist and worker becomes a mere
> semblance of belonging only to the process of circulation, it becomes a
> mere form, which is alien to the content of the transaction itself, and
> merely mystifies it. The constant sale and purchase of labor-power is the
> form; the content is the constant appropriation by the capitalist, without
> equivalent, of a portion of the labor of others which has already been objec-
> tified, and his repeated exchange of this labor for a greater quantity of the
> living labor of others...Now, however, property turns out to be the right,
> on the part of the capitalist, to appropriate the unpaid labor of others or its
> product, and the impossibility, on the part of the worker, of appropriating
> his own product. The separation of property from labor thus becomes the
> necessary consequence of a law that apparently originated in their identity.
>
> Therefore, however much the capitalist mode of appropriation may
> seem to fly in the face of the original laws of commodity production, it nev-
> ertheless arises, not from a violation of these laws but, on the contrary,
> from their application.[216]

---

216. Ibid., 729-30.

11. Overview of the Theory of the Commodity

"Non-Commodities" Can Also Have Prices

Under capitalist relations of production, "things which in and for themselves are not commodities"[217] can also have a price, and thus become "commodities." By examining these special types of commodities *sui generis* we can also provide an overview of Marx's theory of the commodity presented in *Capital*.

Near the beginning of this chapter, we saw how bourgeois scholars such as Böhm-Bawerk criticized Marx by saying that he presented a deceptive, circular argument that took as its object of analysis, or premise, the commodity as a product of labor, and then proceeded to analyze this to discover that the substance or content of value is human labor. (Böhm-Bawerk raises the example of commodities that are not the product of labor, including "gifts of nature, such as the soil, wood in trees, water power, coal beds, stone quarries, petroleum reserves, mineral waters, gold mines, etc."[218]) Certainly it is true that labor-power, capital, land, etc. are "commodified" and appear as commodities in capitalist society. But it would be incorrect to say that Marx did not examine such commodities. In fact, Marx does consider these commodities *sui generis* and position them on the basis of the necessary logical stage and through various mediations.

At the very beginning of *Capital*, Marx analyzes the commodity and discovers that its "value" is abstract human labor that has taken a social form. In this sense, Marx certainly is taking as his object of analysis commodities as the products of labor. This is a matter of course since the commodity is by nature nothing more than the *historical form* taken by products of labor! Under capitalist economic relations, land and capital also take on the appearance, in form only, of commodities. Marx is aware that such commodities are derivative "commodities" and should be distinguished from the commodity proper. For this reason, in his discussion of the commodity at the beginning of *Capital*, he examines the commodity as the product of labor, i.e. only the commodity in this *original* sense. He could not foresee, however, that his theory would be subject to a totally superficial and vulgar criticism from those taken in by the surface phenomena of capitalism, such as Böhm-Bawerk and Uno Kōzō,.

---

217. Ibid., 197.
218. *Karl Marx and the Close of His System*, 70.

In this final section I want to examine in what sense, and in what form, land and capital are commodities (just as we considered labor-power), in order to further clarify the significance of Marx's analysis of the commodity in *Capital*. In the section where Marx explains how value is transformed into price through the functioning of money, he already notes that with this price-form, things emerge that are able to "have a price without having a value."

> The price-form, however, is not only compatible with the possibility of a quantitative incongruity between magnitude of value and price, i.e. between the magnitude of value and its own expression in money, but it may also harbor a qualitative contradiction, with the result that price ceases altogether to express value, despite the fact that money is nothing but the value-form of commodities. Things which in and for themselves are not commodities, things such as conscious, honor, etc., can be offered for sale by their holders, and thus acquire the form of commodities through their price. Hence a thing can, formally speaking, have a price without having a value. The expression of price is in this case imaginary, like certain quantities in mathematics. On the other hand, the imaginary price-form may also conceal a real value-relation or one derived from it, as for instance the price of uncultivated land, which is without value because no human labor is objectified in it.[219]

Marx indicates here that things such as "conscious" and honor," as well as uncultivated land, can come to have a price, and thus assume the commodity-form, and he also discusses the differences between such derivative commodities. Purely "imaginary" prices of things such as conscious and honor require little consideration, but it is worth examining further the prices of things that happen to conceal a value-relation, such as uncultivated land or the price of capital. The question is why and how things with absolutely no intrinsic value come to have prices (even though, as we have seen, price is the "money-expression of value").

Capital also Becomes a "Commodity"

Marx notes that capital also becomes a commodity. This, however, is not something that he was the first to point out, being instead a simple fact of capitalist society. A recent newspaper article I came across quotes a company manager referring to the introduction of "funds" with an inexpensive cost

---

219. *Capital*, vol. 1, 197.

(price), which reflects this person's awareness that "funds" exist as a commodity, with the interest paid on such funds being considered the price. Indeed, it is not accidental that the term "capital market" exists to refer to the market where "capital" is bought and sold at higher or lower prices! For the bourgeoisie (and Unoists as well), anything with a price that is bought and sold is a commodity, and in this sense there is no difference at all between commodities as products of labor (ordinary commodities) and the labor-power commodity, capital commodity, or land commodity. For workers, however, the distinction between these sorts of commodities is important.

Marx examines how things that are not originally products of labor, and thus have no intrinsic value, can appear as commodities, and ponders what the underlying value- or economic-relation is in such cases. Here we also need to consider how capital comes to be a "commodity" and what form this takes. Even if capital becomes a commodity, this is an issue that is entirely separate from the means of production appearing as commodities as the products of labor. At issue here is interest-bearing capital or loan capital. As Marx notes:

> The owner of money who wants to valorize this as interest-bearing capital, parts with it to someone else, puts it into circulation, makes it into a commodity as *capital*; as capital not only for himself but also for others. It is not simply capital for the person who alienates it, but it is made over to the other person as capital right from the start, as value that possesses the use-value of creating surplus-value or profit.[220]

In this case, the parallel between the money being handed over as capital and a "commodity" is complete, with the money-owner handing over a use-value. Of course, unlike typical commodity exchange, what is being handed over is "value" itself, although this "value" is preserved through repayment in the future. Moreover, the actual use-value is handed over unilaterally, while the recipient consumes this use-value, which also coincides with the "law" of commodity exchange. Of course, unlike typical commodities, the use-value of this "commodity" is profit, but the fact that the use-value of each commodity is different, far from being a violation of this law, is in fact its premise.

Still, there is a distinction between this "commodity" and ordinary commodities. The relation of the two parties involved in exchange is not one of sale and purchase, but rather lending and borrowing, and what is paid for is

---

220. *Capital*, vol. 3, 464.

not the commodity's price, but rather interest—and it is obvious at a glance that this is an illogical form of price that contradicts the price-concept of the commodity proper.

The use-value of this "commodity" is the *generation of profit*, and its exchange-value is interest. That is to say, interest is the price of the capital commodity, and the magnitude of this price is determined by changes in the demand for loan capital. However, whereas the basis of the price of general commodities is value, the price of this special commodity does not have any value as its core, and the interest rate is only a "market price" dependent upon demand. This is thus the ideal "commodity" for bourgeois scholars, as it suits their own vulgar outlook and appears in a form completely lacking a concept.

Marx also says that this "commodity" is "to a certain extent analogous" "to labor-power, in its position vis-à-vis the industrial capitalist."[221] In other words, just as the use-value of labor power is the capacity to generate surplus-value, the use-value of the capital commodity is the "capacity to expand value." The "commodity" that appears from the credit relation is money, or money as capital, and this is a commodity in the form of loan capital. Marx says that the credit relation is also, formally speaking, a relation involving purchases and sales, and he analyzes how money *qua* capital appears here as a "commodity." Of course, it is unacceptable to conflate the exchange of such "commodities" with the exchange of commodities in general.

Stocks and Bonds Become "Commodities"

Along with money becoming a commodity as capital, all sums of value appear as the source of the income they generate—i.e. the so-called "capitalization" of income—and they are "bought and sold" as such, thus becoming commodities. Included among these special commodities are credit, stocks, and land, and Marx also lists labor-power as another example.

> Here wages are conceived as interest, and hence labor-power as capital that yields this interest. If the wage for a year comes to £50, say, and the rate of interest is 5 per cent, one annual labor-power is taken as equal to a capital of £1,000. Here the absurdity of the capitalist's way of conceiving things reaches its climax, in so far as instead of deriving the valorization of capital from the exploitation of labor-power, they explain the productivity of

---

221. Ibid., 473.

labor-power by declaring that labor-power itself is this mystical thing, interest-bearing capital.[222]

This point is also clear, for example, when the life of a worker killed in a factory accident is paid for as a "commodity" that is calculated as being worth so many millions of yen.

Like these cases involving labor-power, credit and stocks also become a certain type of "commodity" by coming to have a price arrived at through "capitalization" calculated according to the income they generate and the rate of interest. The commodification of securities (national bonds, stock certificates, etc.) is a general phenomenon of bourgeois society. National bonds, stock shares, etc. are not actual capital, and the capital prices of these securities are purely illusory, so that we can refer to them as examples of "fictitious capital."

State bonds as well can appear as capital. This is the rare case in which the state productively invests the money received from issuing bonds. And for stock shares as well, there are cases where they are the reflection of actual capital as the nominal ownership of a proportional allotment of surplus-value generated by actual capital. Still, this is different from stock certificates that have their face value indicated on them (in addition to their market price at a given time). The "value" of stock certificates exists independently from the capital that is actually invested, and the value of this capital is merely illusory because it does not contain any value (objectified labor) at all, and the stock certificates themselves are mere pieces of paper.

The "price" (market value) and price fluctuations of stock certificates and the like naturally depend upon "the level and security of the receipts [from exploitation] to which they give a legal title."[223] However, as we are well aware, stock prices do not only fluctuate depending on increases or decreases in dividends. "The market value of these securities is partly speculative, since it is determined not just by the actual revenue but rather by the anticipated revenue as reckoned in advance."[224] Moreover, once the shift is made to a situation where stocks are purchased because the price is rising and increase in price because they are being purchased, so that it is a purely speculative price, this will inevitably result in a crash. Thus, on the basis of the credit system, fic-

222. Ibid., 596.
223. Ibid., 598.
224. Ibid.

tional capital also becomes a "commodity" and is bought and sold as such, and the superficial value of these "commodities" is enormous.[225] Marx describes this in the following way:

> In so far as the rise or fall of these securities is independent of the movement in the value of the real capital that they represent, the wealth of a nation is just as great afterwards as before.
>
> "The public stocks and canal and railway shares had already by the 23rd of October, 1847, been depreciated in the aggregate to the amount of £114,752,225." (Morris, Governor of the Bank of England, evidence in the *Report on Commercial Distress*, 1847-8).
>
> As long as their depreciation was not the expression of any standstill in production and in railway and canal traffic, or an abandonment of undertakings already begun, or a squandering of capital in positively worthless enterprises, the nation was not a penny poorer by the busting of these soap bubbles of nominal money capital.[226]

Workers can never overlook the fact that in capitalist society a large part of the "commodities" and "capital" that exist are such fictitious entities, things that merely have "price" but no value. This fact alone clearly reveals the incredibly reactionary nature of the Unoist view that anything with a price is a commodity.

Foreign Currency Becomes a "Commodity"

There is also a lively trade in foreign currency as a "commodity," which becomes an object of speculation like stocks. Indeed, we have the example from a few years ago of the London branch of a trading company losing billions of yen in currency speculation. Foreign currency is bought and sold on the currency market, and the things actually traded on this market are foreign currency drafts. These foreign currency drafts are used when the necessity arises for the payment of currency for the import/export of commodities or inflow/outflow of capital.

---

225. Recently the total market value of the stock of listed companies exceeded 300 trillion yen, and this year [1987], because of the abnormal rise in stock prices, this was increasing at a rate of one trillion yen a day, even though this had almost no relation to actual capital!
226. Ibid. 599.

A corporation or bank in Japan that purchases coal from the United States or U.S. government bonds must transfer so many tens or hundreds of billions of Japanese yen to the United States, and in such cases they appear as a party seeking a bill of exchange (dollar drafts) in New York. Of course, in Japan there are also those who supply dollar drafts. When a corporation such as Toyota sells thousands automobiles in the United States, for example, large banks act as intermediaries and purchase drafts from the suppliers and then sell the drafts to those demanding them. In this case the banks purchase dollar drafts using yen obtained from selling dollar drafts. The banks send dollar drafts they have purchased to their U.S. branches and collect "dollars" from the debtors (such as purchasers of Toyota cars). Meanwhile, import companies that purchased dollar drafts from the main bank in Japan send them to an export company in the U.S., and the export company then sends the drafts to the branch of the Japanese bank and receives payment in "dollars." Since the bank branch receives dollars from import companies in the U.S., it has no problem in paying the exporters in dollars.

Thus, as long as the international balance of payments is coordinated, everything proceeds smoothly in this way, and claims and obligations offset each other. However, as we are well aware, it will be problematic if Japan, for example, runs a trade surplus of tens of billions of dollars. It is fine if the trade surplus is offset by the export of capital, but otherwise the supply of dollar drafts will pile up in the currency market, while demand decreases. If the supply of drafts keeps increasing while demand drops, their price will plummet. When gold existed as the basis for international currency the limit to this depreciation in value was the "gold point"—that is, the point where it becomes cheaper in making payments to actually send gold rather than using credit.

Today, however, the dollar and yen have both lost their "convertibility" to gold. Moreover, whereas up to 1973 there was a "fixed exchange rate system," since that time countries have removed the "obligation" of maintaining "fixed exchange rates" and moved to a "floating exchange rate system," so that it appears as if the "prices" on the currency market fluctuate solely in accordance with supply and demand. Of course, however, the only ones who believe this are bourgeois scholars who lack a concept of value. The currency market is formed through the supply and demand of bills of exchange, but this is also the exchange ratio of the "currency" of each country (the U.S. and Japan), at the basis of which a ratio of value necessarily exists.

Even when gold regulates the movement of currency, there are other corresponding difficulties and contradictions that develop. For example, under a fixed exchange rate system, if the level of imports rises, the government will have to implement strict "austerity" policies, etc. At the same time, even if exports are increasing, it becomes necessary to stimulate business to an extreme point to increase imports, because, for example, a situation where the dollar is weak and yen is strong would be unacceptable to the Japanese government.

On the other hand, under a floating exchange rate system, these kinds of restrictions are eliminated, but in turn this frees up anarchic competition between countries and selfish policies "beggar-thy-neighbor" policies (i.e. arbitrarily devaluing one's currency so as to engage in "currency dumping"). This means that on a theoretical level there is a gap to some extent between the exchange ratio of each country's currency and its value ratio. Furthermore, as this gap increases, and exchange-rate fluctuations intensify, the currency of each country becomes the object of speculation for finance capital and the wealthy. They buy and sell currency on the basis of expectations—either political or economic—of price increases or decreases, and are thus able to amass enormous profits. Of course, if the gap separating the exchange ratio and value ratio of each country's currency widens in this manner, this in turn generates a different, serious contradiction, but the theoretical task here does not include addressing this question.

"Commodification" of Land

According to statistics, the price of all of the land within Japan in 1985 was one thousand trillion yen—one half of the "national wealth"!—and this figure has increased 2.6-fold in the past ten years. But what is the significance of this enormous increase in land prices? Use-values that are not the product of human labor cannot possess value. For example, air and sunlight are use-values of paramount importance to human beings, and yet they have no price.

The same is true in the case of land. Of course, in the case of agricultural land various types of social labor are objectified within it such as investment for irrigation and land improvements, and land is also the "product of labor" if clearing is carried out to construct factories or housing. But it would not be possible for a one-square-meter piece of land to have an intrinsic value of hundreds of thousands or even millions of yen. Clearly such prices are completely separate from the actual social labor (value) objectified in the land.

Marx says that land price presupposes rent—i.e. landowners receiving one part of surplus-value *gratis*—and thus it conceals a value relation. On the basis of commodity-capitalist production, the nominal right to privately own a piece of land bestows a certain income (rent), but here we won't touch on the form in which this rent is generated and accrues to the landowner.[227]

When landed property generates rent, the land comes to be a "commodity" with a certain price. For example, if there is a piece of land that generates 100,000 yen in rent annually, and the rate of interest is five percent, the land would be seen as a capital-value that brings in an "income" of 100,000 yen and would thus sell for a price of two million yen. This is called the "capitalization" of rent (or income in general).

If we look at recent developments, it is big capital that is taking the lead in the formation of land price. In major urban areas, the price of land is skyrocketing, but real-estate companies and landowning capitalists are still very willing to pay for land no matter how expensive, given the demand and the current lack of office space and rental buildings. This increase in the price of land is spreading nationwide, leading to an abnormal expansion in social inequality between landowners and non-landowners. Even if it is said that land in Japan has a total price of one thousand trillion yen, this does not mean that this land has the same intrinsic value (as objectified social labor). The actual value would likely be one-tenth or one-hundredth that figure.

Companies are very satisfied when the prices of land and stocks (fictitious capital) increase so that "hidden assets," that is superficial assets, expand. But what a distorted and parasitical society! Those who actually work suffer alienation and neglect, the risk of unemployment, and the collapse of their livelihoods, while land and stocks, which have no inherent value (social labor), are fawned over, steadily increase in price, and appear to make up the bulk of social wealth.[228] People forget that land and stocks only appear to have "value" on the basis of capitalism. If this basis is shattered, so that the relations of credit and land-ownership disappear, it would become immediately apparent that they in fact do not contain an ounce of value. If this were to occur, the "propertyless" [*musan*] workers would have no cause for apprehension or regret.

Value is the objectification of a certain quality of social labor, and land by nature cannot appear as the expression of this quantity of social labor. How-

---

227. For a detailed discussion of this see chapter four.
228. But just two or three years after these lines were written, the collapse of the "bubble economy" revealed that most of the "value" of land had no real basis!

ever, the relations of landed property—the nominal right of private owners to land—make capitalist rent necessary, both differential and absolute rent, and as a result there is the formation of land price. This private ownership of land, however, is increasingly acting as an enormous fetter on the development of social production and the lives of people. Marx said that with increasing capitalist development, landowners come to appropriate an enormous, parasitical profit, and this appears as the steady rise in land prices, which even capital experiences as a hindrance.

If the earth is the common asset of its five billion inhabitants, then land as the precondition for our direct existence must become our common possession. Only socialism, however, will make it possible to completely end the private ownership of land along with the private ownership of the means of production.

The Great Significance of "Science"

We have already seen how Böhm-Bawerk and other bourgeois economists attempt to explain, all at the same time, "commodities" such as land or stocks and their price (i.e. the fact that things without value are "commodities"). Marx, however, points out the following:

> It is also quite correct that "the value or price of land," which is not produced by labor, appears directly to contradict the concept of value and cannot be derived directly from it…Ricardo sets forth [in his theory of rent] how the nominal value of land is evolved on the basis of capitalist production and does not contradict the definition of value. The value of land is nothing but the price which is paid for capitalized rent. Much more far-reaching developments have therefore to be presumed here than can be deduced *prima facie* from the simple consideration of the commodity and its value, just as from the simple concept of productive capital one cannot evolve fictitious capital, the object of gambling on the stock exchange, which is actually nothing but the selling and buying of entitlement to a certain part of the annual tax revenue.[229]

It is laughable that Uno Kōzō and Kuroda Kan'ichi—new left ideologues!—who sneer at the stupidity of Böhm-Bawerk, end up displaying the same ignorance as bourgeois scholars when it comes to discussing the labor-power commodity. Uno says that it is not possible to analyze the general com-

229. *MECW*, vol. 32, 299.

modity itself (because it is a "circulation-form"), childishly believing that one can determine the value of commodities in general only after labor-power has been commodified and through its mediation. Kuroda for his part, in his inimitable manner, says that the commodity Marx describes at the beginning of *Capital* is the initial form [*tansho keitai*] of the commodification of labor-power, and he promotes this nonsense under the label of "subjective philosophy." Ōtsuka Hisao, meanwhile, offers up the silly view that, "in the case of Marx's economics, it is living, human individuals that form the object of cognition for economics,"[230] revealing how poorly he grasps the great historical and social significance of human social labor taking the form of value, i.e. products of human labor taking the commodity-form.

These radical, liberal ideologues ultimately share in common a cheap and superficial "humanism." But no matter how much one may advocate such views, it does not bring us even one step closer to a correct and true understanding of Marxism, which is the only true "social science."

Böhm-Bawerk argues that to explain commodities it is necessary to deal with *all* commodities, including land and the like, and that it is incorrect to merely examine commodities as products of labor. And this is basically the same view held by Uno and other petty-bourgeois intellectuals. Marx, by contrast, explains how—through various mediations—value-less land comes to appear as a "commodity" with a price. He was aware that the attempt to provide a "general" concept of the commodity that also encompasses every commodity *sui generis*, would only result in being taken in by appearances, like the Uno school, and offering a superficial and empty definition of the commodity as "anything with a price," which reveals a complete failure to understand the *concept* of the commodity.

Marx knew that anything can be "commodified" in capitalist society, but he was able to distinguish between essential and derivative aspects. What is essential is that products of labor take the commodity-form, whereas land and other "commodities" can only be accounted for scientifically on the basis of a number of mediations. It is a blatant lie to claim that Marx failed to explain commodities such as land, when in fact he carried out this explanation at the correct place, in the correct form, and by following the necessary steps. This is precisely what is meant by *science*. But bourgeois and petty-bourgeois scholars,

---

230. *Shakaigaku no hōhō* (Tokyo: Iwanami Shinsho, 1966).

whose thought is quite alien to science, can do nothing more than twist and distort the truth.

Workers need to be aware of the great historical significance (and profound contradictions) pertaining to the fact that products of labor take the commodity-form and their own social labor appears as "value." This is the precise starting point and basis of workers' socialist consciousness, and herein lies the true significance of the Marxist theory of the commodity.

2

Adam Smith's "Theory of Value"

Structure of Smith's Theory of Value

Here my aim is to examine Smith's theory of value, but this task is not an easy one. In general, Smith's theory of value is understood as having a dual nature in terms of combining an "embodied-labor" theory of value and a "commanded-labor" (or purchased-labor) theory of value—which can also be referred to, respectively, as a deduction (breaking-down) theory of value and a composition (adding-up) theory of value. This duality represents a contradiction within Smith's thought, and this is the reason why his theory represents one "moment" in the transition to both Marxism and the subjectivistic theory of value of Malthus and others. The Marxist theory of value, needless to say, is a *labor* theory of value, and therefore also an embodied-labor or deduction theory of value. Alongside or intertwined with Smith's "correct" theory of value, however, is an "incorrect" one. Here we need to consider the historical significance and necessity of Smith's two theories of value, or rather his *dualistic* theory of value.

At first glance, Smith's theory of value has a peculiar composition. To begin with, in chapter five of *The Wealth of Nations*—entitled "Of the Real and Nominal Price of Commodities, or of their Price in Labour, and their Price in Money"—Smith touches on the exchange-value and use-value of commodities, and sets the theoretical task of uncovering the law that governs exchange-value. But what he offers us is extremely complicated and confusing.[1] Smith

---

1. This is clear from the title of the chapter alone, since by saying that the "real price" is the price in labor and the "nominal price" is the price in money, it seems as if Smith is developing a labor theory of value, but what he is in fact saying is not so straightforward.

does speak of a labor theory of value in a form that is somewhat simple and clear, and thus correct, but this appears, not in this fifth chapter, but rather at the beginning of the sixth chapter, which is entitled "Of the Component Parts of the Price of Commodities." However, this discussion of the labor theory of value is not essential to this sixth chapter and is simply mentioned in passing as a sort of preliminary remark to the ideas subsequently developed there.

I would like to begin by looking at Smith's labor theory of value in its correct form, and then examine his various other theories of value. In a sense, it can be said that within Smith's theory of value we can come in contact with every sort of value theory advanced in bourgeois society and the moments that compose these theories.

Smith's Theory of Value

In several passages of *The Wealth of Nations*, Smith brilliantly develops a *labor* theory of value. The best known, as well as the simplest and clearest of these, appears at the beginning of chapter six:

> In that early and rude state of society which precedes both the accumulation of stock and the appropriation of land, the proportion between the quantities of labour necessary for acquiring different objects seems to be the only circumstance which can afford any rule for exchanging them for one another. If among a nation of hunters, for example, it usually costs twice the labour to kill a beaver which it does to kill a deer, one beaver should naturally exchange for or be worth two deer. It is natural that what is usually the produce of two days or two hours labour, should be worth double of what is usually the produce of one day's or one hour's labour.[2]

Another representative passage comes at the beginning of chapter eight ("Of the Wages of Labour"):

> In that original state of things, which precedes both the appropriation of land and the accumulation of stock, the whole produce of labour belongs to the labourer. He has neither landlord nor master to share with him.
>
> Had this state continued, the wages of labour would have augmented with all those improvements in its productive powers to which the division of labour gives occasion. All things would gradually have become cheaper.

---

2. Adam Smith, *The Wealth of Nations* (Chicago: University of Chicago Press, 1976), 53.

They would have been produced by a smaller quantity of labour; and as the commodities produced by equal quantities of labour would naturally in this state of things be exchanged for one another, they would have been purchased likewise with the produce of a smaller quantity.[3]

In chapter eight, Smith goes on to develop his idea further, explaining that even if all commodities were to become cheaper in value, some relatively expensive commodities might also exist; and this explanation is also based on a consistent labor theory of value. Smith says, for example, that as a result of a rise in the productive power of labor, the value of a certain commodity may fall, but that if the productive power of the labor that produces money were to rise even higher, relatively speaking, the price of the commodity (its nominal or monetary price) would rise, since it would exchange for a greater amount of gold or silver (money). What we have here, essentially, is identical to Marx's labor theory of value, i.e. an embodied-labor theory of value. Moreover, by referring to the labor that "usually" determines exchange-value, Smith is even elucidating the fact that the labor governing exchange-value is not something accidental or individual, but *socially-average* labor (but here we will not consider the degree to which Smith was consciously aware of this fact or not).

There is no need to dwell on Smith's correct theory of value, since it presents us with no difficulty. What we need to note, however, is that for Smith this theory of value only applies to the "early and rude state of society" prior to the accumulation of capital, or in what we can tentatively refer to as a "simple" pre-capitalist society. Therefore, this correct labor theory of value is said to only apply to a simple commodity production society. With the dissolution of this society—i.e. under capitalism—Smith believed another law had to be uncovered. But before we consider what this law is according to Smith, and why another theory of value was considered necessary in addition to a labor theory of value, we need to first consider the other correct view Smith held. Here I am referring to his idea that first there is the existence of value, and that this value is in turn resolved or "broken down" into various moments, which is opposed to his other, incorrect, view that value is the composite or result of the "adding-up" of the various moments (wages, profit, and capital[4]).

---

3. Ibid., 72
4. It is worth noting, however, that Smith tends to overlook "capital" here.

Deduction (Breaking-Down) Theory of Value

Already in chapter six, Smith clearly says that with the end of the "early and rude state of society" and the beginning of the age of capital, the value which workers add to the materials resolves itself into two parts: wages and profits:

> As soon as stock has accumulated in the hands of particular persons, some of them will naturally employ it in setting to work industrious people, whom they will supply with materials and subsistence, in order to make a profit by the sale of their work, or by what their labour adds to the value of the materials. In exchanging the complete manufacture either for money, for labour, or for other goods, over and above what may be sufficient to pay the price of the materials, and the wages of the workmen, something must be given for the profits of the undertaker of the work who hazards his stock in this adventure. The value which the workmen add to the materials, therefore, resolves itself in this case into two parts, of which the one pays their wages, the other the profits of their employer upon the whole stock of materials and wages which he advanced. He could have no interest to employ them, unless he expected from the sale of their work something more than what was sufficient to replace his stock to him; and he could have no interest to employ a great stock rather than a small one, unless his profits were to bear some proportion to the extent of his stock.[5]

In chapter eight, just following the passage we quoted earlier, Smith also emphasizes that, with the development of capitalist production, land and capital demand a "share" of the products of labor:

> As soon as land becomes private property, the landlord demands a share of almost all the produce which the labourer can either raise, or collect from it. His rent makes the first deduction from the produce of the labour which is employed upon land.[6]

Smith adds that since capital is also employed for production, naturally the profits of capital are "a second deduction [made] from the produce of the labour which is employed upon land."[7] In other words, he clearly says that one part of the value produced by workers becomes rent and profit. In other words,

---

5. Ibid., 54.
6. Ibid., 73.
7. Ibid.

first there is the existence of value, which is then broken down or divided into rent and profit (as well as wages), rather than value merely being "composed" of rent, profit, and other elements. From this perspective, Smith explains that there are cases where production does not take place under capital, such as the example of "a single independent workman," but that even in this case the situation is essentially the same:

> He is both master and workman, and enjoys the whole produce of his own labour, or the whole value which it adds to the materials upon which it is bestowed. It includes what are usually two distinct revenues, belonging to two distinct persons, the profits of stock, and the wages of labour.[8]

This view is perfectly correct, and Smith goes on to stress the opposition between capital and wage-labor, showing us how a correct theoretical standpoint can have revolutionary significance. Instead of independent workmen, Smith considers "workmen serving under a master," i.e. the relation between wage-workers and their employers:

> What are the common wages of labour, depends everywhere upon the contract usually made between those two parties, whose interests are by no means the same. The workmen desire to get as much, the masters to give as little as possible. The former are disposed to combine in order to raise, the latter in order to lower the wages of labour.
>
> It is not, however, difficult to foresee which of the two parties must, upon all ordinary occasions, have the advantage in the dispute, and force the other into a compliance with their terms. The masters, being fewer in number, can combine much more easily; and the law, besides, authorises, or at least does not prohibit their combinations, while it prohibits those of the workmen. We have no acts of parliament against combining to lower the price of work; but many against combining to raise it. In all such disputes the masters can hold out much longer. A landlord, a farmer, a master manufacturer, a merchant, though they did not employ a single workman, could generally live a year or two upon the stocks which they have already acquired. Many workmen could not subsist a week, few could subsist a month, and scarce any a year without employment. In the long-run the workman may be as necessary to his master as his master is to him, but the necessity is not so immediate.[9]

---

8.   Ibid., 74.
9.   Ibid., 74-5.

Smith then provides a lively explanation of the characteristics of the "combinations" of employers ("masters") and those of workers, reaching the following conclusion:

> But whether [workers'] combinations be offensive or defensive, they are always abundantly heard of. In order to bring the point to a speedy decision, they have always recourse to the loudest clamour, and sometimes to the most shocking violence and outrage. They are desperate, and act with the folly and extravagance of desperate men, who must either starve, or frighten their masters into an immediate compliance with their demands. The masters upon these occasions are just as clamorous upon the other side, and never cease to call aloud for the assistance of the civil magistrate, and the rigorous execution of those laws which have been enacted with so much severity against the combinations of servants, labourers, and journeymen. The workmen, accordingly, very seldom derive any advantage from the violence of those tumultuous combinations, which, partly from the interposition of the civil magistrate, partly from the superior steadiness of the masters, partly from the necessity which the greater part of the workmen are under of submitting for the sake of present subsistence, generally end in nothing, but the punishment or ruin of the ringleaders.[10]

Smith certainly does not go to the trouble of inserting this passage to "demonstrate" the impotence of workers' struggles. Rather, this shows that conflict between capital and labor is inevitable under capitalism, and objectively characterizes the nature of this struggle. One can even sense some vague sympathy on his part toward workers and their fate.

In any case, based on a perfectly correct deduction or breaking-down view of value, Smith advances a scientifically valid theory and provides us with a magnificent description of the position of workers and their struggles. This is certainly no accident. If it is true that value is created by workers, with its substance or essential content being productive labor expended in a social form, which is then broken down into wages and profit (and rent), this means that labor is in fact exploited by capital (and landed property), and under such relations of production class struggle is inevitable since it has a real, "material" basis. It seems likely that this passage written by Smith would have left a strong impression on Marx. We can see the same spirit expressed in Marx's writing, but of course he writes from a consistently proletarian standpoint.

---

10. Ibid., 75-6.

From a Deduction to a *Composition* Theory of Value

Smith, however, was unable to maintain his correct theory of value for historical and class-related reasons. His position shifted from a labor theory of value (an embodied-labor theory of value), to a commanded- or purchased-labor theory of value. In other words, he moved from a deduction (breaking-down) theory of value to a composition (adding-up) theory of value. And in the case of Smith this was an unavoidable path.

We will begin by looking at Smith's theory of the composition (make-up) of value and then examine his commanded-labor theory of value. In chapter seven—"Of the Natural and Market Price of Commodities"—for instance, Smith says that wages, profit, and rent each have their "natural price" or average price:

> When the price of any commodity is neither more nor less than what is sufficient to pay the rent of the land, the wages of the labour, and the profits of the stock employed in raising, preparing, and bringing it to market, according to their natural rates, the commodity is then sold for what may be called its natural price.[11]

In other words, the price of a commodity is the sum of the profit and wages that it is made up of, so that it is *composed* of these parts. This clearly represents an overturning of the deduction theory of value. Smith argues that a commodity is in fact sold at the value (cost) that is expended on it:

> The commodity is then sold precisely for what it is worth, or for what it really costs the person who brings it to market; for though in common language what is called the prime cost of any commodity does not comprehend the profit of the person who is to sell it again, yet if he sell it at a price which does not allow him the ordinary rate of profit in his neighbourhood, he is evidently a loser by the trade; since by employing his stock in some other way he might have made that profit. His profit, besides, is his revenue, the proper fund of his subsistence. As, while he is preparing and bringing the goods to market, he advances to his workmen their wages, or their subsistence; so he advances to himself, in the same manner, his own subsistence, which is generally suitable to the profit which he may reasonably expect from the sale of his goods. Unless they yield him this profit,

---

11. Ibid., 62.

therefore, they do not repay him what they may very properly be said to
have really cost him.[12]

Here we have an extremely commonplace, general bourgeois, concept of commodity price, since for the bourgeoisie price is the cost expended within production plus added profit. The composition theory of value is just another
name for a "cost theory of value" in which the value of a commodity is said to
represent the total cost expended on it. Here Smith adopts a completely ordinary concept and develops a vulgar view of capitalist society that justifies profit
by claiming that the bourgeoisie also helps to ensure profit and has a need to
make a living. Needless to say, however, determining the price (value) of a
commodity on the basis of the cost of producing it is an illogical and circular
theory. Smith, after introducing this theory of the composition of value—i.e. a
theory of cost-price—seeks refuge in a theory of supply and demand.[13]

Commanded-Labor Theory of Value

Smith proposed another well-known theory of value generally referred to as
the commanded- or purchased-labor theory of value. This theory is distinguished from, or opposed to, the embodied-labor theory of value. Already at
the outset of his presentation of the theory of value, Smith introduces a commanded-labor theory of value:

> The power which that possession immediately and directly conveys to him,
> is the power of purchasing; a certain command over all the labour, or over
> all the produce of labour which is then in the market. His fortune is greater
> or less, precisely in proportion to the extent of this power; or to the quan-
> tity either of other men's labour, or, what is the same thing, of the produce
> of other men's labour, which it enables him to purchase or command. The
> exchangeable value of everything must always be precisely equal to the
> extent of this power which it conveys to its owner.[14]

Just following the passage on the "early and rude state of society" at the beginning of chapter six, Smith says that in general equal exchange of labor is the

---

12. Ibid. 62-3.
13. See pages 63-65 of *The Wealth of Nations* [the first part of chapter
     seven].
14. Ibid., 35.

norm, but adds that some "allowance" will naturally be made when labor is expended that "requires an uncommon degree of dexterity and ingenuity," or is "more severe":

> In this state of things, the whole produce of labour belongs to the labourer; and the quantity of labour commonly employed in acquiring or producing any commodity, is the only circumstance which can regulate the quantity exchange for which it ought commonly to purchase, command, or exchange for.[15]

What Smith calls "this state of things" could occur in both "the advanced state of society" and "the early and rude state of society," so the commanded-labor theory of value is said to be universal.

This commanded-labor theory of value is of course incorrect. It is a circular argument to set out to determine a commodity's exchange-value while presupposing its purchasing power, since it is perfectly clear that the exchange-value of the commodity *is* its purchasing power. The purchasing power of a commodity can only be scientifically determined after the concept of exchange-value (and therefore value) is first provided. To explain exchange-value by means of purchasing power, by contrast, is a backward approach that amounts to nothing more than explaining exchange-value by means of exchange-value. It is a tautology to say that a given commodity has a certain degree of purchasing power, such as the power to purchase 1,000 yen worth of commodities, and that for this reason it has an exchange-value of 1,000 yen. "Purchasing power" is clearly nothing but another form of exchange-value, its concrete form, one of its phenomenal forms.

Great wealth "is able to purchase" products of great value, but this does not elucidate the law that *determines* exchange-value. If great wealth is able to possess great value, it is a matter of course that it can "purchase" or "command" products of great value, and this stems directly from the principle of exchange-value where equal value is exchanged. At issue, however, is the question of what determines this exchange-value; the question of why a commodity of little value exchanges for—or to borrow Smith's terminology, "purchases" or "commands"—a commodity of little value, while a commodity of great value exchanges for a value of great value.

---

15. Ibid., 54.

Smith is unable to explain this, and instead says that great wealth can purchase or command a great quantity of products. But such reasoning bears no relation to the explanation of the law that determines or governs exchange-value. If Smith is trying to say that a product is great in magnitude in terms of its use-value or wealth, then this would be nonsense, since a commodity with an insignificant use-value can also have great value. On the other hand, if he is speaking of a commodity having a great value, then this is nothing but a tautology, since it is obvious that an asset of great value can "command" or "purchase" a product of great value.

Thus, while Smith says that labor is the "real measure of the exchangeable value of all commodities,"[16] this is certainly not a clear embodied-labor theory of value. Despite including aspects of such a theory, Smith's advances what is in fact a purchased-labor theory of value, or a theory of labor evaluated subjectively (according to the degree of "toil and trouble"); or a mixture of both aspects.

Smith, at the beginning of chapter six, in connection with the so-called "early and rude state of society," introduces an embodied-labor theory of value. It is interesting to consider why this correct theory is introduced in the sixth chapter, rather than the fifth, and why it is only introduced as the law of exchange-value in the "early and rude state of society." For Smith, the embodied-labor theory of value is ultimately only a law in the subordinate sense, a law applicable only to a period in the past, not modern capitalism. The more valid and correct theory under capitalism, he says, is the commanded- or purchased-labor theory of value. Smith's theory of value thus displays a dual nature. For the "early and rude state of society" it is a labor theory of value (embodied-labor theory of value), while in the case of the "advanced" state of society (i.e. capitalism) it is a composition or purchased-labor theory of value.

But what does it mean to say that the value of a commodity is equal to the labor that can be purchased with it? Smith is thinking of capitalist society, and the labor he is speaking of is *labor-power*. Therefore, what Smith has in mind, or the commodity exchange he is thinking of, concerns the exchange between a commodity as capital and the labor-power commodity. This exchange is only a realistic relation under capitalism and is essentially different from normal commodity exchange, because it is certainly not an exchange carried out according to objectified (or embodied) labor. In other words, this is not an

---

16. Ibid, 35.

"exchange of equivalents" because capital is able to receive a certain amount of extra value, while labor-power hands over a certain amount of value. This is the reason why Smith felt an embodied-labor theory of value could not be established under capitalism.

Of course, in what Smith calls the "early and rude state of society," the embodied-labor theory of value and the purchased-labor theory of value are not necessarily in contradiction with each other. It is not without reason that Smith views the two theories of value as being identical. Certainly in a society of simple commodity production, viewed from the outcome, both in fact end up being the same. Take the example of two commodities—commodity A and commodity B—that are produced with equal amounts of labor. Being of equal value, the two commodities are exchanged for each other. Seen from the result of this exchange, commodity A has "commanded" or "purchased" the amount of labor necessary to produce commodity B, and this amount of labor was the same amount expended to produce commodity A. Thus, in this case, it appears that both the embodied-labor and the commanded-labor are the measure of value. In dealing with simple commodity exchange, therefore, Smith senses no difficulty or contradiction in viewing these as identical and parallel. This, however, does not alter the fact that the commanded-labor theory of value remains irrational.

What, then, would be the case when dealing, not with this exchange of commodity for commodity, but rather the exchange between capital and a commodity (the labor-power commodity)? Since here it is a case of unequal exchange that is generally carried out, it could not be said that the embodied-labor and purchased-labor theories are equivalent. The embodied-labor in the capital, and labor as the expenditure of labor-power, are certainly not equal, and therefore one cannot make the labor that is embodied the "measure of value." Capital "commands" more labor than the labor embodied within itself, since, seen from the result, what capital purchases includes surplus-labor. Here, therefore, it is not the embodied labor, but the labor commanded or purchased that has to be the measure of value. Smith recognizes that with the development of capitalism, so that profit becomes the aim of production, something is given above the cost, above the labor embodied, which demonstrates how the purchased-labor theory of value comes to have an actual basis in reality. Of course, viewed from a rational theory of value, his theory is nonsense. Still, Smith—not to mention Malthus—feels compelled to introduce not only an embodied-labor theory of value, but also a purchased- or commanded-labor theory of value. Marx has the following to say about this:

Secondly, however, this contradiction in Adam Smith and his passing from one kind of explanation to another is based upon something deeper, which Ricardo, in exposing this contradiction, overlooked or did not rightly appreciate, and therefore did not solve. Let us assume that all laborers are producers of commodities, and not only produce their commodities but also sell them. The value of these commodities is determined by the necessary labor-time contained in them. If therefore the commodities are sold at their value, the laborer buys with one commodity, which is the product of twelve hours' labor-time, another commodity, which is the product of twelve hours' labor-time, another twelve hours' labor-time in the form of another commodity, i.e., twelve hours' labor-time which is embodied in another use-value. The value of his labor is therefore equal to the value of his commodity, i.e., it is equal to the product of twelve hours' labor-time. The selling and buying again, in a word, the whole process of exchange, the metamorphosis of the commodity, alters nothing in this. It alters only the form of the use-value in which this twelve hours' labor-time appears. The value of labor is therefore equal to the value of the product of labor. In the first place, equal quantities of objectified labor are exchanged in the commodities—in so far as they are exchanged at their value. Secondly, however, a certain quantity of living labor is exchanged for an equal quantity of objectified labor, because, firstly, the living labor is objectified in a product, a commodity, which belongs to the laborer, and secondly, this commodity is in turn exchanged for another commodity which contains an equally large quantity of labor. In fact, therefore, a certain quantity of living labor is exchanged for an equal amount of objectified labor. Thus it is not only the commodity exchanging for commodity in the proportion in which they represent an equal quantity of objectified labor-time, but a quantity of living labor exchanging for a commodity which represents the same quantity of labor objectified.

On this assumption the value of labor (the quantity of commodities which can be bought with a given quantity of labor, or the quantity of labor which can be bought with a given quantity of commodities) could serve as the measure of the value of a commodity just as well as the quantity of labor contained in it, since the value of labor always represents the same quantity of objectified labor as the living labor requires for the production of this commodity; in other words, a definite quantity of living labor-time would always command a quantity of commodities which represents an equal amount of objectified labor-time.[17]

---

17. *MECW*, vol. 30, 378-9.

The Vulgar "Moment" in Smith's Theory

We have pointed out that within Smith's theory of value there is both an embodied-labor and a commanded-labor theory of value. But the question is not quite so simple. Here I would like to look at the confused, vulgar "moment" within Smith's theory of value. In the fifth chapter of *The Wealth of Nations*, Smith sets the task of investigating what governs or determines exchange-value, and to a certain extent he begins to correctly pose the question. However, he first defines the "value of a commodity" in the following way:

> Every man is rich or poor according to the degree in which he can afford to enjoy the necessaries, conveniences, and amusements of human life. But after the division of labour has once thoroughly taken place, it is but a very small part of these with which a man's own labour can supply him. The far greater part of them he must derive from the labour of other people, and he must be rich or poor according to the quantity of that labour which he can command, or which he can afford to purchase. The value of any commodity, therefore, to the person who possesses it, and who means not to use or consume it himself, but to exchange it for other commodities, is equal to the quantity of labour which it enables him to purchase or command. Labour, therefore, is the real measure of the exchangeable value of all commodities.[18]

Here Smith speaks for the first time of the value of a commodity, but he reveals a tendency to adopt a commanded- or purchased-labor theory of value. He sets the task of finding the "real measure" of the exchange-value of a commodity, offering "labor" as the answer—and in this sense seems to be correct—but his argument is not at all convincing.

First he proposes the concept of "wealth," but there is no need to speak of wealth (use-values) here. It is true, in a sense, that people are considered rich or poor according to the amount of their disposable wealth. But why is labor then said to govern exchange-value, and what relation is there between labor and exchange-value? From the statement that a person is rich or poor according to the quantity of labor that he can command (or purchase), can the conclusion be drawn that "therefore" the value of a commodity is equivalent to the quantity of labor it can purchase. It is true in a sense that wealth or poverty

---

18. *The Wealth of Nations*, 34.

depend on the quantity of labor that can be purchased, but what relation does this have to the *determination* of a commodity's value? It seems outrageous to claim such a relation, but Smith is very much in earnest when he makes this argument.

Here the unfolding of Smith's logic is as follows: Wealth refers to the goods necessary to sustain human life, and all such wealth is the outcome of human labor, therefore labor is the measure of the value of wealth. Smith, however, is supposed to be investigating the laws that determine exchange-value. How can the law that determines exchange-value be explained by saying that all wealth is the outcome of labor? The magnitude of the "value" (read: utility) of the products measured as wealth (use-values) is different from the magnitude of the exchange-value of wealth (commodities), and it is nonsense to line up the two and view them as being identical.

Even if we interpret Smith's "purchased labor" to mean the purchase of the labor-power commodity—i.e. capital purchasing labor-power as one commodity or the exchange of a commodity *qua* capital for the labor-power commodity—his view remains irrational. If this were indeed the case, Smith would be saying that the magnitude of wealth determines the purchase of the labor-power commodity. This would mean, in other words, that the greater the magnitude of wealth the greater the amount of the labor-power commodity that could be commanded or purchased, with this thus determining exchange-value.

To begin with, however, how can this magnitude of wealth be measured? This would be possible if we were dealing with the same commodity, such as 14 fish being half of 28 fish. But what would be the situation if we are talking about wealth represented in different use-values, such as fish and automobiles? Certainly, if it were the case that 100 fish could "purchase" one worker, and one car could also "purchase" one worker, it would seem a "law" had been discovered whereby 100 fish and one car are equal—that is, the discovery of a law determining commodity exchange. However, this is a theoretical deception, and in fact a circular argument, since this example presupposes that the 100 fish and one car have the same exchange-value, and it is for this precise reason that 100 fish and one car can both be exchanged for one worker. One could hardly claim that such an arbitrary method makes it possible to establish the law governing exchange-value. Exchange is not established on the basis of (the quantity of) the "wealth" of the fish and the "wealth" of the car. Rather, it is because both have equal exchange-value that they are able to "command" the one worker.

One can certainly not compare 100 fish and one automobile as use-values since there would be little point, for instance, in comparing their weight.[19] It should be perfectly clear that a commodity with greater weight than another commodity will not necessarily have a greater exchange-value. For example, in terms of weight, the car should "command" a hundred or a thousand times more workers than the 100 fish, but this is not the case. On the basis of Smith's theory, we could only say that this is due to the exchange-value of the fish and that of the car—or to use a more vulgar expression, their "purchasing power"—being equal. But in this way, Smith is presupposing the exchange-value to begin with.[20]

As we can see, Smith's theory of value, from the outset, confuses value (exchange-value) and use-value, so that he is easily able to develop the irrational "commanded-labor" theory of value. In evaluating the overall significance of Smith's theory of value, we cannot overlook the fact that this sort of vulgar "moment" lies at its very basis.

The Meaning of the "Value of Labor"

In the passages quoted above, Smith offers what at first sight seems to be a correct view in referring to labor as the "real measure of the exchangeable value of all commodities," but his explanation is insufficient. Smith then goes on to introduce the following, extremely problematic concept of the value of labor, which in a sense exposes an essential aspect of his theory of value:

> The real price of everything, what everything really costs to the man who wants to acquire it, is the toil and trouble of acquiring it. What everything is really worth to the man who has acquired it, and who wants to dispose of it or exchange it for something else, is the toil and trouble which it can save to himself, and which it can impose upon other people. What is bought with money or with goods is purchased by labour, as much as what we acquire by the toil of our own body. That money or those goods indeed save us this toil. They contain the value of a certain quantity of labour which we exchange for what is supposed at the time to contain the value of

---

19. Here we are ignoring the empty theories proposed by the marginal utility school concerning the subjective significance or utility a commodity has for a particular person

20. And his theory would have been even more arbitrary and meaningless had he not presupposed exchange-value, and instead only compared two use-values in the subjectivistic manner of the marginal utility school.

an equal quantity. Labour was the first price, the original purchase-money that was paid for all things. It was not by gold or by silver, but by labour, that all the wealth of the world was originally purchased; and its value, to those who possess it, and who want to exchange it for some new productions, is precisely equal to the quantity of labour which it can enable them to purchase or command.[21]

This is the famous definition of the value of a commodity as being equal to "the toil and trouble to acquire it."[22] On the one hand, Smith defines the value of a commodity as "the toil and trouble of acquiring it," while on the other hand it is said to be worth "the toil and trouble which it can save to himself. However, are these two things the same? The former expression can be said to represent, albeit awkwardly, a labor theory of value to a certain extent, but what about the latter expression?

A person may, for example, have a need for rice but decide to pay for it rather than obtaining it through his own labor.[23] However, can what is purchased be called the value of the rice? Expressed in simpler terms, this is the idea that the sum of money used to purchase a commodity is equivalent to the value of the commodity, which is a typical circular argument that presupposes the very exchange-value that one sets out to demonstrate, thereby opening up the path to every sort of vulgar theory of value.

Smith, here for the first time, introduces the concept of the "value of labor." However, setting aside other passages in his book, it is hard to imagine that here he is simply referring to the value of the labor-power commodity, i.e. wages, as there is nothing at all to suggest this. The content of Smith's "value of labor" is clearly not labor as abstract human labor, or socially average labor, as understood by Marx. This does not have an objective meaning as it does with Marx, and is rather an extremely subjectivistic concept. Smith says that money and commodities contain a certain quantity of labor-value, and that we can exchange them for what is thought to have the same quantity of value. Therefore, labor can be said to be the measure of value. To get a better idea of

---

21. Ibid., 34-5.
22. This view, incidentally, is related Kawakami Hajime's idea, widely debated in prewar Japan, that "value is equal to the sacrifices made by human beings."
23. Smith defines the substance of human labor, which is a social thing, by the subjective moment of "toil and trouble," which exposes his own limitations.

how Smith's notion should be understood, consider the following passage where he discusses the value of labor:

> But as a measure of quantity, such as the natural foot, fathom, or handful, which is continually varying in its own quantity, can never be an accurate measure of the quantity of other things; so a commodity which is itself continually varying in its own value, can never be an accurate measure of the value of other commodities. Equal quantities of labour, at all times and places, may be said to be of equal value to the labourer. In his ordinary state of health, strength and spirits; in the ordinary degree of his skill and dexterity, he must always lay down the same portion of his ease, his liberty, and his happiness. The price which he pays must always be the same, whatever may be the quantity of goods which he receives in return for it. Of these, indeed, it may sometimes purchase a greater and sometimes a smaller quantity; but it is their value which varies, not that of the labour which purchases them. At all times and places that is dear which it is difficult to come at, or which it costs much labour to acquire; and that cheap which is to be had easily, or with very little labour. Labour alone, therefore, never varying in its own value, is alone the ultimate and real standard by which the value of all commodities can at all times and places be estimated and compared. It is their real price; money is their nominal price only.[24]

Smith says that the same amount of labor will, in whatever time and whichever place, have the same value for the laborer because, under normal conditions of mental and physical strength and skill, the worker will have to sacrifice the same amount of "liberty, ease, and happiness." Therefore, the price that the worker is paid will always be the same regardless of the amount of commodities he may receive as compensation. The compensation received will at times be more or less, but this is said to be due to a change in the value of the commodities exchanged for labor, not because of a change in the "value of labor." Thus, labor is said to be "the ultimate and real standard" by which value can be measured.

Here the "value of labor" is understood in the subjectivistic or idealistic sense of the liberty, ease, and happiness the worker must sacrifice. This is different for each person and cannot be *quantitatively* defined. How could a worker quantitatively evaluate or express how much "liberty, ease, and happiness" has been sacrificed? Would this be "identical" for everyone? Clearly,

---

24. Ibid., 37.

depending on the time and place, the view of a person's ease and liberty would be different.[25] How can personal sacrifice be quantified?

In discussing the "value of labor," Smith ultimately poses the question in terms of the subjective value for the producer or seller of the commodity. In other words, what significance does the commodity have for a particular person? As long as one argues from this starting point, there can only be two responses.

First, what is the significance of this product as a use-value for the person involved in its production? Since this is something that must be exchanged, i.e. a commodity, the value of the product would be its utility for this person (in terms of how much "ease" and "liberty" is sacrificed for its production, since it is produced for another person). Smith says that for a worker the subjective "value" of his own labor is always the same. This is a view that is hard to deny, since no one else can become this person and determine the value of labor based on the ease and liberty that was sacrificed in the production of the commodity. If the person says that this is always the same value—or is the same under identical conditions—then this would indeed be the same value.

The second possible view is that the value of a product is equivalent to the value of the products that it is exchanged for. But this amounts to saying that the value of a commodity is the price for which it is sold. This logic is the starting point for every sort of vulgar theory of value, and basically boils down to a purely circular argument.

Smith here advances the plausible argument that labor itself is the first price. In other words, it is the original purchase price paid for all things; or all of the wealth in the world is originally purchased through labor rather than gold or silver. Theoretically speaking, however, this is irrational. What is Smith trying to say in this passage? Is he arguing that the wealth purchased through exchange with labor-power is the starting point of commodity production? Or is he implying that a person—i.e. a worker—by selling his own labor (power) as a commodity, for the first time is able to obtain wealth, and that this is the beginning of something? Even if this beginning refers to the beginning of commodity production, this would still not be true, as in fact

---

25. Under the monopoly-capitalist stage, there is the vulgar marginal utility school that claims that this can be quantifiably determined, and in Smith's theory we can see the embryo or initial moment or such theories.

commodity production itself historically predates the sale and purchase of labor-power (capitalist production) by a considerable period of time.

We have seen how Smith's concept of "the value of labor" is extremely subjectivistic, and is thus a theory of the value of labor for a *particular* worker. On the other hand, however, Smith seems to be saying that this is the value of labor-power, which is an objective definition, thus confusing the issue further.

> But though equal quantities of labour are always of equal value to the labourer, yet to the person who employs him they appear sometimes to be of greater and sometimes of smaller value. He purchases them sometimes with a greater and sometimes with a smaller quantity of goods, and to him the price of labour seems to vary like that of all other things. It appears to him dear in the one case and cheap in the other. In reality, however, it is the goods which are cheap in the one case, and dear in the other.
>
> In this popular sense, therefore, labour, like commodities, may be said to have a real and a nominal price. Its real price may be said to consist in the quantity of the necessaries and conveniences of life which are given for it; its nominal price, in the quantity of money. The labourer is rich or poor, is well or ill rewarded, in proportion to the real, not the nominal price of his labour.[26]

The "real price" of labor is the quantity of use-values—"the necessaries and conveniences of life"—that the worker can obtain in exchange for the price of labor, whereas the "nominal price" is the money-expression for the value of labor-power. In other words, Smith says that for the worker the "value of labor" is subjectively determined, and therefore its value is constant, but for the capitalist who employs workers, the value of labor (wage) is objective and seems to fluctuate like other commodities. The value of labor is thus subjective and unchanging on the one hand, and objective and changing on the other. From the workers' perspective it is unchanging, whereas its "value" fluctuates like that of other commodities when viewed from the perspective of the user of labor, the capitalist who employs workers and pays them for the "value of their labor." Smith speaks of a subjective and irrational value of labor, while at the same time introducing the concept of the value of labor as the objective value of labor-power.

This is a strange view, but for Smith it is unavoidable. On the one hand, he has to provide a basis for labor to be the measure of value, but at the same time

---

26. Ibid., 37-8.

he also feels compelled to recognize that the value of labor, like other commodities, is subject to change. In this way, Smith is unable to establish, in absolute terms, that labor is the measure of value.

Money and Corn as the "Measure of Value"

Smith emphasizes that labor is the measure of value, while at the same time he claims that money or corn are also measures of value. He introduces several measures of value, saying that each has its drawbacks and merits, but his arguments essentially bear little fruit. Smith begins by considering money, but the explanation of how money can be a measure of value is an extremely expedient one, based simply on the fact that money is exchanged with other commodities more frequently than labor.

> Every commodity besides, is more frequently exchanged for, and thereby compared with, other commodities than with labour. It is more natural therefore, to estimate its exchangeable value by the quantity of some other commodity than by that of the labour which it can purchase. The greater part of people too understand better what is meant by a quantity of a particular commodity, than by a quantity of labour. The one is a plain palpable object; the other an abstract notion, which, though it can be made sufficiently intelligible, is not altogether so natural and obvious.
> But when barter ceases, and money has become the common instrument of commerce, every particular commodity is more frequently exchanged for money than for any other commodity.... Hence it comes to pass that the exchangeable value of every commodity is more frequently estimated by the quantity of money, than by the quantity either of labour or of any other commodity which can be had in exchange for it.[27]

This reasoning is odd. Smith says that money can be used to "estimate" the value of a commodity because it is exchanged more frequently for other commodities. But in this case, why didn't Smith choose money as the measure from the outset? Is his "measure of value" what Marx calls the function of money as the measure of value, the expression of a commodity's value using money? If this were the case, and there is some indication of this, Smith would be correct in a sense, but he does not properly pose the question in this way at all.

---

27. Ibid., 36.

Smith realistically—that is, expediently—emphasizes the significance of money as a measure of value, but then says that since money (gold or silver) fluctuates in value, with high or low prices, it is not an appropriate measure of value. In this case, the value of gold or silver is determined by the labor expended in production. In other words, here Smith is actually applying a labor theory of value, an "embodied-labor" theory of value. On the basis of an embodied-labor theory of value, fluctuations in the value of gold and silver are natural. With a rise in productive power, the value of gold or silver would fall, just as in the case of other commodities. However, in terms of value being expressed through money, these fluctuations in the value of money are completely beside the point. Smith confuses the following two things: (1) the question of what determines the exchange-value of a commodity, and (2) the issue of the expression of a commodity's value (its money-expression).

Smith makes a further mistake when he says that although the value of gold and silver fluctuate, and would not purchase or command the same amount of labor, this would not be the case for corn. He develops the following argument:

> Equal quantities of labour will at distant times be purchased more nearly with equal quantities of corn, the subsistence of the labourer, than with equal quantities of gold and silver, or perhaps of any other commodity.[28]

Smith says that corn is the "subsistence of the labourer" and that even in a distant time corn would be able to purchase the same amount of labor, making corn more suitable than other commodities, or than gold and silver, as a measure of value. But what exactly is Smith trying to say here?

Clearly, it is not possible to say that corn can always purchase the same amount of labor (or does Smith mean workers?). This would only be true if the changes in the value of corn and labor-power run parallel, so that their values rise or fall at the same rate. Or is Smith trying to say that the value of corn *is* the value of labor-power, and since the value of labor-power is the value of corn, the same amount of corn could purchase the same amount of labor(ers)? Or perhaps he is saying that since workers always need roughly the same amount of grain in order to live, this grain would be equivalent to measuring the value of labor-power, so that corn could purchase the same amount of

---

28. Ibid., 40.

labor and would be more effective than money as a measure of value. However, even if workers were to require the same amount of corn, and this would be roughly the same in different time periods,[29] this would not be identical to the *value* of corn. If the average social labor needed to produce corn were to double, the value of corn would also double even if workers consumed the *same amount* of corn, and in this case workers would clearly have to pay twice the value. According to Smith's explanation, however, the value of corn would not have changed because it would be exchanged for the same amount of labor. He manages to come up with such a silly idea because he confuses exchange-value with use-value.

The argument advanced by Smith is a simple tautology—of explaining value with value—and at the same time he reduces value to use-value, or confuses value with use-value, by saying that the value of labor-power is determined or measured by the quantity of the use-value of corn. Smith's theory of value ultimately revolves around these two errors. It is precisely because his theory is tangled up in these errors that it becomes increasingly difficult to understand.

Smith determines the "value of labor" subjectively, and therefore according to (the quantity of) corn as a use-value, and in this way corn is viewed as the best measure of value. This, however, is complete nonsense, and Unoists have based their own theory of value on this view—which Uno Kōzō does not hesitate to admit publicly—because they are repulsed by Marx's labor theory of value. They reject and seek to bury this theory by making use of the confused and vulgar aspects of Adam Smith's theory, thereby revealing their reactionary, philistine natures.

Why Smith Introduces the "Measure of Value"

Here we need to examine Smith's use of the term "measure of value." Needless to say, this is not used in the Marxist sense. For Marxists, the "measure of value" is one of the functions of money. A commodity *expresses* its value, relatively, through money (as so many dollars or yen, etc.). Marx calls this the function of money as the measure of value, whereas Smith uses this same expression to refer to the *determination* of exchange-value, i.e. the universal

---

29. In the case of Japan, per-capita consumption of rice has decreased by one-third or one-half, and this example alone reveals a serious flaw in Smith's theory of value.

standard to measure value. Smith says that if such a measure were to exist, the value of a commodity could also be measured. For this reason, Smith searches, endlessly, for such a standard. First he considers labor as the measure of value, but finding this inadequate, moves on to money, which is in turn rejected in favor of corn. It is no accident that Smith speaks of the "real measure of value." He uses this expression because he does not understand the essence of value and believes there is a need for such a *real* measure. Smith imagines that there must be a commodity that can function as the measure of value which would have an unchanging value, but he can do little more than point out that the value of money is not constant since it fluctuates along with changes in the productive power of the labor that produces gold. Smith here at least says that labor determines exchange-value, but he then argues that the labor-based measure is problematic and value is usually not estimated by labor:

> But though labour be the real measure of the exchangeable value of all commodities, it is not that by which their value is commonly estimated. It is often difficult to ascertain the proportion between two different quantities of labour.[30]

On the basis of this argument, Smith says that "there may be more labour in an hour's hard work than in two hours easy business,"[31] but that it is difficult to find a measure of "hardship or ingenuity." Smith concludes that labor is insufficient or incorrect as a measure of exchange-value. In other words, he often mistakenly—or essentially?—views the labor that determines exchange-value in a subjectivistic manner, and is thus unable to determine this labor quantitatively, reaching the conclusion that labor does not determine exchange-value. Smith adheres to an embodied-labor theory of value, on the one hand, but in addition to being vague, this view is immediately negated and overturned by his other concepts. Subsequent vulgar economists, represented by Malthus, seized upon the contradictions and confusion within Smith's thought to construct a completely nonsensical theory of value, while even offering up the sophistry that they had somehow "purified" Smith's theory.

If the labor that determines exchange-value is reduced to social labor, i.e. abstract labor, one will not end up rambling on about a "measure of value" in the manner of Smith, and it becomes possible to rationally understand com-

30. Ibid., 35.
31. Ibid.

plex and simple labor. But for Smith, it was historically impossible to grasp social labor, and this understanding was also hindered by his class position.

Marx analyzes exchange-value and reveals that the "expression of value" is included within the exchange-value relation, and that this relation between commodities continues to develop until a certain commodity emerges that is established as the general equivalent, as the independent existence of value (money). Once this occurs, money plays the role of expressing the value of commodities, as a certain quantity of money, i.e. price. To this extent, the function of money as a measure of value is clear, but this is theoretically separate from the question of what *determines* exchange-value. It is contradictory to say that money determines exchange-value, since money is also a commodity. The fact that a car exchanges for one million yen *is* the exchange-value itself, not an explanation of what determines exchange-value, and this point should be clear. To answer this question of what determines exchange-value, it is necessary to explain this sort of relationship between one automobile and one million yen.

The classical school was obsessed with the "measure of value," but this was only the reverse side of the fact that they lacked a concept of value. The more they perceived this lack, the more inclined they were to adhere to a "real" measure of value, and in this way they sought something that could "estimate" value. But it was not clear whether they were attempting to measure value according to quality or quantity?

In terms of the concept of value as quality, this refers to the social labor, or abstract human labor, necessary to produce a commodity, its quantity being given in labor-time. If the concept of value is clarified, its quantitative definition easily follows. However, the classical school did not provide such a clear explanation, and did not even feel the necessity to do so. Even though they came close to a labor theory of value, it was incomplete and unclear, and above all they failed to grasp its significance. In considering what determines exchange-value, they were exclusively concerned with the quantitative aspect, and failed to show any interest in the question of why labor takes the form of value. Smith was no exception, and indeed he is the one who expresses this tendency in characteristic fashion. If we grasp the following point made by Engels in his introduction to *Wage Labor and Capital*, we will have no need for Smith's views on the "measure of value":

> And this is the economic constitution of our entire modern society: the
> working class alone produces all values. For value is only another expression

for labor, that expression, namely, by which is designated, in our capitalist society of today, the amount of socially necessary labor embodied in a particular commodity. But, these values produced by the workers do not belong to the workers. They belong to the owners of the raw materials, machines, tools, and money, which enable them to buy the labor-power of the working class. Hence, the working class gets back only a part of the entire mass of products produced by it. And, as we have just seen, the other portion, which the capitalist class retains, and which it has to share, at most, only with the landlord class, is increasing with every new discovery and invention, while the share which falls to the working class (per capita) rises but little and very slowly, or not at all, and under certain conditions it may even fall.[32]

Historical Evaluation of Smith's Theory

We have seen that Smith's "theory of value" contains correct moments as a labor theory of value—i.e. as an embodied-labor theory of value—and therefore as a deduction theory of value. On the other hand, however, Smith emphasizes a purchased- or commanded-labor theory (i.e. a composition theory), while also introducing a "cost theory" (of labor) and the issue of supply and demand. He even goes so far as to propose a subjectivistic explanation of value as one essential moment of his theory, resulting in an extremely vulgar view.

Of course, in a sense, the issue of supply and demand, as well as cost, represent moments within the unfolding of human understanding leading up to a labor theory of value. In considering the question of what determines price (exchange-value), an initial understanding looks to supply and demand, before moving on to a cost theory, where the price of a commodity is said to be determined by the cost of producing it. When it becomes clear that the cost explanation merely determines cost by means of cost, and is thus a circular argument, human thought must in turn move on toward the correct (scientific) understanding that necessarily results in the labor theory of value.

It is not surprising, then, that all of these various moments appear within Smith's theory. Smith blends together all of these different elements, and thus operates within confusion and contradiction. This represents the essence of his thought. Marx points out that Smith, instead of a theoretical and intrinsic analysis of economic relations within capitalism, describes and evaluates these

---

32. *MECW*, vol. 27 (1992), 200-1.

relations as they appear to human consciousness. Smith's theory even includes moments of the irrational theory of value prevalent in the monopoly stage of capitalism—namely, the subjectivistic theory of "marginal-utility" value—but it is not certain whether this should be seen as a point in his favor, in terms of the range of his theory reaching all the way to the stage of monopoly capitalism, or as something that exposes its limitations.

We have repeatedly seen the fundamental twofold nature of Smith's theory of value, which combines an embodied-labor theory of value and a labor-purchased theory of value. Clearly it is this duality that determines the historical significance and limitations of his theory of value. In this sense, grasping Smith's theory of value can lead to an understanding of the significance of the Marxist theory of value, highlighting the rational developmental process through which this latter theory emerged and was formed. Bearing in mind the commanded-labor theory of value—which is particular to Smith and characteristic of his theory despite being illogical and "mistaken"—Marx summed up the positive significance of Smith's theory in *Theories of Surplus Value*:

> [Under capitalism, unlike simple commodity production society,] the product or the value of the product of labor does not belong to the laborer. A definite quantity of living labor does not command the same quantity of objectified labor, or a definite quantity of labor objectified in a commodity commands a greater quantity of living labor than is contained in the commodity itself
>
> But as Adam Smith quite correctly takes as his starting-point the commodity and the exchange of commodities, and thus the producers initially confront each other only as possessors of commodities, sellers of commodities and buyers of commodities, he therefore discovers (so it seems to him) that in the exchange between capital and wage labor, objectified labor and living labor, the general law at once ceases to apply, and commodities (for labor too is a commodity in so far as it is bought and sold) do not exchange in proportion to the quantities of labor which they represent. Hence he concludes that labor-time is no longer the immanent measure which regulates the exchange-value of commodities, from the moment when the conditions of labor confront the wage laborer in the form of landed property and capital.[33]

In any case Adam Smith feels the difficulty of deducing the exchange between capital and labor from the law that determines the exchange of

---

33. *MECW*, vol. 30, 379-80.

commodities, since the former apparently rests on quite opposite and contradictory principles. And indeed the contradiction could not be solved so long as capital was set directly against labor instead of against labor capacity [labor power].[34]

Conversely, the money with which the capitalist buys labor contains a smaller quantity of labor, less labor-time, than the quantity of labor or labor-time of the workman contained in the commodity produced by him. Besides the quantity of labor contained in this sum of money which forms the wage, the capitalist buys an additional quantity of labor for which he does not pay, an excess over the quantity of labor contained in the money he pays out. And it is precisely this additional quantity of labor which constitutes the surplus-value created by capital.

But as the money with which the capitalist buys labor (in the actual result, even though mediated through exchange not with labor directly, but with labor capacity) is nothing other than the converted form of all other commodities, their independent existence as exchange-value, it can equally well be said that all commodities in exchange with living labor buy more labor than they contain. It is precisely this more that constitutes surplus-value. It is Adam Smith's great merit that it is just in the chapters of Book I (chapters 6, 7, 8) where he passes from simple commodity exchange and its law of value to exchange between objectified and living labor, to exchange between capital and wage labor, to the consideration of profit and rent in general—in short to the origin of surplus-value—that he feels some flaw has emerged. He senses that somehow—whatever the cause may be, and he does not grasp what it is—in the actual result the law is suspended: more labor is exchanged for less labor (from the laborer's standpoint), less labor is exchanged for more labor (from the capitalist's standpoint). His merit is that he emphasizes—and it obviously perplexes him—that with the accumulation of capital and the appearance of property in land—that is, when the conditions of labor assume an independent existence over against labor itself—something new occurs, apparently (and actually, in the result) the law of value changes into its opposite. It is his theoretical strength that he feels and stresses this contradiction, just as it is his theoretical weakness that the contradiction shakes his confidence in the general law, even for simple commodity exchange; that he does not perceive how this contradiction arises, through labor capacity itself becoming a commodity, and that in the case of this specific commodity its use-value—which therefore has nothing to do with its exchange-value—is precisely the energy which creates exchange-value.[35]

---

34. Ibid., 380.
35. Ibid., 393-4.

Marx then offers a summary of the relation between Smith and Ricardo, as well as the reaction led by Malthus against the scientific aspects of their theories, which I will use to bring this discussion of Smith's theory to an end:

> Ricardo is ahead of Adam Smith in that these apparent contradictions—in their result real contradictions—do not confuse him. But he is behind Adam Smith in that he does not even suspect that this presents a problem, and therefore the specific development which the law of value undergoes with the formation of capital does not for a moment puzzle him or even attract his attention. We shall see later how what was a stroke of genius with Adam Smith becomes reactionary with Malthus as against Ricardo's standpoint.[36]

---

36. Ibid., 394.

3

Theory of Credit

What is Credit?

This chapter examines the question of credit, and of course here I am referring to the Marxist theory of credit. This issue is closely connected to the discussion of the commodity in chapter one, with Marx's theory of value being the fundamental premise, but the theory of credit has a more direct relation to the logic of capital that was only touched on slightly in the chapter on the commodity, including the issue of the exploitation of labor (production of surplus-labor). The issue of credit merits our attention because under capitalist production in general, and modern or state-monopoly capitalism in particular, credit comes to have extremely great significance. This point is illustrated by the fact that the Japanese government issues bonds in excess of tens of trillions of yen annually, with an outstanding debt amounting to hundreds of trillions of yen.[1] These government bonds represent the debt of the state, and are thus deeply connected to the issue of credit.

Central banks today have become closely aligned with governments, basically acting as subordinate government agencies. However, although banknotes (Bank of Japan notes) have increasingly become *quasi* paper money under capitalism, the starting point for such banknotes is credit money, and the "yen" today has certainly not lost this character. In other words, banknotes have not—and could not—completely become paper money.[2] The development of government credit and the connection between the state and credit is

---

1. [See note 199 in chapter one for figures on government debt.]

thus a fundamental characteristic of modern capitalism, and one essential aspect or moment of the "managed currency system." Indeed, modern capitalism has formed a sort of "addiction" to credit. In this sense, we cannot hope to correctly understand modern capitalism without becoming familiar with credit. But what exactly is credit to begin with?

In our everyday lives we frequently borrow or loan money, such as borrowing from a bank or purchasing goods on credit. Most bourgeois scholars treat credit as something that is suprahistorical, existing in every type of historical society, thus understanding credit merely in terms of being a relationship of "trust" between people, similar to a person borrowing a bit of sugar from a neighbor.

But here we are not dealing with "credit" in this sense. Certainly credit does involve a relationship of trust, but this is separate from the mere question of trust between human beings. For instance, the simple extension of payment in conjunction with the sale of a commodity stems from an acknowledgement of the social character of commodities—the fact that they can be realized as value—and is certainly not merely a question of trust between individuals or some sort of abstract human quality. The "credit" we are concerned with here is a historical and socio-economic relation that emerges and expands within the creation and development of commodity-capitalist production. Although this does involve an element of trust, this is an issue that is quite distinct from the example of a child loaning video-game software to a friend.

In part five of the third volume of *Capital*, Marx presents a broad discussion of credit, with a focus on interest-bearing capital.[3] The starting point for the development of this theory is the fact that, on the basis of capitalist produc-

---

2.   [The concept of "paper money" refers to non-convertible money that is given forced currency through the backing of the state.]

3.   [Readers should note that with the recent publication of Marx's original manuscript for the third volume of *Capital*, it has become apparent that Engels made a number of changes (additions and deletions) that were not explicitly noted, and which reflect at times an understanding that differs from that of Marx. This controversy has been examined—and continues to be examined—by Hayashi and the Marxist Comrades Group. This series of articles was written before he was aware of this problem, but as far as I am aware there is relatively little negative impact from the reliance on what may come to be known as the "Engels edition" of *Capital*.

tion, money assumes the use-value of "creating profit" in addition to its use-value as money, and in this way comes to be traded as a "commodity." This is of course natural to the extent that capitalist credit develops overall with interest-bearing capital (the loaning of capital) as its central axis, but this does not negate the significance of the more fundamental concept of commercial credit which, according to Marx, "forms the basis of the credit system."[4] For this reason, we also must begin by looking at commercial credit.

"Natural Basis" of the Credit System

Since commercial credit is credit that develops under conditions of commodity circulation, Marx refers to it as the "natural basis" of the credit system. In *A Contribution to a Critique of Political Economy*—as well as in chapter three of the first volume of *Capital*—Marx provides a fundamental explanation of commercial credit.

> No proof in detail is needed to show that such *purchases on credit*, in which the two poles of the transaction are separated in time, evolve spontaneously on the basis of simple circulation of commodities…This gives rise to relations of creditor and debtor among commodity-owners. These relations can be fully developed even before the credit system comes into being, although they are the natural basis of the latter.[5]

With the development of commodity circulation, a relation emerges in which, for instance, even if a commodity owner sells a coat, the buyer is allowed a certain period of time before payment is made. This is "purchasing on credit," in which "the alienation of the commodity becomes separated by an interval of time from the realization of its price."[6] In this way, the seller becomes a creditor and the buyer a debtor, and money comes to have the new function of being a means of payment.

However, Marx also refers to commercial credit in chapters twenty-five and thirty of the third volume of *Capital*. This is because capitalism is a society of commodity production—commodity production developed to its highest level—and "capital" also appears in the exchange process simply as a commod-

---

4.   *Capital*, vol. 3, 610.
5.   *A Contribution to the Critique of Political Economy*, 375.
6.   *Capital*, vol. 1, 232.

ity or money. In this way, commercial credit is a reality under capitalist production, and develops greatly within this mode of production.

> I have already shown (vol. 1, chap. 3, sec. 3-b) how the function of money as a means of payment develops out of simple commodity circulation, so that a relationship of creditor and debtor is formed. With the development of trade and the capitalist mode of production, which produces only for circulation, this spontaneous basis for the credit system is expanded, generalized and elaborated. By and large, money now functions only as a means of payment, i.e. commodities are not sold for money, but for a written promise to pay at a certain date.[7]

This already is no longer credit between simple commodity producers, but rather "the credit that capitalists involved in the reproduction process give one another" by means of "the bill of exchange, a promissory note with a fixed date of payment."[8] What needs to be noted here is that commercial credit differs from the loaning of money. It is ultimately credit that commodity owners (capitalists) "give one another" so that "each person gives credit in one direction and receives credit from another."[9]

Commercial credit is "buying on credit" since the buyer receives a commodity although the payment of money is delayed. Therefore, some scholars have argued that this must be seen as the loaning of money. However, the buyer already has money accumulated in some form and does not loan this as "capital." The buyer is also a commodity owner—or a merchant as the "agent of circulation"[10]—and can only obtain money by selling the commodity that he has purchased, i.e. the important distinction here is that this is credit that commodity owners (capitalists) or merchants "give one another." If this distinction is overlooked, it is not possible to correctly understand the concept of commercial credit. Some may say that it is all the same in terms of loaning some sort of value, and it is not mistaken to say that credit is indeed the lending and borrowing of value, but at issue here are the relations under which this credit exists and the form it takes.

---

7.   *Capital*, vol. 3, 525.
8.   Ibid., 610.
9.   Ibid.
10. Ibid., 406.

The role of creditor or of debtor results here from the simple circulation of commodities. The change in its form impresses this new stamp on seller and buyer. At first, therefore, these new roles are just as transient as those of seller and buyer, and are played alternately by the same actors.[11]

Money Credit

Our next topic is money credit. Marx refers to money credit as an antecedent form of bank credit. This money credit is, necessarily, also usurer's credit. Along with commercial credit, money credit is the most fundamental form of credit, which appeared widely in pre-capitalist society. The reason for this is that "usurer's capital requires nothing more for its existence than that at least a portion of the products is transformed into commodities and that money in its various functions develops concurrently with trade in commodities."[12]

With the development of commodity production to a certain extent, and the appearance of money, the hoarding of money naturally occurs. Commodity producers themselves feel the need to maintain some money, but this subsequently reaches the point where the hoarding of money becomes a goal in and of itself. Thus, with a certain development of commodity production, there emerges the formation of money hoarders who do not use money, on the one hand, and people who need money but do not possess it, on the other. The former loan out money to the latter, and in this way we have the crystallization of professional moneylenders.

The idea that money capital necessarily takes the form of usurer's capital should be fairly straightforward. With the development of commodity production, there is the penetration of a money-based economy, so that the need for money increases among society's wastrels (former aristocrats), while on the other hand there is also an increase in the demand for money among small producers. The former require money to satisfy a boundless desire for luxury, while the latter seek money in the hope of recovering from setbacks suffered in production or to respond to the increasing need to pay taxes in cash.[13] Marx notes the following:

---

11. *Capital*, vol. 1, 233.
12. *Capital*, vol. 3, 728.
13. A classic example of this phenomenon can be seen in the history of Japan.

Two of the forms in which usurer's capital exists in phases prior to the capitalist mode of production are particularly characteristic. I deliberately use
the word "characteristic," for the same forms recur on the basis of capitalist
production, though here they are merely subordinate forms. In the latter
case they are no longer forms that determine the character of interest-bearing capital. These two forms are, firstly, usury by lending money to extrava-
gant magnates, essentially to landed proprietors; secondly, usury by lending
money to small producers who possess their own conditions of labor,
including artisans, but particularly and especially peasants, since, wherever
pre-capitalist conditions permit small autonomous individual producers,
the peasant class must form their great majority.[14]

Although both commercial credit and money credit are only generated on the
basis of commodity circulation, we have to draw a clear distinction between
the two concepts. The former emerges from the process of the sale and purchase of commodities, in which the roles of creditor and debtor are assumed in
turn by those involved in the transactions. In the case of money credit, by contrast, the sale and purchase of commodities do not comprise its direct
moments, and the role of the creditor and debtor are separate and fixed in
opposition to each other. In the case of money credit in particular, loans are
made directly in the form of money, and the aim, unlike the case of commercial credit, is to obtain interest.

Both commercial credit and money credit are the most primitive or original
forms of credit, but from the perspective of their relation to capitalism, an
important distinction between them exists. That is, under capitalist production, commercial credit exists as the most basic form of credit and has great
significance and prominence, whereas money-capital (usurer's capital) is
superceded by capitalist loan-capital (interest-bearing capital), and thus only
exists as a historical form with the significance of being an antecedent to bank
credit. Like interest-bearing capital, commercial credit has real significance
under capitalism, but it cannot be called the characteristic type of credit under
capitalism. Capitalist credit, fundamentally speaking, must develop as loan-
capital (interest-bearing capital), which can be considered the characteristic
form of bourgeois credit. In the case of this form, "capital" is shown in its most
"externalized" and superficial shape as such.

---

14. Ibid., 729.

Loaning and Borrowing of "Capital"

The fact that Marx's theory of credit, presented in the third volume of *Capital*, begins directly with the definition of the concept of interest-bearing capital (loan-capital) can be interpreted in various ways, if one pauses to consider it. Marx touches on the issue of commercial credit in the first volume of *Capital* as part of his discussion of the commodity, but in the third volume of *Capital* he does not deal with commercial credit until chapter thirty,[15] and then only in passing, and money credit (usurer's credit) is only referred to one single time, in a historical fashion, in his discussion of pre-capitalist society.

This reflects the fact that interest-bearing capital—the borrowing and loaning of "capital"—is a form of credit particular to capitalist production, symbolizing this mode of production. In terms of form, commercial credit is the same as usurer's credit, but its content is completely different. This is the reason why Marx prefaces his remarks on interest-bearing capital by saying that this occurs "on the basis of capitalist production."[16] The major precondition for this form of credit is the existence of capitalism, and the starting point is that money "on the foundation of capitalism" is transformed into capital, thus becoming "self-valorizing" value.

> [Money] produces profit, i.e. it enables the capitalist to extract and appropriate for himself a certain quantity of unpaid labor, surplus product and surplus-value. In this way the money receives, besides the use-value which it possesses as money, an additional use-value, namely the ability to function as capital. Its use-value here consists precisely in the profit that it produces when transformed into capital. In this capacity of potential capital, as a means to the production of profit, it becomes a commodity, but a commodity of a special kind. Or what comes to the same thing, capital becomes a commodity.[17]

When considering money, Marx emphasizes in his criticism of Samuel Overstone that an important distinction exists between simple money (money *per se*) and money as "capital." In addition to money having a use-value as such, which is the function of being a means of purchase or payment, etc., it also comes to have a function as capital, as the potential to create profit, with a use-

---

15. [The *tenth* chapter of part five (Marx's theory of credit).]
16. Ibid., 459.
17. Ibid., 459-60.

value as "potential capital." In this way, money becomes a type of "commodity." Of course, this is different from the commodity in the original or genuine sense,[18] being instead a commodity *sui generis* or fictitious commodity.

Under capitalism, money *as capital* generates profit (average profit). For this reason, a person who has a certain quantity of money possesses, *in potentia*, the power to create profit. If the owner of money transfers it for a certain period of time to someone who puts it to actual use to create profit, he has handed over to this person the capability of producing profit, and by actually using this as capital it becomes possible to obtain the average rate of profit. Therefore, the owner of capital is entitled to receive a certain compensatory sum of money from out of this profit. This is the manner in which the category of interest-bearing capital is created. In terms of form, this is identical to usurer's capital, but the content is quite different.

Interest-bearing capital is lent out *as capital*, rather than for consumption as in the case of usurer's credit. This is why even though there is no "natural" rate of interest, its maximum level is posited by the limit of the average rate of profit. Ultimately the interest obtained from interest-bearing capital is nothing more than one part of the profit created by productive capital (functional capital). There is no way for only interest-bearing capital, and therefore the *rentier* class, to expand without productive capital also increasing—which means that financial bubbles are bound to burst!

The reason or necessity underlying the fact that this form of credit resembles the purchase or sale of a commodity is that those involved in the borrowing and loaning of such "capital" view this as a type of purchase or sale. In other words, purchasers (debtors) enter into "transactions" involving money as a cheap or costly commodity on the "capital markets." This is reflected by the common use of expressions such as "inexpensive" or "expensive" funds. Marx discusses in detail how capital as a commodity *sui generis* is similar and different from genuine commodities, but I will leave it to the reader to examine this issue further, and instead move on to the next topic.

---

18. [See chapter one for Hayashi's discussion of the distinction between the commodity in the "genuine" or "original" sense (i.e. the *concept* of the commodity) and derivative commodities (commodities *sui generis*) such as "money *qua* capital" discussed here.]

Uno's Concept of Interest-Bearing Capital

We can come to a better understanding of the concept of interest-bearing capital by critically examining Uno Kōzō's views on this subject. However, as we saw in the first chapter, Uno's theories are not particularly easy to understand, and it is often exceedingly difficult to decipher what he is trying to say.

Uno first of all criticizes Marx's concept of interest-bearing capital by saying that "money itself becomes a commodity, but capital does not." He adds that the basis for interest is not profit (the exploitation of labor), but rather the fact that the money—certainly not capital!—loaned out is employed by the functional capitalist, which "enhances the power of capital and increases the surplus-value produced by a certain quantity of his own capital [*jiko shihon*]." Uno goes on to say that the "funds" [*shikin*] that become the basis of loan-capital are fundamentally formed in the circulation process of industrial capital, and should be considered as money-capital (idle capital) *qua* circulation-form of industrial capital, and that it is incorrect to view this broadly as being social money-capital in the manner of Marx.

Turning to Uno's views on the commodification of capital, he argues that this pertains not to loan-capital but rather to stock shares. Uno claims that since stocks are bought and sold on the stock market as "capital" this represents the true commodification of capital. However, if Uno is going to offer up such a view, there seems to be little need to employ the terms "interest-bearing capital" and "loan-capital" in the first place. Considering the fact that he is not speaking of "capital" in any sense, but rather money (funds), the word "capital" itself becomes unnecessary, and we have to wonder why he insists on using the term "interest-bearing capital."

It is evident, even without Uno pointing it out for us, that in the case of interest-bearing capital what is directly being bought and sold is money, and I am not sure who he believes is claiming that this is capital (or industrial capital?) *directly* speaking. At issue is the nature of the money that is being bought and sold. Money is not simply being bought and sold as money. Rather, this is money whose-use value is the production of surplus value. In other words, money is being sold from the beginning as capital, or more precisely as "potential capital." Uno has completely failed to understand the concept of interest-bearing capital, where money as capital (not money as such) is bought and sold and handed over.

This rather astounding view held by Uno stems from his total failure to understand that the basis for interest is that the money loaned out (as capital) is invested as capital (industrial capital), which seeks surplus-value in the relation between capital and wage-labor, and that in the case of interest-bearing capital the "fetishistic" form of capital as self-valorizing value attains its most complete manifestation. According to Uno, interest is the outcome of the "enhanced capital-power" of a capitalist's own capital [*jiko-shihon*] by means of the loaned "funds," so that it is merely a result of the efficiency of capital, with no basis in the exploitation of labor.

The reactionary nature and class basis of this sort of "theory" should be clear. Under capitalism, money comes to have the use-value of generating profit and is the object of transactions as this sort of use-value—as (potential) capital—so the empty, concept-free nature of Uno's view that what is being bought and sold is money *as such* should be self-evident.

Uno's objective role is clearly to generate confusion regarding Marx's scientific explanation, obscuring the secret of exploitation and the significance of the upside-down development of society indicated by interest-bearing capital (which is the pinnacle of fetishized consciousness). In this way, Uno renders an invaluable service to capital!

It is absurd for Uno to counter Marx with the pretentious theory that the "capital" which is bought and sold takes the form of stock shares, rather than money ("funds"). In the first place, the price of fictitious capital is derived from the "capitalization" of dividends and fixed income calculated on the basis of interest rates, and this presupposes the relation of interest-bearing capital. Moreover, fictitious capital is referred to as such precisely because it is *not* capital in reality, whereas interest-bearing capital represents an actually existing relation that is thus distinct from such fictitious capital.

Distinction between Interest Rate and Profit Rate

Along with capital in the form of money (loan-capital) appearing as a commodity, interest presents itself as the price of this commodity and is seen as being nothing more than the "price" of money.

> We have seen that although it is a category absolutely different from the commodity, interest-bearing capital becomes a commodity *sui generis* with interest as its price, and this price, just like the market price of an ordinary commodity, is fixed at any given time by demand and supply.[19]

---

19. Ibid., 489.

Of course, interest can only be considered the "price of money" in a fictional way, and it cannot be forgotten that interest-bearing capital is "a category absolutely different from the commodity." In the case of the commodity in the *original* sense, price is the money-form of a commodity's value, but in the case of interest-bearing capital it certainly cannot be said that interest is the money-expression of the "value" of interest-bearing capital. Interest is only the sale and purchase of a commodity in the sense that the purchaser of this commodity "buys" it through the payment of a certain quantity of money, and the seller hands over a certain use-value (the potential to generate profit).

At first glance it seems odd that in the case of interest-bearing capital a certain quantity of money is bought and sold with money. Needless to say, the reason that this may occur is that what is being bought and sold is not simply money, but money as capital.[20] Thus, this "price of money" has no nodal point (value) to fluctuate around as in the case of genuine commodities, nor does it have a "natural" rate as in the case of profit (average profit). The interest rate is only determined within the push and pull of supply and demand, and therefore this category is particularly attractive to vulgar economists, perfectly suiting their inclinations. Here such economists are not obliged to concern themselves with the essential relations underlying the phenomenon of price or the bothersome issue of value. Marx notes for instance:

> The prevailing average rate of interest in a country, as distinct from the constantly fluctuating market rate, cannot be determined by any law. There is no natural rate of interest, therefore, in the sense that economists speak of a natural rate of profit and a natural rate of wages.[21]

The uppermost limit of the interest rate is posited by the average rate of profit. Since interest is one part of profit, there is no way for the interest rate to exceed the rate of profit Logically speaking, it is not possible for a functional capitalist to pay interest on money borrowed at a rate exceeding the rate of profit. Marx emphasizes the difference between the profit rate and rate of interest. The rate of interest is "directly and immediately determined"[22] by the relation between the money-capitalist as supplier of the money and the functional capitalist who requires it, but this is not true of the rate of profit. The

---

20. I only point this out because of the prevalence of Unoist ideas.
21. Ibid., 484.
22. Ibid., 490.

rate of profit cannot appear as this sort of "direct determination." An examination of the establishment of production price, i.e. the equalization of the rate of profit, reveals that the rate of interest is not mediated by a movement of equalization, but rather is formed (or exists) directly.

> The rate of profit, on the other hand, can vary even within the same sphere, given the same market price, according to the different conditions in which individual capitals produce the same commodity; for the profit rate on an individual capital is not determined simply by the market price of the commodity, but rather by the difference between the market price and cost price. And these various rates of profit, firstly within the same sphere and then within the various different spheres, can be equalized only through constant fluctuations.[23]

In the case of interest-bearing capital, however, the situation is different. Here "as far as the form of demand goes, loan capital is faced with the entire weight of a class [industrial capital as a whole], while, as far as supply goes, it itself appears *en masse* as loan-capital ["a concentrated and organized mass, placed under the control of the bankers as representatives of the social capital"]."[24] Thus, the rate of interest is directly determined by a "simultaneous effect on a mass scale,"[25] appearing socially as a clear and specified rate.

"Qualitative Division" of Profit

Marx emphasizes that along with the establishment of (the category of) interest, the quantitative division of profit turns into a qualitative one. This is important, not only for the concept of interest-bearing capital, but also to understand modern capitalism in which there is a separation between capital ownership and functioning capital, so that the income of the functional capitalist appears as a "wage of supervision." We need to consider exactly what Marx saying here, and why he goes to the trouble of introducing this particular concept.

The issue here revolves around how we should understand the "qualitative division of profit." The quantiative division of profit is not a difficult concept to understand, since it is an easily understood fact that the profit of the capi-

---

23. Ibid., 491.
24. Ibid.
25. Ibid., 489.

talist entrusted with loan-capital is divided up. The *qualitative* division of profit refers to the division between interest as the portion of aggregate profit belonging to capital ownership as such, and the "profit of enterprise" as the portion of aggregate profit that belongs to functional capital—"and this mutual ossification and autonomization of the two parts of the gross profit, as if they derived from two essentially separate sources, must now be fixed for the entire capitalist class and the total capital."[26]

In the first place, the category of interest "lies outside the movement of industrial capital itself"[27] since interest is one part of average profit that only has to be paid to the loan-capitalist if the functional capitalist makes use of loan-capital rather than using his own capital, and thus this does not necessarily have to exist. To examine the transformation of an arbitrary, quantitative division of profit into a *qualitiative* division, Marx says we must address the "real starting point of interest formation," i.e. the fact the that the money-capitalist and the productive capitalist "actually do come face to face," so that "the one simply lends the capital, the other applies it productively."[28] Thus, for the productive capitalist, gross profit is divided into two parts: interest and net gain. The latter "necessarily appears to him as the product of capital in its actual functioning; and this really is the case for him, since he represents capital only as functioning capital."[29]

On the other hand, interest is obtained by the loan-capitalist, who has merely possessed the capital (and then let go of it for a period of time). It appears that the income of the loan-capitalist is derived solely from the ownership of capital. Interest and profit of enterprise appear not merely as a division of profit between creditor and debtor, but as something beyond this, a relation with different determinations than capital, so that there are two different categories of profit. This is the social culmination of the phenomenon of interest appearing as the fruit of capital ownership and profit of enterprise as the fruit of functioning capital.

This phenomenon conceals the fact that the capitalist money-owner (loan-capitalist) also has a connection to the exploitation of labor by collaborating with the functional capitalist and obtaining the outcome of this exploitation (one part of the surplus-value), while at the same time the illusion spreads that

---

26. Ibid., 498.
27. Ibid., 493.
28. Ibid., 495.
29. Ibid., 496.

the functional capitalist's profit is not the result of exploitation but rather compensation for management labor ("wages of supervision"). In place of the confrontation between capital and wage-labor, we now have the confrontation between the owner capitalist and the functional capitalist, the relation between the money-capitalist and industrial capitalist. This phenomenon of the profit accruing to the functional capitalist appearing as a sort of wage develops even further with the spread of joint-stock companies, so that the functional capitalist generally appears as a manager.

> Joint-stock companies in general (developed within the credit system) have the tendency to separate this function of managerial work more and more from the possession of capital...But since on the one hand the functioning capitalist confronts the mere owner of capital, the money-capitalist, and with the development of credit this money-capital itself assumes a social character, being concentrated in banks and loaned out by these, no longer by its direct proprietors; and since on the other hand the mere manager, who does not possess capital under any title, neither by loan nor in any other way, takes care of all real functions that fall to the functioning capitalist as such, there remains only the functionary, and the capitalist vanishes from the production process as someone superfluous.[30]

Bank Credit

We all know that in capitalist society credit is concentrated in the hands of banks (or "finance capital") as the representatives of credit. Normally speaking, however, people are baffled by the complexity and diversity of capitalist credit and the functions of banks, assuming that this must be difficult to understand or even viewing such things as mystical entities. If correctly approached, however, bank functions are not exceedingly complicated. The correct approach when considering the operations of banks is to "reduce" them to their simplest forms.

We have in fact, already discussed the simplest function of credit, in its two most fundamental forms—namely, commercial credit and money (capital) credit. The seemingly complex credit of banks fundamentally comes down to these forms of credit (although in reality this is "complexly" manifested as something intertwined and interconnected). It is not correct, however, to think of these two forms as being equivalent. As Marx notes, banker's credit

---

30. Ibid., 512.

refers to the "monetary loans that bankers, as intermediaries, make to the industrialists and merchants" and is "an entirely separate and essentially different element [from commercial credit]."[31] We have also already seen that commercial credit is credit that capitalists involved in the reproduction process and commercial capitalists "give one another," in the form of an advance of money at the time of the sale of commodities.

Bank credit, as money credit, is based on the lending of "idle" money disengaged from the reproduction process, and is credit in the form of a loan of money or interest-bearing capital. Unlike commercial capital, the aim is to obtain interest, so that for the bankers the money loaned out is capital from the beginning. This is the reason that userer's capital is the antecedent form of banking capital, and seen historically bankers are the transformation of money dealers, originally taking the form of "money-changing and the bullion trade."[32] However, the reason for the existence of bank credit is not limited to this sort of orignal loaning of money, and "the banker also deals in credit in every other form, even if he advances money deposited with him in cash."[33] In other words, bank credit at the same time deals with commercial credit—or rather intervenes in or subrogates this—through the discounting of bills.

Commercial credit is generally carried out through commercial bills of exchange, but since banks appear as the intermediaries to shoulder or subrogate commercial credit, the capitalist who sells a commodity for credit has a bank discount (or "purchase") the promissary note being held, receiving money in return. The credit between capitalists has today been replaced by the credit between banks and capitalists who purchase commodities, and between the two parties a credit relation of claims (credit) and obligations (debt) emerges. Of course, the bank becomes the creditor, while the capitalist who purchases commodities becomes the debtor. This sort of commercial credit is also mixed up with bank credit. The mediation and subrogation of commercial credit becomes an important function of banks. By means of this, a bank is also able to transform its money into interest-bearing capital, so that this can be valorized (with interest advanced in the form of a discounting fee).

We can easily see that the mediation of banks also makes possible a large expansion of the boundaries of commercial credit. Capitalists are able to

---

31. Ibid., 610.
32. Ibid., 434.
33. Ibid., 529.

obtain a great advanatage and this also can spur capitalist development. Unlike commerical credit, bank credit takes the form of being loaned as money, but this is not necessarily cash that is loaned. It is customary to provide loans with the promise of payment in cash, and normal to have cash at hand in reserve when it is required to fulfill the promise of payment. Marx says that the credit that the banker provides as this sort of promissory note "can be provided in various forms, e.g. in bills and cheques on other banks, credit facilities of a similar kind, and finally, if the bank is authorized to issue notes, in its own banknotes."[34]

The Role of Banks

In *Imperialism*, Lenin provides the following concept of "finance capital":

> As banking develops and becomes concentrated in a small number of estab-
> lishments the banks become transformed, and instead of being modest
> intermediaries they become powerful monopolies having at their command
> almost the whole of the money-capital of all the capitalists and small busi-
> nessmen and also the larger part of the means of production and of the
> sources of raw materials of the given country and in a number of coun-
> tries.[35]

And from this time, the original work of banks as "modest intermediaries" comes to occupy a less prominent position, although this still constitutes the foundation of the banks—in particular in Japan where "banking" and "securities" operations are divided. Lenin also notes:

> The principal and primary function of banks is to serve as an intermediary
> in the making of payments. In doing so they transform inactive money-
> capital into active capital, that is, into capital producing a profit; they col-
> lect all kinds of money revenues and place them at the disposal of the capi-
> talist class.[36]

Marx wrote that the modern banking system "on the one hand robs usurer's capital of its monopoly, since it concentrates all dormant money reserves

---

34. Ibid.
35. Lenin, *Imperialism: The Highest Stage of Capitalism* (New York: Interna-
    tional Publishers, 1939), 31.
36. Ibid.

together and places them on the money market, while on the other hand restricting the monopoly of the precious metals themselves by creating credit-money.[37] All of society's idle money and money-capital flow into the banks, to function as "loanable money-capital" on an enormous scale that is integrated and socialized.

According to Marx, "the loan-capital which banks have at their disposal accrues to them in several ways."[38] First, since banks are the "cashiers of the industrial capitalists,"[39] the inactive money-capital that is disengaged from the process of circulation (reserve money for payment, etc.) is concentrated in the banks. Second, this stems from the "deposits made by money-capitalists." In other words, the money-capital of the orignal loan capitalists is concentrated within the banks, but this already existed as loan-capital prior to the appearance of the banks, and in this case banks only play a mediating role, so that "a bank represents on the one hand the centralization of money-capital, of the lenders, and on the other hand the centralization of the borrowers."[40] Third, when the bank comes to pay out interest, the money hoards of all classes and money not being used for the moment are concentrated, but according to Marx "this collection of small amounts, as a particular function of the banking system, must be distinguished from the bank's function as middlemen between actual money-capitalists and borrowers."[41] Finally, "revenues that are to be consumed only gradually are also deposited with the banks."[42] This includes rent as well as the portion of capitalists' profit intended for individual consumption.

Banks lend out the money and money-capital that is concentrated from such sources. The form of this lending, as we saw in the previous section, includes such things as the discounting of bills of exchange and loans. Of course, as long as a bank is also a capitalist enterprise, its capital is composed of its own capital [*jiko shihon*], but this is of little significance compared to the sum of deposits. Recently in Japan, for example, there has been a debate over whether banks should raise the level of their own capital to ten percent.

---

37. *Capital*, vol. 3, 738.
38. Ibid., 528.
39. Ibid.
40. Ibid.
41. Ibid., 529.
42. Ibid.

Marx quotes J.W. Gilbert regarding how "the trading capital of a bank may be divided into two parts: the invested capital, and the borrowed banking capital"[43]; the former being the money spent by the founders of the bank, while the later concerns deposits. Gilbert says of the latter: "There are three ways of raising a banking or borrowed capital. First, by receiving; secondly, by the issuing of notes; thirdly, by the drawing of bills."[44]

(Incidentally, if we look at outstanding deposits and loans at the thirteen Tokyo banks last year [1986], deposits were 144 trillion yen while loans were 145 trillion yen, with the top bank Dai-Ichi Kangyo Bank having deposits and loans of around 19 trillion yen. Last year loans among the thirteen banks rose by around 18 trillion yen, while deposits rose by close to 5 trillion yen. For this reason, the banks were compelled to cover this margin through procurements of bills of exchange and the call market, as well as borrowing from the Bank of Japan.)

"Creation" of Credit and Capital

In addition to mediating credit, banks also *create* their own credit. Marx says that "banks create credit and capital."[45] We have already seen that money loaned out by banks is provided as self-valorizing money, through which interest is accrued, but progressing further, banks issue tokens of value that neither have value themselves nor are backed up by a metal reserve, and they obtain interest through these tokens of value.

> In as much as the Bank [of England] issues notes that are not backed by the metal reserve in its vaults, it creates tokens of value that are not only means of circulation, but also form additional—even if fictitious—capital for it.[46]

Immediately after this, Marx quotes from the record of parliamentary testimonies in England:

---

43. Ibid., 530-1.
44. Ibid., 530.
45. Ibid., 676.
46. Ibid. 675.

"Then whatever profit he derives from that circulation is a profit derived from credit, and not from a capital which he actually possesses?"—"Certainly."[47]

The person responding is the Bank of England official William Newmarch. Marx has the following to say about his testimony:

The same holds true of course for note-issuing private banks...Newmarch considers two-thirds of all these issued notes (for the last third, these banks must have metal reserves) as the "creation of so much capital" because this amount of metal money is saved.[48]

This is the view, in other words, that as long as banks issue banknotes that are not guaranteed by their metal reserves, they are issuing tokens of value, which in addition to forming the means of circulation also create additional "capital." Of course, in this case, whether it is the issuing of banknotes or the establishment of deposits, it is essentially the same. In terms of the bank deriving profit that does not stem "from a capital [the bank] actually possesses,"[49] this is the same as present-day banks following the end of convertibility.

Banking capital consists of (1) cash, in the form of gold or notes; (2) securities. These latter may again be divided into two parts: commercial paper, current bills of exchange that fall due on specific days...and public securities such as government bonds, treasury bills and stocks of all kinds, in short interest-bearing paper, which is essentially different from bills of exchange...The capital which has these as its tangible component parts can also be broken down into the banker's own invested capital, and the deposits that form his banking or borrowed capital. Notes must also be added here, in the case of banks which have the right to issue them.[50]

Today there is the issue of the ratio of cash reserves to deposits in excess of the bank's own capital. For instance, if the reserve requirement for cash reserves compared to deposits is 10 percent, and the bank has 100 million yen in deposits, the amount of money that could be loaned out would be 90 million

47. Ibid.
48. Ibid.
49. Ibid.
50. Ibid., 594.

yen, but in this case no credit is created by the bank. The bank is loaning out money within the range of its customer's deposits. In other words, the bank is doing nothing more than providing credit within the limits of the credit received. However, if a bank designates all of the 100 million yen in deposits as the reserve fund, so that a current deposit of 900 million yen is established, this would still be a reserve of 10 percent compared to deposits, but the bank has thereby *created* credit worth 900 million yen—or what Newmarch calls the creation of "capital."

In other words, with the establishment of the form of interest-bearing capital, whatever yields interest is viewed as interest-bearing capital, and under such conditions it is possible for "capital" to be created by means of credit. Of course, here "capital" is not truly capital, and not even loan-capital in the original sense, but rather fictitious loan-capital (fictitious capital), because actual capital can only be "created" (augmented) in the process of production. For banks, however, this is the formation of additional "capital" and a great source of profit. By means of this, capitalist credit expands by leaps and bounds, and in this respect capitalist production is developed to an extreme point.

What is Credit Money?

If we take a look at the money used in Japan, we can see the words "Bank of Japan note" printed on it. This indicates to us that the money we use is different from genuine paper money, which is "given forced currency"[51] by the state, and instead has its basis in credit-money. The fact that the starting point of Bank of Japan notes is credit money, rather than genuine paper money, is an extremely important point in terms of understanding the various characteristics of modern capitalism. For example, the fact that the abundance of "idle capital" (money-capital that finds no investment) does not directly lead to inflation—although this does not preclude the possibility that inflation will be aggravated in the near future—is deeply connected to the fact that Bank of Japan notes are not directly paper money, but rather credit money that increasingly functions as paper money, a *quasi* paper money.

Bank of Japan notes are based upon credit, issued in line with the conditions of capitalist production and circulation, and are thrown into circulation by the state depending on its needs, and are therefore distinct from paper money which "has value because it circulates."[52] These banknotes are not ran-

---

51. *Capital*, vol. 1, 224.

domly put into circulation by the government, nor does this introduction of banknotes directly increase the amount of "currency" by the same amount or decrease in value in proportion to the amount of banknotes issued (inflation). Here banknotes have a law of movement that differs from that of genuine paper money. If, for instance, companies that gain a profit from foreign trade and others exchange Bank of Japan notes for dollars, a similar quantity of notes would be issued. If the Bank of Japan extends a loan to the government—by taking on government debt, for example—or makes loans to general banks, it has to issue banknotes. This is done on the basis of credit and the actual economic conditions, and has a content and impact that differs from paper money circulated through the forced backing of the state (and also has a different nature from *proper* paper money in terms of inflation, etc.).

Needless to say, the Bank of Japan notes are banknotes issued by the Bank of Japan, but what were banknotes originally? Unlike state-issued paper money—which appears in the function of money as a means of circulation—banknotes are a type of credit money that emerges from the function of money as a means of payment, and originally these were bills of exchange and debt securities that banks issued themselves, and which then entered into circulation where they were able to function as a circulating medium.

> A banknote is nothing more than a bill on the banker, payable at any time to its possessor and given by the banker in place of private drafts…this kind of credit money emerges from commercial circulation into general circulation and functions here as money; also because in most countries the major banks that issue notes are a peculiar mishmash between national banks and private banks and actually have the government's credit behind them, their notes being more or less legal tender; and because it its evident here that what the banker is dealing in is credit itself, since the banknote merely represents a circulating token of credit.[53]

This is what is meant by bankers issuing banknotes "in place of private drafts." With the development of commodity production and exchange, commerical credit also develops, and at the same time promissory notes are created that enter into circulation when the claim is turned over to a third party by the

---

52. *A Contribution to the Critique of Political Economy*, 356.
53. *Capital*, vol. 3, 529.

creditor, thus becoming a type of money (credit money). This "actual commercial money" first circulates among merchants and producers.

Banknotes appear upon the basis of the wider circulation of such promissory notes. Banks discount these bills and issue their own banknotes, which have the characteristic of needing no endorsement, being payable on sight, having unlimited duration, and existing in round figure denominations. Because banknotes have such characteristics they extend beyond the realm of commercial transactions, entering into general circulation. Banknotes appear as the debt of the bank that issues them. In other words, this is a promissory note from a bank that allows the holder to receive an equivalent sum of money from the bank upon request, and is thus a "convertible" note. Therefore, in addition to the function as a means of circulation, banknotes, unlike paper money, are also able to function as a means of payment and as hoarded money (and completely so within a give country).

Crisis is Not Overcome by Issuing More Banknotes

The experience of the English Bank Legislation (Peel Act) established in 1844 and abolished some years later has great practical signifiance. The "currency school" (Overstone, et al.) claimed that by means of this law, the issuing of money (banknotes) would be regulated, and that by "strictly" subordinating this circulation to the principles of the circulation of metallic money, excessive credit expansion could be prevented and crisis forever abolished. Underlying this view was Ricardo's dogmatic "quantity theory of money," according to which a rise in prices is due to the easy availability of money (means of circulation), while a drop is due to its scarcity.

What, then, did the policy of "strictly" subordinating banknotes to the principles of the circulation of metallic money mean in practice? To begin with, this meant that the Bank of England was divided in into an Issue Department and a Banking Department. The Issue Department was given government bonds and the metal reserves, and only issued banknotes for this amount, providing the public gold in exchange for banknotes and banknotes in exchange for gold. This department held the banknotes, while "all other dealings with the public [were] the concern of the Banking Department."[54]

What was the outcome of this policy? Did it really abolish crisis foreever? The reality was in fact the exact opposite. In 1848 it became clear that this

---

54. Ibid., 688.

legislation, far from eliminating crisis, was actually intensifing it. This was because the Peel Act controlled and restricted the means of circulation, which are in particular demand at the moment of a crisis. The Issue Department held a large store of government bonds, gold, and silver, but as long as no new gold came in, it was unable to throw more banknotes into circulation. Instead, if a great amount of gold were to leave the country, as is almost always the case in a crisis, the Bank of England was obliged to defray this cost, which meant that a large portion of the banknotes were withdrawn from circulation.

> In reality...the separation of the Bank into two independent departments withdrew the directors' power of free disposal of their entire available means at decisive moments.[55]

> The Bank Act of 1844 thus directly provokes the entire world of commerce into meeting the outbreak of a crisis by putting aside a reserve stock of banknotes, thereby accelerating and intensifying the crisis...Thus instead of abolishing crises, it rather intensifies them to a point at which either the entire world of industry has to collapse, or else the Bank Act. On two occasions, 25 October 1847 and 12 November 1857, the crisis reached such a height; the government then freed the Bank from the restriction on its note issue, by suspending the Act of 1844, and this was sufficient on both occasions to curb the crisis.[56]

This final sentence about freeing the Bank of England from the restriction placed on the issuing of notes merits particular attention, as the bourgeoisie today responds to crisis by increasing the means of circulation through expansionary financial and credit policies. The experience of 1847 is an example of how the fixed ideas of the bourgeoisie can artificially intensify a crisis; but has the present-day bourgeoisie truly freed itself from such prejudices, and therefore freed itself from crisis? Marx offers the following evaluation of the dogma of the currency school:

> [In] the commercial crises of the nineteenth century...it was no longer a matter of single economic phenomena, but of big storms of the world market, in which the antagonism of all elements in the bourgeois process of production explodes; the origin of these storms and the means of defense

---

55. Ibid., 689.
56. Ibid.

against them were sought within the sphere of currency, the most superficial and abstract sphere of this process.[57]

Marx mocked the superficiality of the currency school, which sought fundamental solutions to crisis "within the sphere of currency"—and this criticism applies likewise to the adherence of the modern bourgeoisie to such schools of thought as Keynesianism. Even if it can be said that the elimination of the Peel Act—the free infusion of banknotes—was able to lessen the impact of a crisis, this did not eliminate crisis altogether. The fact remains that the managed currency system is a means for the bourgeoisie to combat crisis, but it is far from representing the actual uprooting of the source of crisis.

Relation between Real Capital and Loan-Capital

Today [1987], one often hears talk about the "overabundance of money," with this overflowing money used speculatively to invest in land and the stock market, resulting in skyrocketing land and stock prices. The "money" we are speaking of here is loan-capital, i.e. loanable money-capital. We need to consider what, exactly, is the significance of the enormous accumulation of this loan-capital. Or, to borrow the words of Marx, "how far is it, and how far is it not, an index of genuine capital accumulation, i.e. of reproduction on an expanded scale?"[58] We also need to examine the extent to which a shortage of money-capital coincides with a shortage of money as a means of circulation. Marx refers to these as "difficult questions."

What is important first of all, however, is to arrive at a correct concept. If this can be done, our difficulties will be considerably reduced. It is thus necessary to grasp the differences between the following pairs of concepts: money as money and money as capital; the money-form of capital and its real form; money-capital as the circulation form of capital and money-capital as loan-capital; loan-capital and real capital; fictitious capital and real capital, etc.

It is clear that shortages in loan-capital and real capital—i.e. commodity capital and productive capital—do not always coincide, and Marx explains that the accumulation of loan-capital advances independently of the accumulation of real capital, so that a shortage of real capital and a shortage of loan-

---

57. Ibid., 681.
58. Ibid., 607.

capital can occur at opposite times, and he also explains the various processes related to the business cycle.

The accumulation of real capital is the actual accumulation of capital (expanded reproduction), which is nothing more than the various value elements of reproductive capital and material accumulation. By contrast, the accumulation of loan-capital is not merely the accumulation of money, but rather involves various sorts of real money entering the hands of bankers to be transformed into loanable money-capital, and the "idle funds" that are used as a "financial lever" for large companies can also be considered as a type of loan-capital.

If one looks at the relation between real capital and loan-capital in terms of the business cycle, in the early stages of a business downturn, an abundance of loan-capital corresponds to a restriction in productive capital. When the next business upturn occurs, however, the excess of loan-capital recedes somewhat and corresponds with the real capital that is beginning to accumulate, but the increase in loan-capital is not yet manifested in the accumulation of real capital. Periods of prosperity are the only time when the relative abundance of loan-capital corresponds with an increase in real capital, but in the subsequent crisis (particularly its latter stages), it is exactly the opposite, so that a shortage of loan-capital is manifested in an excess of real capital, with capitalists frantically searching for money. Of course, the relation between real capital and loan-capital is not limited solely to the various aspects of the business cycle, but we do not have time here to go into this in more detail.

Marx notes:

> The accumulation of loan-capital simply means that money is precipitated as loanable money. This process is very different from a genuine transformation into capital; it is simply the accumulation of money in a form in which it can be transformed into capital. As we have shown, however, this accumulation can express elements that are very different from genuine accumulation. With genuine accumulation constantly expanding, this expanded accumulation of money-capital can be in part its result, in part the result of elements that accompany it but are quite different from it, and in part also the result even of blockages in genuine accumulation. The very fact that accumulation of loan-capital is augmented by these elements that are independent of genuine accumulation, even if they accompany it, must lead to a regular plethora of money-capital at certain phases of the cycle, and this plethora develops as the credit system improves. At the same time as this, there develops the need to pursue the production process beyond its

capitalist barriers: too much trade, too much production, too much credit. This must also happen always in forms that bring about a reaction.[59]

Dictinction between Loan-Capital and "Currency"

Marx criticized Tooke and Fullarton for not correctly distinguishing between money as capital (loan-capital) and money as the means of circulation. This distinction is particularly important in the case of contemporary capitalism. To begin with, Marx speaks of the relation between loan-capital and currency:

> The volume of loan-capital, moreover, is completely different from the quantity of circulation. By quantity of circulation, here, we mean the sum of all banknotes in circulation in a particular country, together with all metal money, including precious metal in the form of bullion. A part of this quantity forms the banks' reserve and is constantly fluctuating in size...
>
> Variations in the rate of interest...depend on the supply of loan-capital...i.e. of capital lent in the form of money, in metal or notes; as distinct from industrial capital that is lent as such, in the commodity-form, by commercial credit among the reproductive agents themselves.
>
> But the volume of this loanable money-capital is still different from and independent of the quantity of money in circulation.[60]
>
> In countries where credit is highly developed, we may assume that all money-capital available for loan exists in the form of deposits with banks and money-lenders.[61]

Marx then examines the quantitative relationship between the the "quantity of circulation" and the "sum of deposits," which refers to currency and loan-capital, respectively. Marx has the following to say about this:

> In the other case, a low or full circulation is never more than a different distribution of the same mass of means of circulation between active circulation and deposits, i.e. as an instrument for loans.[62]

---

59. Ibid., 639-40.
60. Ibid., 630.
61. Ibid., 632.
62. Ibid., 662.

Marx views the "means of circulation" in a given country as being fixed, as the sum of the banknotes and money (gold) issued. He refers to this money that is actually in circulation as "active circulation," and there is a split between this and deposits, which Marx calls "an instrument for loans."[63]

> It should never be forgotten that although a fairly constant sum of £19-20 million in notes is ostensibly in the hands of the public, yet the portion of these notes that is actually circulating, on the one hand, and the portion that lies unoccupied in the banks as a reserve, on the other, are both constantly and substantially changing. If the reserve is large, i.e. the actual circulation is low, it is said from the standpoint of the money market that the circulation is full, or money is plentiful; if the reserve is small, i.e. the actual circulation full, the money market call it low and say money is scarce, i.e. only a small amount represents unoccupied loan-capital.[64]

Immediately following this passage, Marx discusses various points, including the fact that circulation can even expand or contract because of the payment of taxation or interest on the national debt, and that this can control the quantity of "unoccupied loan-capital."

Currently there is a great deal of talk about the "overabundance of money," which means that the banks have an excessive accumulation of loanable money-capital. But no matter how many banknotes the Bank of Japan issues, or what enormous quantities of loan capital the banks accumulate, this would not signify inflation, and if this is loaned out as capital and invested in the hands of businesses—then flowing back to the banks after a certain period of time—this would also not signify inflation. It is clear, however, that this could signify inflation if the Bank of Japan notes that are accumulated in the hands of the banks are issued in response to the increased need for circulation means, accompanying a general rise in prices,[65] in which case the Bank of Japan notes would function as a means of circulation rather than as capital.

Of course, the concrete moments that transform a superabundance of money into inflation are complex, and in reality this must be mediated by a number of "crises." What is important here for us is the conceptual distinction. Without correctly understanding the distinction between money as capi-

---

63. Ibid.
64. Ibid.
65. Even in this case, however, banks would understand this as the loaning out of "capital."

tal and money as the means of circulation—as well as the various characteristics of the managed currency system and central banknotes under this system—it is not possible to truly grasp the nature and characteristics of inflation in modern-day capitalist society. In this sense, Marx's criticism has great contemporary significance.

Joint-Stock Companies and Credit

Generally speaking, capital today takes the form of joint-stock companies, i.e. the form of integrated capital, but the development of these joint-stock companies is inseparably linked to credit. Indeed, without the mediation of credit, there is certainly no way that joint-stock companies would have been able to achieve such large-scale and universal development. Joint-stock capital itself is the integration of capital owned by several people into a single capital, and in this way "receives the form of social capital (capital of directly associated individuals), in contrast to private capital, and its enterprises appear as social enterprises as opposed to private ones."[66] But in bourgeois society, with the establishment of interest-bearing capital, "any definite, regular monetary revenue appear as the interest on a capital,"[67] and in this way all of the sums of money invested to obtain money revenue come to appear as interest-bearing capital. Thus, stocks as well, like claims on credit, become a place to invest loanable capital.

If five capitalists each invest 200 million yen in a joint-stock company, for a total capital of one billion yen, and jointly manage the company, this signifies nothing more than the integration of their capital. But if the stock of this company "goes public," with many money-capitalists purchasing the stock—solely out of a desire for dividends and no concern for the rights of ownership or control of the company—these stockholders become *rentiers*, and stocks, which are ownership titles to a share of the capital and surplus-value, represent nothing more than another field of investment for money-capitalists. Marx explains how stocks "become forms of interest-bearing capital" in the following passage:

> As we have seen, the ownership titles to joint-stock companies, railways, mines, etc. are genuinely titles to real capital. Yet they give no control over

66. Ibid., 567.
67. Ibid., 595.

this capital. The capital cannot be withdrawn. They give only a legal claim to a share of the surplus-value that this capital is to produce. But these titles similarly become paper duplicates of the real capital, as if a bill of lading simultaneously acquired a value alongside the cargo it refers to. They become nominal representatives of non-existent capitals. For the actual capital exists as well, and in no way changes hands when these duplicates are bought and sold.[68]

In addition to representing the combination of capitals, joint-stock companies also have the significance of acting as a tremendous lever for the concentration and development of capital in the sense of mobilizing and combining all of the social capital. This is not merely concentration, however, but concentration mediated by credit. Joint-stock companies also decisively push forward a separation between the ownership and functioning of capital, which is latent to the nature of joint-stock capital. For instance, in the example above, it is possible for the five capitalists who each invested 200 million yen to choose one person to manage the operation so that the remaining four merely receive dividends, and in fact this is a necessary tendency. If even such large capitalists view the capital invested in the stock market as the same as interest-bearing capital, this means that the "general investor" has an interest in stocks solely because they are considered as a safer or more advantageous field of investment at a given time.

This does not mean, of course, that it would be correct to view claims on credit and stocks as being identical. The fact that many stockowners become *rentiers* does not mean that the distinction between the original characteristics of stocks and claims on credit is dissolved. In the first place, unlike claims on credit, stock shares are not issued on the basis of credit. At the same time, we cannot overlook the important point that the joint-stock company would not have been able to develop into such an overwhelmingly dominant form without the credit system and the mediation of credit.

"Fictitious Capital"

In capitalist society, an enormous amount of "fictitious capital" is formed upon the basis of credit. This fictitious capital is seen as capital (particularly by its owners), but it is not capital in the original sense, and this includes such things as securities. Capital is self-valorizing value, that is to say, value that bears sur-

---

68. Ibid., 608.

plus-value. Understood in this precise way, capital in the genuine sense is industrial capital. However, when Marx speaks of fictitious capital he is not referring to commercial capital or interest-bearing capital. The latter has value and is capital as a reapportionment of the surplus-value produced by industrial capital, and is thus completely different from "capital" that lacks real content.

In the previous section we saw that with the establishment of interest-bearing capital, "any definite and regular monetary revenue appear as the interest on a capital."[69] First, monetary revenue is transformed into interest, and along with this "capital" appears as the source of this interest. "Likewise, with interest-bearing capital, any sum of value appears as capital as soon as it is not spent as revenue; i.e. as a 'principal' in contrast to the possible or actual interest it can bear."[70] For example, if the average rate of profit is five percent and 50,000 yen is the regular annual revenue, this sum of money is seen as the "interest" on a capital of one million yen. Marx notes that this "formation of fictitious capital is known as capitalization" so that "any regular periodic income can be capitalized."[71]

Fictitious capital—such as bonds or stocks—is probably understood by its owners as "capital," but in fact this is not really capital at all. A government bond is a manifestation of the state's debt, and in and of itself is merely a claim of credit upon this debt. The state that issues bonds has already consumed the money borrowed (mainly in unproductive ways!), so that "the capital itself has been consumed, spent by the state" and in the case of the "capital of the national debt...a negative quantity appears as capital."[72]

Stocks as well are seen as "capital" by their owners and indicate real capital, but they are in reality merely ownership titles and represent the *dual* existence of capital. Thus, no matter how much stock prices may skyrocket—such as the recent monthly increases in Japan of as much as one trillion yen—this bears no relation to the true magnitude of a nation's wealth. Even if there are national surpluses totaling hundreds of trillions of yen, this has nothing to do with a nation actually being prosperous, and is rather merely an increase in fictitious capital. Even if this nominal "capital" were to drop in price and lose its value, workers, and society as a whole, would not become any poorer:

69. Ibid., 595.
70. Ibid.
71. Ibid., 597.
72. Ibid., 595-6.

All these securities actually represent nothing but accumulated claims, legal titles, to future production. Their money or capital value either does not represent capital at all, as in the case of national debts, or is determined independently of the real capital value they represent.

In all countries of capitalist production, there is a tremendous amount of so-called interest-bearing capital or "moneyed capital" in this form. And an accumulation of money-capital means for the most part nothing more than an accumulation of these claims to production, and an accumulation of the market price of these claims, of their illusory capital value.[73]

Stocks are the expression of real capital, its copy, which means in this sense that an increase in stock prices reflects an increase of real capital, but the stock price itself is not real capital, and a rise in this price through speculation represents a movement quite separate from that of real capital. This is even more the case for government bonds, which can expand alongside the squandering of real capital. The fact that "capital" within bourgeois society, and the greater part of wealth in this society, is composed of completely substance-less elements, reveals in part the limitations of this mode of production and its reactionary nature!

Interest-Bearing Capital Conceals Capital's True Nature

At the beginnning of the first volume of *Capital*, Marx speaks of commodity fetishism, and in the theory of credit developed in volume three he argues that interest-bearing capital, which takes the form of M → M′ (money → greater magnitude of money), is the culmination of the fetishism that is essential to, and characteristic of, bourgeois society. To begin with we need to consider the meaning of *fetishism*.

In the period of human history when the productive power of labor was still extremely low, there was only a small realm where human beings had actually gained mastery or control over nature, whereas for the most part it could be said that man was instead controlled by nature. Nature thus became a god and an animistic belief arose within ancient society, according to which the sun, moon, mountains, and other natural elements were seen as gods.

In the commodity-capitalist world, similarly, commodities, money, and capital—which are nothing more than the manifestation of social relations within human production—come to appear as autonomous things endowed

73. Ibid., 599.

with their own independent life, and human beings view such things not as the expression of social relations, but rather as being the intrinsic properties of natural things. People thus come to worship these objects as if they were gods (mamonism!). Marx refers to this as the fetishism of commodity-capitalist society. Human social relations take on the illusory form of relations between things, and the social relations between people in their labor—first the relation of the equal exchange of labor, followed by the relation of exploitation—are concealed and manifested in an upside-down form.

In the case of commodities, first of all, social relations involving the private labor of producers appear not as direct social relations, but rather "as material [*dinglich*] relations between persons and social relations between things."[74] In the case of money, its character of being exchangeable with every other commodity, i.e. money as the general equivalent form, is understood as being a quality inherent to gold itself, with no thought given to the fact that this is the outcome of certain social relations. Likewise, capital can certainly take the form of the means of production, but these production means themselves are not identical to capital. The transformation of means of production into capital is one specific social relation, namely self-valorizing value by means of the exploitation of others' labor. As Marx points out, "a negro is a negro" and "only under certain conditions does a negro become slave."[75] Already in the case of capital, the source of surplus-value is concealed, since surplus-value in its relation to the total capital is profit, so that one can no longer perceive that this is unpaid labor (surplus-labor) as opposed to paid labor (necessary labor).

This fetishism of commodity-capitalist society reaches its highest or completed stage with interest-bearing capital. Here every trace of exploitation has vanished, so that capital as self-valorizing value—capital as an "automatic fetish"—appears in a naked form without any apparent mediation. The fetish-worship or idolatry vis-à-vis capital is the view that a certain quantity of labor products accumulated in the fixed form of money possesses the inherent, natural property or capacity of exponentially augmenting surplus-value in a purely automatic fashion. This is precisely the spontaneous consciousness of the bourgeoisie within the capitalist world. In the case of this idolatry of capital, interest-bearing capital comes to be the primary object of worship.

---

74. *Capital*, vol. 1, 166.
75. *MECW*, vol. 9, 211.

In interest-bearing capital, the capital relationship reaches its most superficial and fetishized form. Here we have M-M', money that produces more money, self-valorizing value, without the process that mediates the two extremes...Capital appears as a mysterious and self-creating source of interest, of its own increase. The *thing* (money, commodity, value) is now already capital simply as a thing; the result of the overall reproduction process appears as a property devolving on a thing in itself...In interest-bearing capital, therefore, this automatic fetish is elaborated into its pure form, self-valorizing value, money breeding money, and in this form it no longer bears any marks of its origin. The social relation is consummated in the relationship of a thing, money, to itself. Instead of the actual transformation of money into capital, we have here only the form of this devoid of content.[76]

In this form of interest-bearing capital, interest appears as the intrinsic fruit of capital, while profit is transformed into the form of "profit of enterprise," and thus "appears as a mere accessory and trimming added in the reproduction process."[77] There is nothing particularly surprising about that fact that vulgar economists "discover" this interest-bearing capital form and become particularly attached to it.

Historical Significance of Credit

This section brings to an end our discussion of Marx's theory of credit. This chapter may have been somewhat hard to understand in parts, but I hope that it has at least helped spark an interest in this topic. The modern credit system is characteristic of capitalism, but without understanding its nature it can appear as a sort of enormous and complex monstrosity. The most general and typical form of modern credit is interest-bearing capital (loan-capital), but this is the most "externalized" form of capital, an extreme expression of the upside-down nature (and fetishism!) of capitalism.

Capital as such obtains interest, a certain gain, but entirely overlooked or concealed by this is the fact that this is one portion of surplus-value. If one recognizes that interest is also one part of the surplus-value produced by workers, it should become clear that there is no reason to fear the enormous edifice of finance capital and the system and power based upon it. If workers were to cease production—such as during a general strike—not only industrial capital,

---

76. *Capital*, vol. 3, 515-6.
77. Ibid. 516.

but finance capital as well, would face collapse! At the same time, however, it is not sufficient to merely express "moralistic" outrage against credit and the fact that an enormous superstructure is raised and prosperity enjoyed upon the basis of the exploitation of workers and their sacrifices, because the modern credit system also has historical necessity and great significance for the development of capitalism and the victory of socialism.

It is not difficult to grasp that credit propels forward the development of capitalism. Indeed, without the modern credit system no sound capitalist development would be possible, and it is precisely for this reason that the Soviet Union and China are devoting so much attention to creating or "upgrading" their credit systems!

More than simply hastening the general development of capitalism, credit also has great significance for the modern system of joint-stock companies. On this subject, Marx points out that the credit system "forms the principal basis for the gradual transformation of capitalist private enterprises into capitalist joint-stock companies."[78] The fact that a joint-stock company is created and pays dividends to shareholders is still not credit. However, with stocks being "made public" and sold on the market, so that loan-capitalists invest in the stocks, the development of joint-stock companies advances rapidly along with the expansion of the credit system. The system of joint-stock companies is able to achieve great development through its ties with credit, but at the same time this "reproduces a new financial aristocracy, a new kind of parasite in the guise of company promoters, speculators and merely nominal directors; an entire system of swindling and cheating with respect to the promotion of companies, issue of shares and share dealings," which Marx refers as "private production unchecked by private ownership."[79] He notes the following "dual character immanent"to credit:

> On the one hand it develops the motive of capitalist production, enrichment by the exploitation of others' labor, into the purest and most colossal system of gambling and swindling, and restricts ever more the already small number of the exploiters of social wealth; on the other hand however it constitutes the form of transition towards a new mode of production.[80]

---

78. Ibid., 571.
79. Ibid., 569.
80. Ibid., 572.

We can see that credit has become a "colossal system of gambling and swindling" from the example of Tateho Chemical Industries Co., Ltd., which lost the enormous sum of over 28 billion yen in bond futures trading, despite having annual sales of only around six billion yen. In this process, as Marx points out, "little fish are gobbled up by the sharks."[81]

Credit has the character of being a transitional form toward socialism since it is connected to money, which is the conspicuous "material" [*busshitsu-teki*] form of social labor (its accumulation), and is the most abstract and thorough representation of the social nature of labor within bourgoies society. In this sense, credit is the extreme form of the "alienated" labor that produces commodities, while at the same time representing a step toward the realization of directly socialized labor. Marx offers the following concluding remarks on credit, which I would also like to use to bring this chapter to a close:

> If the credit system appears as the principal lever of overproduction and excessive speculation in commerce, this is simply because the reproduction process, which is elastic by nature, is now forced to its most extreme limit; and this is because a great part of the social capital is applied by those who are not its owners, and who therefore proceed quite unlike owners who, when they function themselves, anxiously weigh the limits of their private capital. This only goes to show how the valorization of capital founded on the antithetical character of capital production permits actual free development only up to a certain point, which is constantly broken through by the credit system. The credit system hence accelerates the material development of the productive forces and the creation of the world market, which it is the historical task of the capitalist mode of production to bring to a certain level of development, as material foundations for the new form of production. At the same time, credit accelerates the violent outbreaks of this contradiction, crises, and with these the elements of dissolution of the old mode of production.[82]

---

81. Ibid., 571.
82. Ibid.

4

Theory of Ground-Rent

Premises of Marx's Theory of Ground-Rent

In chapter forty-seven of the third volume of *Capital*, where Marx discusses rent, he frames the question of ground-rent as follows: "It is necessary to clarify the exact nature of the difficulty faced by modern economics, as the theoretical expression of the capitalist mode of production, in its treatment of ground-rent." He then offers the following response:

> The difficulty consists rather in showing how, after the equalization of surplus-value between the various capitals to give the average profit, whereby they receive a share in the total surplus-value produced by the social capital in all spheres of production together that is corresponding and proportionate to their relative sizes—in showing how, after this equalization, after the distribution of all the surplus-value that there is to distribute has apparently already taken place, there is still an excess part of this surplus-value left over, a part which capital invested on the land pays to the landowner in the form of ground-rent…
>
> The whole difficulty in analyzing rent thus consisted in explaining the excess of agricultural profit over average-profit; not surplus-value as such, but rather the extra surplus-value specific to this sphere of production; i.e. not even the "net product," but rather the extra net product over and above the net product of other branches of industry.[1]

---

1.   *Capital*, vol. 3, 917-8.

The meaning of this passage could be summarized by saying that all of the sur-plus-value created through capitalist production should be equalized into *average profit* by means of competition between different capitals, but despite this, landed property, based on its titular rights, is clearly able to receive a portion of the sur-plus-value without compensation, namely ground-rent. The question thus revolves around why this occurs, and where this surplus-value is derived from.

In other words, after the total surplus-value has been apportioned as aver-age profit, how can we account for this special surplus-value? Is this somehow in contradiction with, and completely separate from, the laws pertaining to value and capital? Should this be treated as a purely arbitrary relation that bears no connection to theory *per se*, as simply excess profit arising from a sim-ple or "genuine" monopoly price? These are the theoretical tasks that Marx sets for himself in approaching the question of ground-rent.

If ground-rent stems from genuine monopoly price, there would be little theoretical difficulty, since it would be sufficient to pose the question of ground-rent in terms of it being a deposit, accruing as rent, from the special profits generated from high prices, based upon the needs of consumers and their ability to pay. Ground-rent, however, is not determined by such a "genu-ine monopoly price."

In a sense, of course, all rent can be considered a special profit derived from monopoly price, one part of the surplus-value which landed property "extracts" on the basis of its rights of ownership. Marx, however, explains the "normal" forms of rent—differential rent and absolute ground-rent—in distinction from what he calls "genuine monopoly price." He makes such a distinction because the com-modity price that results in rent is not simply a (market) price determined by sup-ply and demand. He develops his theory of rent within the framework of the theory of value and production price (the transformed form of value), as a particu-lar application of this theory. This fact is clear in the case of differential rent, but absolute rent is also positioned within the determinations of the law of value.

Marx's theory of ground-rent was consciously developed as a theory of cap-italist ground-rent, and therefore it presupposes an understanding of value, surplus-value, and the transformation of surplus-value into profit. It is thus necessary to understand the formation of the average rate of profit and the transformation of profit into production price,[2] and therefore an overall grasp

2.   For a detailed discussion of this, see part six of the third volume of *Cap-ital*.

of the theory of value and surplus-value are essential to an understanding of Marx's theory of rent. However, these premises cannot be fully explained in the space we have here, so I will only touch on them when necessary.

The issue for Marx is *capitalist* ground-rent—whose two "normal" forms are differential rent and absolute ground-rent—but at the same time he does not completely neglect the question of ground-rent in general or the various historical forms that it has taken. Along with capitalist ground-rent, and in relation to it, Marx elucidates and scientifically determines ground-rent in general and its many historical forms.

Since Marx fundamentally deals with the question of capitalist ground-rent, or ground-rent in agricultural production (grain production), this may appear to be a purely abstract theory that bears no direct relation to the question of rent in present-day Japan. In a sense this is true, because today in Japan, capitalist agriculture has not been fully established and small-scale production remains predominant. Rent has developed to some extent within Japanese agriculture in the form of *ukeoi-kōsaku* "contracted cultivation,"[3] but this cannot be considered the dominant relation within the agricultural sector (and even this relation is forcefully regulated by the state).

Every day, however, in every aspect of the production of capital and the life of working people, we are reminded that the question of rent—either in its independent, pure form or in combination with various forms of profit and interest—is certainly not an inconsequential matter. Most workers, for example, are obliged to pay a huge sum of money, roughly one-third of their income, on housing rent. It is clear that this sum includes a *tribute* (rent or interest on "capital") made to an unproductive class, namely the owners of land and residential buildings, who hold a parasitic relation vis-à-vis the working class. Furthermore, the price of land is also determined by rent, since land "price" is essentially the "capitalization" of rent on the basis of interest rates. Here, however, we will limit ourselves to the theory of ground-rent developed by Marx, and leave to another time the discussion of its applications in present-day Japan. Still, there is no question that Marx's theory of ground-rent has great practical significance, and this point will be made clear in the

---

3. [*Ukeoi-kōsaku* refers to the system in Japan for landowners to hire others to cultivate and harvest their rice crop, who are then paid from the money generated from the landowners' sale of the rice. There is no direct renting of the landowners' land, but this "contracted cultivation" is basically a payment of rent.]

final section of this chapter, where we examine the conditions necessary for the elimination of ground-rent.

To begin with, I would like to say a word about Marx's method or manner of developing his theory of ground-rent. After clarifying the premises of this theory—namely, that capitalist production adapts and subordinates landed property to suit its own needs—he begins by analyzing how one sector of industrial capital can make use of the natural force of a waterfall, which can be monopolized, in order to generate the excess profit connected to differential rent. This overview of differential rent is followed by a concrete and comprehensive explanation of differential rent within agriculture and a definition of absolute rent. (These discussions are in turn followed by an examination of the rent of buildings and mines, the price of land, as well as a historical overview of rent.) In *Theories of Surplus Value,* Marx describes the significance of his "method" in the following way:

> The element in which the capital employed in agriculture is invested, is the soil (nature), etc. Hence rent is here equal to the excess of the value of the product of labor created in this element, over its average price. If, on the other hand, an element of nature (or material) which is privately owned by an individual, is employed in another sphere of production whose (physical) basis it does not form, then the rent, if it only comes into being through the employment of this element, cannot consist in the excess of the value of this product over the average price, but only in the excess of the general average price of this product over its own average price. For instance, a waterfall may replace the steam-engine for a manufacturer and save him consumption of coal. While in possession of this waterfall, he would, for instance, constantly be selling yarn above its *average price* and making an excess profit. If the waterfall belongs to a landowner, this excess profit accrues to him as rent. In his book on rent, Mr. Hopkins observes that in Lancashire the waterfalls not only yield rent but, according to the degree of natural motive power, they yield *differential rent.* Here rent is purely the excess of the *average market price* of the product over its *individual average price.*[4]

> [Hopkins: "A *stream,* favorably situated, furnishes an instance of rent being paid for an appropriated gift of nature, of as exclusive a kind as any that can be named."[5]]

---

4.   *MECW,* vol. 31, 355-6.
5.   Th. Hopkins *The Economical Enquiries Relative to the Laws which Regulate Rent, Profit, Wages, and the Value of Money,* quoted in ibid., 368.

From this passage we can see why Marx begins with differential rent and the form of differential rent in industrial capital, rather than directly in agriculture. This is because differential rent can be formed in any of the sectors in which capital is invested, whereas absolute rent only characteristically appears in agriculture and is not general to capital. Differential rent, to the extent that it is penetrated by the laws of capitalism, can arise anywhere provided the necessary conditions exist, but absolute rent only arises in situations where agriculture generally lags behind industry so that the price of agricultural products exceeds their production price.[6] In other words, differential rent is the outcome of the penetration of the capitalist economic system, whereas absolute ground-rent can only be obtained when this penetration is prevented. This is one essential distinction. The formation of the special profit that makes up differential rent can be explained from the laws of capital, but the explanation of absolute ground-rent is mediated by landed property, and to this extent its explanation is more specific. Thus, following Marx, we will also begin our discussion with the issue of differential rent.

Differential Rent

Prior to Marx, Ricardo had already developed a theory of differential rent, and his understanding was comparatively good.[7] Still, to fully understand this form of rent, it is important to grasp the scientific concept of capital, not to mention value. Marx has the following to say about Ricardo's theory of rent:

> Value is labor. So surplus-value cannot be earth. The land's absolute fertility does nothing but let a certain quantum of labor give a certain product, conditioned by the natural fertility of the land. The differences in the land's fertility have the effect that the same amounts of labor and capital, i.e. the same value, are expressed in different quantities of agricultural products; so that these products have different individual values. The equalization of these individual values to give market values means [to quote Ricardo] that "the advantages of fertile over inferior lands are…transferred from the cultivator, or consumer, to the landlord."[8]

---

6.   *Production price* equals cost price plus average profit.
7.   Of course, Ricardo's theory contains many defects and mistakes, such as combining this theory with the "law diminishing returns," etc.
8.   *Capital* vol. 3, 954.

Here the category of differential rent is not yet strictly determined, but its essence is clearly defined. Marx, in explaining differential rent in general, draws examples not from agriculture but from the use of waterfalls. His reason for doing so is that differential rent can arise anywhere that a natural force which is quantitatively limited so as to be monopolizable raises productivity to a particular extent.[9]

After having "established the general concept of differential rent," Marx moves on to "consider this rent in agriculture proper." We need to begin, however, by recognizing the significance of the fact that he posits the concept of differential rent within capitalist production in general, rather than solely within agriculture. This teaches us that the form of excess profit that is transformed into differential rent is merely the outcome of capitalist production—the fruit of capitalist conditions—including the free competition of capital, transferability of capital from one sphere of production to another, formation of average profit, and the consequent transformation of value into production price. Thus, the theory of ground-rent must be preceded by a theory of value and its transformation into production price. Without this correct theory of value and capital, it is impossible to gain a correct understanding of ground-rent.

As is well known, Marx demonstrated that with the establishment of capitalist production, commodities are exchanged not on the basis of value (a certain quantity of socially determined labor or objectified social labor), but rather on the basis of production price. What Marx refers to as production price is basically what Adam Smith calls "natural price," namely the cost necessary for the production of the commodity plus average profit. Here an understanding of the concept of average profit is necessary. Commodity production is not limited to simple commodity production, but rather is transformed into capitalist-commodity production, where each individual capital demands profit in proportion to its own magnitude (and this is enforced through competition). However, the "organic composition of capital"[10] differs greatly between each sector of production, and therefore if the rate of surplus-value (exploita-

---

9. See the quote from Marx in the first section of this chapter.
10. [The "organic composition of capital" refers to the ratio between the value of the constant capital and the value of the variable capital; with a *high* organic composition referring to cases where the value of the constant capital is relatively high compared to that of the variable capital, while a *low* organic composition describes the opposite case.]

tion) remains constant, the rate of profit will certainly not appear in proportion to the magnitude of capital. This is a self-contradiction for capital as value; and capital—as aggregate capital—redistributes the overall surplus-value in proportion to the size of each individual capital. If, for instance, the total capital is 500 and the total amount of surplus-value 110, the profit rate for each individual capital will settle at the level of 23 percent regardless of the particular organic composition of each capital. This, in short, is the formation of a general (average) rate of profit, so that the commodities produced under each individual capital are sold according to production price rather than value. There thus arises a certain divergence between the value of a particular commodity and its production price. Nevertheless, seen overall, value and production price correspond, as do aggregate surplus-value and profit. A more detailed explanation of the rate of profit and production prices, however, lies beyond the scope of this chapter, and I will leave it up to the reader to pursue this matter further, proceeding instead with the topic at hand.

When commodities, as the products of capital, come to be sold in this way on the basis of production price rather than value, products of the land also come to be sold on the basis of production price, since our premise is that agriculture is carried out under the direction of farmer-capitalists. At issue is the nature of the agricultural production price. In the case of products of the land, their different production prices would differ depending on the natural productivity of the given land. Moreover, unlike the industrial sector, such differences in productivity do not exist as temporary, constantly dissolving differences. Given this condition, the prices of products of the land are determined by the sales price of the products of the worst (least-fertile) land, whose individual production price becomes the market-adjusted production price.

Differential rent is a special profit that ends up in the pockets of the landowners, formed from the products of the land being produced on soil with different levels of fertility. In simplest terms, differential rent can be explained as follows: Assume that A and B represent two types of land, with A being the less fertile and B the more fertile soil. What determines the market price of the product of the land—wheat, for example—is the price of the wheat produced on land A, not B. This is because wheat is wheat, and there is no essential difference between the wheat produced on land A and B, being the same commodity sold at the same price. If the demand for wheat could not be met by production on B alone, making it necessary to also produce on A, wheat would have to be sold at a price sufficiently high to ensure an average profit (cost price + average profit = production price) for the capitalist who uses land A.

If the product could not be sold at this price, then this individual capital would cease production of wheat and shift to another sector. If this average rate of profit can be obtained, capital would produce on land A, and in this way the market sales price (production price) of A would determine the price of wheat. In this case, it is not a question of whether A or B produces a greater quantity of wheat. Even if A were to produce ten percent of the total wheat while B produced the remaining ninety percent, the production cost determining the market price of wheat would still be the production price of A, not B. Here we are not dealing with the case of market price determined by the commodities produced under average conditions or the commodity produced in the greatest quantity.

This can be expressed numerically in the following way: The production cost of wheat—its market-adjusted production cost—is determined by the production price of wheat produced on land A; for instance: $100Kp + 15P = 115$ (with Kp signifying cost price, and P the average profit). On the other hand, land B is more fertile (productive), so its cost price would be 90 rather than 100. Therefore, if products produced on land B were sold at their market-adjusted production price of 115, the result would be a profit of 25 rather than 15, for an *excess profit* of 10. This excess profit would pass into the hands of the owner of land B rather than the farmer-capitalist since the higher productive power that generated this surplus profit stems from landed property rather than capital. In short, this difference of 10, which is the difference between the individual profit and the average profit, forms differential rent. As Marx points out, "the surplus profit that arises from this use of the waterfall thus arises not from the capital but rather from the use by capital of a monopolizable and monopolized natural force."[11]

Concerning differential rent, Marx says that, "it does not contribute to determining the general production price of the commodity, but takes this as given."[12] This ground-rent arises from a difference in the level of fertility or productivity of a monopolizable natural force, but Marx emphasizes that this natural force "is not the source of the surplus profit, but simply a natural basis

11. *Capital*, vol. 3, 785.
12. Ibid.

for it."[13] He then goes on to explain the relation between differential rent and landed property in the following way:

> Landed property does not create the portion of value that is transformed into surplus profit; rather it simply enables the landowner, the proprietor of the waterfall, to entice this surplus profit out of the manufacturer's pocket and into his own. It is not the cause of this surplus profit's creation, but simply of its transformation into the form of ground-rent, hence of the appropriation of this portion of profit or commodity price by the land-owner or waterfall-owner.[14]

The passage above is particularly important in terms of the distinction between differential rent and absolute rent. Here we will not go into detail concerning the differences between Form I and Form II of differential rent, the theory of differential rent Ricardo developed in relation to this (his law of diminishing returns to land, etc.), or Marx's fundamental criticism of such theories. Here it is sufficient to note that Form I of differential rent is, theoretically speaking, the rent arising from a situation in which the same amount of capital invested in the same quantity of land yields different harvests, whereas Form II is the rent that arises when capital is invested continually and intensively in the same land, thus yielding different rates of productivity. Marx draws a number of conclusions from his detailed examination of examples of differential rent, but we will not deal with this here.

Absolute Rent and "Genuine Monopoly Price"

Absolute rent, as the term implies, is rent that is absolute, or ground-rent in general, which can be generated from every type of land, even the least fertile. This rent is "absolute" to the extent that "landed property acts as an absolute barrier." As we know empirically, even the poorest land is not provided free of charge to the capitalist by the landowner to be managed so as to generate profit. Instead, the capitalist confronts an "alien power and a barrier."

> Here landed property is the barrier that does not permit any new capital investment on formerly uncultivated or unleased land without levying a toll, i.e. demanding a rent, even if the land newly brought under cultivation

---

13. Ibid., 786.
14. Ibid.

is of a kind that does not yield any differential rent, and which save for landed property could have been cultivated already with a smaller rise in the market price, so that the governing market price would have paid the tiller of this worst land only his price of production. But as a result of the barrier that landed property sets up, the market price must rise to a point at which the land can pay a surplus over the price of the production, i.e. a rent.[15]

Absolute rent, in other words, is a rent obtained by actively raising the price of a product above its price of production, and in this case "it is not the rise in the product's price that is the cause of the rent but rather the rent that is the cause of the rise in price."[16] The excess value of the product over its production price," i.e. absolute rent, is one determining moment of the general market price. Here landed property raises the price of agricultural products to create rent, and this is a fundamental difference from differential rent.

> Landed property, whenever production needs land, whether for agriculture or for the extraction of raw materials, blocks this equalization for the capitals invested on the land and captures a portion of surplus-value which would otherwise go into the equalization process, giving the general rate of profit. Rent then forms a part of the value of commodities, in particular of their surplus-value, which simply accrues to the landowners who extract it from the capitalists, instead of to the capitalist class who have extracted it from the workers. It is assumed in this connection that agricultural capital sets more labor in motion than an equally large portion of non-agricultural capital. The extent of this gap, or its existence at all, depends on the relative development of agriculture vis-à-vis industry. By the nature of the case, this difference must decline with the progress of agriculture, unless the ratio in which the variable part of the capital declines vis-à-vis the constant part is still greater in industrial capital than in agricultural.[17]

The concept of absolute rent should be more or less clear from the explanation above, but the tricky question still remains of determining how this ground-rent is different from a "genuine monopoly price." Indeed, it may seem more succinct to explain absolute rent as a genuine monopoly price. Since absolute rent has been defined as ground-rent created by the monopoly of landed property, which becomes a barrier to capital, it would seem that this is rent based

---

15. Ibid., 896.
16. Ibid., 897.
17. Ibid., 906.

on a genuine monopoly price, and some may wonder why we cannot simply refer to it as such.

Here a number of distinctions arise, however, between absolute rent and genuine monopoly price. First of all, the price component of absolute rent is not merely nominal, but rather is one part of the value of the agricultural products. Generally speaking, the agricultural sector lags behind the industrial sector, and has a lower organic composition of capital. Therefore, when the average rate of profit is formed, and the transformation made into production prices, the production prices of agricultural products are fixed at a level *below their value*. This is because, due to a lower organic composition, there is a higher proportion of variable capital—a greater proportion of directly exploited workers—so that the ratio of surplus-value to capital is higher than in other sectors of production. In the formation of the average rate of profit, the agricultural sector distributes a portion of its surplus-value to other capitals in the industrial sector. Absolute rent is nothing but the excess value over the production price of agricultural products, not an excess price that exceeds the value of the product (which is the fundamental characteristic of a genuine monopoly price). In the following passage in *Capital*, Marx compares the "normal" forms of ground-rent (differential and absolute rent) to ground-rent based on a genuine monopoly price:

> Even though landed property can drive the price of agricultural products above their price of production, it does not depend on this, but rather on the general state of the market, how far the market price rises above the price of production and towards the value, and to what extent, therefore, the surplus-value produced over and above the given average profit in agriculture is either transformed into rent or goes into the general equalization of surplus-value that settles the average profit. In any case, this absolute rent, arising from the excess value over and above the price of production, is simply part of the agricultural surplus-value, the transformation of this surplus-value into rent, its seizure by the landowner; just as differential rent arises from the transformation of surplus-value into rent, its seizure by landed property, at the general governing price of production. These two forms of rent are the only normal ones. Apart from this, rent can derive only from a genuine monopoly price, which is determined neither by the price of production of the commodities nor by their value, but rather by the demand of the purchasers and their ability to pay, consideration of which belongs to the theory of competition, where the actual movement of market prices is investigated.[18]

---

18. Ibid., 898.

Here absolute ground-rent is defined in distinction from differential rent and genuine monopoly price. Marx clearly says that absolute rent—unlike differential rent, which is determined by production price, and genuine monopoly price, which is determined by "the demand of the purchasers and their ability to pay"—is determined by value, and that such rent is the "excess value over and above the price of production" and the transformation of "part of the agricultural surplus-value...into rent." As the portion of this value transformed into rent increases in size, the price of agricultural products rises, thus decreasing to the same extent the amount of surplus-value produced in agriculture that participates in the equalization of average profit.

This means that absolute ground-rent, as a category distinct from rent based on a genuine monopoly price, would cease to exist if the organic composition of agricultural capital were to increase to the point of exceeding that of the socially average capital. This is because the source of absolute ground-rent is the low organic composition of capital within the agricultural sector, where capital is mainly, or almost exclusively, expended on variable capital (labor), thus obtaining greater surplus-value than other capitals of equal size. If these conditions were eliminated, absolute rent would also cease to exist.

The second reason why absolute ground-rent is not simply a monopoly price—nor a purely monopoly-based additional price—is that landed property itself does not eliminate free competition among capitals. If the demand for grain expands, increasing the market price, capital will seek production on newly-cultivated land, thus intensifying competition between capitals on different plots of land, regardless of whether this is an increase in capital investment on already cultivated land or investment in newly cultivated land. As a result, the production of agricultural products will expand and price will settle around the level necessary for rent to be produced for the new landowners (of the inferior land). It is evident that this is not genuine monopoly price. Indeed, genuine monopoly price can only truly exist as such when competition, rather than intensifying, ceases to have any effect. Marx says that absolute ground-rent is determined within the boundaries of the concept of value and production price, as the transformed form of value, not by the theory of competition "where the actual movement of market prices is investigated."

In *Theories of Surplus Value*, Marx discusses absolute ground-rent at length in the course of his critical examination of the ideas of Rodbertus and Ricardo. He recognizes that, in a sense, ground-rent in general is a monopoly price. Just as the monopolization of the means of production provides the right to exploit labor and extract a surplus, so does the monopolization of the land provide the right to obtain ground-rent. At the same time, however, Marx was opposed to defining absolute ground-rent simply as actual monopoly price.

> For it is precisely the competition of capitals amongst themselves which enables the landlord to demand from the individual capitalist that he should be satisfied with "an average profit" and pay over to him the overplus of the value over the price affording this profit.
>
> But, it may be asked: If landed property gives the power to sell the product above its cost price at its value,[19] why does it not equally give the power to sell the product above its value, at an arbitrary monopoly price. On a small island, where there is no foreign trade in corn, the corn, food, like every other product, could unquestionably be sold at a monopoly price, that is, at a price only limited by the state of demand, i.e., of demand backed by the ability to pay...
>
> Leaving out of account exceptions of this kind—which cannot occur in European countries; even in England a large part of the fertile land is artificially withdrawn from agriculture and from the market in general in order to raise the value of the other part—landed property can only affect and paralyze the action of capitals, their competition, in so far as the competition of capitals modifies the determination of the values of the commodities. The conversion of values into cost prices [production prices] is only the consequence and result of the development of capitalist production. Originally commodities are (on the average) sold at their values. Deviation from this is in agriculture prevented by landed property.[20]

In other words, landed property creates absolute rent, but this is not achieved by means of genuine monopoly price. Rather, landed property, while being subordinate to the actions (competition) of capital, creates absolute rent by acting as a barrier to the transformation of value into production price. This is premised on the competition between capitals, and therefore the explanation of absolute rent cannot be derived from genuine monopoly price, which presupposes the absence of such competition. Marx, for instance, writes:

> The view that rent arises from the monopoly price of agricultural products, the monopoly price being due to the landowners possessing the monopoly

---

19. Marx uses the term "production price" rather than "cost price" in *Capital*. Moreover, this is not necessarily a sale of a commodity "at its value," but rather according to the part of value that exceeds the production price—i.e. at some point between the production price and value.
20. *MECW*, vol. 31, 542-3.

of the land. According to this concept, the price of the agricultural product is constantly above its value. There is a surcharge of price and the law of value of commodities is breached by the monopoly of landed property.

Rent arises out of the monopoly price of agricultural products, because supply is constantly below the level of demand or demand is constantly above the level of supply. But why does supply not rise to the level of demand? Why does not an additional supply equalize this relationship and thus, according to this theory, abolish all rent?[21]

He also criticizes Rodbertus in the following manner:

It is wrong to say, as Rodbertus does: If—according to the general law—the agricultural product is sold on an average at its value then it must yield an excess profit, alias rent; as though this selling of the commodity at its value, above its average price, were the general law of capitalist production. On the contrary, it must be shown why in primary production—by way of exception and in contrast to the class of industrial products whose value similarly stands above their average price—the values are not reduced to the average prices and therefore yield an excess profit, *alias* rent. This is to be explained simply by property in land. The equalization takes place only between capitals, because only the action of capitals on one another has the force to assert the inherent laws of capital. In this respect, those who derive rent from monopoly are right. Just as it is the monopoly of capital alone that enables the capitalist to squeeze surplus labor out of the worker, so the monopoly of landownership enables the landed proprietor to squeeze that part of surplus labor from the capitalist which would form a constant excess profit. But those who derive rent from monopoly are mistaken when they imagine that monopoly enables the landed proprietor to force the price of the commodity above its value. On the contrary, it makes it possible to maintain the value of the commodity above its average price; to sell the commodity not above, but at its value.

Modified in this way, the proposition is correct. It explains the existence of rent, whereas Ricardo only explains the existence of different rents and actually does not credit the ownership of land with any economic effect.[22]

From the passages above it is clear that the price brought about by absolute rent is not a simple monopoly price determined solely by demand. If it were, such rent could appreciate without limit, in excess of the value of the commodity, but in fact landed property does not have the power to bring this

21. Ibid., 387-8.
22. Ibid., 326-27.

about. Although landed property is able to place a certain barrier that confronts competition between capitals—thereby preventing the use of land without payment in compensation—this does not in itself eliminate such competition or even fundamentally restrict it. If capital is able to obtain average profit after paying rent, then it will be "freely" invested in the agricultural sector, and landowners do not have the power to prevent this. To this extent, competition between capitals also functions within the agricultural sector, and it can in fact be said that ground-rent is one outcome of such competition.

Distinctions between the Different Forms of Rent

We have already introduced the concepts of differential ground-rent and absolute ground-rent, which Marx calls the "only normal forms" of ground-rent, but now I would like to compare these two forms in order to deepen our understanding. Such a comparison can be seen in some of the passages cited in the previous section, and the following passage is another example where Marx compares the two forms:

> Differential rent has the peculiarity that here landed property seizes only the surplus profit that the farmer himself would otherwise pocket, and under certain circumstances does pocket for the duration of his tenancy. Here landed property simply causes the transfer of a portion of the commodity price that arises without any effort on its part (rather as a result of the determination by competition of the production price governing the market), a portion reducible to surplus profit, from one person to the other, from the capitalist to the landowner. Landed property is not in this case a cause that creates this component of price or the rise in price that it presupposes. But [in the case of absolute rent] if the worst type-A land cannot be cultivated—even though its cultivation would yield the price of production—until it yields a surplus over and above this production price, a rent, then landed property is the creative basis of this rise in price. Landed property has produced this rent itself.[23]
>
> Absolute rent is the excess of value over the average price of raw produce. Differential rent is the excess of the market price of the produce grown on favored soils over the value of their own produce.[24]

---

23. *Capital*, vol. 3, 889.
24. *MECW*, vol. 31, 370.

Of course, the terminology used here by Marx was not strictly followed later in *Capital*. "Average price" more precisely speaking is "production price," and what determines differential rent is the difference between the market-adjusted production price and the individual production price. However, if one is aware of the fact that production price itself is the transformed form of value, Marx's manner of expression here does not impede an understanding of differential rent in any way.

Simply put, the value of the grain produced on the better land is naturally lower than the market price of grain, and thus by selling this grain at the market price a special profit clearly emerges. When the landowner grabs this special profit on the basis of his ownership rights this becomes differential rent. To better understand differential rent and absolute ground-rent, we can consider the distinction between the two forms under a number of conditions.

First of all, the price component (surplus-profit) that accrues as ground-rent is fundamentally different from relations pertaining to landed property. In the case of differential rent, the price is not actively formed by landed property itself. Rather, this presupposes the transformation of profit into average profit and value into production price—the transformation into an adjusted average market price—and this results from the products of land with varying degrees of fertility being sold at the same market price (market-adjusted production price) despite having different value, or more precisely, different individual production prices. To this extent, landed property does not actively participate in price formation. The principle operating here is not the use of coercion on the part of landed property, but rather the pure and simple principle of capital whereby all identical commodities obtain an average profit and are sold at the same price. In short, this is the determination of market-adjusted production prices through competition. The fact that the products produced on the more favorable land receive a special profit is the outcome of this principle, the outcome of this price, and is not due to the price being generated by landed property. Based on the right of private ownership, landowners line their own pockets by transforming this special profit into differential rent.

On the other hand, in the case of absolute ground-rent, landed property actively creates the price of the agricultural product. In other words, rent alone pushes the price above the production price. By not allowing cultivation until rent is produced, landed property forces this rent upon capital. Here, more than in the case of differential rent, landed property insists on its own rights.

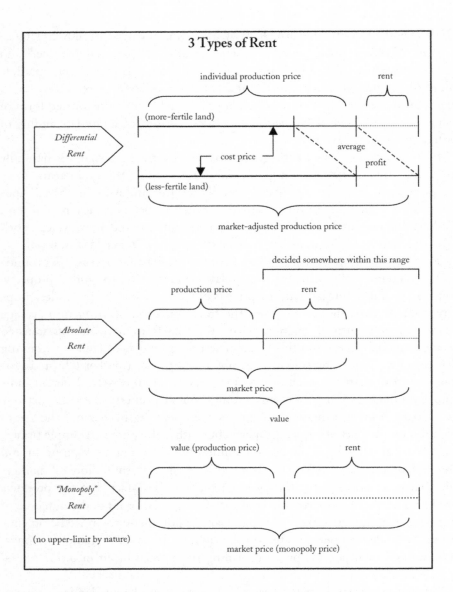

Therefore, the following distinction naturally emerges between these two kinds of rent. In the case of the price of an agricultural product that creates differential rent, the issue centers on the production price, and the difference between the market price of the agricultural product in question and the individual prices. In the case of the price for absolute rent, by contrast, the issue revolves around the excess of value above the production price. This "excess of value" does not exceed the value of the agricultural product, and is rather determined at some point in between the magnitude of the production price and the magnitude of value.[25] Therefore, absolute rent is determined by value rather than production price, since it stems from the excess value over the production price that does not exceed the boundaries of the agricultural product's value.

Another difference arises between the two forms of rent in terms of the source of the special profit (rent). In a famous line from the third volume of *Capital*, Marx describes differential rent as a "false social value," and there was a major debate in Japan over the meaning of this expression.[26] Marx employs a chart to illustrate that 10 quarters of wheat with a value of 240 shillings could sell for 600 shillings, thus yielding a differential rent of 360 shillings. He then adds:

> This is determination by a market value brought about by competition on the basis of the capitalist mode of production; it is competition that produces a false social value. This results from the law of market value to which agricultural products are subjected. The determination of the market value of products, i.e. also of products of the soil, is a social act, even if performed by society unconsciously and unintentionally, and it is based necessarily on the exchange-value of the product and not on the soil and the differences in its fertility. If we imagine that the capitalist form of society has been abolished and that society has been organized as a conscious association working according to a plan, the 10 qrs represent a quantity of autonomous labor-time equal to that contained in 240 shillings. Society would therefore not purchase this product at 2.5 times the actual labor-time contained it; the basis for a class of landowners would thereby disappear.[27]

Differential rent is not surplus-value formed in the agricultural sector, but rather a social surplus-value paid to landowners by society. This is a "false" value because even though it is manifested as the market value it lacks substance. What seems to have a value of 600 shillings in fact has a value of 240

---

25. See the diagram in this chapter describing the three forms of rent.

26. For the most part, however, this debate did not rise above the level of pedantic blather, particularly in terms of the ideas expressed by of followers of Uno Kōzō and Ōchi Hideaki.

27. *Capital*, vol. 3, 799.

shillings. The difference of 360 shillings is the part paid by society to land-owners, who are a purely parasitic class. It is clear that this false social value is not necessarily one part of the surplus-value produced in the agricultural sector. A total production price of 240 shillings is actually transformed into 600 shillings due to the fact that society "considered as a consumer" pays this amount, and this bears no direct relation at all to the part of the surplus-value produced by agriculture.

On the other hand, in the case of absolute rent, the surplus-value that is produced in agriculture is transformed into rent through the power of landed property. This rent stems from the excess of the value of the agricultural product above its production price. Theoretically speaking, this is nothing more than the transformation of the surplus-value formed through agricultural production into rent. Unlike differential rent, this is the part of surplus-value that exceeds the commodity's own production price.

The distinction between differential rent and absolute ground-rent is as described above, but we also need to provide an overview of the difference between these two forms of rent *and* genuine monopoly price. In particular, the distinction between absolute rent and rent based upon monopoly price poses a certain degree of difficulty because, in a sense, rent itself is premised on the monopoly (private ownership) of land, which is a restricted element of nature.

The first thing we need to point out is that genuine monopoly price can be formed regardless of the particular type of landed property. For example, an extremely precious wine that can only be produced in a certain geographic area can come to have a high monopoly price on the market. In other words, as Marx notes, this is a price "determined neither by the price of production of the commodities nor by their value, but rather by the demand of the purchasers and their ability to pay, consideration of which therefore belongs to the theory of competition, where the actual movement of market prices is investigated."[28] This monopoly price can generate a certain amount of rent. However, this is fundamentally different from the case of differential rent and absolute ground-rent, which are determined by production price and value, respectively, and can therefore be explained theoretically, including the magnitude, limitations, and nature of such rent.

---

28. Ibid., 898.

Not only can genuine monopoly price diverge from the price of production, it can also exceed the limitations of value, having no inherent limits, and in this sense the difference between genuine monopoly price and the two kinds of "normal" rent is clear. Marx defines absolute ground-rent as a rent that is ultimately created through the restrictions placed by landed property, rather than stemming from monopoly price, and this point holds great significance. In terms of creating a special profit that boosts the price, genuine monopoly price is similar in one respect to absolute ground-rent. At the same time, genuine monopoly price is similar to differential rent in terms of price being presupposed and landed property simply grabbing the excess profit that is created, with "society considered as a consumer" paying for this. Nevertheless, the price that makes monopoly price possible, and that which makes differential rent possible, belong to essentially different dimensions.

We must recognize that the law of value is not set aside when we deal with the question of rent—even the case of monopoly price. All forms of rent are a certain portion of the total surplus-value of society. In other words, profit, interest, rent, etc. are the sum of unearned income. This is nothing more than the sum of the surplus-labor of workers. Moreover, the difference between absolute ground-rent and differential rent becomes apparent if one considers their elimination. That is to say, it is possible for absolute ground-rent to be "eliminated" on the foundation of capitalist production—setting aside the question of whether this will occur in reality—whereas differential ground-rent cannot disappear as long as capitalism continues to exist. This issue, however, already brings us to the topic of the final section of this chapter.

Elimination of Rent and Socialism

Rent is essentially a historical social relation, one relation of human beings within a society based on private property in which "the monopoly of a piece of the earth enables the so-called landowner to exact a tribute, to put a price on it."[29] Therefore, it is perfectly clear that rent will disappear along with the elimination of private property. On the other hand, however, for capital, landed property is something superfluous, a relation that is not always necessary for the development of capital. It is clear, of course that land is indispensable to the movement of capital as one of the objective conditions needed for production, but for capital this does not represent an essential "moment."

---

29. Ibid., 762.

What is essential for capital is the relation between capital and wage-labor—the social relation between the labor accumulated in the past (production means) and living labor—whereas land as a merely natural object is a moment that, albeit important, is external to this relation.

As long as capitalism continues, differential rent will not disappear, but absolute ground-rent could disappear even upon the basis of capitalist production, and herein lies an important distinction between these two forms of rent. The elimination of absolute ground-rent is possible under two scenarios. This could occur first of all through the abolishment of the private ownership of land and its nationalization. This would only be the nationalization of land that forms one part of the means of production, with capitalist production continuing on as before. Under such conditions, absolute ground-rent would disappear because there would be no private ownership of the land. In fact, the removal of the resistance and barriers to the movement of capital on the land could lead to even further capitalist development. As we have already seen, absolute ground-rent, unlike differential rent, directly exerts an influence on the price of agricultural products, raising their prices, and in this way drags down the general rate of profit. This means that the benefit to landed property comes at the expense of the bourgeoisie. For capital, the nationalization of the land represents getting rid of this unnecessary element, and thus the "radical bourgeoisie" have not hesitated to raise the slogan of land nationalization.

> The difference between the productive power of steam and that of the soil is thus only that one yields unpaid labor to the capitalist and the other to the landowner, who does not take it away from the worker, but from the capitalist. The capitalist is therefore so enthusiastic about this element "belonging to no one."
>
> Only this much is correct:
>
> Assuming the capitalist mode of production, the capitalist is not only a necessary functionary, but the dominating functionary in production. The landowner, on the other hand, is quite superfluous in this mode of production. Its only requirement is that land should not be common property, that it should confront the working class as a condition of production, not belonging to it, and the purpose is completely fulfilled if it becomes State property, i.e., if the State draws the rent. The landowner, such an important functionary in production in the ancient world and in the Middle Ages, is a useless superfetation in the industrial world. The radical bourgeois (with an eye besides to the suppression of all other taxes) therefore goes forward theoretically to a refutation of the private ownership of the land, which, in the form of State property, he would like to turn into the

common property of the bourgeois class, of capital. But in practice he lacks the courage, since an attack on one form of property—a form of the private ownership of a condition of labor—might cast considerable doubts on the other form. Besides, the bourgeois has himself become an owner of the land.[30]

There is a second situation under which absolute ground-rent could be eliminated on the basis of capitalism. Absolute rent, as we have seen, necessitates that agriculture lag behind industry, so that the value of agricultural products is comparatively high. If agriculture were to develop more rapidly than industry, resulting in this gap being overcome, absolute rent would be unable to exist, theoretically speaking.

> Due to landed property, the "raw product" is distinguished by the privilege that its value is not reduced to the average price. If, indeed, its value did decrease, which would be possible despite your "value of the material," to the level of the average price of commodities, then rent would disappear.[31]

> The absolute rent may rise because the general rate of profit falls, owing to new advances in industry...
> The absolute rent can fall, because the value of agricultural produce falls and the general rate of profit rises. It can fall, because the value of the agricultural produce falls as a result of a fundamental change in the organic composition of capital, without the rate of profit rising. It can disappear completely, as soon as the value of the agricultural produce becomes equal to the cost price [production price], in other words when the agricultural capital has the same composition as the non-agricultural average capital.
> Ricardo's proposition would only be correct if expressed like this: When the value of agricultural produce equals its cost price, then there is no absolute rent. But he is wrong because he says: There is no absolute rent because value and cost price are altogether identical, both in industry and in agriculture. On the contrary, agriculture would belong to an exceptional class of industry, if its value and cost price were identical.[32]

Here Marx clarifies an essential aspect of absolute ground-rent, namely that it can only exist at a historical stage where the development of agriculture is lower than that of industry. Thus, absolute rent can be eliminated if land is

---

30. *MECW*, vol. 31, 278.
31. Ibid., 381.
32. *MECW*, vol. 32, 30.

nationalized or agriculture ceases to lag behind industry—although in present-day Japan it seems highly unlikely for either situation to occur.

Differential rent, by contrast, cannot be eliminated under capitalism since it is determined by more fundamental capitalist principles. For instance, even if "the state appropriated the land and capitalist production continued, then rent from II, III, IV[33] would be paid to the state, but rent as such would remain."[34] In other words, even if ground-rent were to disappear due to the productive power of agriculture increasing to the point where it equaled, or surpassed that of industry, differential rent would still remain.

However, if capitalist production were abolished—and socialism achieved—differential rent would also disappear. In the previous section, we already quoted a passage from the third volume of *Capital* where Marx refers to landed property as a "a false social value" since an agricultural product with a value of 240 shillings can be sold for 600 shillings, thus creating an excess profit (differential rent) of 360. In the same chapter, he says that if socialism were realized, "society would therefore not purchase this product at 2.5 times the actual labor-time contained in it [10 qrs. of grain]"[35] Marx basically makes the same point in *Theories of Surplus Value*:

> Differential rent is linked with the regulation of the market price and therefore disappears along with the price and with capitalist production. There would remain only the fact that land of varying fertility is cultivated by social labor and, despite the difference in the labor employed, labor can become more productive on all types of land. But the amount of labor used on the worse land would by no means result in more labor being paid for [the product] of the better land as now with the bourgeois. Rather would the labor saved on IV be used for the improvement of III and that saved from III for the improvement of II and finally that saved on II would be used to improve I. Thus the whole of the capital eaten up by the landowners would serve to equalize the labor used for the cultivation of the soil and to reduce the amount of labor in agriculture as a whole.[36]

---

33. Marx defined I as inferior land, and II, III and IV according to increases in fertility.
34. *MECW*, vol. 31, 335.
35. *Capital*, vol. 3, 799.
36. *MECW*, vol. 31, 337.

Of course, not only differential rent, but rent in general and all forms of rent—as well as the general appropriation of surplus-labor—would be eliminated with the superceding of capitalism. Although it is possible for absolute ground-rent to disappear under capitalist production, this does not mean that this could occur in reality, since aggregate rent only exists practically as the sum of absolute ground-rent and differential rent.

Up to now we have mainly looked at the distinction between the different forms of rent, but to conclude we need emphasize that the three types of rent share an essential identity as such. Rent, regardless of the form it takes, is nothing more than landowners receiving from society a special surplus-value free-of-charge (!) on the basis of their rights of private ownership. In a passage criticizing the famous "trinity formula," Marx writes:

> These means of production are in and for themselves, by nature, capital; capital is nothing but a mere "economic name" for those means of production; and similarly the earth is in and for itself, by nature, the earth as monopolized by a certain number of landed proprietors. Just as the products become an independent power vis-à-vis the producers in capital and in the capitalist—who is in actual fact nothing but personified capital—so land is personified in the landowner, he is the land similarly standing up on its hind legs and demanding its share, as an independent power, of the products produced with its aid; so that it is not the land that receives the portion of the product needed to replace and increase its productivity, but instead the landowner who receives a share of this product to be sold off and frittered away. It is clear that capital presupposes that labor is wage-labor. It is just as clear, however, that once you proceed from labor as wage-labor, so that the coincidence between wage-labor and labor in general appears self-evident, capital and the monopolized earth must also appear as the natural form of the conditions of labor vis-à-vis labor in general. It now appears as the natural form of the means of labor that they should be capital, as a purely material character which arises from their function in the labor process in general. Capital and produced means of production thus become identical expressions. Likewise land and land monopolized by private property. The means of labor as such, being capital by nature, thus become the source of profit in the same way as the earth as such becomes the source of rent.[37]

---

37. *Capital*, vol. 3, 963-4.

Marx clearly says that just as profit is a tribute demanded by capital on the basis of its monopolization of the means of production and its rights and power of ownership, so is rent a share of the product demanded by landed property through its monopolization of land. Moreover, in the case of landed property, even the functional character seen in capital for the realization of surplus-value vanishes, leaving only the pure and simple relation of landowners demanding a certain tribute on the basis of ownership.

At the beginning of his theory of ground-rent, Marx clarifies the premises of his discussion. He notes that he does not intend to discuss rent in general (or rent in its historical forms), but rather capitalist ground-rent, and he promises to purely consider this issue independent from the many impurities included within what is generally called rent (such as interest on fixed capital or the deductions from labor). Still, Marx was aware that the essence of the problem is that "the monopoly to a piece of the earth enables the so-called landowner to exact a tribute."[38] It would be an error to treat capitalist ground-rent as rent in general, dissolving it within this concept and thereby abandoning the specific independent analysis of ground-rent under capitalism and its determinations. At the same time, however, Marx does not question for a moment the fact that ground-rent is the outcome of landed property and a certain type of private ownership.

> Whatever the specific form of rent may be, what all its types have in common is the fact that the appropriation of rent is the economic form in which landed property is realized and that ground-rent in turn presupposes landed property, the ownership of particular bits of the globe by certain individuals.[39]

In order to understand Marx's theory of ground-rent it is necessary to be clearly aware of the fact that landed property obtains a tribute of *free* labor from those who utilize the land, so as to exploit a portion or all of the surplus-labor of others, and this therefore presupposes a type of private ownership whereby portions of the earth can be exclusively owned or monopolized. For Marx, this was a clear premise, and he saw no need to emphasize it. What he did emphasize, however, was the error of explaining capitalist rent from landed property in general, thereby overlooking the specific historical charac-

---

38. Ibid., 762.
39. Ibid., 772.

ter (*differentia specifica*) of capitalist rent. Unoists distort the content and development of Marx's theory of rent, casting aside the radical (fundamental), critical awareness of rent—and thus the awareness of the private ownership of land—to instead drone on endlessly about a "purely economic" theory of rent.

As we have already pointed out, capitalist ground-rent has its own particular economic laws—just as in the case of the realization of surplus-value or the exploitation of labor—and it is important to understand these laws, but at the same time we certainly cannot overlook that "the appropriation of rent is the economic form in which landed property is realized[40] and that ground-rent in turn presupposes landed property, the ownership of particular bits of the globe by certain individuals." Differential rent, not to mention absolute ground-rent, makes its way into the pockets of landowners as rent because of the power of the private ownership of land, and this is the "economic form" in which rent is *actualized*. A theory of ground-rent that lacks this fundamental awareness (criticism) of the private ownership of land can only end up being deceptive and of questionable worth. We might go so far as to say that Marx's theory of ground-rent is the theoretical form in which his character as a communist is *actualized*. Marx wrote the following beautiful passage, as a communist, and I would like to use it to bring this chapter on ground-rent to an end:

> The fact that it is only the title a number of people have to property in the earth that enables them to appropriate a part of society's surplus labor as tribute...[The title] was entirely created by the relations of production. Once these have reached the point where they have to be sloughed off, then the material source, the economically and historically justified source of the title that arises from the process of life's social production, disappears, and with it all transactions based on it. From the standpoint of higher socio-economic formation, the private property of particular individuals in the earth will appear just as absurd as the private property of one man in other men. Even an entire society, a nation, or all simultaneously existing societies taken together, are not the owners of the earth. They are simply its possessors, its beneficiaries, and have to bequeath it in an improved state to succeeding generations, as *boni patres familias*.[41]

---

40. Marx says that this can take any number of forms, and he mentions a few concrete historical examples.
41. Ibid., 911.

5

Concept of Productive Labor

Introduction

Why is it necessary, in the first place, to make a distinction between productive and unproductive labor? The bourgeoisie and petty bourgeoisie are completely unaware of the real necessity of this distinction, or think that concern over it reflects a dogmatism or nonsensical detachment from reality. They would like to eliminate this distinction, and are in fact doing so. For the bourgeoisie, the distinction between productive and unproductive labor does not actually exist. Every sort of labor under capitalism—no matter how empty or contemptible the "labor" may be—is seen as productive labor, so that any conceptual distinction between productive and unproductive labor is dissolved. For socialists, however, this distinction is essential. It is no exaggeration to say that socialism is not possible without such a distinction. This is because socialism is, above all, the reorganization of productive labor that has reached a great level of productivity under capitalism, and is only feasible on the basis of productive labor that has attained the highest social level.

In bourgeois society, this issue has been approached from the extremely distorted perspective of considering what is the source of "national income." In this sense, the modern bourgeois theory of national income is not unrelated to the concept of productive labor, but the understanding of productive labor within this theory is "somewhat" different than the Marxist concept of productive labor. The Marxist concept of productive labor—or so-called "original definition"—refers to labor that produces material goods, and not simply labor, but *social* labor. This concept, moreover, does not generally include service labor. The bourgeois concept of productive labor, by contrast, includes both labor in general that is exchanged against capital to produce a profit, as well as labor that "produces" some sort of "socially useful" service despite not being exchanged against capital and therefore creating no profit for capital (e.g. the "labor" of police officers and soldiers, as well as the "labor" of general employees within the state apparatus, etc.).

Of course, Marx considers not only the "original" definition of productive labor, but also this latter, historical or formal definition. His examination, however, is based upon the understanding that labor exchanged against capital also coincides—by and large, as the predominant form—with productive labor in the original sense. At the same time, Marx fully understands the limitations or restrictions of the historical definition of productive labor, which stem from the nature of a historical, formal definition.

It may be worthwhile here to provide a brief introduction of the bourgeois concept of productive labor. By "bourgeois" I am *not* referring to the theories of Adam Smith, which Marx critically examines at length, but rather to post-classical bourgeois economics, or "vulgar" economics. Contemporary theories of national income date back to the emergence of Keynesianism, but Keynes' teacher Alfred Marshall already wrote in *Principles of Economics*:

> The labour and capital of the country, acting on its natural resources, produce annually a certain *net* aggregate of commodities, material and immaterial, including services of all kinds. This is the true net annual income, or revenue, of the country.[1]

This view held by Marshall is the original form of the bourgeois concept of national income. Today, in all of the bourgeois conceptual definitions of productive labor, we can find, almost word for word, this same notion that the concept of productive labor includes "material and immaterial [commodities], including services of all kinds."

The "official" view of productive labor held by the state is precisely the same. For instance, a 1963 government white paper in Japan describes national income as being "the sum of the (value-added) net product produced by the people of a given country within a certain period."[2] Here, however, pro-

---

1. Alfred Marshall, *Principles of Economics*, 2 vols. (London: Macmillan, 1907), 2: 524.
2. *Kokumin shotoku hakusho* (Tokyo: Tōyō Keizai Shinpō-sha, 1963), 222.

duction is not limited to material production, and includes whatever "creates any sort of good or service." Another common view of national income is the following:

> The net outcome produced by the activity of the national economy over a certain period of time (for example one year) can be viewed from one of two perspectives: production or income. In terms of production, this is the sum total of the value of new goods and services added through production in a certain period within a given country. In terms of income, this is the total of all of the income (wages, profit, interest, rent, etc.) earned through production in a certain period...National income, in the so-called wider sense of the term, is a concept that encompasses both of these aspects."[3]

Such views, however, are not held solely by bourgeois scholars, and are also shared by many "Marxist economists." The view of the Japanese Communist Party, for instance, is essentially the same as that of the bourgeoisie, in the sense that they are happy to consider the "labor" of anyone and everyone as being productive. In this way, even soldiers receiving salaries from the state are considered productive workers based on the view that they are engaged in the "sacred" task of protecting the state and are therefore providing a valuable "service," so that there is no reason to regard their "labor" as unproductive. For the bourgeoisie (and the JCP), "labor" existing in present-day society is seen as something absolute and unsurpassed, with the actually existing relations seen as the best of all possible relations. Within this view, all fundamental and essential criticism of capitalist society vanishes, and what holds sway is the attitude of simply adhering firmly to the current status quo.

Such views of productive labor closely resemble the manner in which the bourgeoisie defines a commodity as anything with a price that is provided through exchange. In other words, for the bourgeoisie "a commodity is a commodity," even if we are dealing with land, stocks, bonds, or Marx's example of "honor."[4] Likewise, "sex" gains currency as a commodity, as evidenced by the existence of an enormous "adult-entertainment industry." Those who hold such views, however, are unaware of the limitations of a formal definition, and thus completely forfeit any sort of critical perspective.

---

3.   Miyazawa Ken'ichi, *Kokumin shotoku riron* (Tokyo: Chikuma Shobō, 1976), 19.
4.   See *Capital*, vol. 1, 197.

The modern bourgeoisie—as well as the petty bourgeoisie and the JCP who curry favor with them—even fail to understand why Adam Smith made a distinction between productive and unproductive labor and considered this distinction to be so important. If "service labor" is indeed an example of productive labor, there would have been little reason for Smith to be so particular about this distinction. If both labor that produces material wealth and labor that only accompanies consumption are productive, then there is no need at all to make an essential distinction between the two by placing the formation of "national wealth" on one side and the consumption of this wealth on the other. Smith, however, attempts to demonstrate that productive labor is the real basis of national wealth, and that through its increase, either relatively or absolutely, a nation prospers, whereas a decrease in productive labor leads to the impoverishment or ruin of a nation.

Smith clearly considers the expenses provided for government workers and the military to be unproductive. The labor of government workers is neither exchanged against capital, nor does it augment capital, representing instead a deduction from the profit of capital that is paid for from revenue. Smith's clear conclusion is that unproductive labor is that labor exchanged against revenue rather than against capital. The wealth of a nation thus increases to the extent that there is an increase in the amount of labor exchanged against capital, whereas this wealth contracts when such labor decreases. The ideal for Smith is to decrease the proportion of unproductive labor and the expenses that impede the accumulation of capital; in other words, the creation of an "economical" state. Smith knew that the expansion of state expenditures and the maintenance of a massive military force would definitely not enrich a nation, concluding that such a state would be a parasitic, decadent state in decline, which would place an increasingly heavy burden on the working population. For Smith, then, the distinction between productive and unproductive labor, far from being a matter of indifference, is of decisive importance for his theory of national wealth.

Marx, for his part, does not place particular emphasis on the concept of productive labor in *Capital*, treating it instead as a self-evident premise. He does offer something of an overview of productive labor in chapters seven and sixteen of the first volume of *Capital*, where he defines the "original" and "formal" concepts of productive labor, but this is not developed in much detail. A detailed treatment of productive labor can be found in "The Distinction Between Productive and Unproductive Labor" in *Theories of Surplus Value* as well as in "The Results of the Immediate Process of Production," which was written as a preliminary manuscript to *Capital*. Marx, of course, discusses productive labor in passing in other books and articles, and from these fragments we can basically understand his views on the subject. The bulk of the references to productive labor can be found in the notebooks later published as *Theories of Surplus Value*, where Marx critically examines Smith's concept of productive labor and develops his own concept by means of this criticism. Owing to the notebook format, however, it is natural that Marx's comments would be open to various interpretations, with different writers often drawing polar-opposite conclusions from the same passages.

It was natural for Marx to take up Adam Smith's views when examining the concept of productive labor, because of all the classical economists, it was Smith who emphasized and developed this concept to the greatest extent as one of the fundamental concepts and theoretical pillars of *The Wealth of Nations*. When we briefly examine Smith's concept of productive labor later, it will become clear how bold and vibrant the classical school was, unlike today's vulgar bourgeois economics. The classical economists were theoreticians who represented the "healthy" bourgeoisie in its period of development, and thus made a firm distinction between productive and unproductive labor, defending productive labor for the sake of the accumulation of capital and prosperity, and clearly recognizing the need to emphasize its significance.

In the modern era, however, even supposed Marxists oppose Smith's views and argue that examples of unproductive labor are actually productive labor. These theorists clearly exist at a level below that of Smith, and have slipped into the standpoint of the decadent bourgeoisie, even while advancing the ludicrous claim of "developing Marxism." Marx, for his part, while recognizing the historical significance and justification of Smith's theory, correctly understood and exposed its bourgeois limitations, revealing the contradictions and confusion within this theory. He did this, of course, not in a moralistic manner, but rather in terms of historical and class necessity.

"Original" Definition of Productive Labor

Marx emphasizes that there are two concepts of productive labor: (a) productive labor in the sense of a metabolic relationship between man and nature to produce material wealth, and (b) productive labor in the sense of exchange against capital and the self-valorization of capital. He calls the former the "original definition" [*die ursprüngliche Bestimmung*] and the latter the "formal" or "historical" definition. We will begin here by looking at the original definition. In the first volume of *Capital*, in discussing the labor process, Marx writes:

> In the labor process, therefore, man's activity, via the instruments of labor, effects an alteration in the object of labor which was intended from the out-set. The process is extinguished in the product. The product of the process is a use-value, a piece of natural material adapted to human needs by means of a change in its form. Labor has become bound up in its object: labor has been objectified, the object has been worked on. What on the side of the worker appeared in the form of unrest [*Unruhe*] now appears, on the side of the product, in the form of being [*Sein*], as a fixed, immobile characteristic. The worker has spun, and the product is a spinning.[5]
>
> If we look at the whole process from the point of view of its result, the product, it is plain that both the instruments and the object of labor are means of production and that the labor itself is productive labor. [Marx's footnote:] This method of determining what is productive labor from the standpoint of the simple labor process, is by no means sufficient to cover the capitalist process of production.[6]
>
> The labor process, as we have just presented it in its simple and abstract elements, is purposeful activity aimed at the production of use-values. It is an appropriation of what exists in nature for the requirements of man. It is the universal condition for the metabolic interaction [*Stoffwechsel*] between man and nature, the everlasting nature-imposed condition of human exist-ence, and it is therefore independent of every form of that existence, or rather it is common to all forms of society in which human beings live. We did not, therefore, have to present the worker in his relationship with other workers; it was enough to present man and his labor on one side, nature and its materials on the other. The taste of porridge does not tell us who grew the oats, and the process we have presented does not reveal the condi-tions under which it takes place, whether it is happening under the slave-owner's brutal lash or the anxious eye of the capitalist, whether Cincinnatus undertakes it in tilling his couple of acres, or a savage, when he lays low a wild beast with a stone.[7]

Marx is referring here to the simpler determination of productive labor or the definition "from the standpoint of the simple labor process." This is a concept

---

5. [According to the footnote in the English edition of *Capital*, "spinning" is "a quantity of thread or spun yarn."]
6. *Capital*, vol.1, 287.
7. Ibid., 290-1.

that presents no difficulty and can be readily understood by anyone. Human beings, in order to satisfy their needs, act upon nature, and nature is altered and processed through their social labor. Productive labor is this sort of labor as the "universal condition for the metabolic interaction between man and nature." Therefore, essentially speaking, this is labor that produces *material wealth*.

It is easy to grasp the inseparable relation between this original concept of productive labor and the materialist conception of history. Already in *The German Ideology*, Marx had pointed out that "life involves before everything else eating and drinking, a habitation, clothing and many other things," and the "the first historical act is thus the production of the means to satisfy these needs, the production of material life itself, which is "a fundamental condition of all history."[8]

And in a letter to Kugelmann (July 11, 1868), Marx wrote that, "any nation that stopped working, not for a year, but let us say, just for a few weeks, would perish."[9] In this way, Marx emphasizes that productive labor is the necessary material condition for, or moment within, the existence and development of human history and culture, constituting the fundamental process of all human history and society—and capitalist society is certainly no exception to this. At the beginning of *Capital*, Marx indicates that the substance of a commodity's value is abstract human social labor, but since he felt that it was perfectly clear that this labor was "productive labor" (in the "original" sense) he saw no particular need to add a further explanation.

"Formal Definition" of Productive Labor

Marx, however, was not satisfied with only the original concept of productive labor as seen from the standpoint of the simple labor process. The issue for Marx is labor under capitalism, how to evaluate wage-labor in such a society. He thus emphasizes that the original concept of productive labor alone is insufficient, and goes on to examine the "formal definition." In other words, from the simple or abstract definition of productive labor, Marx moves on to the concept of productive labor under capitalism. This formal definition of productive labor is qualitatively different from the concept seen from the sim-

---

8.   Karl Marx, *The German Ideology* (New York: International Publishers, 1947), 16.
9.   *MECW*, vol. 43, 68.

ple labor process, its content being more complex. Although it has a basis in the original definition, the formal definition involves a more complex and realistic determination of productive labor, which depends upon the formal essence of capitalist production. In *Theories of Surplus Value*, Marx writes:

> Productive labor, in the meaning of capitalist production, is wage labor which, exchanged against the variable part of capital (the part of the capital that is spent on wages), reproduces not only this part of capital (or the value of its own labor capacity), but in addition produces surplus-value for the capitalist. It is only thereby that commodity or money is transformed into capital, is produced as capital. Only that wage labor is productive which produces capital. (This is the same as saying that it reproduces on an enlarged scale the sum of value expended on it, or that it gives in return more labor than it receives in the form of wages. Consequently, only that labor capacity is productive which produces a value greater than its own.)"[10]

Only labor that produces capital is productive labor. Commodities or money become capital, however, through being exchanged directly for labor capacity, and exchanged only in order to be replaced by more labor than they themselves contain. For the use-value of labor capacity to the capitalist as capitalist does not consist in its actual use-value, in the usefulness of this particular concrete labor—that is spinning labor, weaving labor, and so on. He is as little concerned with this as with the use-value of the product of this labor as such, since for the capitalist the product is a commodity (even before its first metamorphosis), not an article of consumption. What interests him in the commodity is that it has more exchange value than he paid for it; and therefore the use-value of the labor is, for him, that he gets back a greater quantity of labor-time than he has paid out in the form of wages. Included among these productive workers, of course, are all those who contribute in one way or another to the production of the commodity, from the actual operative to the manager or engineer (as distinct from the capitalist). And so even the latest English official report on the factories "explicitly" includes in the category of employed wage-workers all persons employed in the factories and in the offices attached to them, with the exception of the manufacturers themselves (see the wording of the report before the concluding part of this rubbish). Productive labor is here defined from the standpoint of capitalist production, and Adam Smith here got to the very heart of the matter, hit the nail on the head. This is one of his greatest scientific merits (as Malthus rightly observed, this critical differentiation between productive and unproductive labor remains the basis

10. *MECW*, vol. 31, 8.

of all bourgeois political economy) that he defines productive labor as labor which is directly exchanged with capital; that is, he defines it by the exchange through which the conditions of production of labor, and value in general, whether money or commodity, are first transformed into capital (and labor into wage labor in its scientific meaning). This also establishes absolutely what unproductive labor is. It is labor which is not exchanged with capital, but directly with revenue, that is, with wages or profit (including of course the various categories of those who share as co-partners in the capitalist's profit, such as interest and rent). Where all labor in part still pays itself (like e.g. the agricultural labor of the peasants on *corvée*) and in part is directly exchanged for revenue (like the manufacturing labor in the cities of Asia), no capital and no wage labor exists in the sense of bourgeois political economy. These definitions are therefore not derived from the material characteristics of labor (neither from the nature of its product nor from the particular character of the labor as concrete labor), but from the definite social form, the social relations of production, within which the labor is realized. An actor, for example, or even a clown, according to this definition, is a productive laborer if he works in the service of a capitalist (an entrepreneur) to whom he returns more labor than he receives from him in the form of wages; while a jobbing tailor who comes to the capitalist's house and patches his trousers for him, producing a mere use-value for him, is an unproductive laborer. The former's labor is exchanged with capital, the latter's with revenue. The former's labor produces a surplus-value; in the latter's revenue is consumed.

Productive and unproductive labor is here throughout conceived from the from the standpoint of the possessor of money, of the capitalist, not from that of the workman."[11]

And Marx provides the following overview of this concept in *Capital*:

Yet the concept of productive labor also becomes narrower. Capitalist production is not merely the production of commodities, it is, by its very essence, the production of surplus-value. The worker produces not for himself, but for capital. It is no longer sufficient, therefore, for him simply to produce. He must produce surplus-value. The only worker who is productive is one who produces surplus-value for the capitalist, or in other words contributes towards the self-valorization of capital. If we may take an example from outside the sphere of material production, a schoolmaster is a productive worker when, in addition to belaboring the head of his pupils, he works himself into the ground to enrich the owner of the school That the latter has laid out his capital in a teaching factory, instead of a sausage

---

11. Ibid., 12-3.

factory, makes no difference to the relation. The concept of a productive worker therefore implies not merely a relation between the activity of work and its useful effect, between the worker and the product of his work, but also a specifically social relation of production, a relation with a historical origin which stamps the worker as capital's direct means of valorization. To be a productive worker is therefore not a piece of luck, but a misfortune. In Volume 4 of this work [*Theories of Surplus Value*], which deals with the history of the theory, we shall show that the classical political economists have always made the production of surplus-value the distinguishing characteristic of the productive worker. Hence their definition of a productive worker varies with their conception of the nature of surplus-value. For the Physiocrats, indeed, surplus-value exists exclusively in the form of ground rent.[12]

The essence of the formal definition of productive labor is labor exchanged against capital rather than against revenue, labor that leads to the self-valorization of capital, thus constituting capital as such. We need to consider, however, whether this formal definition of productive labor would also include service labor.

Certainly when Marx says that an actor working under capital would be a productive worker, it appears that service labor is also being considered productive labor in the sense of being subsumed within capital and contributing to its self-valorization. However, we need to draw a distinction between the fundamental concept and derivative concepts. The essential point in the formal definition is that labor is exchanged against capital and leads to the self-valorization of capital. In this definition, the qualitative content of labor is abolished or dissolved. In other words, for the moment, it is a matter of no concern whether such labor is productive or unproductive labor according to the original definition.

Stated on a more profound level, in the case of the capitalist, formal definition, as long as labor is subsumed within capital, any labor (formally speaking) can appear to be productive labor. This indeed is one of the essential characteristics or limitations of bourgeois society, and exposes the vacuous or concept-free nature of this society. In the formal definition, labor is separated from its concrete content and defined in a manner that is purely abstract and lacking in a concept. In other words, labor is evaluated solely in terms of whether it serves to augment value or is useful to the self-valorization of capital. This is the actual image of wage-labor under capitalism. In capitalist soci-

---

12. *Capital*, vol. 1, 644.

ety, any unsocial labor or service labor can appear to be productive provided that it is subsumed within capital and augments it. Of course, the fact that labor can *appear* to be productive does not mean that such labor is actually productive labor in the original sense.

For Marx, it is self-evident that service labor is unproductive labor according to the original definition. Such labor is unproductive not only because it does not produce material wealth, but also because even in terms of its form, service labor has the clear characteristic of being fundamentally exchanged against revenue rather than against capital. The formal definition has the same content and is fundamentally the same as the original definition, in terms of viewing labor as productive if it is exchanged against capital and unproductive if it is exchanged against revenue. This is because labor exchanged against capital is, for the most part, labor involved in material production, whereas labor exchanged against revenue is fundamentally service labor. There are of course exceptions to this, but such exceptions do not invalidate the conceptual definition, and therefore the following can be said:

> It is, however, in any case clear: the greater the part of the revenue (wages and profit) that is spent on commodities produced by capital, the less the part that can be spent on the services of the unproductive laborers, and vice versa.
>
> The material determination of labor, and therefore of its product, in itself has nothing to do with this distinction between productive and unproductive labor. For example, the cooks and waiters in a public hotel are productive laborers, in so far as their labor is transformed into capital for the proprietor of the hotel. These same persons are unproductive laborers as menial servants, inasmuch as I do not make capital out of their services, but spend revenue on them. In fact, however, these same persons are also for me, the consumer, unproductive laborers in the hotel.[13]

> The labor capacity of the productive laborer is a commodity for the laborer himself. So is that of the unproductive laborer. But the productive laborer produces commodities for the buyer of his labor capacity. The unproductive laborer produces for him a mere use-value, not a commodity; an imaginary or a real use-value. It is characteristic of the unproductive laborer that he produces no commodities for his buyer, but indeed receives commodities from him.[14]

---

13. *MECW*, vol. 31, 15.
14. Ibid., 16.

The significance or characteristic of the formal definition is that under capitalist relations of production service labor is also subsumed within capital, and therefore appears as productive labor, but this is not the essence of the matter. However, the JCP philistines make a lot of noise on the basis of this misunderstanding. The following crucial passage can be found in "The Results of the Immediate Process of Production":

> Productive labor is merely an abbreviation for the entire complex of activities of labor and labor-power within the capitalist process of production. Thus when we speak of productive labor we mean socially determined labor, labor which implies a quite specific relationship between the buyer and seller of labor. Productive labor is exchanged directly for money as capital, i.e. for money which is intrinsically capital, which is destined to function as capital and which confronts labor-power as capital. Thus productive labor is labor which for the worker only reproduces the value of his labor-power as determined beforehand, while as a value-creating activity it valorizes capital and confronts the worker with the values so created and transformed into capital. The specific relationship between objectified and living labor that converts the former into capital also turns the latter into productive labor.
>
> The specific product of the capitalist process of production, surplus-value, is created only through an exchange with productive labor.
>
> What gives it a specific use-value for capital is not its particular utility, any more than the particular useful qualities of the product in which it is objectified. Its use to capital is its ability to generate exchange-value (surplus-value).
>
> The capitalist process of production does not just involve the production of commodities. It is a process which absorbs unpaid labor, which makes the means of production into the means for extorting unpaid labor.
>
> From the foregoing it is evident that for labor to be designated productive, qualities are required which are utterly unconnected with the specific content of the labor, with its particular utility or the use-value in which it is objectified.[15]

Thus, productive labor is not only labor involved in the production of material things, but essentially must be defined within a certain set of social relations, within capitalist relations of production. This is indeed a historical concept. In *Theories of Surplus Value*, we can come across an almost identical passage:

---

15. Karl Marx, "Results of the Immediate Process of Production," in *Capital*, vol. 1, 1043-44.

It is only this particular relation to labor [the exploitative relation between capital and labor] which converts money or commodity into capital, and that labor is productive labor which—by means of this relation it has to the conditions of production, to which there corresponds a particular position in the real production process—converts money or commodity into capital, i.e. preserves and increases the value of the objective labor which has attained an independent position vis-à-vis the labor capacity. Productive labor is only an abbreviation for the whole relation in which, and the manner in which, labor capacity figures in the capitalist production process. It is however of the highest importance to distinguish between this and other kinds of labor, since this distinction brings out precisely the determinate form of labor on which there depends the whole capitalist mode of production, and capital itself.

Productive labor, therefore, is labor which—in the system of capitalist production—produces surplus-value for its employer or which converts the objective conditions of labor into capital, and their owners into capitalists, hence labor which produces its own product as capital.

Hence in speaking of productive labor we are speaking of socially determined labor, labor which implies a highly definite relation between the buyer and the seller of labor.[16]

As we can see from the passage above, Marx is pointing out that productive labor according to the formal definition is also naturally labor that produces material wealth. However, in the case of the formal definition, this is a matter of indifference, and slips into the background as something non-essential. Still, this does not mean that the original definition is somehow cast aside.

We have already seen that abstract human labor as the substance of value contains more active determinations than the concept of simple labor. In the concept of value, labor as the substance of value is not simple labor but abstract labor, and human labor takes a thoroughly social form as money. In other words, Marx elucidates that human labor taking the form of value clearly appears as a decisively *social* thing, and in this sense the concept of labor comes to have an important, positive determination that the concept of simple labor lacks. At the same time, of course, as a historical, formal definition of human labor, the concept of value is also fundamentally determined by the concept of human labor in general.

The historical or formal concept of productive labor likewise has a positive aspect. This definition states that only labor exchanged against capital is pro-

16. *MECW*, vol. 34 (1993), 131.

ductive labor, and that labor exchanged against revenue is unproductive. In this way, even in the capitalist form, a distinction exists between social labor and unsocial labor. The fact that this bourgeois definition also has a positive aspect is seen characteristically in the example of a servant's labor that produces some material thing and yet is categorized as unproductive labor. Labor that is not exchanged against capital is said to make no contribution to the accumulation of capital, and it is even seen as a barrier to such accumulation (or to what Smith calls the augmentation of "national wealth"). Such labor is viewed as unsocial labor that does not augment capital, and instead occupies a parasitical position vis-à-vis capitalist prosperity, being human activity that cannot be considered (productive) "labor" in the original sense.

A Discussion of the Two Definitions

We have taken a look at the two definitions of productive labor, but now we need to consider what sort of relation exists between them, and whether or not they should be considered as two separate and distinct definitions that can be simply lined up next to one another. Even within the Marxist camp, there is no consensus regarding the concept of productive labor (and therefore the concept of unproductive labor), or the relation between the two definitions. Indeed, views on this subject have become tangled up and confused, and increasingly so, to the point of moving further and further away from Marxism toward bourgeois theory. This seems to be a reflection of the political confusion generated by the JCP, and at the same time an outcome or theoretical reflection of the parasitism and decay of modern capitalism. With the expansion of the service sector within the economy, a need also arose for a corresponding theory and such a theory has actually emerged. In this sense, there is nothing particularly strange or unexpected about the phenomenon of JCP theorists, who have politically assimilated to bourgeois society, uncritically focusing on and tailing after this economic reality of modern capitalism.

One of the "Marxist" views concerning the two concepts of productive labor, which was even considered the "official" view for a good part of the postwar period, is the notion that the definition of labor in terms of producing material wealth (Marx's original definition) is from the standpoint of *society*, whereas the definition of labor in terms of being exchanged against capital, rather than revenue, and creating profit (Marx's formal definition) is from the perspective of *individual capital*. However, the limitations of this view should be clear at a glance. Needless to say, this formalistic understanding, which mechanically sets society and the individual in opposition, cannot provide us with a correct concept of productive labor. There are also those who speak of the need to "integrate" the two definitions. For instance, Kaneko Haruo offers the following argument:

> The fact that Marx was able to establish the original definition of productive labor was the outcome of understanding, first of all, capitalist production in its particular, historical form and establishing the historical definition of productive labor, thus making possible the "logical abstraction" of "labor in general"—which becomes clear in particular through a comparison with Smith—and therefore, these two definitions must not be grasped separately, but rather in a unified manner.[17]

Even given the fact that the two definitions should not be grasped separately, this in itself does not pertain to the actual nature of the concept of productive labor itself. On this point, Kaneko's theory resembles Uno's idea that it is through the establishment of historical materialism that dialectical materialism is also ultimately grasped, thereby insisting on the priority of historical materialism, within which it is said that dialectical materialism is superceded (or dissolved!).

Even if we say that the two concepts must be understood in a "unified" manner, it is not clear at all what this means, concretely. There certainly is a need for a unified understanding of the two concepts, but on the other hand they must also be clearly distinguished between, and this is the precise reason that they exists as *two* concepts in the first place. One need only flip through the pages of Marx's *Theories of Surplus Value* to verify that he clearly distinguishes between the two concepts. A standpoint that only concentrates on unity at the expense of grasping distinctions opens the path to all sorts of non-sensical dogmas. At best, this leads to the position of being satisfied with merely juxtaposing the two definitions, which is also clearly a non-conceptual approach. Kaneko, for example, makes the following claim:

> In the capitalist production process, the labor process and the valorization process are integrated. Therefore, in this production process, productive labor, in line with the dual nature of the capitalist production process, must be grasped as a dual definition encompassing the original definition posited

---

17. Kaneko Haruo, *Seisanteki rōdō to kokumin shotoku* (Tokyo: Nihon Hyōċ ron-sha, 1966), 2.

by the labor process and the capitalist, formal definition posited by the valorization process. However, since valorization is the main aspect of capitalist production, it is the capitalist, formal definition of producing surplus-value that determines the essence [of productive labor]. By contrast, since the labor process is a secondary aspect within the capitalist production process, the original definition of producing use-values cannot determine this essence. In other words, the original definition forms the general foundation [of the concept] as the bearer of the capitalist, formal definition.[18]

Of course, this view is nonsense. If what Kaneko is saying were true, then the fact that workers in the munitions industry, for example, also appear as productive workers would "determine the essence" of the concept, but any worker would know that this is ridiculous. The issue does not revolve around which definition is the "essential" one. (Although if this were the question, it would have to be said that labor mediating the material metabolism between nature and man is the most fundamental, and precisely because this does not *directly* coincide with the capitalist meaning of productive labor, there is a need for a formal concept that is distinct from this fundamental concept of productive labor.) Marx emphasizes both of the definitions separately, since he does not recognize either one as being predominant. However, by calling the labor that produces material wealth the "original" definition of productive labor, his intention can be seen to some extent.

Certainly, in examining Smith's concept of productive labor, Marx values his historical, formal definition, but this is because Smith had recognized that the concept of productive labor involves *social* labor, not labor expended individually or exchanged against revenue (even if such labor produces material wealth). On this point, Marx recognizes the positive significance of Smith's (formal) definition. If productive labor were merely defined as labor that produces material wealth, then the individual labor of producing some sort of material thing for a capitalist, exchanged against revenue, would have to be viewed as productive labor. Smith, however, insists that labor exchanged in this manner against revenue, as some sort of individual service, cannot be considered productive labor even if a material good is produced. This stems directly from Smith's primary definition of productive labor as labor exchanged against capital, and Marx also values this definition and emphasizes that it is it justified.

---

18. Ibid., 91.

Here the fact that labor is exchanged against capital and generates profit also encompasses the fact that such labor is socially expended labor and thus *objectified* as the value of the commodity. It is precisely because this labor is objectified as commodity-value that it becomes the source of profit. In other words, Smith's definition of productive labor presupposes that labor is expended as socially-abstract human labor, rather than merely being any sort of human activity that creates a "thing."

Marx is of course aware that the formal definition has essential limitations, and that from this formal, bourgeois definition all sorts of nonsense could result. According to the formal, bourgeois definition of productive labor as profit-generating labor exchanged against capital, any "labor" whatsoever, even that involved in prostitution or munitions production, could be defined or evaluated as productive labor. However, even JCP theorists, who completely lack the concept of productive labor, would have to recognize that such labor is not productive at all. The examples of prostitution and munitions production are a thorn in the side of such theorists which they are quite incapable of removing. According to their own theories, such "labor" would indeed be productive since it is self-evident that this is carried out as wage-labor (and exchanged against capital to generate a profit) or provides some sort of "service."

Marx, on the one hand, seems to insist that the formal definition is essential, while on the other hand emphasizing that, in terms of the simple [original] definition, labor is productive if it produces commodities or material wealth. In discussing the formal definition, Marx often adds expressions such as "under the capitalist mode of production," or "from the capitalist perspective," while at the same time noting that it is an example of bourgeois narrowmindedness to believe that any labor that produces a material thing is directly equivalent to productive labor. For instance, there is the following passage:

> Only bourgeois narrowness, which considers the capitalist forms of production to be the latter's absolute forms—and therefore the eternal natural forms of production—is able to confuse the question of what productive labor is from the standpoint of capital with the question of what labor is productive in general, or what productive labor is in general, and therefore esteem itself very wise in giving the reply that all labor which produces anything at all, results in anything whatsoever, is *eo ipso* productive labor.[19]

---

19. *MECW*, vol. 34, 128.

We need to be careful, however, not to misunderstand Marx here. He finds it self-evident that a commodity is a certain use-value or useful thing, and therefore a material thing. In the passage above, he is pointing out that "bourgeois narrowness" stems from failing to see the essence of the labor objectified in commodities—i.e. failing to see that this is not concrete useful labor but abstract human labor, labor abstracted from quality—and thereby ignoring or wiping out the characteristic aspects of the historical form of productive labor. Herein lies the origin of every sort of narrowness, he says. For Marx, it was a clear premise that commodity-producing labor, in addition to producing profit, produces a use-value in terms of the labor being objectified within a given use-value. However, in the case of capitalist society the question centers on the form that this takes historically, not simply the fact that some "thing" is produced. This is the point Marx is emphasizing.

Therefore, it would be wrong to conclude from the passage above that productive labor is not, primarily speaking, labor that produces some material thing. Productive labor is, essentially, labor that produces material things, but this cannot be understood in a mechanical fashion. This is because, first of all, under capitalist production there is the production of things through exchange against revenue, i.e. labor that is unproductive even though it produces some material thing. At the same time, there is productive labor that does not directly produce a thing (such as transport labor, which is a part of the extended production process) or that is connected to the circulation of commodities, but originally the labor involved in storage, processing, and packaging *was* a part of the production process.[20] On this point, as Marx notes, "the materialization, etc., of labor is however not to be taken in such a Scottish sense as Adam Smith conceives it."[21]

Reciprocal Relation or Unity between Two Definitions

It may seem that Marx merely compares or juxtaposes two independent and completely distinct concepts of productive labor—with the concept of productive labor determined from the perspective of the general labor process,[22] on one hand, and the concept of productive labor that appears on the basis of

---

20. We will discuss this in more detail later.
21. *MECW*, vol. 31, 26.
22. This corresponds to Adam Smith's secondary definition, i.e. the idea of productive labor as commodity-producing labor.

capitalist production, on the other. But is this really the case? Are these two concepts essentially separate, mutually-exclusive, and independent concepts? This is the precisely the question that we need to consider!

In reality it could be said that these two concepts are, in a sense, the same; or even if they are not directly the same, they cannot simply be juxtaposed and defined as separate concepts. Here we need to examine the relation between the two. In the "Results of the Immediate Process of Production," Marx provides us with the concept of productive labor, and he in fact discusses the relation that exists between the two concepts:

> Looked at from the simple standpoint of the labor process, labor seemed productive if it realized itself in a product, or rather a commodity. From the standpoint of capitalist production we may add the qualification that labor is productive if it directly valorizes capital, or creates surplus-value. That is to say, it is productive if it is realized in a surplus-value without any equivalent for the worker, its creator; it must appear in surplus produce, i.e. an additional increment of a commodity on behalf of the monopolizer of the means of labor, the capitalist. Only the labor which posits the variable capital and hence the total capital as $C + \Delta C = C + \Delta v$ is productive. It is therefore labor which directly serves capital as the agency of its self-valorization, as means for the production of surplus-value.
>
> The capitalist labor process does not cancel the general definitions of the labor process. It produces both product and commodity. Labor remains productive as long as it objectifies itself in commodities, as the unity of exchange-value and use-value. But the labor process is merely a means for the self-valorization of capital. Labor is productive, therefore, if it is converted into commodities, but when we consider the individual commodity we find that a certain proportion of it represents unpaid labor, and when we take the mass of commodities as a whole we find similarly that a certain proportion of that also represents unpaid labor. In short, it turns out to be a product that costs the capitalist nothing.
>
> The worker who performs productive work is productive and the work he performs is productive if it directly creates surplus-value, i.e. if it valorizes capital.
>
> It is only bourgeois obtuseness that encourages the view that capitalist production is production in its absolute form, the unique form of production as prescribed by nature. And only the bourgeoisie can confuse the questions: what is productive labor? and what is a productive worker from the standpoint of capitalism? with the question: what is productive labor as such?"[23]

---

23. "Results of the Immediate Process of Production," 1038-9.

As we can see, Marx emphasizes that the formal definition of productive labor exists as such as the *historical form* of the original definition of productive labor. He criticizes the "obtuseness" of the bourgeoisie in terms of their inability to either distinguish between the formal and original definitions, or correctly position the two. Because bourgeois scholars end up confusing the two definitions, they treat the capitalist, formal definition as an absolute and are quite incapable of stepping outside this capitalist framework (just like present-day JCP scholars).

Marx emphasizes the formal definition and recognizes its importance, but at the same time he underlines that this is the concept of productive labor seen from the standpoint of capital. Clearly for Marx the concept of productive labor in general is essential, while the concept seen from the standpoint of capitalism must be evaluated within its historical limitations. Just as the capitalist labor process does not in any way negate the general determinations of the labor process itself, the capitalist concept of productive labor does not supercede the general definition of productive labor. Concretely speaking, the historical, formal definition of productive labor concerns labor that produces surplus-value—labor with the essential "moment" of extending beyond necessary labor. Along with this a distinction arises, so that productive labor is labor that produces surplus-value rather than merely commodity-value. This is the concept of productive labor as a historical, formal definition.

For Marx it was a self-evident premise that commodity-producing labor—labor that produces value, and developed further, labor that produces surplus-value—is fundamentally labor that produces material wealth. Marx is concerned simply with the historical form that productive labor takes, and thus the question centers on the fact that a product takes the form of the commodity, or productive labor takes the form of wage-labor. At issue here is the historical form of social production, with this social production existing as the main premise.

This is true not only for the concept of productive labor, but also—first of and foremost—for the value-determination of the commodity. We are familiar with the fact that the definition of the commodity as value contains more determinations than the definition of the commodity as mere use-value, because the former is determined simultaneously as use-value and as value. Moreover, the definition of the socio-historical form of the product (as commodity) includes elements that go beyond the boundaries of the definition as product (as use-value). For instance, things that originally were not commodities can come to be formally defined as commodities, so that purely formal commodities such as land or "capital" can also appear. In this way, the essential concept of the commodity, as the historical form taken by products, is distorted so that it no longer coincides with its content. Similarly, in the case of the historical, formal definition of productive labor, the concept of productive labor comes to include labor that originally was not productive labor. However, in terms of the conceptual definition of productive labor (and even the formal definition), this phenomenon is not something essential. And those who treat it as being essential, end up completely severing the formal definition of productive labor from the original definition, rendering it independent, and thus opening the path to every brand of theoretical confusion and opportunism (such as the idea that service labor is also essentially productive labor). In his examination of the views of Adam Smith, Marx basically argues that the most fundamental point is commodity-producing labor:

> Apart from such cases, productive labor is such as produces commodities, and unproductive labor is such as produces personal services. The former labor is represented in a vendible thing; the latter must be consumed while it is being performed. The former includes (except for that labor which creates labor capacity itself) all material and intellectual wealth—meat as well as books—that exists in the form of things; the latter covers all labors which satisfy any imaginary or real need of the individual—or even those which are forced upon the individual against his will.
>
> The commodity is the most elementary form of bourgeois wealth. The explanation of "productive labor" as labor which produces "commodities" also corresponds, therefore, to a much more elementary point of view than that which defines productive labor as labor which produces capital.[24]

For capitalist production, however, the standpoint of defining productive labor as value-producing labor is insufficient. This is because the characteristic of such production is the production of surplus-value, not simply value. The view of productive labor as commodity-producing labor must be replaced by the idea of productive labor as labor that produces surplus-value. Still, this does not alter the fact that the former definition has more "fundamental" significance.

Marx speaks of the manner in which the two definitions of productive labor are integrated. Here we have already adequately discussed the distinctions between the two, while also recognizing that they must be integrated and

---

24. *MECW*, vol. 31, 28.

essentially defined rather than simply juxtaposed. Marx emphasizes that in capitalist society these two definitions coincide in the sense that labor producing things (material wealth) is for the most part labor that produces profit for capital, so that in reality the two definitions are integrated. He writes:

> To the extent that capital conquers the whole of production, and therefore the home and petty form of industry—in short, industry intended for self-consumption, not producing commodities—disappears, it is clear that the unproductive laborers, those whose services are directly exchanged against revenue, will for the most part be performing only personal services, and only an inconsiderable part of them (like cooks, seamstresses, jobbing tailors and so on) will produce material use values. That they produce no commodities follows from the nature of the case. For the commodity as such is never an immediate object of consumption, but a bearer of exchange-value. Consequently only a quite insignificant part of these unproductive laborers can play a direct part in material production once the capitalist mode of production has developed. They participate in it only through the exchange of their services against revenue...
>
> The labor capacity of the productive laborer is a commodity for the laborer himself. So is that of the unproductive laborer. But the productive laborer produces commodities for the buyer of his labor capacity. The unproductive laborer produces for him a mere use-value, not a commodity; an imaginary or a real use-value. It is characteristic of the unproductive laborer that he produces no commodities for his buyer, but indeed receives commodities from him.[25]

As soon as capital has mastered the whole of production, revenue, in so far as it is at all exchanged against labor, will not be exchanged directly against labor which produces commodities, but against mere services. It is exchanged partly against commodities which are to serve as use-values, and partly against services, which as such are consumed as use-values.

A commodity—as distinguished from labor capacity itself—is a material thing confronting man, a thing of a certain utility for him, in which a definite quantity of labor is fixed or materialized.

So we come to the definition already in essence contained in point I: a productive laborer is one whose labor produces commodities; and indeed such a laborer does not consume more commodities than he produces, than his labor costs...By producing commodities the productive worker constantly reproduces the variable capital which he constantly consumes in the

---

25. Ibid, 15-6.

form of wages. He constantly produces the fund which pays him, "which maintains and employs him."[26]

In considering the essential relations of capitalist production, therefore, it can be assumed—since this tends to occur more and more, is the principal purpose, and the productive powers of labor are developed to the highest point in this case alone—that the whole world of commodities, all the spheres of material production—the production of material wealth—have been subjected (either formally or really) to the capitalist mode of production. In this presupposition, which expresses the limit, and therefore approximates ever more closely to exact accuracy, all the workers engaged in the production of commodities are wage laborers and the means of production confront them as capital in all spheres of production. It can then be described as the characteristic feature of productive workers, i.e. of workers producing capital, that their labor is realized in commodities, material wealth. And thus productive labor would have obtained a second, subsidiary determination distinct from its decisive characteristic, for which the content of labor is a matter of complete indifference and which is independent of that content.[27]

Here the relation between the two definitions is indicated. That is, under capitalism the concept of productive labor is defined as labor exchanged against capital that is capable of valorizing capital. Therefore, labor that is exchanged against revenue—not only service labor but also labor involved in producing material things—is unproductive labor. Fundamentally speaking, however, capital encompasses "the whole world of commodities, all the spheres of material production," and therefore labor exchanged against capital is at the same time labor that produces material things, and appears as such. Today, of course, under decaying, parasitical state-monopoly capitalism, an enormous amount of unproductive labor is subsumed within capital, and the phenomenon arises of unproductive labor appearing to valorize capital, but this does not alter the essence of the problem in the least.

What does Marx mean when he emphasizes that the definition of productive labor as labor exchanged against capital is already encompassed within the first definition, and is therefore a "second, subsidiary determination"?

Here, as we will subsequently see, it is necessary for us to think *dialectically*. Marx emphasizes that the commodity is the foundation of capital, but that

26. Ibid., 19.
27. *MECW*, vol. 34, 143.

under capitalism, in a sense, the commodity determination becomes secondary. This is because the essential moment that distinguishes capitalism from production relations under other historical societies is not that capitalist society produces products as commodities, but rather that commodities are produced within the relationship between capital and wage-labor, so that production is carried out for the sake of profit through the exploitation of labor. Of course, the fact that the aim of capitalist production is to obtain surplus-value (the exploitation of labor) also encompasses the fact that labor products are produced as commodities, since without being produced as commodities surplus-value could not be realized. Thus, the commodity determination is presupposed, or already included in fact, within the capital determination. This is what Marx means when he speaks of "the production of a surplus-value, which in itself implies the production of an equivalent for the value consumed."[28]

Marx, in this way, provides us with a synthesis or overview of the two definitions. For Marx, the two definitions are not separate, but rather two aspects of the same thing. Certainly he places an emphasis on Adam Smith's definition of form, but this does not mean that the other definition is seen as being incorrect or is rejected. He is simply recognizing the realistic, historical, and class-related significance of each definition, and positioning them correctly. The following passage from Marx is crucial in this respect:

> It is however clear that in the same measure as capital subjugates to itself the whole of production—that is to say, that all commodities are produced for the market and not for immediate consumption, and the productivity of labor rises in the same measure—there will also develop more and more a material difference between productive and unproductive laborers, inasmuch as the former, apart from minor exceptions, will exclusively produce commodities, while the latter, with minor exceptions, will perform only personal services. Hence the former class will produce the immediate, material wealth consisting of commodities, all commodities except those which consist of labor capacity itself. This is one of the aspects which lead Adam Smith to put forward other points of difference, in addition to the first and in principle determining *differentia specifica*.[29]

---

28. *MECW*, vol. 31, 17.
29. Ibid., 16-7.

With the development of capitalism, productive labor is generally commodity-producing labor that is exchanged against capital, i.e. labor that produces material wealth, whereas unproductive labor is labor exchanged against revenue that provides some service. This is how Marx basically synthesizes and summarizes the two definitions. Of course, everyone knows that labor exchanged against capital and labor that produces material wealth are not, directly speaking, identical. It is also common knowledge that some labor exchanged against revenue is involved in material production. Still, fundamentally speaking, labor exchanged against capital *is* commodity-producing labor and productive labor in the original sense, as the "material metabolism" between man and nature.

How, then, should we evaluate labor exchanged against capital that does *not* produce material wealth, yet inescapably comes to be included within the definition of form? How can such labor be considered productive labor according to this formal definition?

This phenomenon reveals the fact that even though the formal definition is the more developed definition, its content remains abstract as a definition of form, and thus has certain limitations. Therefore, one should not treat this formal definition as an absolute and end up carelessly saying that those employed as singers, artists, soldiers (mercenaries), or prostitutes are involved in productive labor simply because they are employed by capital and produce a profit for capital. Rather, we must clearly be aware of the limitations and one-sidedness of this formal definition. In this sense, the JCP scholars who, far from seeing such limitations, actually discover positive significance in the definition of form, have grasped nothing. The fact that service labor also comes to be counted as productive labor, according to the definition of form, represents an essential limitation of the formal definition as such, which exposes how this definition is distinguished from and in contradiction with the original definition.

The original definition and the formal definition fundamentally coincide and are integrated, but at the same time, the distinction between the two is important, even critical. This is not a question of which definition is fundamental or superior to the other. Unoists, for instance, say that historical definitions of form are fundamental and must be given precedence because the present-day society is a capitalist one, and the contradictions of this society and their development are the primary issues. And when they deal with the issue of productive labor, they adopt this same mistaken view.

In *Capital*, where Marx discusses the historical, formal definition of productive labor, he notes that "a schoolmaster is a productive worker when, in addition to belaboring the heads of his pupils, he works himself into the ground to enrich the owner of the school."[30] This example of a teacher does not imply, however, that the labor of teachers is productive labor in the original sense, but rather simply shows that from the standpoint of capitalism this labor can also *appear* as productive labor. According to the capitalist, formal definition, labor that is not originally productive labor can appear and be evaluated as such. It could be said that Marx cites the example of a teacher's labor being productive labor according to the capitalist, formal definition because here the characteristics of this formal definition are clearly manifested and its limitations revealed. Here Marx focuses on the distinction between the two definitions and what arises from this distinction.

In the capitalist, definition of form, "productive and unproductive labor is throughout conceived from the standpoint of the possessor of money, of the capitalist, not from that of the workman."[31] From this alone, it is clear that Marx always views this formal definition as representing the standpoint of the capitalist, and he recognizes its limitations, so nothing could be sillier than to treat this formal definition as an absolute or suprahistorical concept.

Marx draws a distinction between the original concept of productive labor and the historical, formal (bourgeois) concept, and it is precisely this distinction that sets Marx apart from Adam Smith and underlies the Marxist concept of productive labor. For the bourgeoisie, who lack a conceptual approach, commodity-producing labor as well as service labor can appear as productive labor, but this is certainly not the case from a worker's perspective. Overlooking this fact is tantamount to casting Marxism aside.

Corrupt intellectuals aligned with the JCP, however, are partial to this bourgeois view and happily adopt it as their own. Now they have even gone so far as to include labor that does not produce a profit, such as the labor of government workers, within the category of productive labor, and this is the inevitable outcome of the fact that they have begun considering service labor that produces profit under capital as productive labor, not only from the capitalist perspective, but also according to the original definition. In order to be consistent, these reactionary intellectuals—who amazingly continue to parade

---

30. *Capital*, vol. 1, 644.
31. *MECW*, vol. 31, 13.

around as "communists"—would have to refer to the "service" labor of soldiers as productive labor as well, since there is no question that they carry out "important" service labor and receive wages. Theorists of such low caliber are capable of little more than obstinately treating the upside-down bourgeois world—a society in which unproductive labor can also appear to be productive—as representing the absolute truth as is, which exposes the great distance that separates them from what Marx refers to as the "standpoint of the workman."

Extension and Contraction of Productive Labor Concept

Marx says that under capitalist production, the concept of productive labor expands, on the one hand, with products becoming social products as "the joint product of a collective laborer" (combination of workers), while on the other hand the concept contracts. Here we need to consider this point, which is particularly important considering how opportunists have introduced a heap of nonsense to obscure the distinction between productive and unproductive labor, thus defining examples of unproductive labor as being productive. They seize, for example, on the fact that Marx includes transport labor within the category of productive labor, or they point to managerial, supervisory, or technical labor (and even the labor of capitalists) as being productive labor—not only in the historical, formal sense, but in the original sense as well—in order to advance the argument that Marx himself never claimed that only labor involved in material production is productive labor, and that such a view is a distortion of Marxism.

This issue is connected to Marx's comments about the "extension" of the concept of productive labor. On this point Marx's view is clear, and contains nothing that could justify the views of opportunists. In fact, it immediately becomes apparent how Marx's view undermines their arguments. In *Capital*, for example, the following point is emphasized:

> In so far as the labor process is purely individual, the same worker unites in himself all the functions that later on become separated. When an individual appropriates natural objects for his own livelihood, he alone supervises his own activity. Later on he is supervised by others. The solitary man cannot operate upon nature without calling his own muscles into play under the control of his own brain. Just as head and hand belong together in the system of nature, so in the labor process mental and physical labor are united. Later on they become separate; and this separation develops into a

hostile antagonism. The product is transformed from the direct product of the individual producer into a social product, the joint product of a collective laborer, i.e. a combination of workers, each of whom stands at a different distance from the actual manipulation of the object of labor. With the progressive accentuation of the cooperative character of the labor process, there necessarily occurs a progressive extension of the concept of productive labor, and of the concept of the bearer of that labor, the productive worker. In order to work productively, it is no longer necessary for the individual himself to put his hand to the object; it is sufficient for him to be an organ of the collective laborer, and to perform any one of its subordinate functions. The definition of productive labor given above, the original definition, is derived from the nature of material production itself, and it remains correct of the collective laborer, considered as a whole. But it no longer holds good for each member taken individually.[32]

Marx argues that the product of labor becomes the common outcome of collective labor, and for the individual worker "it is no longer necessary to put his hand to the object; it is sufficient for him to be an organ of the collective laborer." This means that there is no longer a necessity to be directly involved in the productive action of processing the raw material. For example, in "Results of the Immediate Process of Production," Marx says that in the labor process, productive labor is labor that coincides with "the productive consumption of labor-power," and then adds that "two things follow from this." He explains the "first thing" as follows:

First, with the development of the real subsumption of labor under capital, or the specifically capitalist mode of production, the real lever of the overall labor process is increasingly not the individual worker. Instead, labor-power socially combined and the various competing labor-powers which together form the entire production machine participate in very different ways in the immediate process of making commodities, or, more accurately in this context, creating the product. Some work better with their hands, others with their heads, one as a manager, engineer, technologist, etc., the other as overseer, the third as manual laborer or even drudge. An ever increasing number of types of labor are included in the immediate concept of productive labor, and those who perform it are classed as productive workers, workers directly exploited by capital and subordinated to its process of production and expansion. If we consider the aggregate worker, i.e. if we take all the members comprising the workshop together, then we see

---

32. *Capital*, vol. 1, 643-4.

that their combined activity results materially in an aggregate product which is at the same time a quantity of goods. And here it is quite immaterial whether the job of a particular worker, who is merely a limb of this aggregate worker, is at a greater or smaller distance from the actual manual labor.[33]

As the representative of productive capital engaged in the process of self-expansion, the capitalist performs a productive function. It consists in the direction and exploitation of productive labor. In contrast to his fellow-consumers of surplus-value who stand in no such immediate and active relationship to their production, his class is the productive class par excellence. (As the director of the labor process the capitalist performs productive labor in the sense that his labor is involved in the total process that is realized in the product.) We are concerned here only with capital within the immediate process of production. The other function of capital and the agents which it employs within them form a subject to be left for later.[34]

Productive labor includes labor involved in the transport industry, as well as labor engaged in the storage, processing, and packaging related to the circulation process of commodities. In *Theories of Surplus Value*, Marx notes that "in addition to extractive industry, agriculture, and manufacturing, there exists yet a fourth sphere of material production." This is the "transport industry" in which "the object of labor undergoes a material alteration—a spatial alteration, or change of place."[35] And in the second volume of *Capital*, Marx refers to the transport industry as an "additional production process,"[36] which of course increases the value of the commodity. He defines storage, processing, packaging, etc. as productive labor that forms one part of the labor process, in distinction from labor involved in the realization of commodities (the functions of merchants). Thus, here as well, there is an "extension" of the concept of productive labor, in a sense. In *Theories of Surplus Value*, Marx provides the following overview:

With the development of the specifically capitalist mode of production, in which many workers cooperate in the production of the same commodity, the direct relations between their labor and the object under production

---

33. "Results of the Immediate Production Process," 1039-40.
34. Ibid., 1048-9.
35. *MECW*, vol. 34, 145.
36. *Capital*, vol. 2, 226.

must of course be very diverse. E.g. the assistants in the factory, mentioned earlier, have no direct involvement in the treatment of the raw material. The workers who constitute the overseers of those who are directly concerned with this treatment stand a step further away; the engineer in turn has a different relation and works mainly with his brain alone, etc. But the whole group of these workers, who possess labor capacities of different values, although the total number employed reaches roughly the same level, produce a result which is expressed, from the point of view of the result of the pure labor process, in commodities or in material product, and all of them together, as a workshop, are the living production machine for these products; while, from the point of view of the production process as a whole, they exchange their labor for capital, and reproduce the money of the capitalist as capital, i.e. as self-valorizing value, self-multiplying value.[37]

Here various kinds of labor are viewed as being productive. First, labor that plays an assisting role, not directly involved in production, such as workers engaged solely in transporting raw materials or supervisors and instructors. Seen individually, these are workers who are not involved at all in the "treatment of the raw material," but it cannot be said that they are not productive workers. Marx says that the labor within the factory is carried out as combined, collective labor, with the outcome appearing as a commodity or group of commodities, so that the labor of the assistants, supervisors, and technicians is also productive since it forms one link or part of the combined labor-power.

Of course, this does not mean that *any* labor can be considered productive. If the concept were extended to the point of lacking a determination, any "labor" could appear as productive labor. The labor Marx is speaking of, however, is the restricted sense of labor involved in the production of the *same* material commodity, i.e. labor related to the "treatment of the raw material" and labor involved in the production of the same commodity at the same workplace. To extend beyond this limitation, so that the concept of productive labor is expanded in an unrestricted manner, would open up the path to those wishing to pass off any sort of labor as being productive. We need to keep in mind that Marx is ultimately talking about "all of [the workers] together, as a workshop."

Under capitalist production, the concept of productive labor at the same time "contracts." This is a point that is easy to grasp. Productive labor seen from the standpoint of capitalist production is labor exchanged against capital

---

37. *MECW*, vol. 34, 144–5.

that creates a profit, so that, for example, the labor of small-scale farmers does not appear as productive labor. It is clear, however, that agricultural labor is productive labor in the original sense, but such labor is not directly productive labor according to the capitalist concept of productive labor since it is certainly not labor exchanged against capital to create a profit, nor labor that augments capital. Here, again, we can see the narrowness and limitations of the concept of productive labor in the bourgeois sense.

Is Educational Labor Productive?

The question of the nature of educational labor is also interesting. This concerns whether such labor is productive, and if so, to what extent and in what sense. From the capitalist perspective, the matter is quite simple: educational labor is unproductive if exchanged against revenue and productive if exchanged against capital to augment it in the educational sector. As Marx speaks of "educational factories" and the teachers employed in such factories as wage-laborers for capital, teachers would seem to be productive workers. But what about the case of educational workers employed at public schools? Marx offers the following view:

> The product is not separable from the act of producing, as with all execu-tant artists, orators, actors, teachers, doctors, clerics, etc. Here too the capi-talist mode of production only occurs to a slight extent, and can in the nature of things only take place in certain spheres. E.g. teachers in educa-tional institutions may be mere wage laborers for the entrepreneur who owns the institution; there are many such education factories in England. Although they are not productive workers vis-à-vis the pupils, they are such vis-à-vis their employer. He exchanges his capital for their labor capacity, and enriches himself by this process. Similarly with enterprises such as theatres, places of entertainment, etc. Here the actor's relation to the public is that of artist, but vis-à-vis his employer he is a productive worker. All the phenomena of capitalist production in this are so insignifi-cant in comparison with production as a whole that they can be disregarded entirely.[38]

Here is the same idea mentioned earlier, that is to say, in terms of carrying out service labor teachers are unproductive, but they are considered productive if employed by capitalists to work in an "educational factory," so that they pro-

---

38. Ibid., 144.

duce profit for capital and constitute one moment in the self-valorization of capital. Capitalist production does not call into question the quality of labor, so that all profit-creating labor is equally manifested as productive labor regardless of whether it is productive labor in the original sense.

One characteristic view expressed in the passage above is the idea that since "the capitalist mode of production only occurs to a slight extent" in the fields of art and education, and the people engaged in such work generally do not appear as productive workers, this can be "disregarded." However, does this remain true in present-day capitalism? Even today, investment of capital in the educational sector is relatively small compared to production as a whole, and if this were not the case a country would be in a state of decline. But it is true that compared to Marx's own time the educational sector has taken on increased significance. The development of the productive power of social labor, the increase in the mass of profit, the relative growth in the amount of labor exchanged against revenue, and the swelling of the ranks of the parasitical classes are all noticeable aspects of modern capitalism, and capital attempts to make rapid inroads within the service sector. These are the real conditions that can be said to underlie the strong tendency to defend service labor as being productive labor.

The discussion of whether educational labor is productive labor in the original sense includes such issues as whether this labor produces commodities, whether it is abstract human labor, and whether such labor is included within the value of commodities. Needless to say, educational labor does not directly produce commodities, and in this sense it is clear that it is not productive labor. However, the issue centers on the fact that there are two important types of commodities (commodities in general and the labor-power "commodity"), and that educational labor entering into the value of the labor-power commodity could thus indirectly enter into the value of general commodities. In *Capital*, Marx discusses the "costs of education" in relation to the value-determination of the labor-power commodity:

> In order to modify the general nature of the human organism in such a way that it acquires skill and dexterity in a given branch of industry, and becomes labor-power of a developed and specific kind, a special education or training is needed, and this in turn costs an equivalent in commodities of a greater or lesser amount. The costs of education vary according to the degree of complexity of the labor-power required. These expenses (exceedingly small in the case of ordinary labor-power) form a part of the total value spent in producing it.[39]

Here Marx's idea is expressed concisely and correctly. The cost of education or training forms one part of the value of labor-power, since it is necessary for "labor-power of a developed and specific kind." The use-value (labor) of the higher labor-power, as "intensified" or "multiplied"[40] labor, has greater value objectified within it. To this extent, therefore, labor providing education or training can appear as productive labor. But Marx also notes that such costs are insignificant in the case of "ordinary" labor-power. Clearly his view was influenced by the fact that workers at the time received very little formal education, but it still remains true today that educational costs pertaining to workers (and the value of their labor-power) should not be overestimated. In *Theories of Surplus Value*, Marx basically advances the same view that is stated above:

> The whole world of "commodities" can be divided into two great parts. First, labor capacity; second, commodities as distinct from labor capacity itself. As to the purchase of such services as those which train labor capacity, maintain or modify it, etc., in a word, give it a specialized form or even only maintain it—thus for example the schoolmaster's service, in so far as it is "industrially necessary" or useful; the doctor's service, in so far as it maintains health and so conserves the source of all values, labor capacity itself, etc.—these are services which yield in return "a vendible commodity, etc." namely labor capacity itself, into whose costs of production or reproduction these services enter. Adam Smith knew however how little "education" enters into the production costs of the mass of working men. And in any case the doctor's services belong to the *faux frais de production*. They can be counted as the cost of repairs for labor capacity. Let us assume that wages and profit fell simultaneously in total value, from whatever cause (for example, because the nation had grown lazier), and at the same time in use-value (because labor had become less productive owing to bad harvests, etc.), in a word, that the part of the product whose value is equal to the revenue declines, because less new labor has been added in the past year and because the labor added has been less productive. If in such conditions capitalist and workman wanted to consume the same amount of value in material things as they did before, they would have to buy less of the services of the doctor, schoolmaster, etc. And if they were compelled to continue the same outlay for both these services, then they would have to restrict their consumption of other things. It is therefore clear that the labor of the doctor and the schoolmaster does not directly create the fund out of which they

---

39. *Capital*, vol. 1, 275-6.
40. Ibid., 135.

are paid, although their labors enter into the production costs of the fund which creates all value whatsoever—namely, the production cost of labor capacity.[41]

Marx also writes:

> If I buy the services of a teacher, not in order to develop my own capacities, but to acquire skills with which I can earn money—or if other people buy this teacher for me—and if I really learn something—which is entirely independent of me paying for his services—these costs of learning form as much a part of the costs of production of my labor capacity as do my subsistence costs. But the particular utility of this service changes nothing in the economic relation; and this is not a relation in which I convert money into capital, or by which the performer of the service, the teacher, converts me into his capitalist, his master. Whether the doctor cures me, the teacher is successful in instructing me, or the lawyer wins my case, is therefore a matter of complete indifference for the economic determination of this relation. What is paid for is the performance of a service as such, and its result cannot by its nature be guaranteed by the person performing it. A large part of services belong to the costs of consumption of commodities, as with cooks, maids, etc.[42]

Marx is noting that educational labor is not originally productive labor, but is productive to the extent that it enters into the value of labor-power. The fact that such labor is not productive labor is made clear, for example, by the fact that people generally cut back on educational and medical expenses when the value of other, indispensable items grows dear, preferring to expend their resources in other ways. Marx emphasizes that educational labor barely enters into the formation and production costs of labor-power (although we should note that this was written more than 150 years ago). He also points out:

> It remains true, however, that the commodity appears as past, objectified labor, and that therefore, if it does not appear in the form of a thing, it can only appear in the form of labor capacity itself; but never directly as living labor itself (except only in a roundabout way which in practice seems the same, but this is not so in the determination of different wages). Productive labor would therefore be such labor as produces commodities or directly produces, trains, develops, maintains or reproduces labor capacity itself.

---

41. *MECW*, vol. 31, 22-23.
42. *MECW*, vol. 34, 140.

Adam Smith excludes the latter from his category of productive labor; arbitrarily, but with a certain correct instinct—that if he included it, this would open the flood-gates for false pretensions to the title of productive labor [*nota bene!*].

In so far therefore as we leave labor capacity itself out of account, productive labor is labor which produces commodities, material products, whose production has cost a definite quantity of labor or labor-time. These material products include all products of art and science, books, paintings, statues, etc., in so far as they take the form of things. In addition, however, the product of labor must be a commodity in the sense of being "a vendible commodity," that is to say, a commodity in its first form, which has still to pass through its metamorphosis.[43]

Marx feels that Adam Smith's exclusion of educational labor from productive labor was mistaken from a strictly theoretical perspective, but that his decision displays a "certain correct instinct." In other words, Smith was instinctively concerned that including educational labor within productive labor would foster the temptation to include any sort of service labor within this concept, ultimately opening the path to ill-intentioned attempts to defend and justify every sort of unproductive labor. Adam Smith's "instinct" was in fact correct, since today's "communists"—the JCP and its lackey scholars—started off by defending the productive nature of educational labor, and now have gone so far as to say that service labor in general is productive.

In the passages quoted above, Marx is clearly saying that if we exclude cases involving the labor-power commodity, productive labor is labor that produces commodities in the original sense, i.e. "labor that produces commodities—or material products—whose production has cost a definite quantity of labor or labor-time." One would have imagined such a clear concept could not be ignored, but JCP scholars treat this as something irrelevant and shun anything that does not conform to their own ideas. Of course, to say that Marx's views are irrelevant represents one standpoint, but we can hardly be indifferent in the face of attempts by people claiming to be true Marxists, and the most faithful adherents of "scientific socialism," to attach Marx's name to a concept that is the polar opposite of the view he actually held. Such people, to be blunt, can only be referred to as charlatans or fools.

---

43. *MECW*, vol. 31, 27.

Concept of Household Labor and Productive Labor

Another question to consider is the debate over whether domestic labor performed by housewives is productive or unproductive. If productive labor refers to labor exchanged against capital that makes possible the self-valorization of capital, while unproductive labor is exchanged against revenue and bears no relation to self-valorization, then domestic labor is clearly unproductive labor. Such labor is not even exchanged against revenue, but rather is labor that is dependent upon revenue (since the labor of the housewife is generally not directly compensated by the husband).

There is no point in arguing that such domestic labor is productive labor in the sense of being necessary for the consumption of "things"—i.e. goods that are the object of some human need—because, as is clear from the positive aspects of the formal definition, productive labor is not merely labor to make "things," but rather labor to produce commodities (a "thing" as the unity of use-value and exchange-value), and therefore labor that produces surplus-value. In this sense, productive labor is not just labor that makes some material thing (since labor exchanged against revenue appears as unproductive labor no matter what "thing" may be produced), but rather profit-creating labor exchanged against capital through which some "thing" *qua* social use-value (commodity) is produced. Here, indeed, we are dealing with a question of a "social relation"!

It is clear that there are cases where labor "fixed in a thing" is unproductive rather than productive. For instance, if a capitalist hires a gardener to care for and trim a tree in his garden, this labor is fixed in a thing, yet as labor exchanged against revenue, it is unproductive. The same is true if the capitalist hires a servant to make a chair or a maid to cook dinner.

> Even though capital has conquered material production, and so by and large home industry has disappeared, or the industry of the small craftsman who makes use-values directly for the consumer at his home—even then, Adam Smith knows quite well, a seamstress whom I get to come to my house to sew shirts, or workmen who repair furniture, or the servant who scrubs and cleans the house, etc., or the cook who gives meat and other things their palatable form, fix their labor in a thing and in fact increase the value of these things in exactly the same way as the seamstress who sews in a factory, the engineer who repairs the machine, the workers who clean the machine, or the cook who cooks in a hotel as the wage laborer of the capitalist. These use-values are also, potentially, commodities; the shirts may be sent to the pawnshop, the house resold, the furniture put up to auction, and

so on. Thus these persons have potentially also produced commodities and added value to the objects of their labor. But this is a very small category among unproductive workers, and does not apply either to the mass of menial servants or to parsons, government officials, soldiers, musicians and so on."[44]

Some feminist theorists, unfamiliar with the *concept* of productive labor, argue that if a housewife carries out domestic labor as the final stage of consumption and is involved in processing material things, there is no reason to not consider this as being productive labor. They fail to note, however, that the question here is not simply whether a "thing" is processed or not, but rather involves the important question of a social relation, i.e. what the labor of housewives is exchanged against. Domestic labor, although not in fact paid for, is exchanged against the income of the spouse, and in this sense it is a classic example of unproductive labor. In a bourgeois household, for example, such labor would be done by a maid, but this would make no difference in terms of the economic category itself. It is a matter of complete indifference, insofar as the economic concept is concerned, whether this is the labor of a housewife exchanged against revenue or that of a maid (although the work of the housewife appears as a purely volunteer activity since it is unpaid, whereas the work of the maid appears as unproductive labor).

Although I just mentioned that the labor of housewives is unpaid, some feminists have calculated the cost of a housewife's labor and argue that such labor should receive compensation. These theorists seem unaware of the fact that are essentially "digging their own grave" with such arguments, since this amounts to saying that such labor is not a purely private service but rather is unproductive labor. If a housewife's labor is paid for, this would come from the income of the husband, and therefore this would have to be seen as unproductive labor that is qualitatively equivalent to the labor of a servant exchanged against the revenue of the master. Here the "pecuniary" relation between the two parties is not one of a husband and wife, but rather a "master-servant" relationship. Stuck within this framework of personal dependence upon the "master" (husband),[45] and being paid for such labor, is hardly a fortunate set of circumstances.

---

44. Ibid., 20.

Here one positive element of the formal definition of viewing labor exchanged against revenue as unproductive labor becomes clear. Marx emphasizes this "moment" because it encompasses a social relation, recognizing that it is problematic to simplistically distinguish between productive and unproductive labor on the basis of whether or not a material product is produced.

Of course, the fruit of the housewife's labor, as Marx points out, is "potentially" a commodity, and this domestic labor is gradually being replaced by social labor. If the meals that housewives once cooked at home can be bought at supermarkets, or the clothes that were once made at home purchased at a store, this means that potential commodities are being transformed into actual commodities. Furthermore, the fact that the labor objectified in these commodities is productive labor, in the sense that they are produced by labor exchanged against capital that is objectified as the commodity's value, also clearly shows that this labor comes to have a social aspect.

Marx concludes that the amount of labor exchanged against revenue that also produces some material "thing" is negligible, whereas most of the labor exchanged against revenue is service labor, and he does not delve much further into the matter. However, to those feminist theorists today who argue that domestic labor is also productive labor and claim that this represents an enormous segment of the overall productive labor, I feel obliged to point out, along with Marx, that the concept of productive labor is not a "simple" concept, and that in bourgeois society this concept encompasses a social relation that certainly cannot be ignored.

The Significance of Adam Smith

For Marx the concept of productive labor was a matter of course, appearing as a perfectly natural concept, but Adam Smith felt that the distinction between productive and unproductive labor was extremely important, and in a sense a concept of decisive significance. In the introduction to *The Wealth of Nations*, Smith clearly says that all of the "necessaries and conveniences" supplied to a nation depends first on "the skill, dexterity, and judgment with which its labour is generally applied," and secondly "by the proportion between the number of those who are employed in useful labour, and that of those who are

---

45. [In Japanese, one of the words for "husband" (*shujin*) also has the meaning of "master," and here Hayashi places the term in quotation marks to refer ironically to this.]

not so employed."[46] Smith argues that as the proportion of productive labor grows, so does the wealth of a nation, whereas a nation becomes poorer if there is an expansion in the proportion of its unproductive labor and parasitical elements.

It is no accident that Smith raises this argument at the very beginning of *The Wealth of Nations*, as it corresponds with the task and theoretical aim of his book. He sets out to clarify which countries attain wealth, and how this occurs. His response is that wealthy nations are those that accumulate capital, and that such nations must necessarily have a high proportion of productive labor compared to unproductive labor. Smith calls unproductive workers "idle people" and does not hesitate to even call them loafers. In chapter three of book two, Smith discusses in detail the issue of productive and unproductive labor, and the first thing he emphasizes is that there are these two types of labor. One might wonder why labor has to be clearly divided into two types, since it would seem to be the same as labor, or why it is not possible to just refer to both as "labor." Smith responds to such questions in the following way:

> There is one sort of labour which adds to the value of the subject upon which it is bestowed; there is another which has no such effect. The former, as it produces a value, may be called productive; the latter, unproductive labour. Thus the labor of a manufacturer adds, generally, to the value of the materials which he works upon, that of his own maintenance, and of his master's profit. The labor of a menial servant, on the contrary, adds to the value of nothing. Though the manufacturer has his wages advanced to him by his master, he, in reality, costs him no expense, the value of those wages being generally restored together with a profit, in the improved value of the subject upon which his labour is bestowed. But the maintenance of a menial servant never is restored. A man grows rich by employing a multitude of manufacturers: he grows poor by maintaining a multitude of menial servants.[47]

> The labor of some of the most respectable orders in the society is, like that of menial servants, unproductive of any value, and does not fix or realize itself in any permanent subject, or vendible commodity, which endures after that labor is past, and for which an equal quantity of labor could afterwards be procured. The sovereign, for example, with all the officers both of

---

46. *The Wealth of Nations*, 1.
47. Ibid., 351.

justice and war who serve under him, the whole army and navy, are unproductive laborers. They are the servants of the public, and are maintained by a part of the annual produce of the industry of other people. Their service, however honorable, how useful, or how necessary soever, produces nothing for which an equal quantity of service can afterwards be procured. The protection, security, and defense of the commonwealth, the effect of their labor this year, will not purchase its protection, security, and defense for the year to come. In the same class must be ranked, some of the gravest and most important, and some of the most frivolous professions: churchmen, lawyers, physicians, men of letters of all kinds; players, buffoons, musicians, opera-singers, opera-dancers, &c.[48]

Here Smith says that productive labor is not just labor that produces value, but labor that augments value and creates profit for capital. Such labor is productive because workers produce in excess of their own value, creating a profit or something additional for capital. Capital is augmented and the wealth of society is thus increased, and unlike the labor of servants, which does not increase social wealth (capital), this does not vanish into thin air. Smith emphasizes that payment for unproductive labor does not increase production for the subsequent year, but rather represent a deduction from this. The labor of soldiers is exchanged against the annual revenue, on a state scale, and therefore "produces nothing for which an equal quantity of service can afterwards be procured," which reveals the fact that this is unproductive labor. The labor of soldiers offers nothing that can be exchanged against the labor of soldiers the following year, so their work the following year can only be sustained on the basis of the productive labor of others. There is no question that without productive labor none of the soldiers' labor the following year would be possible. This is because their labor itself clearly generates nothing that can support the labor carried out in subsequent years. Here Smith's view is absolutely justified.

Of course, what is important to Smith is the accumulation of capital, and clarifying the factors that determine its accumulation. According to his view, the fundamental condition for the accumulation of capital, and an increase in wealth, is for more and more of the profits to be exchanged against productive labor *qua* capital, rather than expended as revenue on unproductive labor.

> If the society were annually to employ all the labour which it can annually purchase, as the quantity of labour would increase greatly every year, so the

---

48. Ibid., 352.

produce of every succeeding year would be of vastly greater value than that of the foregoing. But there is no country in which the whole annual produce is employed in maintaining the industrious. The idle everywhere consume a great part of it; and according to the different proportions in which it is annually divided between those two different orders of people, its ordinary or average value must either annually increase, or diminish, or continue the same from one year to another.[49]

Regardless of whether unproductive workers are useful or not, they are "maintained" by productive workers and appear as an encroachment upon capital, and to this extent Smith feels that such labor should be restricted to a minimum. For this reason, he is an ardent defender of the "cheap" state. He finds it economically advantageous to limit the scope of the state, and keep its expenses (e.g. military budget) to a minimum. Smith no doubt would have found the modern state, with its enormous military expenditures, terrifying and grotesque. For Smith, a nation prospers by increasing its productive labor, and declines with the swelling of unproductive labor. In short, the decisive question for him is whether labor is exchanged against capital or revenue. For instance, he offers the following view:

> The proportion between capital and revenue, therefore, seems everywhere to regulate the proportion between industry and idleness. Wherever capital predominates, industry prevails: wherever revenue, idleness. Every increase or diminution of capital, therefore, naturally tends to increase or diminish the real quantity of industry, the number of productive hands, and consequently the exchangeable value of the annual produce of the land and labour of the country, the real wealth and revenue of all its inhabitants.[50]

> That portion of his revenue which a rich man annually spends, is in most cases consumed by idle guests, and menial servants, who leave nothing behind them in return for their consumption. That portion which he annually saves, as for the sake of the profit it is immediately employed as a capital, is consumed in the same manner, and nearly in the same time too, but by a different set of people, by labourers, manufacturers, and artificers, who reproduce with a profit the value of their annual consumption.[51]

---

49. Ibid., 61.
50. Ibid., 358.
51. Ibid., 359.

Smith's view is, of course, subordinated to his ultimate goal of capital accumulation, and in this sense it is thoroughly bourgeois and alien to socialist thought. He emphasizes that "a rich man" (capitalist) should not expend his profit as revenue, but rather transform it into capital, and instead of paying for unproductive labor, which does not increase the social wealth but rather consumes it, he should pay for productive labor, thereby enriching the nation.

At the same time, however, this does not mean that Adam Smith holds little interest for the working class. Smith's thought represents the bourgeoisie in its period of robust health, and as such has important content from the workers' perspective. The school of Marxism has learned a great deal from Smith, and his views take on even greater significance in the modern period as a declining bourgeoisie and petty bourgeoisie ardently seek to justify and defend "idle people." Socialism, as we have pointed out, can only exist on the basis of the rational reorganization of productive labor. For this reason, workers aiming for socialism have a great interest in the concept of productive labor. Smith, for the sake of the bourgeoisie and their "correct" behavior, as well as for the further prosperity of capitalism, elucidated the distinction between productive and unproductive labor, advising the bourgeoisie to adopt "healthy" ways. Class-conscious workers, meanwhile, for the sake of achieving socialism, and to clarify its theoretical basis, need to clearly distinguish between productive and unproductive labor, and call on the working class to fight for socialism.

In the period when capitalism was still healthy, the bourgeoisie defended productive labor and lashed out at unproductive labor in order to foster capital accumulation, since the exploitation of productive labor is the essential moment of capitalism. Socialists, for their part, also recognize the significance of productive labor, but this is from the starting point of viewing productive labor as the material foundation of society. And socialists, unlike the bourgeoisie, seek to overcome the system of exploitation (capitalism).

In the following passage, Marx presents reasons why Smith's theory of distinguishing between productive and unproductive labor sparked such great debate among the classical school—albeit its second-rate representatives—and this passage can also be considered Marx's conclusion to the problem of productive labor:

> The great mass of so-called "higher grade" workers—such as state officials, military people, artists, doctors, priests, judges, lawyers, etc.—some of whom are not only not productive but in essence destructive, but who know how to appropriate to themselves a very great part of the "material" wealth partly

through the sale of their "immaterial" commodities and partly by forcibly imposing the latter on other people—found it not at all pleasant to be relegated economically to the same class as buffoons and menial servants and to appear merely as people partaking in the consumption, parasites on the actual producers (or rather agents of production). This was a peculiar profanation precisely of those functions which had hitherto been surrounded with a halo and had enjoyed superstitious veneration. Political economy in its classical period, like the bourgeoisie itself in its parvenu period, adopted a severely critical attitude to the machinery of the State, etc. At a later stage it realized and—as was shown too in practice—learnt from experience that the necessity for the inherited social combination of all these classes, which in part were totally unproductive, arose from its own organization.

In so far as those "unproductive laborers" do not provide pleasure, and therefore whether they are purchased or not depends entirely on the way in which the agent of production chooses to expend his wages or his profit—in so far on the contrary as they are necessary or make themselves necessary partly because of physical infirmities (like doctors), or spiritual weakness (like parsons), or because of the conflict between private interests and national interests (like statesmen, all lawyers, police and soldiers)—they are regarded by Adam Smith, as by the industrial capitalists themselves and the working class, as *faux frais de production*, which are therefore to be cut down to the most indispensable minimum and provided as cheaply as possible. Bourgeois society reproduces in its own form everything against which it had fought in feudal or absolutist form. In the first place therefore it becomes a principle task for the sycophants of this society, and especially of the upper classes, to restore in theoretical terms even the purely parasitic section of these "unproductive laborers," or to justify the exaggerated claims of the section which is indispensable. The dependence of the ideological, etc., classes on the capitalists was in fact proclaimed.[52]

In this matter even such people as Malthus are to be preferred, who directly defend the necessity and usefulness of "unproductive laborers" and pure parasites [compared to despicable JCP theorists, Kunio Akobori, and others].[53]

---

52. *MECW*, vol. 31, 30.
53. Ibid., 31. [Here Marx is comparing Malthus somewhat favorably to subsequent "sycophantic underlings of political economy" who "felt it their duty to glorify and justify every sphere of activity by demonstrating that it was 'linked' with the production of material wealth." (Ibid.) And Hayashi compares the latter group to pseudo-Marxist theorists in Japan.]

6

Service Labor and the Concept of Productive Labor

(A criticism of the theories of Akabori and Isagai)

Introduction

Akabori Kunio provides an overview of his own concept of productive labor in the preface to his book:

> In Marx's explanation, even the price of a natural thing such as land is elucidated on the basis of the labor theory of value as being the capitalized price of one part of the surplus-value (excess-profit = rent) generated by industrial labor carried out on the land. Moreover, there is no need to point out that the prices of services such as storage and transport, which are sold as commodities and unmistakably the product of labor, are determined by labor-value.
>
> Despite this, however, the common view among Marxist economists up to now has been that storage and transport services produce value because they are services involved with material things, whereas personal services, such as education or the performing arts, are said to not produce value because they are not examples of labor objectified in things. What, then, is the fee paid for services such as education or the performing arts? The response of Marxists to this question has been that in this particular case price without value is formed, with money, which is the embodiment of exchange-value, being paid for something that has no exchange-value.

Within the modern economy, industries related to personal services are thriving, including those industries involved in bus and taxi transportation, radio and TV broadcasting, education, music, film, theater, and hotel lodging, but present-day Marxist economists have insisted that Marx's labor theory of value cannot be applied to this sector. From their perspective, labor expended on material things produces value, but service labor provided for people, even if provided as a commodity, does not.

According to Marx's explanation, value is the social quality of each bit of the (social) labor expended by human beings for commodity production. Marxist economists, however, argue that only labor expended on the production of material commodities assumes the quality of value, whereas labor expended on the production of immaterial service commodities does not take on this quality of social value because such labor is not objectified in things. Therefore, according to this explanation, the price of service commodities cannot be explained according to the labor theory of value, which represents the bankruptcy of this theory within the context of the modern economy.[1]

Here Akabori argues that the concept of value is not restricted to labor embodied in things, and that value has a "social quality," so that it makes no difference whether we are dealing with service labor or commodity-producing labor,[2] with service labor also being able to generate value. He believes that Marxists economists today, by failing to recognize this fact, are theoretically bankrupt, and for this precise reason there is a need to construct a concept of productive labor that encompasses service labor. Of course, Akabori is saying quite a lot here, and it is not possible to deal with all of his untruths at once, but even from this one short passage his non-Marxist stance should be apparent.

First of all, Akabori speaks of land price. But this is an example of price without value, and therefore it is evident that pointing to this example does not lend support to his dogma, since the issue revolves around whether it is possible for something to have price without having value. By bringing up the issue of land price, Akabori should feel compelled to recognize that under capitalist relations of production there is nothing particularly strange about the

---

1.   Akabori Kunio, *Kachi to seisanteki rōdō* (Tokyo: San'ichi Shobō, 1971), 2-3.

2.   Or rather we might say that his conception of the commodity itself is vague.

common derivation or appearance of price without value, and therefore nothing strange about service labor having a price without having value.

However, this fraudulent theorist raises the issue of land price in order to claim that no price can exist that is not founded upon the theory of value and surplus-value, thus creating the impression that he has demonstrated that there can be no price that does not have value. But the question of whether land price can be *explained* from the theory of value and surplus-value, and the question of whether the price of land is a price that is *backed up* by value (a price *with* value), are two totally separate issues. Certainly, land price can be "explained" from the theory of value and surplus-value, but this does not change the fact that land price is a price without value, that valueless price is formed, and that money is paid for this (and therefore the income generated is completely parasitic). Akabori says that land price is determined by labor-value, but what exactly does he mean by "determined"? If he is saying that this land price is determined by labor-value[3] in the same manner as general commodities, then this is an astounding misconception. In the very first pages of his book, Akabori, in this manner, reveals to us that he is completely incapable of understanding Marxism!

Since Akabori himself approves of Marx's explanation of the price of land, he is basically recognizing that Marxism cannot be deemed bankrupt for pointing out that a price without value is paid for in the case of land (a price for something in which labor is not objectified). Where, then, is the basis for his slanderous claim against Marxism? If he insists that this is because Marxism generally recognizes the existence of price without value, he would be in contradiction with himself, since he has just recognized this to be the case for land price. Or is Akabori trying to say that he does not agree with the Marxist concept of land price? In this case, it would only reveal that he is consistently opposed to the concepts of Marxism, and we would have to say that it is not Marxism but his own views that are bankrupt! Clearly Akabori, should not speak so casually of the bankruptcy of Marxism.

Saying that service labor is not objectified as value can hardly be said to signify the bankruptcy of Marxism, just as pointing out the unproductive nature of the "labor" of soldiers or prostitutes does not. Rather, it is Akabori's own theory, which claims that such labor—i.e. service labor in general—is productive, that is quite flimsy. He conceives of value as being a "social quality of

---

3.   The meaning of "labor-value" for Akabori here is not clear.

labor" or as labor that "assumes the quality of value," but it is the height of concept-free thought to refer to labor objectified as value as being labor that "assumes the quality of value." To claim that the labor theory of value does not elucidate the price of service labor is a nonsensical view that stems from a failure to truly understand the nature of this theory. The labor theory of value denies that service labor is objectified as value, but this does not mean that it fails to explain *why* service labor comes to have a "price."

Finally, Akabori points to the fact that the service sector is "thriving" in today's society in order to claim that "orthodox" Marxism—which he refers to as "vulgar, fetishistic Marxism"[4] or "crude Marxism that worships at the altar of the commodity"—is unable to account for this. In fact, however, it is only the Marxist thought, denounced by Akabori, that is able to elucidate the actual significance of the blossoming service sector within present-day society!

The reactionary nature of Akabori's theory should be evident just from the short passage cited above from the preface to his book, which is a typical example of bourgeois theories that reflect contemporary prejudices. Akabori, a quintessential philistine, is now esteemed as the pioneer in the field of productive labor, and his theory has paved the way for the defense of unproductive labor (as being productive) by the Japanese Communist Party, which has completely embraced a bourgeois standpoint. In this way, the JCP effectively serves as an apologist for capitalist decay and parasitism. An examination of Akabori's theory, therefore, can help us come to a better understanding of the practical standpoint of the JCP. And later we will also examine the views of Isagai Nobuo, as a typical example of a theorist who has further developed Akabori's theory. In our discussion, however, the issue of the two men's specific political standpoints or whether they are members or supporters of the JCP is of little concern.

Akabori's Concept of "Productive Labor"

Akabori "valiantly" advances the view that the concept of productive labor held by Marxists up to now has been mistaken:

> The original definition of productive is the "material" [*sozaiteki*] or substantial [*ji'shitsu-teki*] definition according to which labor that produces

---

4.   It is also evident that Akabori has no grasp of the meaning of "commodity fetishism," nor any capacity to discuss this issue.

material things is productive labor. But the formal definition of productive labor in capitalist society is a different type of definition, from a totally different perspective. Despite this, however, the majority of Marxist economists today combine the definition stemming from the natural properties of products with the definition from the perspective of social production relations. As a result, they claim, first of all, that the value of a commodity cannot be formed without labor being objectified in a material commodity, and secondly, that even in the case of labor under production relations of capitalist exploitation, the production of material commodities is the necessary precondition for the production of surplus-value.[5]

It should be quite clear that although there are particular transitional aspects of the overall production process—such as the "transport process"—where labor does not involve transforming the natural character of an object (use-value), productive labor is fundamentally labor that acts upon nature, to transform and alter it. Even the capitalist, formal definition of productive labor, where labor is productive if it produces surplus-value, is restricted by the original definition. By viewing this capitalist definition as something undetermined or absolute, Akabori shows that his thought lacks a concept, thus revealing a mediocre mind incapable of stepping beyond a bourgeois framework.

Proceeding to Akabori's conclusion, he claims that only labor that produces surplus-value is productive, which effectively means that the concept of productive labor would disappear under socialism, as there would be no labor generating surplus-value. According to Akihiro's high-flown conclusion, productive labor is *superceded* under socialism, ceasing to exist. But how does he imagine that socialism would be possible without being rooted in the concept of productive labor? The fact is that the Marxist concept of productive labor actually comes to take on decisive importance under socialism. Akabori's theory is a peculiar one, and it has precious little in common with that of Marx. Akabori claims, for instance:

> For Marx, the capitalist, formal definition of productive labor is that labor which directly produces surplus-value for capital, and this alone is sufficient. This definition, directly speaking, bears no relation at all to the substantial [original] definition of productive labor. In order for this point to

---

5. Ibid., 23.

be correctly understood, Marx provides a detailed explanation that draws upon various examples regarding what types of labor produce surplus-value.

According to Marx's explanation, the labor of teachers, singers, and the like, is labor involved in immaterial production, but if such labor that produces useful services is carried out under a capitalist entrepreneur, so that surplus-value is directly created for the capitalist by means of unpaid labor-time exceeding necessary labor-time, this would become productive labor.[6]

According to Akabori's incredibly reactionary theory—since it ultimately defends and prettifies every sort of unproductive labor—the "labor" of prostitutes could also be considered productive, since it is no secret that they are hired by pimps (capitalist "entrepreneurs") and that their "labor" generates a profit. Even the military, which is engaged in the most reactionary sort of unproductive labor that could only exist in a class-divided society, could be openly defended as being engaged in productive labor, since even though a nation's soldiers do not produce profit, there are "mercenaries" who generate enormous profits for their employers! According to Akabori's concept, soldiers and those involved in security work are also very much engaged in productive labor, since the question of whether or not profit is created becomes the litmus test for determining which labor is productive. All profit-creating labor is thus seen as productive, and therefore even labor that is involved in immaterial production—even the soldier's job of killing other human beings—can be deemed productive.

It should be clear at a glance, however, that such a concept bears no connection at all to Marx's understanding of productive labor. Akabori's standpoint is very similar to the claim that since value and surplus-value are concepts that are only valid under capitalist production relations, they bear no relation to social production in general. But capitalist production relations only exist as such as one *historical form* of social production. Since capitalist production is only a historically limited form of social production, it does not supercede the bounds of social production itself. What we have, rather, is a historical form that penetrates social production, with capitalist production itself as one type of social production. To deny this would be to strip the concept of capitalist production relations of its basis, turning it into something hollow, which is precisely what Akabori does.

---

6.   Ibid., 24.

The only positive claim that Akabori makes is that unproductive labor *becomes* productive labor under capitalist production relations. Certainly, a person selling "sex" also produces profit if hired by a capitalist, and certainly a prostitute's labor appears as productive labor to this capitalist involved. But this stems from the capitalist form of productive labor—what I would call the subordinate form—and this capitalist concept of productive labor is not something unconditional, having instead clear limitations. For Akabori to uncritically accept this reality, and consider this sort of capitalist notion to be equivalent to science, only shows us how he has been taken in by phenomenal aspects of capitalism. He thinks that the concept of productive labor, with its capitalist restrictions, is the concept *per se*, and in this way declares every sort of unproductive labor to be productive (including that performed by soldiers and prostitutes), arguing in effect that such labor is both necessary and important to human social life! This view may be appropriate for a bourgeois professor like Akabori, but it must be said that for workers such an idea is a totally alien one!

The notion that any sort of labor whatsoever is productive, provided that it generates profit, is the view of the bourgeoisie, not the working class. Certainly, for individual capitalists, such as managers of brothels and those involved in the prostitution industry, the "labor" of prostitutes creates profit and is therefore productive. However, for society as a whole, in what sense can this be considered productive? Akabori must prove in what sense the labor of prostitutes is productive, but he finds this exceedingly difficult. He is able to elaborate on the example of singers when discussing the arts, but he has to throw up his hands when it comes to the case of prostitutes or soldiers. Economically speaking, however, singers and prostitutes essentially belong to the same category—even though they can be distinguished from a moral standpoint in terms of the one being the expression of some lofty human feeling, and the other the satisfaction of a more carnal desire.

When Marx defines productive labor in terms of workers generating profit, he always makes a point to says that this is "within the capitalist form" or "under capitalism," but Akabori gives no thought to the significance of such qualifying phrases. Even when critically examining the theories of Adam Smith, Marx essentially adopts this perspective, but Akabori pays no attention to this decisively important point. Marx discovers many ideas within Smith's theory that are limited by a bourgeois framework, and he examines the concept of productive labor by critically analyzing such ideas. What Akabori offers, however, are basically the same notions held by the classical school,

namely the bourgeois view that only profit-generating labor is productive. Of
course, this idea does not lack a basis and is not totally mistaken,[7] but to overlook the restrictions that stem from the historical definition of form would
mean falling into a completely mistaken, bourgeois standpoint, and this inevitably results in an unmediated defense of unproductive labor (precisely as carried out by Akabori and the JCP!).

According to Akabori's reasoning, in the case of productive labor according
to the capitalist, formal definition, there is absolutely no reason to distinguish
between labor that produces material things and the "labor" of prostitutes,
with both being treated as the same type of productive labor. From Akabori's
theoretical standpoint, this point seems self-evident, but what could better
reveal the bankruptcy of his theory? Anyone should know that there is a distinction between productive labor and the "labor" of prostitutes, or at least
have an inkling that this is the case. But Akabori dares to take on such views,
saying that science exists as such for the very reason that it challenges common
sense, and here I must extend a round of applause to our brave Don Quixote.

Actually, Akabori is aware that service labor is unproductive labor, but he
says that this is only according to the "substantial definition" which has no
relation to the formal definition. He argues that what is important in the case
of service labor is the definition of form, not the substantial definition, since
the issue centers on the definition of labor under capitalism, not the general
definition, and thus according to this capitalist definition of form, service labor
is also very much productive labor (or transformed into productive labor).
Akabori clearly accepts that service labor is in fact unproductive, and that productive labor is fundamentally labor that produces some material thing. For
this reason, he only calls service labor "productive" according to the "purely
formal" definition under capitalist society. However, we need to consider what
exactly Akabori means by a "purely formal definition" in the first place. He
writes:

> It is evident that service labor, from the standpoint of the substantial defi-
> nition, is unproductive labor. This is because service labor is not labor that
> produces material things. Rather, the production of a service, as in the case
> of taxi-driving, from the perspective of material things, involves the con-
> sumption of a use-value (the passenger vehicle), by means of which a form-

---

7.   Marx examines in detail how and to what extent this view is correct or
     mistaken in *Theories of Surplus Value*.

less, useful effect or useful service is produced, [in this case] movement from one place to another. Since from the perspective of material things, this is the consumption of things, such labor, substantially speaking, is unequivocally unproductive labor.

The labor of a taxi-driver, seen from the perspective of society, involves providing, as a commodity, a service with the useful effect of moving a passenger from one place to another, but from the perspective of things there is no difference between this and a taxi-driver taking a weekend drive in his own passenger vehicle, thereby consuming the use-value of the car. This type of labor, seen from the perspective of things, is labor that only involves consumption and is not in any sense labor that produces things. According to the substantial definition, the taxi-driving labor that provides a ride to a shopper or tourist is unproductive labor. From the perspective of the relation of labor to material things, not only the labor of taxi-driving, but all typical service labor is labor that does not produce things. Thus, seen from the substantial definition, this is unproductive labor. On this point there can be no doubt. However, what about from the perspective of the definition of form? That is the next question.[8]

As is well known, in Marx's theory of productive labor, a distinction is made between the substantial definition and the formal definition. According to the substantial definition of productive labor, only labor that produces material things is deemed productive, which is the most obvious definition concerning the workings of human labor.

The educational labor of school teachers or the labor of musical performers are examples of labor that produces useful services, but since this is not labor that produces use-value things [*shiyō-kachi butsu*] such labor is unproductive according to the substantial definition (of the nature of labor). In the case of the substantial definition, which concerns the substantial [material] nature of human labor, the deciding factor in determining whether labor is productive or not is the question of whether it produces a use-value *qua* thing. With the development of the productive power of labor and the greater specialization and cooperation within the concrete labor process to produce use-value things, the sphere of productive labor in terms of the substantial definition expands to include supervisory and planning labor that is not directly engaged in material production, but this does not alter the essence of the matter at all. Such labor as freight transport, which takes place outside of the factory, or the transporting of miners to the site of production, is defined as productive labor, substantially speaking, to the extent that it has the character of forming one part of the socially-divided system of labor to produce material things.

8. Ibid., 137.

However, the meaning of productive labor according to the substantial definition is not limited to this. As long as labor functions as one part of the labor that produces things, whether directly or indirectly, it is defined, substantially speaking, as productive labor, whereas labor that does not produce things, no matter how important it may be, is defined as unproductive labor. The substantial definition of productive labor has almost no significance for economics as a social science because it is a definition of a natural process qua natural existence whereby human beings as living nature produce useful things within a metabolic process as an extension of a sort of physiological activity. For this reason, in *Capital* and other economic works, Marx only provides a brief explanation of this definition. He touches on the substantial definition of productive labor only to the minimum extent believed necessary to clarify the social, formal definition of productive labor. This is the reason why so many misunderstandings later arose over this definition.

At any rate, the standard for determining the substantial definition of productive labor concerns the natural properties of the labor product as the outcome of labor, and this is the natural or material [*sozai-teki*] definition of the nature of labor. This definition is thus essentially unrelated to economics.

However, the formal definition of productive labor is completely the opposite. The formal definition of productive labor concerns what sort of labor is productive under the form of capitalist society, and this is very much an economic definition that is particular to the capitalist form of society.

Under the form of capitalist society, only that labor which produces surplus-value for capital is productive labor, while all other labor is unproductive. In a capitalist economy all products are produced as commodities, but the material nature of these commodities bears no relation at all to the formal definition of productive labor under capitalism. Products of a capitalist society, to the extent that they are commodities, must have some use-value and be an object that satisfies some human need, but the nature of such needs, whether intended for the stomach or the imagination, or whether in a definite form or as a formless service, has absolutely no bearing on the formal definition of productive labor.

Productive labor under capitalist society is labor that produces surplus-value directly for capital. According to this formal definition, the natural properties of the product produced by productive labor, whether it be something to please the human eye (artwork) or ear (music), or a useful effect such as moving from one place to another (transport), is a matter of indifference. This is because the formal definition concerns the social properties of the manner of production and is totally distinct from the definition pertaining to the product's natural properties. The formal definition of productive labor is related to valorization, whereas the substantial definition adheres to the standard of whether or not a material use-value is produced. The two are totally separate definitions. Value emerges from a socio-economic relation between people, whereas use-value emerges from a relation between people and external, natural things. The formal definition of productive labor is a definition related to the social nature of labor, whereas the substantial definition of productive labor is a material definition.[9]

I have quoted Akabori at some length here because this passage expresses well the fundamental aspects of his standpoint. Like the classical (bourgeois) school of political economy, Akabori treats "economic categories" such as the commodity, money, and capital as absolutes, thus failing to grasp Marx's socialist standpoint of understanding these categories as *historical forms* of social relations of production.[10]

Akabori casually divides the concepts of productive and unproductive labor into a theory of non-capitalist society on the one hand and a theory of capitalist society on the other. He then declares the two concepts to be "totally separate," which is basically the end of the matter as far as he is concerned. But this theory is a bit strange. If this were indeed the case, why does Akabori feel obliged to have two theories in the first place? A single capitalist, formal definition should suffice (and in reality this *is* the case for Akabori). He speaks of the original concept of product labor, not to confirm its significance, but rather in a ceremonious manner, for the simple reason that Marx also used this expression. Akabori knows nothing of the significance or importance of this concept, and he does not—or is unable to—speak of its necessity.

Naturally for Akabori the distinction between the two concepts, as well as their identity,[11] is a matter of complete indifference, existing outside of his field of vision. He speaks in a concept-free and formalistic—or rather one-dimensional—manner about the "distinction" between the two concepts, but he has no understanding at all of their identity. For Akabori, they are separate things that are not united in any sense; or more precisely, it is as if the original concept of productive labor does not exist for him, and only the formal concept or capitalist definition of productive labor exists. By holding close to and

---

9. Ibid., 133-5.
10. We should note, however, that Smith and Ricardo's theories were historically healthy and progressive, whereas Akabori's ideas only have reactionary significance.
11. For more on these points see the preceding chapter.

emphasizing this definition of form, Akabori is able to convince himself that he has offered some fundamental insight into the truth or essence of productive labor, but the fact remains that he has only managed to come up with an empty and meaningless theory.

The concept of productive labor, according to Akabori, has almost no significance for economics, and Marx is said to have only clarified the capitalist definition of productive labor "to the minimum extent believed necessary." However, he has nothing at all to say about the manner in which Marx's concept of productive labor is necessary for the clarification of the definition of form. He only says that the two definitions are totally separate, placing out of consideration, and treating as a matter of indifference, the relation between them. Akabori should say something—even "to the minimum extent" necessary—about how the original concept is necessary when dealing with the formal definition of productive labor, regardless of whether or not his thoughts agree with Marx's own. Without doing so, he is simply introducing a completely empty theory that is incapable of explaining why Marx spoke of the original concept of productive labor.[12]

The formal definition of productive labor discussed by Akabori is completely detached from the original definition. In other words, he deals with a completely empty concept, while being unaware of how barren this concept is. In this sense, he is similar to those who speak of the concept of the commodity that bears no direct relation to it being a product of labor. In short, Akabori is a "blood relation" of the theorists Hiromatsu Wataru and Uno Kōzō, and their followers.[13] The only thing Akabori is capable of saying is that the formal definition of productive labor bears no relation whatsoever to the substantial nature of the commodity, and he claims that this view was shared by Marx. Certainly this is *part* of the truth, but Akabori understands this in words only and is unaware of its profound content.

---

12. Of course he is incapable of doing this because the original definition of productive labor runs quite counter to his entire argument, and he would be happy if this concept were consigned to oblivion.

13. We will later see how Akabori's theory is often a carbon copy of theories held by the Uno and Hiromatsu, which demonstrates that, politically speaking, the JCP and reformist factions share the same foundation as radical and new left tendencies. [Here Hayashi is referring to the fact that the JCP-leaning Akabori's ideas are close to those held by the two prominent new left ideologues Uno Kōzō and Hiromatsu Wataru.]

Granted, the formal definition of productive labor is labor exchanged against capital that generates profit, and a great deal of unproductive labor could also *appear* as productive labor to the extent that it coincides with this definition. But Akabori seems unaware of the fact that the question concerns *how* to rationally explain this fact, not simply stating the fact itself. The irrationality of this aspect of bourgeois society should be clear at a glance, but Akabori and others who sense no contradiction, present the formal definition as an absolute, while at the same time jettisoning the original definition, thereby freeing themselves to drone on endlessly about a content-less "economics."

Concentrating on the capitalist, formal definition, Akabori neglects to mention what this definition is a form of, or is perhaps unaware of the necessity to do this. When Marx speaks historically of forms—such as value being the form that human labor takes under certain historical relations of production—this concerns the form of certain social relations between human beings. If we do not bear this point in mind, the term "historical form" loses all meaning and becomes nothing more than an empty phrase. This would amount, in other words, to merely treating form *as form*, turning it into an independent entity, thus treating the bourgeois concept—and therefore bourgeois production relations as well—as something absolute and eternal. For Akabori, the capitalist concept alone represents the truth concerning productive labor, since it is said to bear no relation at all to the original definition of productive labor and is not the historical form of this original definition. Here Akabori appears unmistakably as a *pure* bourgeois.

Akabori "boldly" declares that the original definition of productive labor is completely unrelated to economics. Of course, everyone knows that the original concept of productive labor is not an economic category *per se,* but it would be ridiculous, on the basis of this fact, to deny that an economic category *is* a historical concept of certain human social relations. For instance, when Marx says that value is a historical definition of form, this means that value is the historical form that human labor takes. For a person to overlook this and say that the concept of value "has absolutely no relation" to human labor, or that it is "totally separate" from this, would clearly reveal a failure to understand value and the concept of value. Akabori's concept of "historical form" is no different from the view of historical form held by Uno—where the commodity is seen as a mere "circulation-form"—which is to say it is an empty abstraction. Akabori also claims that services are commodities on the basis of the fact that they are also bought and sold. Indeed, for Akabori, a commodity is nothing more something that is bought and sold, which is identical to the concept of Unoists (and the bourgeoisie in general) that a commodity is anything "purchased" with money or anything that has a price and circulates.

Akabori concludes that the original definition of productive labor is the "substantial" (material) definition of the character of labor, whereas the definition of form is the definition that concerns the social character of labor. I must say, however, that Akabori has got it completely wrong. The original definition of productive labor is also very much connected to the "social character" of labor. Under socialism, productive labor would directly appear as social labor, and would therefore thoroughly retain its "social character," but such labor would not—and would have no need to—take the form of value. In other words, there would be no necessity for the "social character" of human labor to appear as value, and further as money, as it does under capitalism. This is the only essential difference, not the question of having or not having a social character. Correctly stated, productive labor under both definitions has a social character, but in capitalist society, owing to the fundamental contradictions within production—namely, private property and private ownership!—this social character must appear as value, and further as money, i.e. in a "material" form. Under socialism, however, there would be absolutely no need for this to occur, and the social character would appear in a direct form, and herein lies an essential distinction. Not only does Akabori utterly fail to understand this fundamental point, his own approach is so far off the mark that this does not even enter his field of vision.

He emphasizes that any labor that does not create profit is unproductive labor. This view, however, comes into contradiction with reality, revealing a defect when faced with the important question of small-commodity producers. For Akabori, small-scale farmers would have to be defined as unproductive workers, but is this truly the case? By excluding the labor of small commodity producers from the concept of productive labor, and therefore excluding one part of the total social labor[14] Akabori exposes the bankruptcy of his own theory.

In the following passage, Akabori claims that to the extent that it also produces services, service labor cannot be essentially distinguished in any way from productive labor:

---

14. Would this mean that Akabori thinks their labor is *not* objectified as value?

In the production of services as well, as long as they are produced as commodities, their production process is the integration of the labor process and the value-formation (or valorization) process. However, the labor process of service production, of course, cannot be human activity for the production of material use-values. In terms of whether or not a material use-value is produced, the labor process for service production is rather, not infrequently, a process of consuming material use-values. This labor process typically utilizes some helpful material means in order to efficiently produce a useful service, and this is a process of the "productive consumption" of such material means for the sake of service production. In terms of the realm of material production, this "productive consumption" of the means of production does not create a material use-value. What is created is not a so-called "use-value," but an immaterial "useful effect" or useful service. This useful service is not a material product that breaks away or splits off from the production process, but rather an immaterial product for which the production process itself is consumed, this sort of immaterial commodity. The production process for service commodities is the unity of the labor process and the value-formation (or valorization) process, but this labor process seen from the perspective of things is not a process of human activity to produce material use-values. This labor process is, however, a process in which a formless useful effect is produced as a desired object for someone, and in this labor process the concrete activity of human beings utilizes the means of labor and specific kinds of useful effects are appropriately created. And this same labor process, in cases where the service created is produced in order to be sold to another person as a commodity, also has a social character in terms of the value-formation process of the service commodity, and the labor expended becomes the value (or surplus-value) of the service commodity.

The labor that produces service commodities is not productive according to the original definition, but it can be productive labor according to the definition of form.[15]

Akabori uses the word "production" in a completely concept-free manner. He casually says that services are also "produced"—although as formless "useful effects"—but from a Marxist perspective, production refers to the production of material goods, and this fundamental term should be used in a strict sense. It is a mere analogy, or playing with words, to say that service labor is the "production" of services, as it should be perfectly clear that service labor does not produce services, but rather is itself an "effect." Akabori is merely making a declaration, as a sort of divine revelation, rather than analyzing reality. He

---

15. Ibid., 121-2.

insists that service labor is also productive labor, and therefore "produces" something, but this is completely unrelated to the question of whether this is in fact the case. To say that service labor "produces" services, is a misuse of the word "production" and represents an expansion of its meaning.

If such usage is acceptable, then one might as well refer to sugar as salt, as both are white and have a loose, granular texture. Our use of the term "productive labor" presupposes that an object undergoes some sort of change, and Marx views this term as referring to one moment in the "material metabolism" between man and nature. The idea that services are also "produced" or are examples of "productive labor" is simply the result of Akabori's arbitrary use of terminology. If the providing of services is called production, then following this sort of logic, any human activity could be considered production (or productive labor); for instance, playing sports "produces" sweat and good health, the excretory process "produces" excrement, love "produces" not only offspring but affection, and fighting "produces" not only scars but animosity, and so forth.

At the same time, Akabori makes use of Marx's discussion of educational labor as forming one part of the reproduction costs of labor-power in order to argue that services also generally form part of the reproduction costs of labor-power. In the following passage he says that the reproduction costs of labor power also include "recreational expenses":

> Just as "man cannot live by bread alone," since labor-power also has a mental aspect, it is necessary, at least at particular moments, to improve one's abilities by means of education or receive mental enjoyment through the consumption of a recreational service, thereby restoring some of one's energy. In this way, the value of services (commodities) from industries involved in providing such things as education, television programs, or films, are included in the production or reproduction costs of the mental aspect of labor-power. Thus, labor-power is reproduced as an element of material productive power within the social reproduction process. For this reason, such services are not "idle expenditures."[16]

This dim-witted fellow wants to include within the reproduction costs of labor-power the media employed to transmit bourgeois culture and ideology, such as education and television programs, which, although not uniformly "vacuous," are in part responsible for keeping workers down. Prewar public

16. Ibid., 256.

education in Japan was essentially nothing more than a state organ used to "drive home" the ideology of the emperor system and imperialism among the citizens as a whole, but according to Akabori's logic, expenses involved for such things would also be considered as one part of the reproduction costs of labor-power. Akabori inevitably ends up prettifying and defending imperialistic bourgeois culture, and the media organs that force this culture upon the people—which are a means of "dumbing-down" the entire population!—and this shows us precisely the reactionary nature and bankruptcy of his views on service labor and productive labor.

Akabori "misuses" Marx's statement about education being included as one part of the reproduction costs of labor-power. Even though Marx includes education within the reproduction costs of labor-power, he does not neglect to point out that this is to a partial extent and dependent upon the circumstances. Why should education as a means of forcing a class ideology upon people be included within the overall reproduction costs of labor-power? One thing that is certain is that Akabori—who is quite unaware of the reactionary aspects of bourgeois, class-based education—does not grasp the concept of the reproduction costs of labor-power.

It should be clear that within the modern, developed bourgeois state, a rather significant part of the overall national production is taken up by leisure-related industries. However, in order to enjoy baseball why should workers have to bear the burden of the enormous salaries of professional athletes? Would Akabori go so far as to insist that the activities of such athletes are examples of "productive labor"? Certainly, Ichiro and Matsui produce, according to Akabori's view, "recreation" for people, but this does not mean that their "labor" is productive. To define such activity as productive labor would amount to abandoning the concept of productive labor itself. In short, Akabori has no concept of productive labor, and this is inevitable for a theorist who represents the urban petty bourgeoisie, which is mainly composed of people who are essentially "consumers" rather than producers. It is astounding for someone to include within productive labor all activities that "produce recreation." Such activities are completely arbitrary, because what is seen as recreation and what is considered unpleasant varies depending on the particular person or situation, so that it cannot be objectively evaluated. For this reason, such "commodities" can be paid for at any price, and this is inevitable for activities that concern "consumption costs."

In the future cooperative society, an increase in the productive power of people's labor would bring about a reduction in the time needed for material production and a vast expansion in personal free time. To understand this merely as the expansion of consumptive activity, however, represents a distorted view, completely determined by bourgeois narrow-mindedness. Marx above all views this increase in free time as the expansion of human self-realization. But contemporary petty-bourgeois ideologues, like Akabori and Isagai, can only understand this historical development as the expansion of consumptive activity, the swelling of the service sector, and they fail to realize how their own views are infected by the vulgarity of bourgeois "mass-culture."

Marx understood this process, first and foremost, as a reduction in the labor-time spent on material production, recognizing the decisive significance of this, and this is precisely because he clarified the distinction between productive and unproductive labor. But Akabori and others give no consideration to this matter. According to Akabori's view, a decrease in labor-time is only seen as being significant in terms of the development and deepening of the social division of labor; i.e. the process whereby the social division of labor extends from productive industries to include the service sector. Needless to say, this is separate from the issue of a rapid reduction in labor-time. For Akabori, labor-time is not essentially reduced, since even if it is reduced in the productive sector, labor-time is expanded in the service sector, so that for society as a whole, and individuals as well, a reduction in labor-time does not appear as an essential moment. What is fundamental for Akabori is that the social division of labor expands to include the service sector, so that people's lives become more "colorful," not only materially but also through the enjoyment of services. This is the sort of small-minded view of a future society that perfectly suits the petty bourgeoisie.

Another characteristic of Akabori is that he considers governmental service labor as unproductive labor, since it is not exchanged against capital and does not create profit for capital. He thinks that any sort of vile labor that produces profit for capital—"labor" in the sex industry or labor producing weapons, etc.—is productive labor, but on the other hand, services, no matter how beneficial or necessary, are unproductive if they are of a governmental nature, because this is not profit-creating labor exchanged against capital. On this point, Akabori's theory can at least be distinguished from the extremely vulgar and banal view of productive labor as any labor that "creates revenue," whether involved services or anything else. Akabori writes:

> How should we view services provided through public expenses, such as national or local government bodies? Since one portion of services, such as

school education, is actually produced and provided in the form of a governmental service, rather than in the form of commodity production, such services can be viewed in the following way. Governmental services are services carried out by government employees, and thus correspond to Adam Smith's discussion of domestic servants, with the cost of procuring such services belonging to what Marx calls the costs of consumption. Therefore, when educational services are provided by private schools, for example, this is commodity production, which produces value and surplus-value, and this forms a component part of national income; whereas the services of public schools, like the administrative services of government employees in general, are not a part of national income, but rather merely one part of the services maintained by means of redistributing national income through taxes. This is the principle of public services.[17]

Akabori considers the definition of productive labor in terms of profit-generating labor exchanged against capital, and he treats this definition alone as an absolute. He overlooks the bourgeois nature of this definition, i.e. how it is the concept of productive labor held by the bourgeoisie. For the bourgeoisie, profit-creating labor is productive labor and any other definition is irrelevant and unessential. And they have a hard time imagining how things could be any other way.

Akabori's Concept of a Service "Commodity"

Akabori says that labor exchanged against capital is productive labor, and that what is exchanged is naturally a commodity, and could not be otherwise. He claims that services are also commodities. But here two questions arise. First of all, are services, as such, actually commodities? And secondly, what is the concept of the commodity? Akabori's concept of the service "commodity" is as follows:

> Labor that produces material things becomes labor-value, not simply because some "material thing is produced," but because this labor becomes one component part of the total social labor within a social relation where things are produced that other people desire and then handed over to them by means of exchange. In terms of commodities, there are material commodities as well as immaterial commodities. A commodity is a useful thing, and as such it is handed over to another person by means of exchange. Services are useful things, and in commodity society they are produced as com-

---

17. Ibid., 282.

modities to be handed over to other people through exchange. The value of a service commodity is created by the character of the service-producing labor as social labor. In commodity-production society, just as the character of human labor as the substance of value, which is based upon the social unity mediated by the commodity-exchange relation, can be manifested in a material commodity-form, as the labor objectified in a material thing, so too can it appear in the shape of a useful service itself, as the value-substance of an immaterial service commodity. Marx included the labor of service workers employed by capital within his concept of productive labor based on the understanding of the theory of value mentioned above. When service labor is carried out under capital, it directly produces surplus-value for capital within the production process of service commodities, and is thus included within the category of productive labor.[18]

In other words, even given the same type of service labor, this is instantly considered productive labor if handed over to another person by means of exchange, whereas otherwise it is viewed as unproductive labor. Akabori claims that the "original" concept of productive labor does not apply to capitalism because service labor, which would be unproductive labor originally, is instantly transformed into productive labor according to the formal definition. He says that as long as service labor is a commodity it also has value, and he presents the odd and irrational view that this value "is created by the character as social labor of the service-producing labor." But the question arises—which we will address later—of how this "character" is able to create value.

Akabori also introduces the ridiculous logic according to which service-producing labor *itself* is said to be value or the substance of value. Akabori has the following to say about the service-labor commodity, which reveals his vulgar and silly concept of the commodity:

> In modern society, services are produced as commodities and provided to society by wage-workers who work under service-industry capital. This is the case for the labor of taxi or tour-bus drivers. In terms of the substantial definition, this labor is unproductive, but seen from a socio-economic perspective this is in fact labor that is functioning under capitalism to augment capital.
>
> The augmentation of capital by service-producing labor within the service industry is a fact that no one would likely deny. This is labor that produces a useful service or utility but does not produce a material good or use-

18. Ibid., 19-20.

value thing. However, these service products, because of their usefulness, are a type of commodity demanded by other people, which are handed over to them for consumption in exchange for money. A commodity is something that (1) is useful and thus (2) is handed over to another person through exchange. On this point, service commodities produced by capitalist companies are no different, in any way, from material commodities. Moreover, service commodities are unmistakably products of labor. Among material commodities, there are things such as garden stepping stones, works of art, and antiques, for which it is difficult to determine the extent to which they are products of labor, whereas in the case of service commodities there is no such ambiguity. In terms of being products of labor, a service commodity is not inferior in any sense to a material commodity.

Therefore, if we summarize the points mentioned above, service commodities (1) have usefulness, can be handed over through exchange, and very much maintain their social character as commodities; (2) are products of wage labor; and (3) augment capital as articles of sale owned by capital that appear on the market; this is the social character of service commodities. On these points, there is not the slightest difference when compared to material commodities. However, this does not mean that material commodities and service commodities are identical in all respects. Whereas material commodities appear as goods, service commodities appear on the market directly as the labor process of the concrete, service-producing labor. From a social perspective, material commodities and service commodities have an identical character, but from a material [*sozaiteki*] perspective, their quality is completely different. However, as we have already pointed out, this does not represent any sort of defect in terms of being a commodity. If this is not clearly understood, it is impossible to grasp the formal definition of labor that produces service commodities.

In a capitalist economy, services are provided to society as commodities and produced as such. Service commodities are the product of wage-labor. However, they are not a tangible, material good. Service commodities are also products of labor, but instead of taking a material form they are commodities in which labor, as it is within the concrete labor process, directly becomes the commodity-body [*shōhin-tai*], as labor in a fluid state. What, then, determines the exchange-value of the service commodity?

The exchange-value of a service is determined by the quantity of human labor expended on its production. The magnitude of the value of a service commodity is determined, just like the value of commodity goods, by the amount of human labor expended on their production.

Service commodities are produced by wage-labor as capitalist commodities containing surplus-value. Under capitalism, therefore, although service-producing labor is unproductive labor in terms of the substantial definition, it is productive labor in terms of the definition of form.[19]

Akabori's concept of the commodity is basically anything that is useful, handed over to another person through exchange, and then consumed. The question of *intrinsic* value, i.e. whether the commodity includes objectified labor, is considered something irrelevant and unessential. For Akabori, things with prices but no intrinsic value—such as land or securities, which come to have prices through capitalization of revenue calculated on the basis of interest rates—are also commodities simply because they are useful things with prices that are purchased with money and provided for exchange. Akabori makes no distinction between commodities in the original sense and derivative commodities or commodities with a price but no value (i.e. commodities with no social human labor objectified in them). In other words, he lacks the concept of the commodity in the *original* sense, and on this point Akabori is no different from modern bourgeois economists and the Uno school.

Akabori mentions the two types of commodities he learned about from Marx; namely, the original commodity, which is the outcome of productive labor, and the service commodity. However, the two types of commodities that Marx actually deals with are the original commodity and the labor-power commodity, which he views as being the essential "moments" of capitalism. By contrast, the "service commodity" and other similar commodities are treated as aspects that are in fact not essential.

Certainly, services also appear as commodities in bourgeois society. However, this is no different from the commodification of things such as land, securities, money-capital, sex, or as Marx says, a person's "honor." Such "commodities" are the outcome of the world of general commodities, representing secondary or derivative phenomena. From a scientific perspective, these commodities must be distinguished from commodities in the original sense which contain objectified human labor.

Only after the concept of the original commodity has been clarified can one for the first time reveal the significance of derivative commodities, thus the concept of the commodity cannot be demonstrated by means of such derivative commodities. Akabori and others like him do not understand that a concept exists as such as the truth concerning an object. If a commodity is merely something that is exchanged, then certainly services would also be commodities, but the commodity *per se* exists as the unity of value (objectified labor) and use-value, and in no sense can a service be considered objectified labor.

---

19. Ibid., 138-9.

Living labor itself is certainly not—and could not be—a commodity. The fact that services, which are not originally commodities, can appear as such, reveals the position of service commodities within capitalist society, and understanding this limitation is the starting point of a theory of services.

Akabori merely offers the dogma that "a commodity is a commodity." Marxists, however, begin by making a distinction between the commodity in the original sense and derivative commodities. In addition to commodities in general, there are commodities—such as the labor-power commodity—that have intrinsic value in a sense, but whose value-determination is only carried out indirectly. There are also commodities—such as the price of land, etc.—whose exchange-value can be derived from the theory of value and surplus-value despite the fact they have no intrinsic value themselves. Furthermore, there are commodity prices that are determined in a completely arbitrary manner, such as those determined solely according to the purchasing power of buyers. To lump all of these different types of commodities together within the concept of the commodity, and attempt to determine all of their exchange-values at the same time, would only result in the tautology that "exchange-value is exchange-value" or the determination of price by means of price (or by means of utility). This is in fact the approach of the Uno school, as well as the approach of bourgeois, vulgar economics in general.

Akabori says that Marx abstracted out value as the thing common to all commodities, but if the commodity is understood in the manner of Akabori, the question here becomes one of *price* not value. Despite using the term "value," he is actually talking about exchange-value or price. If one seeks the thing that every sort of "commodity" has in common within bourgeois society, this would clearly be price rather than value. This is because here the concept of the commodity means nothing more than the fact that something has exchange-value (i.e. price, or to borrow Akabori's expression, the character of "being exchanged for money"). The element that *all* varieties of "commodities" share in common is not value, but exchange-value,. There are any number of commodities that have exchange-value but no value; land is one example, securities another, and various other examples exist, such as the human body (sex), violence and military actions, as well as "honor."

Marx defines value as the social human labor necessary to produce a certain use-value. This is value in terms of being objectified in a commodity. In other words, the substance of value is human labor, but this does not mean that labor itself is value. Furthermore, exchange-value presupposes use-value as its material bearer.

Akabori says that the common element of every sort of commodity is value, in order to suggest that service labor is also a commodity and therefore has "value" (read: price). This is exactly the same concept-free approach of the Unoists, who argue that what commodities have in common first of all is price (and therefore a commodity is merely a "circulation-form"). Although the determination of price itself must be derived from the concept of value, vulgar theorists take the opposite approach, seeking the concept of value directly within the phenomenon of price, and this is the approach of all bourgeois economists. Akabori dissolves the concept of value within the phenomenon of price, and for this reason groups together within the same category, and views as identical, every sort of "commodity," including general commodities, land as a commodity, as well as the labor-power commodity and the "service com- modity" (although the meaning of this last "commodity" is unclear).

The commodity is the unity of use-value and value, and the substance of its value is objectified labor. This is the *concept* of the commodity, and in this sense service labor is certainly not a commodity, but rather merely a sort of pseudo-commodity. However, even though services are not commodities in the original sense, and only pseudo-commodities, as commodities *in the formal sense* their exchange-value is necessarily determined according to certain laws (just as in the case of land or capital as commodities). Marx says that the exchange-value of service commodities is a question that essentially belongs to the theory of wages. In other words, the exchange-value of service labor is determined by the law governing the wages of workers in general, to which it is subordinated. This is an extremely simple, easy-to-grasp law. Marx says that there is no special law for the wages of service-industry workers, which are instead determined or restricted by the wages of industrial workers (of course, due to the particularity of the service industry, there are also some "workers" who obtain high "wages" that amount to hundreds of millions of yen per year).

When workers are hired by service capital, surplus-labor is squeezed out that exceeds necessary labor and this forms one source of profit for service cap- ital, but this is only a source of profit in the *negative sense*. Service labor does not produce surplus-value, and therefore the surplus-labor of service workers merely provides service capital with the right to a larger portion of the total surplus-labor created by capital as a whole. In this sense, service capital discov- ers a decisive benefit in obtaining as much surplus-labor as possible from workers subsumed under it, exploiting workers every bit as cruelly and relentlessly as industrial capital.[20]

Akabori's argument is a simple one; namely, that services are also commodities, appear as such, and that these services are purchased by capital, which they serve to augment. Therefore, the "value" of a service is said to directly be the service itself. Living, functioning labor itself is thus said to be a commodity, and this at the same time is said to be value itself, with the magnitude of value being labor-time. In bourgeois society, then, labor itself is said to be value—directly speaking—rather than taking the form of value due to the contradictions of this society. This view may seem quite ridiculous, but Akabori is arguing very much in earnest. If labor were value directly speaking, however, what need would there be for the concept of value? Akabori's nonsensical idea reveals a limited understanding of the essence of commodity production and the concept of value.

Even setting these points aside for the moment, his view that service labor in modern society is carried out under capital as wage-labor to produce service commodities remains a complete muddle. Here the question revolves around *what* the service worker sells. The worker sells labor-power to the capitalist, not a service. In this case, the service is the use-value of labor-power, and this is no different from the case of productive workers. The capitalist, by selling the service to consumers, obtains a profit. The question is where this profit is derived from. As long as service industries do not produce their own value or surplus-value, it should be clear from the beginning that their profit is one part of the profit created by industrial capital, representing a deduction from it. This is essentially the same as how profits are made in the munitions or luxury-goods sectors. (Of course, the social significance of these industries, and that of the service industry in general, are completely different, but here the question, as Akabori emphasizes, centers on economic meaning.)

The profit of service capital is not derived from forcing workers who provide services to work beyond necessary labor-time, since the labor of service workers does not produce value in the first place and therefore is not a direct source of surplus-value. At the same time, as mentioned above, only paying

---

20. [Marx's discussion of commercial capital and commercial profit in part four of the third volume of *Capital* elucidates the point Hayashi is making here about service labor only being a source of profit for service capital in the negative sense and not actually producing surplus-value.]

workers the value of their labor-power can be a passive or negative source of profit for service capital.

This passive source of profit is a relation involving the social distribution of capital and the concomitant redistribution of overall social profit. Just as capital must be redistributed to service industries, so too is profit also naturally redistributed, and this must occur under capitalism. This is because capital as a self-valorizing value-body, in its abstract existence, seeks (average) profit in proportion to its own magnitude, and does indeed obtain this. With the demand for certain services, capital is distributed to this sector, and naturally profit is also redistributed, but this does not mean that profit is directly produced in the service industry. Akabori thinks that because service capital also obtains profit, this profit is *created* by service capital, as in the case of industrial capital. We must say, however, that it is exceedingly strange to believe that services produce value, and as a result create surplus-value. Akabori looks at a direct phenomenon of capitalism, namely the fact that service capital also obtains profit, and wonders how it could be said that this sector does not also produce or create profit. What he lacks is a true understanding or scientific concept of value.

The ideas of Akabori are in contradiction. He says that the value of a service commodity is the service labor itself, but if this were the case, why does the capitalist pay the worker in the form of wages? If it is the service labor itself that is being paid for, how is surplus-value possible? Or perhaps he is trying to say that the capitalist pays the worker for his labor-power rather than service labor. In this case, however, the service labor would appear as the use-value of the worker's labor-power, and the service labor would not directly be a commodity.

If the capitalist pays workers for service labor rather than labor-power, Akabori would be unable to account for the profit of the service capitalist, since the capitalist would be selling the consumer this same service labor. On the other hand, if the capitalist is said to pay service workers for their labor-power, rather than directly paying for the service labor itself, this would expose the fact that service labor is the use-value of this labor-power, so that the labor itself is not a commodity.

Akabori declares that labor is directly a commodity. But how can labor in a fluid state become a commodity? According to his concept, the use-value of the service commodity is the particular service itself, and the exchange-value is directly the service labor. Thus, ten hours of service labor, as such, represents value. This would basically mean that socialism is in effect within the service sector, since labor is not objectified as value and appears directly as labor-time. There is no need for Akabori to bring up the issue of value, and it would be sufficient for him to declare that value is understood as labor-time.

The idea that labor itself is a commodity is also bizarre. Is he referring to concrete useful labor or abstract human labor? If he is speaking of the former, this would mean that the labor which produces a use-value is value, thus adding on a further contradiction. If Akabori is referring instead to abstract human labor, then what is being sold is labor-time, and that labor-time is directly value. Thus, this would signify socialism, since labor would not appear in the form of value.

According to Akabori, service labor takes the form of value because it is also paid for with money. In fact, however, labor takes the form of value because it is unable to appear directly as labor-time and is objectified. It is clear that one cannot say that labor-time is directly value, while at the same time saying that labor takes the form of value. Akabori totally fails to understand the meaning of labor taking the form of value, as well as the significance and content of this foundation of capitalist relations of production.

Akabori makes the further claim that the exchange-value of a service commodity is determined by "the amount of human labor invested for its production." But didn't he just say a moment ago that this exchange-value is (the magnitude of) human labor provided for exchange as such? Does he think that objectified labor and living labor in a fluid state are identical? If he is saying that service labor itself, as living labor, is directly exchange-value, what exactly is the nature of the human labor that produces this service labor?

All that we have here is a playing with words and Akabori's ill-intentioned attempt to explain his dogma using pseudo-Marxist concepts. This nonsense has no real content and basically amounts to listing up a series of mutually contradictory terms. If service labor itself is the service—or what Akabori calls its use-value—how is he able to envisage labor as "producing" services, and thereby conclude that service labor and the labor that produces material things are identical? To say that "labor produces service labor," is nothing more than the tautology that "labor is produced by labor." This is completely different from human labor under capitalism producing a use-value in its concrete moment and value in its abstract moment.

At any rate, since Akabori defines the value of a service commodity as the service labor itself, he cannot say that the value of this commodity is determined by the amount of human labor objectified within it. This is complete nonsense that could only be written by someone who lacks all knowledge of

Marxism. But revisionists and opportunists like Akabori have no sense of shame, proudly displaying their own ignorance. Of course, this is not simply a question of ignorance. The fact that Akabori offers up such nonsense reveals his own theoretical bankruptcy. Not only is he incapable of consistently developing—to the end—his own theory of service labor and productive labor, but he is also quite unable to explain this using Marxist concepts. No matter how much he tries to dress up his theory to resemble Marxism, he cannot conceal the fact that, from start to finish, his work is simply revisionist blather.

Akabori says that Marx "indicated that labor value, as the substance of a commodity's exchange-value, is the thing that commodities basically have in common, not only material commodities, but service commodities as well."[21] But he is peddling a lie in claiming that Marx's labor theory of value explains what "commodities basically have in common," thus implying that such a theory also encompasses derivative "commodities" that are commodities in form only. And even putting this aside, his description of "labor-value as the substance of exchange-value" is a mess. Marx spoke of human labor as the substance of value, but what on earth does it mean to say that "labor-value is the substance of value"? People who have no qualms about using such irrational and incomprehensible expressions reveal the level of their own knowledge. Akabori's use of language in this manner exposes, in a classic form, the meaningless and empty nature of his own theory.

Actual Meaning of Passages Akabori Quotes

Akabori, in a fundamental sense, rejects the concepts held by Marx and presents views totally opposed to Marxism, but at the same time, in order to justify his dogma, he relies heavily upon Marx's words, offering up a mountain of quotations from his works! We will thus have to spend some time here addressing the actual meaning of the passages that Akabori cites. The following, from *Theories of Surplus Value*, is an example of the sort of passage that Akabori introduces in an attempt to justify his own absurd views:

> Is not the value of the commodities at any time in the market greater as a result of the "unproductive labor" than it would no without this labor? Are there not at every moment of time in the market, alongside wheat and meat, etc., also prostitutes, lawyers, sermons, concerts, theaters, soldiers, politicians, etc.? These lads or wenches do not get the corn and other nec-

21. Ibid., 180.

essaries or pleasures for nothing. In return they give or pester us with their services, which as such services have a use-value and because of their production costs also an exchange-value. Reckoned as consumable articles, there is at every moment of time, alongside the consumable articles existing in the form of goods, a quantity of consumable articles in the form of services. The total quantity of consumable articles is therefore at every moment of time greater than it would be without the consumable services. Secondly, however, the value too is greater; for it is equal to the value of the commodities which are given for these services, and is equal to the value of the services themselves. Since here, as in every exchange of commodity for commodity, equal value is given for equal value, the same value is therefore present twice over, once on the buyer's side and once on the seller's.[22]

Akabori's explanation of the passage above is complete nonsense and utterly wrong. For Akabori, this passage represents Marx himself confirming that services also produce value, and are thus a component part of the productive labor that makes up the national income. He also claims that in this passage Marx is saying that services are commodities because it is stated that services also have both use-value and exchange-value. He basically interprets Marx as saying that the total value of commodities is greater than it would have been without including service labor, and thus services are also value-creating labor.

We must first point out, however, that the fact that services have an exchange-value does not mean that service labor itself is value. It is Akabori, not Marx, who offers this irrational view. Rather, the labor-power that is the subject of service labor also has a "production cost," and for this reason has an exchange-value. This is why Marx says that this is a question that fundamentally concerns the theory of wages, and does not pertain to the theory of value. One cannot use this passage as the basis for claiming that Marx views service labor itself as being a commodity. Marx is only saying that service workers, like workers in general, also sell their labor-power as a commodity, and its exchange-value is determined by the worker's production costs just as in the case of ordinary productive workers. In other words, Marx is emphasizing that what is paid the service worker corresponds to the production costs of the service worker, not to the service labor itself, which is in fact the very opposite of what Akabori claims.

Incidentally, in the case of ordinary productive workers as well, the wage they are paid is certainly not payment for their "labor" but rather for their

---

22. *MECW*, vol. 31, 24.

labor-power—the labor-power commodity and its exchange-value—and any-one claiming to be a Marxist should know this. But Akabori argues that ser-vice workers are paid for their *labor*, and thus his view runs directly counter to Marxism, representing a step backward to the level of classical bourgeois econ-omists, who viewed wages as payment for labor, rather than for labor-power.

Would Akabori also say that the soldiers or religious ministers mentioned by Marx "sell" their services as commodities? If he claims that musicians and lawyers sell their own services as commodities, then naturally he would have to say the same for soldiers and ministers. In order to be consistent, Akabori is obliged to view soldiers and government officials as productive workers employed by the state, to which they sell their services. However, while Akabori includes musicians and others employed by capital within the concept of productive labor, he says that soldiers and bureaucrats are different. Isn't this a blatant contradiction? Isn't it clear that soldiers, whether employed by the state or some other party, provide a "use-value" to the state in exchange for their own services, and receive payment for their own labor-power?

In addition, there is Akabori's misunderstanding, or mistaken interpreta-tion, that Marx in the passage above is saying that the total value of commod-ities is augmented through service labor and therefore service labor is also value-producing productive labor. In fact, Marx is merely saying that through service labor the "total value" is increased *only* by that amount paid in compen-sation for such labor. This does not mean that service labor plays an active role in increasing the total social value that is produced, but rather that it only aug-ments this in a passive sense. If the total value is 500 this would not mean that 50 is added through service labor, but rather that 50 of this total is redistrib-uted to service labor, i.e. this part is deducted, and removing this 50 would only remove the burden borne by productive workers.

Marx is not saying that services produce new value or increase the total value. In the first place, from the beginning he speaks of "prostitutes, lawyers, ministers, musicians, theaters, soldiers, politicians" etc. as "unproductive workers," so there is no reason why he would think that their "labor" could create new value or expands the total social value. How does Akabori imagine that prostitutes produce value? Only a very strange and reactionary person could defend such exceedingly unproductive labor.

As is clear from the passage quoted above, Marx is clearly saying that ser-vices have an exchange-value based on their production cost; namely, the pro-duction cost or wage of the service worker. But Akabori argues in the following passage that what determines the exchange-value of the service commodity is the service labor itself:

> Service labor is certainly labor within the labor process, labor in a fluid state, and in this condition it appears on the market and is demanded by other people. In the case of service labor, labor in a fluid state is itself a use-value and in this state it is a (service) commodity. Its exchange-value is thus determined by the quantity of labor expended on its production.[23]

This is a bizarre view. He says that the exchange-value of the service commodity is the service labor itself, and therefore value is human labor, directly speaking, with the magnitude of this value directly being the labor-time of the service worker. Here labor-time is "purchased" directly with money, or labor-time and money are directly exchanged. In fact, however, what the "consumer" purchases is the service, i.e. a use-value, not its exchange-value. Therefore, here we have the domain of the marginal utility school; that is to say, the theory of value according to utility, a subjective theory of value, not the "objective" theory of value advocated by Ricardo or Marx. It is precisely for this reason that such views are embraced by vulgar scholars of all sorts in the JCP and revisionist camps, including Akabori and Isagai.

Thus far we have examined Akabori's theory of the commodity, but now we need to move on to his understanding of value—which we have already seen one aspect of in connection to his discussion of the commodity.

Akabori's "Theory of Value"

The great premise for Akabori Kunio is that the concept of productive labor refers to labor that produces surplus-value directly for capital. He confuses the historical form of productive labor with the concept of productive labor itself. Starting out from this mistaken premise, he proceeds to analyze the concept of value, and we must therefore also closely consider his understanding of this concept. Akabori says that it is impossible to grasp the concept of productive labor without a correct understanding of the labor theory of value and a concept of value, and I could hardly agree more. But is Akabori's theory of value really correct? Is it truly a labor theory of value? To begin answering these questions, I would like to introduce a few passages where he discusses the theory of value.

---

23. *Kachi to seisanteki rōdō*, 142.

Commodity-producing labor in one aspect is concrete, individual useful labor that creates concrete use-values, but on the other hand, it is a certain quantity of abstract social labor that creates value. Labor that produces the use-values of commodities can take a tangible, material form of existence, such as in the case of shoes or coats, but it can also provide society with immaterial use-values in the form of labor as it appears within the labor process, such as the educational labor of teachers or the medical service labor of doctors. In either case, however, as commodities provided to society for exchange, they are use-values that are the object of some human need, while at the same time having the character of value as a certain amount of human labor expended within social relations.

Just as the use-value of a commodity can take the form of a material good, so can it take the form of an immaterial service. In either case, however, the value of the commodity is something social, and contained within each commodity-body is nothing more than a certain quantity of socially-abstract human labor. This socially-abstract human labor, which is the value-substance of the commodity, can be objectified within a material commodity, but it can also be objectified within the immaterial commodity-body of a useful service.

Marx says that the labor objectified within a thing is value, and as long as one is talking about material commodities this is appropriate. However, in the case of immaterial commodities, since the commodity-producing labor does not assume a material form of existence, useful services in an immaterial shape are commodities in this given state, and this service labor is value as social human labor abstracted from its concrete useful nature.

Therefore, in the case of service commodities, the definition of value as the objectification of labor in material things is not appropriate. This does not mean, however, that service commodities have no value. Service-producing labor has the utility of satisfying the needs of other people, and is handed over to them via exchange; this is labor that produces a useful service, while also having the character of being social labor that produces the value of the service commodity.[24]

A correct understanding of the labor theory of value is the main prerequisite for a theory of productive labor. Correctly understanding the labor theory of value means properly grasping the meaning of what Marx calls "abstract human labor" or "social labor." Abstract human labor, which Marx refers to as the substance of value, and social labor are the same thing. This means that the concrete useful character of the labor that produces the commodity has been abstracted from, and in this sense, this is human labor of an abstract character, labor as one part of the total social labor in general,

24. Ibid., 18-9.

separated from its individual concrete nature. It is as this abstract character that individual labor is expended within commodity production society, and a certain quantity of this labor becomes the value of individual commodities. This is the (social) character of commodities as value. A commodity-production economy is composed of the social totality of individual private labor. Individual private labor is first of all expended as useful labor that produces some sort of useful thing, but by means of the reciprocal, complementary relation formed through the exchange of the product, labor comes to take on a social character and is mutually exchanged because it socially maintains the existence of human beings and their reproduction. In commodity-production society, since labor has this sort of character, when a commodity takes a material form, the "labor objectified in a thing" is value, but when a commodity takes the form of a service, labor in an active state, as it is, takes on the character of value. Those who think that labor is not value if it does not assume the form of a thing, do not understand the meaning of value. Value is the character of human labor within particular social relations, having a social character that does not contain any trace of the elements of things."[25]

According to Akabori, "value is the character of human labor" and labor "takes on the character of value." But since labor itself is not value, how can it take on the "character of value"? If he were saying that human labor *takes the form* of value under capitalist society, we would be able to understand him, but what on earth does it mean for labor to take on the character of value? Is this the irrational view of classical economists that labor itself (not labor power) is purchased, or an even more idiosyncratic concept?

Akabori's understanding of value is exceedingly vulgar. He declares that labor is value if it is one of the component parts of the total social labor. However, in socialist society, for example, individual labor from the outset is expended as one part of the total social labor, but this human labor certainly does not appear in the form of value. This alone reveals the bankruptcy of Akabori's nonsensical theory.

Lacking a concept of both productive labor and value, Akabori groups together productive labor in the original sense with unproductive labor, saying that both are one part of the total social labor, and thus claiming that unproductive labor is actually productive labor. He argues that there is no distinction on average between productive and unproductive labor in the sense of being individual private labor, and that this individual labor can be grouped together

---

25. Ibid., 106-7.

in terms of combining to form the total labor. Akabori believes it is clear that service labor is also *social* labor, one of its constituent elements, since within the framework of capitalist production relations it is expended as one part of the overall labor. In short, Akabori's impulse or motive is to justify and defend all labor, no matter how reactionary and parasitic or bourgeois and empty it may be.

From the outset Akabori feels no need to make a conceptual distinction between productive and unproductive labor. This is natural because he views any labor within society as being productive labor, provided that it produces surplus-value (read: profit). All "labor" under capitalism is thus considered good and useful. Unproductive labor, no matter how ridiculous, is considered productive if it brings about profit for capital. No one could deny that this view is the general standpoint of the bourgeoisie and that Akabori is merely rehashing their views.

Akabori rejects the concept of value in terms of being labor *objectified* within a commodity, on the basis of the argument that value is actually the "character of human labor within particular social relations" which does not "contain any trace of the elements of things." Granted, Marxists accept that value "does not contain any trace of the elements of things," but at the same time no Marxist would deny that value is labor "objectified" within a commodity. Akabori believes that on the basis of value being a social substance and not containing "any trace of the elements of things," he is able to negate the idea that human labor is value to the extent that it is objectified within a commodity. For this reason, he has no qualms about treating labor in its active state as directly being value. What our vulgar scholar fails to realize, however, is that by doing this, he ends up concealing the entire basis of capitalist exploitation.

It would of course be incorrect to understand the objectification of human labor as somehow being objectification in a material sense. This is ultimately the objectification of social relations, or to borrow the view of Marx, the commodity is seen as a certain quantity of labor. Nevertheless, it is precisely because labor is objectified within the commodity that the commodity expresses a certain amount of value. If value were merely a "social character," how exactly would Akabori be able to gauge the determination of a commodity's value? Needless to say, it is impossible to establish a quantitative determination of some character or quality. Clearly, Akabori has forfeited any concept of value, and completely fails to understand the necessity, contradictions, or historical limitations of commodity production in general, where labor is expressed as value—as labor objectified in a commodity—so that it necessarily assumes the form of value. In short, he is ignorant of the very foundations of capitalism. It takes quite a crude and peculiar person to think, as this revisionist scholar does, that the scientific concept of value can be negated on the basis of the observation that the concept of value "does not contain any trace of the elements of things." Indeed, the person who does "not understand the meaning of value" is none other than Professor Akabori himself.

Not every sort of labor in an active state takes on the character of value. (If this were true, human labor under socialism would also "take on the character of value" or, to borrow another expression from Akabori, "produce value.") Akabori's argument is unclear. Is he trying to say that what service workers sell—namely their activity itself—is a commodity? If so, this would amount to viewing what workers sell to capitalists as labor itself, thus losing sight of the secret of exploitation and reverting back to the level of the classical economists, who for the most part instinctively concealed this fact. Or is he trying to say that service activities, directly speaking, have value (or more correctly: price)? It is possible, of course, to examine in what way "labor" has value (read: price), what determines this price, and how it is determined. But this is completely different from saying that service labor is value directly speaking (or "takes on the character of value").

For Akabori, moreover, all "labor" in capitalist society is value or the substance of value, since he defines labor itself as also being value. He views labor directly as value, and therefore value is defined as being the sum of the labor objectified in things *plus* living labor (service labor). Not surprisingly, he does not go so far as to say that service labor is objectified labor, defining it instead as "labor in an active state," i.e. living labor or labor that is not objectified. He says that this labor in an active state is value in terms of being one part of the social labor. Akabori thus claims that living labor, as such, is value.

This, of course, is an outrageous claim. It could be said that the "content" of value is social labor, but the fact that social labor itself is not value should be evident to a Marxist. If social labor were directly value, every notion concerning value would become muddled, and there would be no need to exert an effort to analyze or clarify this concept. This would mean that the issue of why social labor necessarily takes the form of value, and the significance of the value-form of labor, would not even enter into the equation. By saying that social labor is directly value, Akabori has revealed to us that he does not understand the fundamental concept of value. He even neglects the basic distinction between capitalism and socialism—i.e. the concept of the emancipation of labor and the breaking free from the historical stage where labor takes the form of value.

Akabori thinks that the total labor of society, or aggregate social labor, is the sum of the labor objectified in material commodities plus the service labor. Therefore, labor that produces material commodities, and labor that is itself a commodity as service labor, are each one part of the total social labor. Individual labor is thus seen as directly being one part of the total social labor, and in this way the concept of value is dissolved within the concept of total social labor. It is clear that Akabori overlooks the historical form of capitalist labor, which holds little interest for him. He claims that labor is directly one part of social labor, but this is something that can only be realized under socialism. The fact that Akabori introduces a determination of labor that can only exist under socialism, far from being evidence of a revolutionary nature, simply reveals that he has utterly failed to grasp the historical particularity of the labor that produces capitalist commodities. On top of this, Akabori states that value is a "social character" that use-value-producing labor assumes via the exchange of use-values.

> This is because commodity-producing labor, within the exchange relation between commodities, comes into contact with labor that produces other commodities, and through this mediation a social relationship is formed between commodity producers, so that commodity-producing labor takes on the social character of exchange-value within this social relationship. The substance of the exchange-value of a commodity is the quantity of human labor necessary to produce it. The value of a commodity is the labor expended for the production of the commodity, the labor embodied in the course of its production, and the labor objectified in the commodity in this manner. Marx says that labor objectified in a thing is value, but more precisely this is the idea that labor objectified in the commodity *qua* thing is value, or labor objectified in a commodity is value. Since the value of a commodity only appears in the exchange relation with another commodity, value only actually appears as exchange-value. The value of a commodity is labor-value, and exchange-value is the phenomenal form of value. Since labor-value is something with this sort of character, unless labor produces a commodity that appears on the exchange market, no value can be produced.[26]

---

26. Ibid., 225-6.

It may seem that Akabori is offering a valid idea here, but what he is basically saying is that "value is labor." He means this in a direct sense. Value is said to be labor that has "taken on the character" of exchange-value. He is certainly not saying—and is indeed incapable of saying—that labor is the substance of value, which is Marx's definition of value. Even when Akabori says that value is labor objectified in the commodity, this does not refer simply to it being objectified as a substance. Rather, he frames the question in terms of its appearance as a character or quality [*seishitsu*]. There is a fundamental difference, however, between "appearing as a quality" and being "objectified as a substance." In the former case, value definitely cannot appear as money (in a *visible* form). But value exists as such precisely because it progresses to the point of assuming a "physical" form as money. Within money, an essential aspect of value is revealed, but Akabori treats this as an insignificant matter. The issue for Akabori is to emphasize that service labor is also directly value, and for this reason, the idea of value being objectified labor as a "substance" is problematic. For Akabori, everything comes down to the "character" of social labor and nothing more. Of course, Marxists do not deny that labor objectified as value is social labor, with a particular historical "character," but this is a separate issue from defining value *as* the "character of labor," which is childish nonsense.

Akabori openly rejects the idea that value is objectified labor, which is the basis of Marx's concept of value. Value cannot be the activity or active living labor itself. He needs to recall Marx's view that the substance of value is human labor, but human labor itself is not directly value, and cannot be, as this would fly in the face of logic. It should be clear that Akabori has little understanding of the objectification of labor. He vulgarly interprets this as having some sort of physical meaning, despite Marx emphasizing that even if a commodity is held up to the light, "though worn to a thread," it remains impossible to see its value. The issue revolves around a social relation; the question of how a human, social relation penetrates the exchange of social products. What is expressed in the value of a commodity is a social relation between people, not some sort of "material" relation. Akabori naively confuses commodity-value (objectified labor) and labor itself. And on the basis of this confusion, he argues that service labor is directly a commodity. Akabori claims to have "learned from Marx" that value exists not only within a commodity-body, but also within something that is not a commodity-body. That is, he says that labor can still very much be considered productive even without producing a "genuine commodity"—which is the unity of material wealth (use-value) and exchange-value—and he claims this is also the view Marx held.

> Since modern Marxist economists understand the substance of value as always taking the form of thingified labor [*bukkashita rōdō*], where labor is *objectified* or *embodied* within a thing, they claim that only labor that produces surplus-value in the form of material commodities can be considered productive labor. These economists believe that labor which does not produce some material thing, even if carried out as wage-labor under capital, is merely the production of services and not the production of value or surplus-value.
>
> Marx, however, explained that labor that produces surplus-value directly for capital is productive labor, while at the same time strictly rejecting, as completely irrelevant, the question of whether or not labor produces a material thing. This reveals that Marx viewed labor that is the substance of surplus-value, and therefore value, as being social labor with no connection at all to the material [*sozaiteki*] character of the product of labor. This is the reason why Marx criticized the mercantilists and physiocrats, who only recognized value and surplus value in the substantial form of money or agricultural products, while also criticizing Adam Smith, who at best could only see value and surplus-value in the form of tangible commodities in general...Therefore, the ability to correctly understand Marx's theory of productive labor depends on adhering to the labor theory of value, which is the core of Marxist economics, while also being able to recognize value within the immaterial commodity-body.[27]

Akabori is fond of pointing out that value is also created by transport labor, which does not make material things, and this is certainly true. However, it is an elementary principle of science that one cannot take an exceptional case and treat it as having a general character, whereas exceptions can—and indeed must—be explained on the basis of general principles. Even though transport labor does not bring about any "physical" change in its object, since the object of labor is simply the changing of locations, this is one exceptional case, whereas productive labor exists as such precisely because it *generally* acts upon a natural object and alters it.

Akabori says that, "economists prior to Marx, who were unable to grasp value as this sort of social entity, could only understand value as being some sort of 'thing' or as having a connection to things."[28] Akabori also claims,

---

27. Ibid., 16-7.

while quoting from Marx, that "the materialization of labor, etc. should not be understood in the manner of Smith in the Scottish or sensual manner," and that "it is possible for commodity-producing labor to leave no trace within a thing."[29] Certainly the classical economists were wrong to grasp value as being a property of things, but this does not change the fact that the "material bearer" of exchange-value is the commodity as *use-value*.

Even though, in some cases, an actual trace of commodity-producing labor does not remain in the material thing, in general such traces of human labor do remain because the great significance of human labor is that it works upon nature, altering it, so that the object becomes something that is useful to human beings. The fact that petroleum, for instance, can be turned into nylon and other synthetic materials, or transformed into a number of artificial resins, is an example of traces of labor remaining in material things. The possibility that traces of commodity-producing labor will not remain in a thing, such as in the case of transport labor, does not negate the fact that, in general, human labor exists as such for the very reason that it does leave some trace within a material thing, which involves the transformation of nature.

Akabori seizes upon one individual phenomenon, and by emphasizing that such a case can in fact occur, he obscures the essential issue. Even though transport labor, which enters into the commodity as a part of its value, does not leave any trace in the commodity as a thing, it should still be immediately apparent that this does not negate that the particular commodity being transported is an altered form of nature as the outcome of productive labor. Even if traces of the transport labor do not remain in the thing *qua* commodity, it is a matter of course that the labor itself is inseparable from, and forms one part of, the human labor that performs the great role of altering nature to make it useful. If this were not the case, transport labor could not exist as the transporting of commodities in the first place.

The fact that value is not a property of things simply means that the value of a commodity is value as a social substance, not as some sort of material thing. Value takes on a material form and appears as such—for example, as money—but this does not mean that value is actually a material thing (or some quality or property of things). At the same time, however, value cannot exist without the commodity-body, and it is only value *through* it. For this very rea-

---

28. Ibid., 21.
29. Ibid., 87.

son, Marx said that the use-value of a commodity is the "bearer" of value, with the production of a socially useful thing as the premise. The question revolves around this taking the form of the commodity.

Akabori claims that, given the flourishing service sector today, Marxism should somehow be altered, and he tampers with the Marxist labor theory of value. He offers the following reasons for why his own views on this matter were not incorporated within *Capital*:

> In *Capital*, Marx primarily takes the world of material commodities as his object of study, elucidating a theory of labor value in line with the reality of material commodities. But at the time he wrote the manuscript known as *Theories of Surplus Value*, just prior to *Capital*, Marx did take up the study of service commodities, albeit partially, and he examined the exchange-value of commodities based on the reality of both material commodities and service commodities, thereby completing his labor theory of value. The value of a commodity is not the labor congealed within a thing. Value is the social character of the human labor that produces a commodity, which is a product with a social character, and in this sense the value of a commodity is social labor. This is human social labor that is expended uniformly, whether it be for the production of material commodities or for the production of service commodities."[30]

Akabori emphasizes what he considers to be a realistic approach because he mistakes his own vulgar perspective of seizing on superficial phenomena as being realistic, while viewing scientific concepts as unrealistic and abstract. He lacks the ability to understand a scientific concept, only setting his sights on, or paying attention to, phenomena as they appear directly to the senses, and it is from this standpoint that he carries out an attack on Marxism. This is reminiscent of how the defenders of the Ptolemaic system noted how the sun crossed over their heads, and mistaking this for a "sense of reality," deemed it unrealistic to say that the earth instead orbited the sun, and argued that it was idealism or a contradiction of this common sense to consider such a view as science.

Akabori criticizes "dogmatic" Marxists for believing every utterance made by Marx, but in fact he makes a habit of doing this himself, mistakenly interpreting various isolated passages from *Theories of Surplus Value*. He is well aware that when Marx provides the concept of value at the beginning of *Capi-*

---

30. Ibid., 181-2.

tal, commodities are limited to material commodities. Since this fact inconveniences him, Akabori tries to conceal this plain truth by saying that Marx had already provided a concept of value that included immaterial commodities in *Theories of Surplus Value*. In reality, however, this sort of explanation does little to benefit Akabori.

If, as he claims, Marx had already "completed" a labor theory of value that included service labor prior to writing *Capital*, one would have imagined that this view would be manifested or reflected within *Capital*, and it is odd that the "completed" theory presented in *Capital* is restricted to only deal with material commodities. If Marx had already developed a correct labor theory of value that also included service labor at the time of writing *Theories of Surplus Value*, why wasn't this standpoint "applied" to his latter work, considering that *Capital* is the great summation of all his research? Does Akabori believe that Marx regressed to the point of abandoning his earlier, "correct" standpoint; or does he have some other explanation? If Marx did take a step backward, it would be necessary to explain why. Akabori is obliged to account for this, but he seems to prefer viewing it as an "eternal mystery."

In reality, however, the fact that Marx provides a concept of value in *Capital* that is limited to material commodities demonstrates that this is the *essential* concept. It is irrational and unthinkable to argue that Marx, in providing the concept of value in *Capital*, set aside his correct view and regressed to the point of providing a trivial or incomplete concept. How can Akabori explain this rationally? I can't imagine that he means to suggest Marx was being intellectually "stingy." Akabori holds on to his fixed idea that Marx developed a different concept in *Theories of Surplus Value* from the one presented in *Capital*, when it should be perfectly clear that the ideas expressed in both works are fundamentally the same. Granted, *Theories of Surplus Value* is a collection of notes, a manuscript that is not put into exact order, so that there are many ideas presented in an incomplete or somewhat ambiguous manner, and these are the sections that Akabori seizes upon to construct his own dogma. At this point, however, we will have to take leave of Akabori and move on.

Isagai Nobuo's Theory of Service Labor

One person who "developed" Akabori's theory of productive labor is Isagai Nobuo, author of *Seisanteki rōdō no riron: sābisu bumon no keizai*. In this book, Isagai not only defends Akabori's theory, but also attempts to "historically" position the theory of service labor and productive labor, "boldly" and openly attempting to refute Marxism in the name of Marx. At the same time, he clearly advances beyond Akabori by providing a practical foundation for this theory. According to Isagai, the proportional growth of the service industry justifies a (structural-) reformist and opportunist political line.

Isagai is not unfamiliar with the significance of productive labor in the Marxist sense, but like Akabori, he staunchly rejects Marx's idea (the labor theory of value) according to which productive labor alone is the source of commodity-value. He adopts a standpoint similar to Akabori in terms of saying that Marx presented such a view in *Capital*, but proposed a different idea in *Theories of Surplus Value*, where he is said to have recognized service labor as also producing value. Isagai thus directs his attack at the most fundamental position of Marxism. He recognizes the significance of Marx's concept of productive labor, but claims it is mistaken to see it as the substance of value.

> The concept of productive labor according to the original definition indicates the primary role of productive praxis within human activity, as well as indicating that through productive praxis, or labor, human beings demonstrate their capabilities, and that mechanized large-scale industry, the highest developmental stage of human ability (productive power), particularly the system of automated machinery, is the material prerequisite for the future, free community or true human society that sets as its objective the development of the individual's qualities. This can be said to indicate Marx's view of labor as well as his theory of the human essence. Therefore, to understand this as the foundation that demarcates the boundaries of value-creating labor would mean losing sight of its rich, original content.[31]

What Isagai is saying here is a muddle. Why does he recognize the significance of productive labor in the original sense, but then say that this is in contradiction with exposing the essence of value? It should be clear at a glance that there is no contradiction here, since what emerges from the exposure of this essence is an awareness of the "sacred" human obligation and necessity to abolish the historical society in which productive labor takes the form of value. Isagai lacks an awareness of labor taking the form of value, of the historical limitations of this sort of society, and the consequent need and necessity to overturn this society and shift to a type of cooperative society (socialism/communism), and in this way he exposes his own essentially bourgeois nature.

---

31. Isagai Nobuo, *Seisanteki rōdō no riron: sābisu bumon no keizai* (Tokyo: Aoki Shoten, 1977), 27.

Isagai, like Akabori, mechanically separates the concept of original productive labor from the formal (and to this extent, bourgeois) concept of productive labor. While they speak of the distinction between the two concepts, saying both are essentially distinct from one another, both men remain quite unaware of the unity of these concepts, that is to say, how they are the same in one respect. To be more precise, they sever the original concept from the formal concept, and treat the two as being totally distinct concepts, for the sake of constructing their own dogmas.

Isagai's fundamental concept is that labor in the service sector also forms one part of social labor. He claims that this was not true during Marx's own lifetime, but has since become the case under modern capitalism, where productive power has been developed to a higher level. On this point, Isagai surpasses even Akabori, defining service labor in general as productive labor, so that service labor is uniformly productive labor even if it is not exchanged against capital and does not generate a profit.

> The form of service labor is, in the modern period, fundamentally different from the era of Marx, shifting from "labor exchanged against revenue" to "labor exchanged against capital," and since the service sector is one important part of the social division of labor, which has become a wide field for the exploitation of labor by capital, we cannot ignore this sector.[32]

> Modern service labor is incorporated within the system of the social division of labor and subsumed within the law of value and the law of surplus-value. In Marx's own era, service labor fundamentally took the form of individual services provided to the ruling class, and since this was sustained by a redistribution of surplus-value, this was something parasitical. Compared to this, the expansion of the service sector under modern capitalism is, in a way, the development of productive power, possessing the positive aspect of expanding and deepening the social division of labor, while its parasitic or decadent quality arises from the behavior inherent to capital of seeking and expanding profit. This sort of parasitic and decadent quality can also be seen in the sector of material production. Saying that value cannot be created without the production of some tangible product, and that [service labor] is maintained through the redistribution of revenue and is parasitic in this sense, ignores the difference in the developmental stage of the social division of labor between Marx's era and the present one, and overlooks the penetration of capitalist laws within the service sector, which

---

32. Ibid., 72.

in turn potentially leads to the incorrect positing of the class position of educational and medical workers.[33]

Regardless of whether it is exchanged against capital, service labor remains unproductive labor in the original sense. It is only from the bourgeois perspective that such labor is manifested as producing profit, and thus appears to be productive labor.

Isagai says that in the past service labor depended upon redistributed surplus-value, whereas now the situation is different since this labor produces its own value and surplus-value, thus existing as one part of the social distribution of labor. He claims that even if there is a "parasitical quality" of modern service labor, it stems from the nature of capital "seeking and expanding profit" rather than from the essence of service labor itself. This last bit of reasoning is unclear, since Isagai begins by saying that service labor is productive *because* it also creates profit, before going on to say that services take on a parasitic quality because capital pursues profits. Is service labor productive because it produces profit, or does this instead reveal the parasitic nature of service labor? Isagai fails to inform us which view he considers to be correct, offering us instead whichever arbitrary idea he finds convenient. Echoing the ideas of the bourgeoisie, he cheerfully claims that the expansion of services is a manifestation of social progress, while at the same time referring to the deepening parasitism of modern capitalism. Like a bat flying back and forth, Isagai comes up with whatever argument happens to suit him at a particular moment.

Isagai claims that the rise in the productive power of labor appears as the diminishment of the relative importance of material production within the national economy, and the expansion of the relative importance of the service sector." And he praises this as social progress. But it is clear at a glance that this is nothing but a clumsy rehashing of the logic of "economic evolution" advanced by bourgeois scholars, who are fond of portraying social progress as the advance of an "industrial structure" composed of primary, secondary, and tertiary industries, with the tertiary industries mainly corresponding to the service sector. In short, this is a shallow "historical view" that is dazzled by the surface phenomena of bourgeois society. For instance, the rise in the productive power of productive labor is, above all, a drastic shortening of labor-time, and should appear as such, and indeed would appear clearly as such in a social-

---

33. Ibid., 42-3.

ist society. But in bourgeois society, this is manifested as a rise in surplus-value and the swelling of parasitical industries, and therefore in the number of parasitical "workers" as well. Petty-bourgeois theorists end up chasing after such phenomena, and are able to do little more than glorify this status quo.

Isagai depicts this process as being, at the same time, "the deepening and expansion of the social division of labor." He claims that in Marx's own era the social division of labor only included the field of productive labor in the original sense, but that in the contemporary world, this division of labor has expanded and deepened to include the sector of service labor. This philistine seems to have even overlooked the fact that Marx viewed the transcending of the division of labor as one of the most essential elements of socialism. He is thrilled by the prospect of the "expansion and deepening of the division of labor" to include the service sector, but this only underscores his class standpoint and ineptitude, and Isagai is not even aware that he reveals this to his own shame!

Here we will look at a few passages where Isagai develops his rather appalling theory. As one example, I would like to consider a few passages where he comments on the following passage from Lenin's *The Development of Capitalism in Russia*:

> The development of commodity economy leads to an increase in the number of separate and independent branches of industry; the tendency of this development is to transform into a special branch of industry the making not only of each separate product, but even of each separate part of a product—and not only the making of a product, but even the separate operations of preparing the product for consumption.[34]

Isagai writes:

> Here what Lenin calls "the separate operations of preparing the product for consumption" likely refers to workers engaged in the occupations of transport, communication, and commerce which he refers to as the "semi-productive population." Today the sector that provides intangible objects of consumption (education, medicine, transportation, culture, entertainment, etc.) is expanding, and since production and consumption temporally coincide in this sector, this expansionary trend is manifested as the process of

---

34. Vladimir Lenin, *Collected Works*, vol. 3 (Moscow: Progress Publishers 1961), 37.

consumption also being subsumed within the system of the social division of labor. Thus, in addition to Lenin's formula regarding the development of the social division of labor, we must add on a formula according to which "the service sector, which functions within the consumption process of society and creates use-values that do not take a tangible form, undergoes an expansion as a result of the development of social and cultural needs and the social integration of the consumption process."[35]

"Fully-developed individuals" or "developed social individuals" are made possible by means of services such as education, medicine, culture, and entertainment, which act directly upon human beings. Services that formerly were the object of luxury consumption for the ruling class have entered into the formation of the labor capacity as a result of changes in the labor process through large-scale industry. In other words, they have turned into use-values that are again incorporated into social reproduction or incorporated into the system of the social division of labor. The basis for the inevitability of the expansion of the service sector under capitalism is, first of all, that the development of large-scale industry, which is the original material foundation of capitalism, necessitates and demands the development or qualitative improvement of human labor-power with the highest productive power.[36]

The establishment and development of large-scale industry, which is the original material foundation of capitalism, necessitates the expansion of the service sector in order to cultivate the labor capacity. For the working class, the expansion of service consumption brings about the development of intellectual and cultural abilities, fostering workers as the bearers of the future society with the capacity to manage and administer…The rapid expansion of tertiary industries is on the one hand the expression of the relative expansion of the labor process engaged in the joint office work for social production, and therefore of the proletariat that carries out such work, which signifies that the socialization of labor has reached the point where management labor is socialized. This expansion of tertiary industries can be said to have positive significance in terms of creating the material foundation, as well as the subjective conditions, for full socialization.[37]

For Marx, the "moments" that give birth to the full development of the individual, if we set aside the revolutionary change of social organization, are an increase in the productive power of labor, the resulting shortening of labor-

---

35. *Seisanteki rōdō no riron*, 109.
36. Ibid., 119-20.
37. Ibid., 126.

time and expansion of free-time, and material abundance. Isagai, however, views this development as being made possible by the flourishing of the service sector, focusing exclusively on this particular moment.

But the development of productive power and the flourishing of the service sector are two completely different things. This foolish scholar, by using the term "social division of labor," treats a broad sector of service workers as being autonomous and juxtaposes them with the rest of the population. In other words, he says that these workers, by being solely engaged in the service industry, render a service to the rest of the population, dedicating themselves to the noble profession of helping others become "fully developed human beings." What we have here is the typical sort of theory espoused by educators and religious ministers. Isagai has thus fashioned an image of service workers that is sure to please intellectuals.

According to Isagai's view, an entertainment program on TV, any one of the "vulgar" shows that flood the airwaves, could be seen as necessary for the creation of "fully developed individuals," having a role to play and a reason for existing, while also representing an important part of the social division of labor. Of course, this would also be true for the sex industry, and in order to be consistent Isagai is obliged to refer to such examples. Indeed, one could list up examples, *ad infinitum*, of things such as vulgar TV shows, the sex industry, pachinko, horse racing, and so on. According to Isagai's view, such examples would have to be seen, and positively evaluated, as examples of productive industries, as a deepening and expansion of the division of labor, and as forming one part of the total social labor, with the workers engaged in such undertakings viewed as the creators of value and surplus-value.

Isagai says that service labor is something that is produced and then sold. But service labor itself is an activity, not something that is produced through this labor and then sold. His concept of "productive" is an exceedingly forced one. Isagai, like Akabori, directly equates "being sold as a commodity" with "possessing value." Both lack a theory of value and in this sense are essentially on the same level as bourgeois economics ("modern economics"). Like Unoists—as well as Hiromatsu Wataru and his followers—Isagai and Akabori are incapable of understanding the labor theory of value.

Isagai speaks of the "highest productive power of labor-power," but this empty phrase, while similar to expressions used by Marx, is a typical concept held by Stalinists, who have one-dimensionally and abnormally expanded the meaning of Marx's own terminology, and this can be seen as a concept that corresponds to one of the "individualistic" or "humanistic" moments of Stalinism. Productive power is, of course, essentially the productive power of labor, and this is a concept that expresses a certain relation between the worker (labor-power) and the means of production. To this extent, the worker as subject is also one moment, but the emphasis in this concept is placed on the means of production and this stems from the essence of the matter. Moreover, everyone knows that Marx's formulation of the materialist conception of history places the emphasis on the means of production.[38] It is no accident that Isagai would introduce this Stalinist concept here, as he shares their petty-bourgeois "humanism" and has formed a "united front" with them in this sense.

Isagai views the prosperity of the service industry as being a fundamental moment in the shift from capitalism to socialism. He even goes so far as to say that within the flourishing service industry there is a relative expansion of "labor" specializing in the management of workers, which represents one moment in the shift to socialism. With this outrageous theory, Isagai glorifies the workers who bear the functions of capital by supervising other workers for capital's sake, and says that the emergence and expansion of this type of worker—with the "capability to manage and administer workers"—puts in place the "subjective conditions" needed for full socialization, and in this sense the expansion of the service sector has positive significance. This shows the extent to which he has fallen into an opportunistic and bourgeois standpoint.

He also says that the service industry is made up of "labor that exchanges against capital," and therefore (?):

> The service sector is a huge part of the social division of labor, and becomes a wide field for the exploitation of labor by capital. And for this reason, the service sector, which was abstracted from in *Capital*, should be seen as an extension of the definition of the transport industry.[39]

This view is rather extraordinary. Marx views the transport industry as an extension of the labor process, as one part of the production process, and for this reason transport labor was seen as productive labor. It should be clear that service labor in general cannot be posited as an "extension" of the production

---

38. Consider Marx's statement in *The German Ideology* that "the hand-mill gives you society with the feudal lord; the steam-mill, society with the industrial capitalist."
39. Ibid., 112-3.

process. Isagai has no qualms about making use of Marx's theory by distorting its content and interpreting it in an arbitrary manner, just up to the point where Marx's views can no longer co-exist with his own dogma.

Isagai does not openly admit to rejecting Marx's theory, but by mixing up a number of arguments, and treating them in a relativistic and distorted manner, he does in fact reject it. This is done in a variety of ways. Isagai says that Marx's theory only applied to his own era and is no longer relevant today, arguing that Marx did not posit service labor as being productive labor in *Capital* but had already done so in *Theories of Surplus Labor*. Isagai, for instance, advances the following argument:

> In Marx's era, service labor was still not incorporated within the system of the social division of labor, and was fundamentally provided for by the lavishness of the ruling class in the form of individual services performed by those dependent upon this class. It is important to note the fundamental difference between the productive power and development of the social division of labor in Marx's era and that of the present period.[40]

This view does not stand up to scrutiny, however. It should be clear that Marx's concept of distinguishing between labor that is productive or unproductive in the original sense is "applicable" as long as human society continues, regardless of whether it is "Marx's era" or any other, and that in the capitalist "stage" productive labor does not become unproductive labor, or vice versa. The fact that unproductive labor can also be seen as productive labor according to the formal definition under the capitalist mode of production does not imply a difference between capitalism in the era of Marx and in the current period. As long as capitalism remains capitalism, the question will be presented in essentially the same manner, and there is no basis for claiming that a difference has emerged since Marx's time. Marx has already provided us with a clear explanation of this problem, and the fact of the matter is that Akabori and Isagai are incapable of understanding what he has written. Marx, for example, clearly emphasizes that workers in luxury shops "are productive, as far as they increase the capital of their master; unproductive as to the material result of their labor."[41]

---

40. Ibid., 165.
41. *Grundrisse*, 273.

There are many cases where something that is productive for the bourgeoisie is unproductive when viewed from the perspective of society. The classic example of this is the large number of workers engaged in the munitions industry or involved in the sex industry. Everyone knows that these workers ensure profits—indeed, enormous profits—for capital, and according to the view held by Akabori and Isagai, such workers are also very much productive workers because of this. The labor that creates weapons or labor engaged in military affairs would have to also be seen as productive labor, since nothing could be clearer than the fact that this provides some kind of "service."[42] In this way, all kinds of unproductive labor are transformed into productive labor.

Isagai's Theory and Practical Opportunism

Isagai's theory is an explanation of service labor and productive labor, but it takes on special significance in terms of exposing the sort of opportunism that such theories can be practically connected to, and what sort of nonsensical (Stalinist, JCP-style) reformism results from this. Isagai combines his own theory of service labor with contemptible structural reformist opportunism. For instance, he argues:

> The revolutionary change of the labor process requires a rise in the educational level of workers, but under capitalism education is turned into a means of structuring, discriminating, and screening to create a group of workers with abilities that suit the needs of capital rather than aiming for the full development of human capabilities and the cultivation of creative abilities. This is an important aspect of the management of labor-power by the government and monopoly capital. The movement made up of citizens and educational workers seeking to establish and expand the right to learn and democratic education, comes to occupy an important position in terms of the prospects of changing society in a revolutionary way.[43]

> The futurological conception that the contradictions of capitalism will be alleviated or dissolved on the basis of a decrease in the industrial proletariat involved in direct material production is a one-dimensional technological theory that severs the tendency of the social labor process to develop into a process of intellectual and scientific control and regulation from the inherent laws of capitalism and the class struggle. Marx already foresaw the shift

---

42. Soldiers, for instance, provide the indispensable "service of national defense" to a class state!
43. *Seisanteki rōdō no riron*, 37-8.

to a post-industrial society as well as the fact that this was linked to the inevitability of the overall dissolution of capitalism and the shift to socialism…

The emergence of a techno-structure and intellectual workers is not the appearance of a new middle class, but rather essentially a "change in the composition of the working class" in response to a new developmental stage of social labor. The crude theory according to which the proletariat has already been incorporated within the system is just the reverse side of theories that defend the [current] system and speak of the dissolution of the power of capital. The expansion of the so-called techno-structure demonstrates that the working class has already gained the ability to manage society and that capital has lost all of its functions concerning the actual conditions of the labor process, and at this point in time has become a useless parasite that only exists in terms of ownership.[44]

The view expressed above is identical to the so-called theory of the rule of managers—i.e. today's typical reformist ideology which claims that the ownership function of capital has declined and that the influence and rule of technocrats ("techno-structure") within management and the workplace is expanding, which in itself signifies a shift to socialism and is in fact preparing the way for this shift.

What Isagai fails to understand is that managers are in charge of a company only as the bearers of the functions of capital, as the *personification of capital*, and in this sense they are every bit as much capitalists as the owner-capitalists. By referring to functional capitalists as the representatives of the working class, he has in fact fallen into a bourgeois standpoint. Isagai's ultra-optimistic theory that workers are not "co-opted by the system and are still a revolutionary and socialistic class" stems from his belief that functional capitalists are the representatives of the working class, and the fact that he notices that they are the officially recognized bearers of modern capitalism. This is nothing more than the idea that the bearers of modern capitalism can at the same time become the representatives—the vanguard or champions—of the working class, thus presenting a convenient shortcut to the liberation of the working class. This ultra-optimism is a classic example of opportunism that is of no use at all, and in fact quite harmful. Isagai goes on to offer the following view:

---

44. Ibid., 38-9.

The idea that "marketing is consumer-centered" is a fantasy; the substance of which is the imposition of a mass-production, mass-consumption life-style by means of mass advertising, mass consumption, and mass market-ing.

This leads to the enormous waste and squandering of materials and labor-power within the national economy, which is one significant cause of today's urban and pollution problems; namely the worsening of the social living environment and natural environment, the proliferation of traffic accidents and disasters, the overall structural deformation of living space, as well as the decay of spiritual life. This is a manifestation of the aim of pro-duction being the pursuit of profit for capital and the inherent contradic-tions of capitalism in the current stage of capitalist production, where the consumptive activity of the masses does not improve and the achievement of developing productive power is not made use of for the improvement of the welfare of the people. Today, the movement to establish the "sover-eignty of the consumer," which opposes the "dependency effect" generated and manipulated by monopoly capital, and the civic movement against the degradation of the physical and living environment resulting from monop-oly, represent important aspects of the modern class struggle.[45]

The incorporation into the state sector of the branches of labor that origi-nally formed one part of the social division of labor, i.e. the organization of "unproductive workers," is on the one hand the strengthening of the man-agement apparatus, but on the other hand this is something that leads to an expansion in the possibility of people's democratic control over the national economy. The expansion and strengthening of the administrative and financial apparatus of the state consequently results in removing the man-agement of the state structure from the hands of a specially privileged class and placing it instead in the hands of the enormous mass of proletarianized government workers. This tendency shows that "capital ownership" has already become nothing more than a useless outgrowth. The strengthening of the apparatus of rule invariable leads to the social integration of the peo-ple and the development of their management capabilities, and the more that this is strengthened, the more that the conditions ripen for overthrow-ing the monopoly of social wealth maintained by a tiny minority.[46]

It may appear that Isagai has something to say about the contradictions within modern society, or that he is making an appeal to wage a struggle against such a society, but in fact his position is fundamentally that of the petty bourgeoisie

45. Ibid., 53.
46. Ibid., 50.

and the so-called "civic" or "citizen-based" movement [*shimin undo*].[47] Ultimately he is only calling for some cosmetic changes or a reform of society. He claims that the civic movement also represents "an important aspect of the class struggle" and he advances the JCP slogan of "democratic regulation" of the capitalist economy, and these are very characteristic aspects of his position. This silly petty-bourgeois intellectual falls into a confused and non-conceptual position by going so far as to advance the argument that there is positive significance in the expansion of the state apparatus since government workers are entrusted with the management and operation of the state. According to his strange reasoning, one should seek the greatest possible expansion of the state, the skyrocketing of taxes, the state squeezing workers to a greater extent, and for a decrease in the proportion of productive labor, since this would all hasten the liberation of the working class.

This is quite an extraordinary argument. In reality, the state apparatus is connected to monopoly capital, represents its interests, and is led and controlled by a handful of bureaucrats and bourgeois politicians, while the "enormous mass of proletarianized government workers" have absolutely no power over the operation of the state.

> Workers ruling workers is inherently contradictory, and with the intensification of class contradictions and development of the class struggle, the prospect is opened up for the "apparatus that controls workers" to become an "apparatus to control monopoly capital and its apologists." When the proletarianized workers who handle administrative tasks become connected to the social revolutionary movement of wage-workers, it will be possible for the material apparatus that state monopoly capitalism has put in place to come under the democratic control of the members of society. In this way, the "unproductive class" that has borne the functions of maintaining class relations will be transformed into "productive workers" (in the fundamental sense) who control and manage the social division of labor.[48]

---

47. [*Shimin* literally means "city dwellers," while *shimin undō* refers to the "grassroots" or community-based movement that focuses on some particular, pressing issue, often related to the environment or civil rights, with activists not calling into question broader issues related to the nature of capitalist society as a whole or the need to fight for socialism.]
48. Ibid., 59–60.

Isagai directly confuses a bourgeois state with a proletarian one, tossing aside the view held by Marx and Lenin that the bourgeois state, in its current state, cannot shift to become a workers' state, and would rather have to be smashed. He thinks, mistakenly, that in a modern state "workers are ruled by workers." His hopes lie with government workers, thinking that they are the bearers of the bourgeois state and can therefore become the bearers of the proletarian state, and that this would make possible the immediate liberation of the working class. Government workers for Isagai are the latent rulers of the modern state, and it is only a matter of awakening them to a realization of their own position.

There is no limit to the illusions Isagai holds toward government workers. He conceives of the liberation of the working class by means of government workers changing or shifting to become productive workers who "manage and control the social division of labor." This is indeed a theory that suits government workers, and fixes or absolutizes their standpoint.

> So-called "informatization" [*jōhōka*] has certainly expanded the importance of individual human knowledge, but this has not led to a society that respects human dignity. Information is monopolized by the state and monopoly capital, and the information monopoly is the basis for the control apparatus of monopoly capital, militarism, and fascism. Educational institutions, the mass-media, etc. have been twisted into ideological instruments of monopoly capital to manage and control the lives of citizens over the course of their lives. The movement led by the working class that aims for a socio-cultural life "free from capital" has taken on an independent position vis-à-vis the outlook for revolutionary social change. Moreover, within this movement, the struggles of educational workers, government workers, and others upon whom citizens are dependent, are of pivotal importance. Quite a significant segment of the service sector is made up of public institutions. The fact that the bearers of this labor have essentially been proletarianized represents the strengthening of the control apparatus of monopoly capitalism (the expansion of the unproductive class), but at the same time this represents the possibility that this apparatus for managing workers will be overturned so as to become an apparatus to control monopoly capital.[49]

Finally let's reveal our conclusions. From the standpoint that Marx's theory of productive labor can only be grasped on the basis of an understanding of

---

49. Ibid., 128-9.

the theory of value, the relation between the original definition and the formal definition can only be posited in terms of the former criticizing the latter, that is to say, in the form of the mystified criticism in which originally unproductive service labor is historically manifested as being something productive. The systematic understanding of Marx's theory of productive labor, taking the struggle between the labor process and valorization process as its axis, is the logic of how the development of capitalism itself necessitates and makes possible its own sublation. Understanding the development of the service sector within the totality of Marx's theory of productive labor reveals the necessity of the service sector's development (perspective of the labor process), elucidates its capitalist form (perspective of the valorization process), criticizes its decay (perspective of reproduction), clarifies its position within the apparatus of class repression (definition of an unproductive class), and by doing all of this, incorporates the expansionary tendency of the service sector within the logic of the inevitable sublation of capitalism.[50]

As we can see, this is identical to the structural reformist theory that held sway at one time and had a significant impact on the practical standpoint of the JCP—namely, the theory of the democratic reform of capitalism. Structural reformists argued that in a contemporary society of state-monopoly capitalism, due to the swelling of the state apparatus and its increasing importance, revolutionary forces should not adopt the foolish and utopian strategy of fighting this system head on, but rather infiltrate the state apparatus and transform it from being a tool of the bourgeoisie into a tool of the workers. This was said to be not only possible but in fact the only path to workers' liberation. And today this astounding opportunism lives on in the JCP's strategy of the democratic reform of capitalism.

Isagai sees the increase in the proportion of service (unproductive) workers as providing future hope to the working class and putting in place the realistic and subjective conditions needed for the victory of socialism. This is nothing more than his own personal view, however, because in reality this increase reveals a process or stage of the deepening decline of capitalism. In terms of this development revealing the dissolution of capitalism, Isagai is "correct" in a sense. But he sees this deepening decay as being progress and in the interests of the working class, and by viewing this is a step forward toward the liberation of workers, he in fact justifies and prettifies this decay.

---

50. Ibid., 130.

In modern capitalism, for the sake of monopoly capital, as well as because of the corruption and decay of the system, there is an expansion of the state apparatus and a swelling of the service sector and the ranks of unproductive labor. But this "negative phenomenon"—far from being something that should be justified, defended, or perpetuated—must be overcome by the working class. It seems strange that Isagai has come up with such a misconception, but at the same time his theory of service labor is the inevitable result of reaching dead-end, Malthusian conclusions. Isagai sums up the content of his own book in the following passage, where he criticizes the views of Soviet economists:

> In our speculation up to now, we were able to confirm that the expansion of the service sector is, to a certain extent, something that expands the market of a capitalist economy. This is not, however, something that creates conditions for limitless market expansion or that can remove the inherent contradiction between production and consumption within a capitalist economy. The service sector expands the market to the extent that services contribute to the consumption of workers and capitalists. Furthermore, the service sector brings about a qualitative change in the nature of the market. The service sector functions on the basis of the use of material products, but it does not participate in the creation of material wealth. Therefore, the service sector is able to attract commodities from the sector of material production without the flowing back of material equivalents. If the expenditure of revenue on services increases, the outflow of material goods that do not flow back increases in turn. Finally, we need to take note of a number of cases where the service sector becomes a certain means of expanding the channel for realization. First of all, the increase of demand for services is more rapid than the increase of demand for material goods. Secondly, the creation process for services is at the same time the process of their consumption, so there is no difficulty in terms of realization. Furthermore, the growth of the service sector expands not only the commodity market, but also the investment in labor.[51]

Not only does Isagai fail to provide any essential criticism of the views of Soviet scholars, he also claims that Marx's theory offers an "insufficient examination of the position of productive labor," but has "great significance in terms of constructing a theory of value and reproduction that also incorporates the service sector." What we have here—although it is concealed by hedging

---

51. Ibid., 212.

expressions such as "to a certain extent" or "with limitations"—is typical, dyed-in-the-wool Malthusianism, a view that was thoroughly denounced by Marx as being reactionary and corrupt. Akabori holds a "high" opinion of service labor in terms of creating and expanding the market for capital, along with making various effective contributions to the prosperity of capital and profits. This is the actual content of what he refers to as the contribution that service labor makes for the sake of socialism. Through his arbitrary interpretation of Marx's writings, Isagai comes up with the following:

> [Marx points out:] "The bourgeoisie cannot exist without constantly revolutionizing the instruments of production, and thereby the relations of production, and with them the whole relations of society. Conservation of the old modes of production in unaltered form, was, on the contrary, the first condition of existence for all earlier industrial classes. Constant revolutionizing of production, uninterrupted disturbance of all social conditions, everlasting uncertainty and agitation distinguish the bourgeois epoch from all earlier ones."[52] The tendency for the service sector to expand must also be understood as the result of this "constant revolutionizing," that is, as one part of the increase in productive power and expansion and deepening of the social division of labor. The typical view of simplistically regarding the expansion of the service sector as an increase in decay and parasitism must be considered a step backward, which abandons a scientific analysis in favor of a moralistic critique.[53]

At this point, there is little need for us to further examine Isagai's book, as the passage above characteristically exposes the manner in which he understands and treats Marxism. He "utilizes" Marxism in an extremely unserious, egoistical, and arbitrary manner. He does not truly understand Marx, believe in his theories, or respect him, and in turn we find it difficult to place much trust in a person such as Isagai. I would like to conclude this final chapter by citing a passage concerning productive labor from Marx's *Theories of Surplus Value* that I am particularly fond of.

After quoting Adam Smith, Marx emphasizes the following:

---

52. Karl Marx, *The Communist Manifesto* (London: Penguin Press, 1967), 83.
53. *Seisanteki rōdō no riron*, 99.

This is the language of the still revolutionary bourgeoisie, which has not yet subjected to itself the whole of Society, the State, etc. All these illustrious and time-honored occupations—sovereign, judge, officer, priest, etc.—with all the old ideological professions to which they give rise, their men of letters, their teachers and priests, are from an economic standpoint put on the same level as the swarm of their own lackeys and jesters maintained by the bourgeoisie and by idle wealth—the landed nobility and idle capitalists. They are mere servants of the public, just as the others are their servants. They live on the produce of other people's industry, therefore they must be reduced to the smallest possible number. State, church, etc., are only justified in so far as they are committees to superintend or administer the common interests of the productive bourgeoisie; and their costs—since by their nature these costs belong to the *faux frais de production*—must be reduced to the indispensable minimum. This view is of historical interest in sharp contrast partly to the standpoint of antiquity, when material productive labor bore the stigma of slavery and was regarded merely as a pedestal for the idle citizen, and partly to the standpoint of the absolute or aristo-cratic-constitutional monarchy which arose from the disintegration of the Middle Ages—as Montesquieu, still captive to these ideas, so naïvely expressed them in the following passage (*Esprit des lois*, B. VII, Ch. IV): "If the rich do not spend much, the poor will perish of hunger."

When on the other hand the bourgeoisie has won the battle, and has partly itself taken over the State, partly made a compromise with its former possessors, and has likewise given recognition to the ideological professions as flesh of its flesh and everywhere transformed them into its functionaries, of like nature to itself; when it itself no longer confronts these as the representative of productive labor, but when the real productive laborers rise against it and moreover tell it that it lives on other people's industry; when it is enlightened enough not to be entirely absorbed in production, but to want also to consume "in an enlightened way"; when the spiritual labors themselves are more and more performed in its service and enter into the service of capitalist production—then things take a new turn, and the bourgeoisie tries to justify "economically," from its own standpoint, what at an earlier stage it had criticized and fought against. Its spokesmen and con-science-salvers in this line are the Garniers, etc. In addition to this, these economists, who themselves are priests, professors, etc., are eager to prove their "productive" usefulness, to justify their wages "economically."[54]

What Marx says here applies to the standpoint and role of Akabori and Isagai. They are small-minded, cowardly ideological servants of the bourgeoisie, and

---

54. *MECW*, vol. 31, 197-8.

not the bourgeoisie in its progressive stage either, but rather in its present stage of decline.

Glossary of Japanese Names

Akabori, Kunio (1917-)
Professor of economics at Kanto Gakuin University. Mainly known for his writings on productive labor. Author of *Kachi-ron to seisakteki rōdō* (Theory of Value and Productive Labor).

Furihata, Setsuo (1930-)
Former student of Uno Kōzō at Tokyo University and one of the main representatives of the Uno school. Has taught economics at Hokkaido University, Tsukuba University, and Kyoto University. Numerous works include: *Uno riron no kaimei* (Elucidating Uno's Theory) and *Ikiteiru marukusushugi* (Living Marxism).

Hijikata, Seibi (1890-?)
Professor of economics at Tokyo Imperial University and prominent opponent of Marxism. Works include *Meiji zaisei shi* (History of Fiscal Policy in the Meiji Era) and *Senji no zaisei to keizai* (Wartime Fiscal Policy and Economy).

Hiromatsu, Wataru (1933-1994)
Philosopher and author of many works on Marxism and Marxist philosophy. Taught philosophy at Tokyo University, and was well known for his view that Marx's philosophy transcends the opposition between subject and object. Works include *Marukusushugi no chihei* (The Horizon of Marxism), *Benshōhō no ronri* (Logic of Dialectics), and *Marukusushugi no seiritsu katei* (Formative Process of Marxism).

Isagai, Nobuo (1947-)
Professor of economics at Saga University. Has written on the concept of productive labor and the question of service labor. Author of *Seisanteki rōdō no riron: sābisu bumon no keizaigaku* (Theory of Productive Labor: Economic Study of the Service Sector).

Kamakura, Takao (1934-)
Professor of economics at Higashi Nippon International University who is associated with the Uno school.

Works include *Shihonron taikei no hōhō*. (The Method of the System of *Capital*) and *Keizaigaku hōhōron josetsu* (An Introduction to the Methodology of Economics).

Kawakami, Hajime (1879-1946)
Economics professor at Kyoto University who began his career as a bourgeois economist. Gained considerable fame for a series of articles he began writing in 1916 entitled *Binbō monogatari* (Tale of Poverty). Was gradually converted to Marxism in the early 1920s, and subsequently lost his university post for JCP-related activities. Arrested in 1933, he spent the next four years in prison. After his release, Kawakami spent most of his remaining years working on an autobiography, which is a popular work still in print today. In the twenties and thirties he wrote a large number of works on Marx's economic thought, the history of political economy, and the philosophical foundation of Marxism. Best-known work as a Marxist economist is his detailed discussion of Marx's *Capital* in *Shihon-ron nyūmon* (Introduction to *Capital*). A biography of Kawakami's life by Gail Lee Bernstein, entitled *Japanese Marxist*, was published in 1990.

Koizumi, Shinzō (1888-1966)
Taught economics at Keio University, and was president of the university from 1937-1947, during which time he cooperated with the militaristic Japanese government. In the early twenties he was one of the main opponents of Marx's economic theories. Works include *Rikarudo kenkyū* (A Study of Ricardo), *Shakai shisō kenkyū* (Research on Social Thought), and *Marukusu shigo gojū nen* (Fifty Years after Marx's Death).

Kuroda, Kan'ichi (1928-)
Leader of the Japan Revolutionary Communist League (Kakumaru-ha) and writer of numerous works on philosophy. Has attempted to combine elements of idealism and materialism. A number of his books have been translated into English, including *Praxiology: Philosophy of Inter-Human Subjectivity*, *Dialectics of Society*, and *What is Revolutionary Marxism?*.

Kuruma, Samezō (1893-1982)
Marxist economist who started working in the 1920s at the Ōhara Institute for Social Research, a leftwing "think-tank," and later became its chief director. Published articles on the history of political economy and Marx's theory of crisis in the prewar period, and in the late forties and early fifties was the main theoretical opponent of Uno Kōzō's subjective theory of value. After the war, in addition to work for the Ōhara Institute, he taught economics at Hosei

University, and from the late sixties concentrated primarily on editing the *Marx-Lexicon zur Politischen Ökonomie*. Other works include *Kachikeitai-ron to kōkankatei-ron* (Theory of the Value-Form and Theory of the Exchange-Process), *Kyōkō-ron kenkyū* (Studies on Crisis Theory), and *Kahei-ron* (Theory of Money).

Kushida, Tamizō (1885-1934)
Pioneering Marxist economist who studied under Kawakami at Kyoto University, and was instrumental in his teacher's conversion to Marxism. Unlike Kawakami, however, he did not support the JCP. Joined the Ōhara Institute for Social Research, where he pursued research on economic theory, focusing in particular on questions related to agriculture. A four-volume collection of his works was published posthumously in 1935.

Miyamoto, Kenji (1908-)
Former Chairman of the JCP. He was actively involved as one of the organizational leaders of the prewar (JCP-led) proletarian literature movement, after first gaining public attention for a 1929 essay on the writer Ryunosuke Akutagawa. Joined the JCP after graduating from Tokyo University in 1931, was arrested in 1933, and spent the next twelve years in prison. After becoming one of the leaders of the postwar JCP, he eventually gained control of party leadership in 1958, becoming Secretary-General, and later Chairman. Miyamoto still maintains some honorary positions within the JCP today.

Ōtsuka, Hisao (1907-1996)
Influential professor of economics at Tokyo University. Although a Christian, he was politically close to the JCP. He was strongly influenced by the thought of Max Weber and translated Weber's *The Protestant Ethic and the Spirit of Capitalism*. His own works include *Shakai-kagaku no hōhō* (Method of Social Science), Ōbei keizai-shi (Economic History of the West), and *Shakai-kagaku ni okeru ningen* (Man within Social Science).

Ōuchi, Hideaki (1932-)
Tohoku University professor of economics whose works include *Mō hitori no marukusu* (Another Marx), *Uno keizaigaku no kihon mondai* (Key Issues of Uno's Economics), and *Shihon-ron no jōshiki* (Common Sense of *Capital*).

Takata, Yasuma (1883-1972)
A professor at Kyoto University and later at Hitotsubashi University who helped pioneer the study of "modern economics" in Japan. Author of *Shakai-gaku genri* (Principles of Social Science) among other works.

Tsushima, Tadayuki (1901-1979)
An anarchist in his younger days, Tsushima converted to Marxism in the mid-twenties, first associating with the JCP and later with its rival the Rōnō-ha (Worker-Farmer Faction). After the war he was one of the first Marxists to thoroughly criticize Stalinism and the Soviet Union, which culminated in his development of a theory of state capitalism. Tsushima translated works by Trotsky, Tony Cliff, Raya Dunayevskaya, and C.L.R. James, and his own works include *Sutarinshugi hihan* (Criticism of Stalinism) and *Kuremurin no shinwa* (Myths of the Kremlin).

Uno, Kōzō (1897-1977)
Influential professor of economics at Tokyo University, who is known for his three-staged theory of political economy and critical view of historical materialism. Although considered a Marxist, Uno criticized many aspects of Marx's economic theory, including his labor theory of value. Numerous works include *Kachi-ron* (Theory of Value) and *Keizaigaku hōhō-ron* (Methodology of Economics).

Bibliography

Akabori, Kunio. *Kachi to seisanteki rōdō* (Value and Productive Labor). Tokyo: San'ichi Shobō, 1971.

Albritton, Robert. *A Japanese Reconstruction of Marxist Theory*. New York: St. Martins Press, 1986.

—and T. Sekine, eds. *A Japanese Approach to Political Economy: Unoist Variations*. New York: St. Martins Press, 1995.

Böhm-Bawerk, Eugen von. *Karl Marx and the Close of His System*. Edited by Paul Sweezy. Philadelphia: Orion Editions, 1949.

Dowsey, Stuart, ed. *Zengakuren: Japan's Revolutionary Students*. Berkeley: The Ishi Press, 1970.

Hayashi, Hiroyoshi and Ken'ichi Suzuki. *Socialism: Stalinist or Scientific?*—The Marxist Theory of State Capitalism. Translated by Roy West. Tokyo: Zenkokushakensha, 2000.

—et. al. *Rōdō-ha, shakaishugi-ha no daihyō wo kokkai he!* (Send a Representative of Workers and Socialists to the Diet!). Tokyo: Zenkokushakensha, 1976.

Isagai, Nobuo. *Seisanteki Rōdō no Riron: Sābisu Bumon no Keizai* (Theory of Productive Labor: The Economy of the Service Sector). Tokyo: Aoki Shoten, 1977.

Itoh, Makoto. *The Basic Theory of Capitalism: The Forms and Substance of the Capitalist Economy*. London: Macmillan Press, 1988.

—*Value and Crisis*. London: Pluto Press, 1980.

Kaneko, Haruo. *Seisanteki rōdō to kokumin shotoku* (Productive Labor and National Income). Tokyo: Nihon Hyōron-sha, 1966.

Kawakami, Hajime. *Shihon-ron nyūmon* (An Introduction to *Capital*). 3 vols. Tokyo: Sekaihyōronsha, 1946.

Keynes, John Maynard. *A Tract on Monetary Reform*. Amherst: Prometheus Books, 2000.

Kuroda, Kan'ichi. *Essential Terms of Revolutionary Marxism*. Tokyo: Kobushi Shobō, 1998.

Kuruma, Samezō. *Kachikeitai-ron to kōkankatei-ron* (Theory of the Value-Form and Theory of the Exchange-Process). Tokyo: Iwanami Shoten, 1957.

Kushida, Tamizō. *Kachi oyobi kahei* (Value and Money). Tokyo: Kaizōsha, 1934.

Lenin, Vladimir. *Collected Works*. 45 vols. Moscow: Progress Publishers, 1960-1972.

—*Imperialism: The Highest Stage of Capitalism*. New York: International Publishers, 1939.

—*Two Tactics*. New York: International Publishers, 1989.

Marshall, Alfred. *Principles of Economics*. 2 vols. London: Macmillan, 1907.

Marx, Karl. *Capital*. Vol. 1. Translated by Ben Fowkes. London: Penguin Books, 1976.

—*Capital*. Vol. 3. Translated by David Fernbach. London: Penguin Books, 1981.

—*The Communist Manifesto*. London: Penguin Press, 1967.

—*A Contribution to the Critique of Political Economy*. Vol. 29 of *Marx-Engels Collected Works*.

—*Grundrisse*. Translated by Ben Fowkes. London: Penguin Books, 1973.

—*The Poverty of Philosophy*. New York: International Publishers, 1992.

—*Theories of Surplus Value*. Vols. 31-34 of *Marx-Engels Collected Works*.

—*Value: Studies by Marx*. Translated by Albert Dragstedt. London: New Park Publications, 1976.

—and F. Engels. *Marx-Engels Collected Works*. 50 vols. New York: International Publishers, 1975–.

Miyazawa, Ken'ichi. *Kokumin shotoku riron* (Theory of National Income). Tokyo: Chikuma Shobo, 1976.

Moore, Joe. *Japan Workers and the Struggle for Power, 1945-1947*. Madison: University of Wisconsin Press, 1983.

Norman, E. Herbert. *Japan's Emergence as a Modern State*. Vancouver: HBC Press, 2000.

Ōtsuka, Hisao. *Shakaigaku no hōhō* (Method of Social Science). Tokyo: Iwanami Shinsho, 1966.

Ōuchi, Hideaki and Kamakura Takao, eds. *Keizai genron* (Principle Theory of Economics). Tokyo: Yuhikaku, 1976.

Rozenberg, D.I. *Shihon-ron chūkai* (An Explanation of *Capital*). 5 vols. Tokyo: Aoki Shoten, 1962.

Sekine, Thomas T. *The Dialectic of Capital*. 2 vols. Tokyo: Yushindo Press, 1984.

Shima, Shigeo ed. *Bunto no shisō* (Thought of the Bund). 7 vols. Tokyo: Hihyōsha, 1992.

Smith, Adam. *The Wealth of Nations*. Chicago: University of Chicago Press, 1976.

Uno, Kōzō. *Kachi-ron* (Theory of Value). Tokyo: Iwanami Shoten, 1973.

—*Kachi-ron no kenkyū* (Studies on Value). Tokyo: University of Tokyo Press, 1952.

—*Kachi-ron no mondai ten* (Issues Concerning the Theory of Value). Tokyo: Hosei University Press, 1963.

—*Keizaigaku hōhō-ron* (Methodology of Economics). Tokyo: University of Tokyo Press, 1962.

—*Keizaigaku no hōhō.* (Method of Economics). Tokyo: Hosei University Press, 1963.

—*Keizai genron* (Principle Theory of Economics). Tokyo: Iwanami Shoten, 1977.

—*Principles of Political Economy:* Theory of a Purely Capitalist Society. Translated by Thomas Sekine. Atlantic Highlands: Humanities Press, 1980.

—*Shakai kagaku no konpon mondai* (Fundamental Problems of Social Science). Tokyo: Aoki Shoten, 1966.

—et al., *Shihonron kenkyū* (Research on Marx's *Capital*). 6 vols. Tokyo: Chikuma Shobō, 1967.